Mike -

Men like you have
the Battle"

"Born

tive lives, the Veterans Administration encourages fraud and rewards indolence, further marginalizing these men and women and robbing the nation of their potentially robust contributions and continued service post-war. These meticulously researched findings set to compelling human narratives won't make Gade very popular. But they represent the brave effort and convincing factual evidence necessary for the hard work of systemic change when the system is broken."
—**Kevin Sites, author of** *Swimming with Warlords*

"America's veterans, including the most seriously wounded, ill, and injured, have become the latest battleground in a long-standing political war. The political left and right both trip over themselves to 'honor veterans,' not ever considering that their efforts may be misguided or even harmful to those they aim to help. In this bold, groundbreaking new book, Daniel Gade exposes flaws in the disability system that make America's veterans poorer and sicker. This book will be controversial, and it should be read by anyone who seeks to understand the veteran landscape in America."
—**Col (Ret.) Jack Jacobs, US Army, Medal of Honor Recipient and Author of** *If Not Now, When? Duty and Sacrifice In America's Time of Need* **and** *Basic: Surviving Boot Camp and Basic Training*

"[*Wounding Warriors* shows that] the current system promotes waste and abuse not only of VA disability payments but of unnecessary medical appointments. It would almost be better to give soldiers a piece of paper that asks, "Are you willing to lie, cheat, and/or steal to receive 100 percent disability?" and if they check yes, just give them 100 percent because it will free up waste from unnecessary imaging, behavioral health, sleep studies, etc."
—**MAJ [Name Withheld], PT, DPT, MHA, MBA; US Army**

"[*Wounding Warriors*] makes a compelling case for reform. Lincoln's immortal words in his second inaugural address, "To care for him who has borne the battle and for his widow, and his orphan" have

Praise for *Wounding Warriors*

"This revelatory, lens-changing book shows why our VA, though staffed by devoted and capable medical professionals, must change. Institutions get the behavior they reward. Seen through the experience of a clear-eyed, seriously wounded warrior, the current system's design and application guides vets coming in with no intent of becoming wards of the state into that very situation. Those with serious problems are submerged in a sea of others who are rewarded for staying in an unimproved situation. In *Wounding Warriors*, Daniel Gade has made an unflinching appraisal and charted a refreshing path forward for making the VA best in class. A must-read for those committed to caring for our veterans who have borne the battle."
—General (ret.) Jim Mattis, US Marine Corps (Ret), Former US Secretary of Defense

"As a US Army veteran and former Secretary of Veterans Affairs, I find this book to be a breath of fresh air. In *Wounding Warriors*, Daniel Gade, himself a wounded warrior, dissects and critiques some of the serious issues that beset our nation's worthy attempts to care for our wounded, ill, and injured service members and veterans. His credibility is ironclad and his argument is stunning: in attempting to care for veterans, our disability system creates incentives that make them sicker, poorer, and worse off. This is a must-read for policy makers and anyone involved in care for veterans, as well as for veterans and their families."
—Jim Nicholson, 5th Secretary of Veterans Affairs

"Daniel Gade's real education came after losing his leg fighting in Iraq. The most disturbing lesson paradoxically came from the agency that was supposed to help put him back together. What Gade discovered both through his own experiences and extensive research of others' is this: rather than assisting warriors in returning to produc-

served as a beacon, but today are shrouded in fog. It is time to bring the disability compensation program into the twenty-first century and not the century gone by. Reform is never easy, but veterans who have suffered the physical and mental wounds of war, their dependents, and the American people who support this critically important program deserve no less."
—**Anthony Principi, 4th Secretary of Veterans Affairs**

"A vitally important book, written by someone uniquely qualified to tell the story. Reaching all the way back to the post-World War II era (when five-star General Omar Bradley — one of the great leaders of that war — led a commission that identified the "perverse incentive structure" that continues in our current VA disability system), this book shows us how 'the path of care and compensation' has led to a 'quagmire of despair and dysfunction.'

"Astoundingly well documented, with a clarion call for action and clear-cut recommendations, *Wounding Warriors* shows us the road home from dysfunction and despair. This book can transform the way we care for our veterans, from the current methodology that has done great harm, to policies that will give our veterans the care they deserve.

If our nation sincerely cares about our veterans, we will read and heed this book."
—**Lt. Col. Dave Grossman, author of *On Combat, On Killing,* and *On Spiritual Combat***

"I found myself re-reading parts of this book as they strike so deep. [The authors captured] the reality of soldiering as well as anything I've read. This book accurately describes a broken and spectacularly failing VA system, and will make plenty of people squeamish. Between popular culture, wishful thinking, and an untamable bureaucracy, I'm afraid that the only real solution is to blow the whole system up and start over."
—**Matt Eversmann, Army Ranger (Ret.) and Author of *The Battle of Mogadishu: Firsthand Accounts from the Men of Task Force Ranger***

"Gade and Huang provide crucial context to understanding the Department of Veterans Affairs' policies and practices of determining disability ratings. The authors' research and experience tell of a deeply flawed system that incentivizes veterans to 'claim everything.' Perhaps even more concerning is the negative effect the process has on healing and rehabilitation of veterans who often chose financial compensation over recovery.

"The authors masterfully describe the challenges associated with implementing change in this government bureaucracy. *Wounding Warriors* deftly uncovers the current situation within the VA and the history that led to this point. This story should infuriate every veteran for the rampant malingering among our own warrior class and every American citizen that funds these benefits through taxation. If *Wounding Warriors* doesn't result in a demand for congressional reform of this well-intentioned but grossly off-track institution, then perhaps nothing ever will."
—**Lt. Col Wayne Phelps, USMC (Ret.) and author of *On Killing Remotely: The Psychology of Killing with Drones***

"Few people know this issue as well as Daniel Gade, informed by his experience in Washington and on the frontlines. Gade's thorough examination of the VA, from its poorly designed incentive structure to its record of waste and lack of accountability, is a serious indictment that should have American taxpayers demanding reform. In an era when veterans' entitlements are treated as an untouchable third rail of politics, Gade's book is a profile in courage."
—**Paul D. MIller, PhD. Professor of the Practice of International Affairs at Georgetown University's School of Foreign Service and author of *Just War and Ordered Liberty; American Power and Liberal Order;* and more.**

"Daniel Gade was wounded in combat twice and has spent the last fifteen years fighting against the bad policies he saw crippling his fellow veterans. Too often, our wounded warriors have to fight through a system that prematurely labels them 'disabled' without ever making an attempt to help them adapt to their new lives. The system thrives on dependency and creates bad outcomes, making our veterans poorer and sicker. He brings his hard-earned expertise to bear in this vital guide to fixing our broken systems."

—Jim Hanson, Special Forces Veteran and President of Security Studies Group; Author of *Winning the Second Civil War: Without Firing a Shot*

"My friend Daniel Gade is a gravely wounded American war hero and a scholar. In this book, he proffers an antidote for the terrible problem of wounded veterans being treated as broken toys rather than potentially valuable members of our communities. Treating severely wounded veterans as irreparably broken contributes to a catastrophic veteran suicide crisis. We The People can solve this problem. Herein, Daniel Gade describes a broken system and solution for reform."

—Lt. Col. Oliver L. North, USMC (Ret.); CEO Fidelis Publishing.Com

"As a veteran Marine and former Deputy Secretary of the Department of Veterans Affairs, I've seen some of the problems described in these pages close up. Unfortunately, most people in political life don't have the courage to do what Daniel Gade and Daniel Huang have done here: shine a bright light on a system that in many cases creates disincentives for veterans to recuperate and thrive. In some cases, the current system can also encourage distortion of honorable service into a way of seeking financial gain. With its clear call for significant reform, *Wounding Warriors* charts a path toward a system that better promotes wellness and treats veterans like the valuable assets that they are."

—The Honorable Jim Byrne, 8th Deputy Secretary of Veterans Affairs

WOUNDING WARRIORS

How Bad Policy Is Making Veterans Sicker and Poorer

Daniel M. Gade, PhD and **Daniel Huang**
Lieutenant Colonel, US Army (Ret.)   Former *Wall Street Journal* Reporter

Ballast Books, LLC
Washington, DC
www.ballastbooks.com

ISBN 978-1-955026-99-4

Library of Congress Control Number has been applied for

Printed in Canada

Published by Ballast Books
www.ballastbooks.com

For more information, bulk orders, appearances or speaking requests,
please email info@ballastbooks.com

To America's veterans, past, present, and future.

"With malice toward none, with charity for all,
with firmness in the right as God gives us to see the right,
let us strive on to finish the work we are in, to bind up
the nation's wounds, to care for him who shall have
borne the battle and for his widow, and his orphan…"
—Abraham Lincoln's Second Inaugural Address, March 4, 1865

"… ask not what your country can do for you.
Ask what you can do for your country."
—John F. Kennedy's Inaugural Address, January 20, 1961

CONTENTS

PROLOGUE

IT WAS ALL two-lane country roads out of Fort Bragg, North Carolina. Jeff Kisbert[1] sat behind the wheel of his dusty Ford Focus, a maroon beret beside him on the passenger's seat, never to be worn again. He cruised past wild grass and empty lots, his window down. The cold wind felt good after the stress of the last few weeks, the last few years. It was early afternoon, December 28, 2010.

For several weeks, Jeff had been collecting the required signatures for his military separation checklist. First, he had gone to the health center and asked them to sign: yes, he was up to date on all his shots. Then he stopped by the library and hounded them to confirm: yes, all his books had been returned. The biggest headache was the signature to verify he had returned all the items the Army had issued—one helmet, one bulletproof vest, two sleeping bags— across what felt like a lifetime, before everything had been lugged to hell and back through his two deployments. He had tracked it all down and held his breath as the guy behind the supply desk ticked through the lost list. Finally, he had the two dozen signatures he needed. The ordeal had taken longer than Jeff could have imagined. But he was done.

For more than four years Jeff had served as an infantry soldier, one vertebra in the millions-strong backbone of the Army. His first deployment, to southern Afghanistan's Kandahar province, came just as Defense Secretary Robert Gates extended the length of tour to fifteen months. "Our forces are stretched. There's no question about that," Gates said in April 2007, and Jeff found himself among the surge of troops flown in to re-energize the war.

His second deployment took him to Zabul, the poorest province in Afghanistan, and much of his worldview changed after witnessing that level of poverty, where healthcare and education were faraway abstractions and the closest thing to an institution was the village well from which the locals drew water to survive. Rumbling down a cracked road one day, Jeff's Humvee rolled over an Improvised Explosive Device (IED).[2] The blast threw him off the gunner's seat, but he was lucky. He woke up with a concussion. Some friends on patrol with him didn't wake up at all. When Jeff returned, they gave him a Purple Heart.

He felt more satisfaction when he received the stamp releasing him from the Army. On the last day of service, an officer took his checklist and scrutinized it for all the required appointments and signatures, then stamped the sheet with the black print of a dragon head, the emblem of the XVIII Airborne Corps. Headquartered at Fort Bragg, the unit traced its history back to the Battle of the Bulge during World War II. Jeff rubbed his thumb over the emblem and felt a flush of pride. He had earned it. His final stamp of approval.

He brought his leave papers to the battalion headquarters and handed them to a sergeant who nodded absently as he scribbled his signature.

"You didn't even read it," Jeff said. "That's my terminal leave. I'm out of the Army now."

The sergeant's head snapped back in shock.

Jeff realized he was smiling. He walked out of the building and took off his beret.

From the road, he pulled out a flip phone and called his fiancé. "It's done," he said. "I'm out of here." His destination was McLeansboro, a small town in southern Illinois, where his fiancé was staying with her mother. The plan was to pick her up and drive down to St. Louis, where they had met two years earlier and planned to start their new life. "No more driving out for four-day weekends," he told her. "This is the last drive."

But first he had one quick stop to make.

Matt Jackson[2] had joined the Army a couple months after Jeff in 2006. The two met after basic training and quickly became best friends; by the time they had completed two tours in Afghanistan, they might as well have been brothers. At one point they pledged that if they couldn't find wives after leaving the military, they would go to Montana, pitch a tent on some rocks, and inhale cigarettes and Red Bull for their remaining days.

Thankfully, it never came to that.

Matt had gotten married in 2009 and lived with his wife in Fayetteville, twenty minutes outside Fort Bragg. He had achieved his final stamp of separation from the Army a few weeks before Jeff, but they had worked through much of the process together. The freedom they had gone to war for had never felt so sweet. "I was on top of the world when I got out," Matt said. "It's a great feeling when you can do what you want to do again."

His plan was to transfer his infantry skills into law enforcement. A few Army buddies had transitioned out before him and found jobs as police officers and firefighters. Matt liked the idea of serving his country and his community in a new capacity. He felt equipped for the task and eager to get started.

When Jeff arrived at Matt's apartment, he headed straight for the bathroom to change out of his uniform. "Well, you're not waiting for anything, huh?" said Matt's wife. For Jeff it was a cathartic moment, like casting off an old skin—and shedding all the rules and regulations that came with it. In his new skin of jeans and a sweatshirt, he and Matt stepped outside. They each lit a cigarette and savored their first smoke together as civilians. It felt surreal. They were out, back in the real world, their lives in their own hands again.

Yet their paths, intertwined so closely as soldiers, had already begun to diverge. In their final weeks at Fort Bragg, they had attended a mandatory seminar hosted by representatives from the Department of Veterans Affairs.

The representatives glossed over certain services, such as the post-9/11 GI Bill that pays for education and retraining, while doubling down on others—in particular, Jeff noticed, disability compensation. Inside a packed classroom, he listened as the VA official listed condition after condition: "if you have trouble sleeping, if you have nightmares, if you're ever feeling anxious," in order to emphasize one point: "You can get paid for these things."

Jeff left the meeting disgusted. "I didn't want to have anything to do with it," he said. He was moving to a new city, getting married, enrolling in a bachelor's degree program to pave the way for a long-term career. He felt ready "to grab the world by the horns," not file a list of disabilities. "I wanted to get out and get on with my life," he said.

Matt had a different response. He took the VA agent's advice and filed for every condition he could think of. "My thought process was if they want to give it to me, they'll give it to me. If not, they'll deny me." He was not alone. In the twenty years after 9/11, more than 1.3 million veterans from the wars in Iraq and Afghanistan have become compensation recipients on the VA disability payroll. [4]

Some decisions come to define everything that follows. "I was pushing him to go to school," Jeff says, "and he was pushing me to go to the VA."

INTRODUCTION

VETERANS DISABILITY COMPENSATION was conceived in a phrase tucked into the closing of Abraham Lincoln's second inaugural address in 1865. Speaking before thousands on a muddy spring day, the president expressed his gratitude to the grieving families of those who had sacrificed life and limb to keep the nation whole. It was the nation's obligation, he believed, "to care for him who shall have borne the battle." Today, his words are honored by a plaque at the entrance of the Department of Veterans Affairs headquarters in Washington, D.C., which has assumed the charge of helping make former soldiers, and their families, whole.

To this day, the nation stands overwhelmingly behind the sentiment Lincoln conveyed. When men and women are maimed by battle, they deserve the best care we the people can muster to return them to health and compensate them for whatever cannot be restored. Unfortunately, the path of care and compensation leads into a quagmire of despair and dysfunction.

America has allowed itself to grow apart from its service members. The military is respected, honored, even revered in our culture, yet too often the engagements are shallow and insincere. Companies advertise their support for soldiers to boost business. Politicians pay tribute to the troops for an applause line. Most damaging of all, the public's perception of its veterans has become a convoluted caricature, saddled with battle wounds—those that can be seen, and those that can't. Too frequently the picture zooms in to focus on their disabilities. And, on paper, the nation's veterans are sicker today than ever.

- Between 2000 and 2020, the number of veterans receiving disability benefits nearly doubled, even as the overall veteran population fell by about a third, from 26.4 million to 18 million.[1]
- 36 percent of veterans from the post-9/11 service era are disability recipients, compared to 11 percent after World War II.[2]
- They are assessed to be more disabled, on average receiving compensation for 7.96 conditions, compared to the World War II cohort's 2.4.[3]
- Since 2000, the number of veterans rated at 70 to 100 percent disability, the most severe category of impairment, has increased nearly *seven-fold*.[4]
- As a percentage, more veterans today are compensated for disabilities than ever before in the VA's history.

These numbers paint a bleak outlook, but the picture is a distortion. The reality is that the VA disability apparatus has strayed from its purpose and lost sight of its mission. Military physicians balk at the stream of patients who arrive with no desire to improve, wishing only to log their ailments for compensation. VA doctors cringe when they see vets "performing symptoms" and internalizing ailments in response to the incentives offered for being disabled, but fear the backlash they will face if they speak out. "There's a great many veterans pretending to have fictitious conditions," said one VA examiner. "And a great many doctors pretending to treat them."

Millions of veterans have been folded into a VA disability model that reflects a flawed understanding of human nature, an outdated view of current medical capabilities, and an antiquated assessment of the labor market. It operates like a misguided assembly line, churning out diagnoses of disability and applying bandages of cash in lieu of the rehabilitative care veterans deserve.

The impact of a disability diagnosis can be serious and lasting; it can disrupt a person's identity, limit their opportunities, and constrict their vision for the future. But far too often, disability is both a symptom and a disease among veterans. Disability has become a

way to reinforce destructive stereotypes and resist proven methods of recovery. It has become a means of cloaking a grab at entitlements and a back door out of the civilian workforce in a robe of virtue. It has become a story the country is too eager to believe and retell, before even checking to see if it is right.

As more vets are approved for disability, economists rue the shrinking of America's labor supply. Military service members come from among the best and the brightest of our nation's youth. They are physically and mentally capable individuals with the proven tenacity to endure challenges, and they possess valuable skills gained through military training and experience. The significance of their actual and potential contribution to the workforce is hard to overstate, yet an alarming number are taking a seat on the sidelines of society, as if they have nothing to offer and nothing to gain.

Psychologists and medical experts have been sounding alarm bells for years, warning anyone who will listen that the conditions getting the most attention don't have to be disabling at all, and certainly don't have to be permanent. Good science gets shouted down when it conflicts with the overarching narrative that veterans are impaired and broken and cannot hope to be anything more than what is conveyed in their disability rating.

Meanwhile, inside service halls and online chat rooms, vets advise and congratulate one another on raising their disability levels and achieving the ultimate prize: 100 percent disability. Years into dependency, some wonder where their livelihoods have gone. Said one veteran, "I feel like discarded government waste."

Since 2000, VA spending on disability compensation has more than tripled and become the organization's largest expenditure. In 2021, the VA is projected to spend more than $105 billion on disability benefits—twice the combined value of Delta and American Airlines.[5] It is spending more on veterans' disability today than it is spending on rehabilitation programs, than it is spending on education and re-training, than it is spending on all the services covered under veterans' health care. In fact, the VA spends more on

veterans staying sick than on veterans getting better.

Service members returning to civilian life deserve a better system, and so does the country.

Policymakers recall the flashes when reform seemed possible, when a fix appeared within reach and they could have done more, but the path to reform has always been a political minefield, strewn with failed efforts and professional blowback. Powerful interests suppress even the mention of new ideas, and many with the duty to lead have learned to stay away. When a senior VA official was asked about pushing for a more recovery-oriented disability department, she responded, "Oh no, I will not touch that. I am simply focused on making the system run." Anything more, she insisted, "is too hard to do."

Inside the chambers of D.C. politics, the most controversial issues earn the moniker "third rail." Nobody wants to touch them because no one wants to get shocked. Nothing produces quite the same charge as trying to grapple with the growth of veterans' entitlements. The purpose of this book is to shake loose the paralysis and diagnose the problem for what it is. The aim of this book is to seize the third rail of the veterans disability system with both hands.

PART I:
SERVICE

CHAPTER 1
THE VOLUNTEER ARMY

MARCO VASQUEZ JOINED the US Army in the country's last breath of peacetime. The new millennium had just dawned and 2001, he resolved, would be the year he began providing for his young family in the way they deserved. More than anything, he was determined to get out of his hometown of El Paso, Texas.

Marco had grown up playing with his Hot Wheels beneath framed portraits of the Pope on the walls of his grandmother's home. Then, after he turned thirteen, his mother joined the Pentecostal church. "That became very awkward," he says. She tore down his Metallica posters, snapped his Led Zeppelin records, and insisted that he start to attend worship with her. After graduating high school in 1995, he wanted to go to college, but his parents would only support him if he attended a Bible college. He chose one in California to get as far away from them as he could.

The distance from his high school sweetheart was harder, and they saved up for months so that she could visit. They had been introduced by a mutual friend when they were both juniors. He was a musician. She was a dancer. He had almost finished his first year of college when he learned that she was pregnant.

Marco dropped out of school and moved back to El Paso. Their daughter was born in August 1998. He married his girlfriend that year, solidifying the family.

To pay the bills, Marco took a job at a discount tire shop. The work had him on his feet all day—changing tires, repairing flats, taking inventory—but "they were paying pretty good at the time,"

he said, about $12 an hour. Within six months, he was promoted to assistant manager. The promotion came with a small raise, but the workload multiplied. After a while, he realized he was working fifty-hour weeks just to make ends meet.

In 2000, he and his wife had their second child, a boy. Marco knew what it was like to grow up poor in El Paso, and when he looked at the people around him, uncles and older cousins who got married and never left, he saw that the struggle to find—and more importantly, keep—a job never ended. He didn't want that kind of life for his family. Education, he believed, would be his way out. "I need to go back to school," he told himself. "If I don't do it now, I'm never going to do it."

Marco knew the military offered scholarships through its vast Reserve Officers' Training Corps (ROTC) network, and one afternoon, he visited the closest recruiting center inside a nearby shopping mall. There was an office for each of the five branches. Marco had thought about joining the US Coast Guard, but he soon learned that having children hurt his eligibility. He next considered the Marine Corps, but then the recruiter told him that most of his first paycheck would go to paying down his uniform. That wouldn't work; he needed every dollar he could get for his family.

The recruiters in the Army office were more laid-back, Marco remembered, and the benefits, in particular, were attractive to him. "What hooked me was the Green to Gold program," he said. The largest provider of college funding in the country, Army ROTC offered a variety of financial packages to cover tuition, fees, and living expenses. Enrolled students committed to a period of service after graduating.[1] Marco chose a four-year Green to Gold scholarship package, which meant that he would serve for a year in the military, come back to Texas and earn a four-year degree, then return to the Army for three more years of service.[2] The Army would also provide medical benefits for his whole family. "I thought that was great," Marco said.

Then there was the cash. "It was in 2001. There was a lot of college bonus money, and the infantry branch was throwing out a bonus too," Marco said.[7]

He knew a good deal when he saw one: $11,000 for joining the infantry, $3,000 more for airborne. "I was like, 'Let's go for it!'" he said. "Let's do it."

George W. Bush had just been elected president on a campaign against nation-building, and another war in the Gulf seemed as plausible as a space invasion. The events that would change everything were still two seasons away.

On February 3, Marco signed his papers, then recited the oath alongside a dozen other recruits. An officer shook his hand.

"Welcome to the Army, son."

Marco's actions represent the exact intent of the incentives and benefits the military introduced during the twentieth century to attract new recruits.[3] The GI Bill, first signed into law during World War II, offers service members as much as $22,000 per year for college or vocational training after completing their terms.[4] For soldiers with existing student debt, the Army can help them repay up to $65,000 in loans.[5] And like many other federal employees, service members are eligible for the government's Thrift Savings Plan, a retirement program similar to the 401(k)s offered by many private companies, with the Army matching contributions of up to 5 percent for qualified recruits.[6]

THE MILITARY did not always offer benefits or bonuses to attract recruits. Conscription policies in the United States date back to the American Civil War, with draftees serving in both the Union and Confederate armies.

As America prepared to join the Allied war effort during World War I, President Woodrow Wilson signed the Selective Service Act of 1917. The act created a "liability to serve" for all eligible male citizens, and formed the basis for the national conscription system that exists to this day.[8] In World War II, Selective Service expanded its scopeand influence by doling out deferments to channel manpower toward designated areas of "national interest."[9] As one researcher put it, the system held complete authority to determine "whether a young man was more valuable as a father or a student or a scientist or a doctor than as a soldier."[10]

On one hand, occupational deferments exempted scientists and engineers and placed more of the burden of service on poor and working-class men.[11] On the other, the draft served as one of the few mechanisms to actively integrate various American populations. The writer Joseph Epstein praised conscription's blending properties.[12] The draft "took me out of my own social class and ethnic milieu—big-city, middle-class, Jewish—and gave me a vivid sense of the social breadth of my country," he wrote. "I slept in barracks and shared all my meals with American Indians, African Americans from Detroit, white Appalachians, Christian Scientists from Kansas, and discovered myself befriending and being befriended by young men I would not otherwise have met."

Despite its imperfect execution, the draft broke barriers that needed breaking. It mixed disparate groups into a unified class of recruits and taught them to approach objectives as a collective.

The movement to abolish conscription gained strength, though, as the Vietnam War dragged on. The draft became the subject of an intense national debate over defining the nature of the armed forces. At the height of the war, General William Westmoreland, commander of US forces in Vietnam, appeared before a presidential commission to testify against voluntary service. His voice ringing with conviction, he declared that he had no desire to command an "army of mercenaries." Sitting on the commission, Milton Friedman, the future Nobel Prize-winning economist, shot back, "General, would you rather command an army of slaves?"[13]

General Westmoreland struck the more imposing figure, but Friedman's position resonated with the public. Secretary of Defense Melvin Laird announced the end of the draft on January 27, 1973. The last inducted American entered the service that June.[14]

The removal of the draft eventually gave birth to a serious and devoted professional military. Prior to the 1970s, many conscripted troops, wary of commitment, enlisted with poor discipline and low morale. The new force was different. Populated entirely with volunteers who had individually decided to serve, its ranks drew from those who viewed service not as an obligated stint but as a serious profession, perhaps even a long-term career. Subsequent successes in Grenada, Panama, the Persian Gulf War, and Kosovo showcased American soldiers at their most effective.[15] On average, experience levels in the military rose, enlistment periods lengthened, and retention rates grew.[16]

But as the makeup of America's military shifted, so did its relationship with the rest of society. Toward the end of World War II, nearly one in ten Americans had served, and flags with tiny blue stars, signifying a family member on active duty in the military, hung from windows across the country. Today, after nearly twenty years of the "Global War on Terror," about 1 percent of the population—about 2.8 million Americans—has served in Iraq or Afghanistan.[17]

In 1971, near the height of America's involvement in Vietnam, three out of four representatives in the US House and Senate had served in the military. In 2018, the portion of Congressional members with military service had fallen to less than a fifth—half the number of representatives who came from prior careers in business.[18] "A people untouched (or seemingly untouched) by war are far less likely to care about it," wrote the military historian Andrew Bacevich, whose son died fighting in the Iraq War. "Persuaded that they have no skin in the game, they will permit the state to do whatever it wishes."[19]

Not long after the draft was dissolved, two University of Michigan scholars described the development of a "separate military ethos" as career-oriented service members replaced their citizen soldier counterparts. Surveys at the time showed broad public support for a voluntary force, while the majority of Americans favored raising military pay to attract sufficient volunteers. But in a 1975 study, the two scholars reported that few civilians had considered "what kinds of servicemen will, or should, staff an all-volunteer armed force."

By interviewing more than 2,500 Navy personnel, the authors found diverging ideological views between members of the "career force" and the wider public. "It seems inevitable that the military will indeed grow more separate from civilians," they concluded. "As the proportion of career-oriented men in the all-volunteer force increases, the force will be less likely to match the values, perceptions and preferences concerning the military held by civilians."[20]

For generations, conscription had acted as a bridge, flawed but serviceable, that connected the military with the rest of society. Ending the draft not only severed this important tie but initiated a deterioration that ate at other remaining links. These days, service members seemingly detach from the general public and disappear into the removed reality of the armed forces for years, sometimes decades, at a time. When they emerge again, they return to a world that mystifies its soldiers and mythicizes their sacrifices—a world that can never fully comprehend the experiences they've had, the orders they've carried, the bonds they've shared—yet insists on treating them with a deference bordering on idolatry.

Many service members describe the effect as being placed on a pedestal. Civilians celebrate and honor them, but view them as spectacles, treating them as an "other." Cast apart from civilian society, veterans describe living behind a barrier where shallow sentiments and stock phrases like "Thank you for your service" don't reach. They describe a distance that they don't know how to cross.

In America, that psychological distance is growing.

THE GEOGRAPHICAL DISTANCE has also grown, extending across the span of the United States.

In the first half of the twentieth century, as the country prepared for two world wars, a rapidly expanding military acquired huge tracts of land in remote, inexpensive areas of the South, where many of the nation's largest military bases continue to operate today. The bases required massive, open areas for ranges, runways, and training exercises, far from major cities. Multiple rounds of base closures since 1988 have further deepened the military's geographic isolation, concentrating resources and manpower increasingly in the South. This shift has coincided with a higher percentage of military personnel hailing from that region. While southern states have always contributed a greater share of recruits to the armed forces, the disparity has widened over time. In 1976, 32 percent of voluntary service members came from the South; in 2015, the percentage had risen to forty-five.[21]

Less than a week after he took the oath, Marco boarded a plane from El Paso to Fort Benning, a sprawling Southern military base on the Alabama-Georgia border. Assigned to an anti-armor infantry specialty, he learned how to fire an M249 machine gun, aim an Mk19 grenade launcher, and do it all from the back of a roaring Humvee. After sixteen weeks of training, his wife, Amber, flew down with the kids for his graduation.

In July, he arrived at Fort Campbell, another Southern Army base, this one straddling Kentucky and Tennessee, where he reported to his assignment with the 101st Airborne. Known for its brigade-scale air assaults, the 101st Airborne specializes in mobilizing large forces at a moment's notice. Senior military leaders described the unit as the Army's "tip of the spear."[22] Marco received his post to the 502nd Infantry Regiment, nicknamed the "Five-O-Deuce." His division commander was David Petraeus, at the time a two-star general.

On a Tuesday morning, Marco was stomping through fields, slinging equipment for an air assault exercise, when the entire training program suddenly froze. "Radio communication ceased. Everything was grounded. No one was moving," he remembered. "We just sat there."

He looked around. Everybody appeared as bewildered as he was. Marco always carried a flip phone inside his Army rucksack, tucked into a little plastic bag so it wouldn't get wet, and when he took it out to call his wife, her first words to him were, "Oh my god."

His stomach plunged.

"It's worse than Pearl Harbor," she said, then moments later, she screamed. "The second tower just got hit."

Marco still had no idea what was happening. "What do you mean the second tower?"

"We're being attacked," his wife replied.

The details came slowly, but the rumors spread fast. In bits and pieces, Marco and his squad mates learned about the World Trade Center buildings, about the planes, about the attacks on New York and the nation's capital. Ordered to stay where they were, some soldiers started getting angry, others gaped in shock. Then, as if the same thought hit everyone at the same time, a hush came over the camp. A buddy sidled up next to Marco.

"We're going to war."

Marco didn't reply but he knew it was true.

"That's all I was thinking," he said. "We're going to war, dude."

In the days that followed, military recruitment centers around the country received a flood of phone calls. Among high school and college-aged men, willingness to join the service jumped from 21 percent in July to 32 percent by October 2001. Just as in the aftermath of Pearl Harbor, an attack on American soil jolted the public sentiment, and enthusiasm for the nation's armed forces spiked. Nearly half of Americans said they were more likely to enlist.[23]

Yet for all the goodwill, enlistment figures remained little changed. Between 2001 and 2002, the number of young men and women who joined the military's active components actually fell.[24] Many of the individuals who contacted recruiters simply didn't meet the requirements.

The military has long battled perceptions that it draws from lower-achieving segments of society, scooping up misfits with few other options. However, the records have never substantiated this perception, and in recent years, they point to the opposite—a growing worry that fewer and fewer Americans are qualified for service. A 2015 report titled "Ready, Willing, and Unable to Serve" found that

75 percent of the country's youth population was ineligible to join the military. Reasons for disqualification include health and physical issues, drug use and criminal history, poor conduct, low educational attainment, and inadequate aptitude; a third were estimated to have multiple disqualifiers. "As military leaders look ahead to the coming years, they are increasingly concerned that there are not enough qualified candidates to defend our nation," the report said.[25]

Candidates wishing to join the military are first screened to ensure they meet a range of physical, educational, and citizenship requirements. Those who move on must take the Armed Services Vocational Aptitude Battery (ASVAB), a comprehensive exam that covers nine subjects, from 'Arithmetic Reasoning' to 'Mechanical Comprehension.' A sample multiple-choice question might test recruits on how a generator component operates, or which car part contains a vehicle's coolant. Minimum ASVAB scores vary according to a recruit's desired service branch and job function, but all must demonstrate sufficient competency to enter service. Of the military's active service members, 75 percent scored in the top half of the Armed Forces Qualifying Test, a component of the ASVAB, significantly higher than the ability distribution in the general population.[26]

The Department of Defense publishes a series of quality benchmarks to guide recruiting efforts, and consistently demands that recruits meet a higher standard than the civilian population. The military conducts tests to gauge character, requires candidates to be healthier and more fit than civilians, and bars anyone from service who has a history of drug use or criminal behavior.[27]

Enlistees are also typically more educated than the average citizen. According to a 2007 Congressional Budget Office report, 91 percent of recruits were high school graduates, compared with 80 percent for all eighteen-to-twenty-four-year-old US residents.[28]

And despite common misconceptions about the military's "poverty draft," recruits don't typically enlist out of financial need. A 2008 Heritage Foundation study found that only 11 percent of military recruits came from the lowest economic quartile, while 25 percent came from the highest.[29] In 2010, the National Priorities Project reported that more than 50 percent of recruits had lived in ZIP codes from the upper half of the nation's income distribution.[30]

In one of his final speeches as Secretary of Defense, William Cohen capped his comments with a heartfelt endorsement of the nation's armed forces: "On countless occasions I've been asked by foreign leaders, 'How can our military be more like America's?' I'll repeat here today what I've said time and time again. It's not our training, although our training is the most rigorous in the world. It's not our technology, although ours is the most advanced in the world. And it's not our tactics, although ours are the most revolutionary in the world. We have the finest military on Earth because we have the finest people on Earth—because we recruit and retain the best that America has to offer."[31]

MATT JACKSON GREW up in Marion, Illinois, alongside his two cousins and best friends: Dustin, older by a year, and David, fifteen months younger. Dustin joined the Marine Corps first, in 2000, and his brother followed him into the armed forces not long after. When the invasion of Iraq launched in March 2003, Matt and the entire extended family found themselves situated daily in front of the television, following every bit of news that came out.

Marion was a small town, and Matt lived on the same street as his grandfather and two of his uncles. About three miles long, it was spelled two ways, either Link or Linck Road, depending on which end you drove in from. "Obviously, the guy who made the street signs was an idiot," Matt said. If the family wasn't having Sunday dinner together at the church, they met at his grandfather's house to discuss the latest from the war—the little clips they had seen that day, anything they had heard.

One day, Matt's grandfather called for everyone to quiet down. Papa Jim then got out a VHS tape and popped it into the living room's bulky video player. It was a recorded news segment, the reporter giving his dispatch from a US military base in Iraq. Dozens of service members scurried about behind him.

"Right there!" Papa Jim shouted, pointing at the screen. Everyone leaned in and squinted.

Papa Jim was convinced it was Dustin. At 6'3", Dustin had always stood taller than anyone around, and after a decade on the sidelines watching his grandson sprint up and down the court at school basketball games, Papa Jim swore he could spot the kid's movements anywhere—including the background of a dusty military compound halfway around the world.

Plus, Papa Jim insisted, the guy on TV had a long neck, and everyone knew that Dustin, too, has a long neck. Eventually the family let him have it. "Who really knows?" Matt said. "It was probably just a guy in a Marine Corps uniform running with a hundred other guys."

Matt had been in third grade when the first Gulf War began, and he remembers Operation Desert Storm as a blur of photographs and news footage. In February 1991, an American-led coalition pounded into Kuwait, liberated the capital, then drove into Iraq with so much homegrown American moxie that a ceasefire was called within days. One Army unit, Matt heard, took out forty-one Iraqi battalions in less than seventy-two hours.[32] In 2003, as American boots stomped through Iraq once again, "That's what a lot of people were thinking," remembers Matt. "We're going to frickin' show up, break your shit, then leave."

Few proceedings in Operation Iraqi Freedom followed the script of the Gulf War, though. Enthusiasm at home soon became harder to sustain, but Marion was the kind of small Midwestern town that adored its sons and daughters in service. Supporting the troops was "kind of our thing," Matt said, and watching his cousins ship off to war "gave the rest of us an obligation. Like, maybe we should do our part."

Growing up, Matt had one clear role model: Dustin and David's father, Uncle Dennis—a paratrooper in the 101st Airborne who served four years' active duty in the late 1970s and had remained in the National Guard ever since. Uncle Dennis taught Matt how to shoot, how to hunt, how to be a man.

As kids, Matt and his cousins would spend hours rooting around in the attic, looking through Uncle Dennis's old military gear—an old pair of boots, a pocketknife, a compass. Weekends they took everything out into the backyard and staged battles until it got too dark to see. Military service was never far from Matt's mind. "It was something I grew up being interested in," he said. "I always wanted to do my part, also, and serve my country."

After graduating from high school in the spring of 2001, Matt enrolled at a local community college, but passed only about half of his classes. "I was young and immature," he said. Before he could drink legally, he would wait outside bars until somebody left, then ask for their wristband and use a piece of gum to attach it again. After a couple of years, Matt decided school wasn't for him. "I didn't know what I wanted to do. I kind of just dicked around," he said. He dropped out and began to work for his dad's construction business, delivering pizzas on the weekend for extra cash.

Construction slowed as winter set in. With the holidays approaching at the end of 2005, Uncle Dennis called one day and asked Matt if he wanted to drive down to Fort Benning together. David, Matt's younger cousin, was coming back from his first deployment. When they arrived on base, Uncle Dennis suggested that Matt stay in the barracks with David for a few nights. Matt was eager to hang around. "It was just like a giant dorm," he remembered.

Looking out the window, Matt saw soldiers packed tightly into group formation, running, marching, drilling in sync. He noticed how orderly everything was, the entire base grid-like and clean, how there was no trash or even tall weeds anywhere. And he listened spellbound to David's stories—about driving through Iraq, about loading up tanks, about bonding with the other guys. Serving in the Army, he began to understand, was saying yes to a transformation. It was saying yes to direction and structure, something you could be proud of, and he couldn't stop talking about it with Uncle Dennis during the eight-hour drive home. When they got back to Illinois,

Matt was ready to say "yes" to the Army.

Matt's decision to enlist featured several factors common to many veterans. Regardless of service era, vets frequently recount being pulled by a sense of duty—a desire "to serve their country." According to the Pew Research Center, 88 percent of post-9/11 veterans indicated that serving their country was an important reason for why they enlisted, while 93 percent of older vets said the same.[33] A commonly heard phrase among younger recruits is "wanting to make a difference."

More practical motivations exist as well. More than half of veterans say they joined the military to learn skills for future civilian careers, and three out of four post-9/11 vets list educational benefits as an important reason for their enlistment. "I joined for the free shit," said one Iraq War vet, "but I stayed for the people." Explaining her rationale, she continued: "I grew up in a dead-end town where there were no opportunities. I figured the military would pay me to leave my town and learn how to do something new. I knew I would get educational aid, which I needed since my parents were poor. I knew I would get free healthcare, which I needed since I wouldn't be able to stay on my parents' insurance unless I went to school (which I couldn't afford). I wanted to see more of the world, and I knew the military would pay me to see new places and do new things."[34]

Indeed, recent veterans are more likely than their predecessors to join the military in order "to see more of the world," while roughly a quarter of all vets say they enlisted in part because they had trouble finding civilian jobs.[35] "After 9/11 there was all kinds of economic downsizing," said Nicole Gordon, an Army sergeant from South Carolina. "No matter what kind of job you had, you were getting laid off. Businesses were closing. So with that, I had no choice but to serve, because it was either not make it and wonder whether I'm going to have a job or serve my country."[36]

As in Matt's case, a big influence for many enlistees is having family members who served before them. "Grandpa was in Europe for WWII, Dad was a Green Beret, uncle was in Vietnam," said Jon

Davis, a Marine sergeant who fought in the Iraq War. Roughly 80 percent of all recruits have at least one military family member.[37] "There was a great deal of support when I started thinking about joining," said Davis. "It wasn't pressure, but it was support."[38]

Many also join the military in response to a sense of challenge. As a natural athlete, Matt had always relished the special pleasure from pushing his body to conquer new tasks. Growing up, his free time was allocated between half a dozen different sports—soccer, basketball, baseball, track and field, coed volleyball, and softball—and after graduating from high school he took up cross-country. When he was twenty years old, he got on a bike and rode five hundred miles across the state of Iowa. It took about a week—on some days he covered as many as seventy-five miles before sunset—and then the following year, he did it again with no training, "just counting on the fact that I was young and athletic," he said. It was the most fun he ever had. He discovered things about himself he had never known—blissful, bitter lessons earned from forcing his legs to pump against pedals and chains when they screamed for him to stop. "Your body can go further than your brain," he said, and it was a truth he tried not to forget.

Matt decided to enlist as a paratrooper, just like his uncle, even though he was "terrified of heights, absolutely terrified," as he put it. When he was five years old, he was climbing a tree when his foot slipped. A branch gave way and he fell hard, the wind completely knocked out of him. That was how the fear started. Working construction, his team often got sent up to the roof, or the vacant skeleton of some high-level floor, and it was all he could do not to embarrass himself. "I remember sitting on my butt, scooting around, holding onto stuff like I was Spiderman. Like, three to four points of contact," he said. On their drive back from Fort Benning, he asked Uncle Dennis about the scariest moment of his life, and Uncle Dennis said it was when he jumped out of an airplane and his parachute didn't open. He eventually pulled out his reserve, but it was thirty seconds of terror that nothing ever came close to. Matt thought about his uncle's fear, and about his own. He considered joining the airborne infantry as the greatest challenge he would ever face, and realized that he had already made up his mind. "I wanted to do the hardest thing I could think of," he said.

Months later, he lifted himself from the holding deck of a C-130 transport plane and felt the whirlpool suck of air as the latch popped open at three thousand feet. He had been told it wasn't so bad once you were falling; jumping was the hard part.

Forty guys adjusted to face the door and Matt could feel his heart pounding. This was what he had signed up for. "This is your job now," he told himself. "This is your obligation."

He felt the tug from the soldier in front of him, the anticipation of the soldier behind. His mind was still terrified, but he was a soldier now, too. His body belonged to the pack.

He jumped.

CHAPTER 2
INDOCTRINATION

JEFF KISBERT celebrated his mom's birthday on his last night in the house in 2006. The family skipped the festivities, choosing to order a pizza and celebrate the occasion at home. The next day, January 8, Jeff made his way to the airport in Buffalo, New York, and boarded a flight for Atlanta to begin his military training. It was his first time on a plane. The second time would be on a C-130 at Airborne School, and he wouldn't wait for the tires to hit tarmac, he would leap right out the door in mid-flight. In the military, he would learn time and time again, you did a lot of things differently.

From day one at Fort Benning, the training began to change him. "You come in on the bus with whatever physical features you have—your beard, mustache, long hair, wearing your hometown team's baseball cap," Jeff recalled—none of it survived the first day. At twenty-six, Jeff had a few years on most of the other recruits, but when he woke up the next morning, there was no way to tell: he looked the same as everybody else. Same short-buzzed hair, same clean-shaven face, same camouflaged uniforms. For many of them, this dramatic change in appearance would be the first in a long series of new, often unnerving, experiences, occurring at the most formative age in their lives.[1]

Jeff had been eighteen, less than a year out of high school, the first time he tried to enlist. It was 1998, peacetime, and he was working at Applebee's, then meeting up with friends to get stoned after work. The most exciting thing he did that year was advance through the missions on *GoldenEye 007*. Soon, even his Nintendo lost its appeal. Jeff's favorite toy as a child had been G.I. Joe; together with the fearless plastic soldier, he conquered vast enemy forces in epic imaginary clashes inspired by what he had seen in the photo albums of his grandfather, a Korean War-era veteran.

At 6' 4" and over 200 pounds, Jeff's grandfather went by the nickname Big Dave. Jeff admired Big Dave more than any man in the world. The two liked to sit and watch old movies together ("all those iconic Hollywood World War II films, General Patton and stuff," he said) and when Jeff felt his life hitting a dead end, he knew that joining the service would straighten him out. One day he drove to the local recruiting station and asked to sign up. He was allowed to sit for the ASVAB, but when he went in for his medical checkup, the doctor said his acne was too severe. He left dejected and slipped back into his Applebee's polo and smock.

Jeff got married a couple years later and a few months after the wedding, the 9/11 attacks occurred. He felt the call to service again, stronger than ever this time, and went back to the recruiting office. He got the papers he needed, then came home to tell his wife. "Fort Drum is just upstate in New York," he reasoned. He tried to make a case for it. "It's not that far from your parents."

She shut him down. "This is not what I signed up for. You are not going to war."

When the couple split in 2005, Jeff knew exactly what he was going to do, and this time, nothing could stop him. "I didn't want to be somebody who doesn't have a good answer when his family asks, 'What did you do during the wars?' I'm going to be on the front line. I'm going to be in the infantry. I wanted to be out there," he said.

The divorce finalized in September. One month later, he took the ASVAB for the third time, then his oath, then finally found himself a member of the US Army.

The old Jeff began to fade away as soon as he got to basic training. Suddenly he wasn't even "Jeff" anymore but "private" or "soldier," no longer a name but a rank. The first rule: no talking. No talking while in formation, no talking in the mess halls, no talking even in line for food. "There was no input," Jeff, now Private Kisbert, remembered, no expression or communication of any kind—just stare at the back of the guy's head in front of you, and know the guy behind you is doing the same. If there was one message made clear to everyone all through basic training, immediately and repeatedly, this was it:

You are not an individual.

THE INTENT OF military indoctrination is illustrated by a well-known parable from the nineteenth century military theorist Ardant du Picq:

"Four brave men who do not know each other will not dare to attack a lion. Four less brave men who know each other well, sure of their reliability and consequently of mutual aid, will attack resolutely."

While military training cannot influence the innate bravery of individuals, it does transform them into members of a greater whole, able to attack challenges with a combined fortitude that exceeds the sum of its parts.

In the context of the armed forces, indoctrination is a transformative procedure, purposefully calibrated, to produce soldiers. In a 2006 paper, senior military officers Dennis McGurk, Dave Cotting, Amy Adler, and Thomas Britt stated that "the military replaces the recruit's former identity with another identity"—one defined by a capacity for two tasks: comply and execute. Combat soldiers must be rewired so that they are able to carry out orders in extreme circumstances, perhaps requiring extreme actions radically departed from what they had considered acceptable in their prior worldviews. "By the end of basic training," the officers wrote, "a young person will obey all orders, including the order to kill another person without hesitation."[2] Only a rigorous, targeted regime can condition service members for these outcomes.

How does indoctrination happen? The psychologist Robert Baron examined indoctrination rituals across a wide range of institutions, from Soviet gulags to modern cults, and categorized the procedure into four main stages. Stage one, he described in a 2000 paper, is known as the "softening-up" phase. Inductees are inundated with stimuli to create high levels of stress, weakening their natural defenses and making them more vulnerable to a subsequent "assault on [their] attitudes, beliefs, and values."[3]

Research shows that this initial period of disorientation, involving tactics such as sleep deprivation and continuous physical activity, primes an individual to de-emphasize their personal identity while lowering their resistance to the procedure's persuasion attempts. During basic combat training, drill sergeants run recruits through intensive physical exercises all day long, then routinely interrupt them in the middle of the night. Recruits are suddenly roused from their sleep, then given two minutes to dress and line up for an impromptu physical training session. Drained by sleep deprivation and exhausted from physical labor, subjects have reduced cognitive capacity to process new inputs, increasing their susceptibility to messages from a perceived authority.[4]

Sooner or later, recruits must also face the gas chamber. Protected at first by gas masks, trainees line up with their right arm on the shoulder of the person in front of them, proceeding into the chamber as a human chain. In many cases, the fumes are so thick it becomes hard to see. Individually, or assigned into small groups, the recruits are instructed to remove their masks. Some drill sergeants order them to recite the alphabet, or a pledge, or their social security numbers—anything to force them to inhale—until everyone is coughing and hacking, chins steeped with drool, hands clutching at their throats. "All you can think about is how you're going to die," said one former soldier.[5]

Through repeated exposure to such stressors, subjects are prompted to shed their prior group identities, stripping away salient features until they are a blank, uniform slate.[6] At this point, recruits have been disconnected from their home lives, isolated from their loved ones, and immersed in an unfamiliar environment. Previous achievements, relationships, and markers of individuality are actively suppressed. Identical haircuts and attire enforce the group identity. When recruits in the Marine Corps wanted to talk to their drill instructor, they had to refer to themselves in the third person: "The recruit requests to speak."

Known as depluralization, this process is often painful, with many enlistees reporting heightened anxiety and scientists measuring greater cortisol levels during the transition. Military officials say the drills are designed to "promote a sense of anonymity and loss of self-awareness, leading to a greater likelihood of immersion in the social role or group." As recruits struggle with the conversion, it isn't uncommon to hear sobs, sniffles, or prayers rippling through the barracks at the end of a grueling day.[7]

Although these methods might appear harsh and maladaptive, even abusive, they belong to a carefully constructed operation meant to prepare soldiers for the demands of combat and the conditions of functioning in a team. In that sense, this process is invaluable to the survival of the group.

Enlisted training varies in length from six to twelve weeks, depending on the branch of service. For Jeff, basic infantry extended the full three months, divided into red, white, and blue phases. In the red phase, recruits were put through an unrelenting current of fitness exercises, tactical instruction, and learning modules, covering subjects from chemical warfare to landmine defense.[8] As they gradually adapted to the new tempo of boot camp, they entered the second stage of indoctrination: compliance.

Pla-toon! A-ten-shun!

Early on, recruits are instructed to memorize the Army's basic marching commands, then immediately drilled through them dozens of times a day.

About...face!

Left...face!

Right...face!

Mark time...March!

Research shows that by repeatedly reinforcing specific rituals, subjects start to internalize behaviors they may have initially performed in response to lower-level motivations, such as avoiding disapproval or punishment.[9] As the drills continue, recruits move away from paying lip service or simply going through the motions and begin taking the commands to heart.

During the first month, Jeff and his class of recruits were barred from any contact with the outside world, other than letters and a weekly phone call. One of the few times they were allowed to speak was to recite the infantryman's creed:

I am the infantry.

I am my country's strength in war, her deterrent in peace.

I am the heart of the fight—wherever, whenever.

Every morning before sunrise Jeff gathered with his platoon outside its brick, two-floor barracks. They stood in formation, backs straight, arms at their side, and their voices rang in unison:

I am what my country expects me to be: the best trained soldier in the world.

In the race for victory, I am swift, determined, and courageous, armed with a fierce will to win.

Soon they were also expected to know their chain of command, an imposing hierarchy beginning with their drill sergeant, to the company commander, all the way up to the commander-in-chief.

For a long time, these recitals of their creed and the chain of command—and of course, the incessant barking of their drill sergeants—were the only voices they heard. They were completely starved of stimuli. There was no television, no music, no internet, no newspapers, no books, no posters. All they had to stare at were their bunker's pocked cement walls, and hanging from them, a pyramid of framed portraits—the military's top brass—topped by a headshot of George W. Bush.

By the second month, the red phase was over and the white phase began. The recruits were allowed to go to the store, where Jeff bought a James Patterson novel for company at night. They were also permitted a five-minute phone call, and swarms instantly formed around the camp's pay phones. Social restrictions were relaxed. "As opposed to sitting there and just cleaning your rifle in silence, we could sit in the bay and clean our rifles and chit-chat," Jeff said. "It was a more relaxed manner that allowed storytelling and joking around and bullshitting."

Perhaps more than any other factor, this group cohesion is the key that activates indoctrination's next and crucial step, internalization. Humans are social creatures, driven by the need to belong to a group and form meaningful relationships with others; it is among the most simple and powerful determinants of individual behavior.

During basic training, the constant presence of others can initially be distracting, even a hindrance. One recruit described the chaos of his first shower experience after arriving. "We only had twenty minutes [...] for over a hundred recruits to shower and shave and get into bed. There were only fifteen shower heads and we were all fighting each other. Fifty naked men crammed into one head, trying to make sure we did not lose our clothes all the while stripping bare ass naked. It was mayhem."[10]

But no inconvenience, however frustrating, compares with the pain from feeling left out of the group—a sensation that most people would do anything to avoid. Over time, the desire for inclusion comes to override all else, enabling the three types of group conformity that researchers have identified in military indoctrination: "conformity to the actions of fellow unit members, conformity to the demands of authorities (e.g., drill sergeants), and conformity to the more abstract values emphasized by the particular branch of the armed service." Peer-shaming and other psychological penalties reinforce the group's dominant culture.[11]

Social psychologist Henri Tajfel states that identity is also dependent on the emotional significance a person attaches to that membership. This process of attachment accentuates the perceived similarities between the in-group members, while simultaneously emphasizing perceived differences between the in- and out-group. Recruits embrace their inclusion into one group, the armed forces, by minimizing their attachment to another, the civilian sphere. A sense of "us" is strengthened against the perception of "them." They are no longer who they were, civilians hailing from various walks of life. They have become soldiers, bound to a single cause.

During the blue phase in their final weeks of training, Jeff and his company were rewarded with a day entirely to themselves. After more than two months in which every movement was mapped, every exchange was monitored, every minute was planned, suddenly, they had twenty-four hours of freedom.

It was a Friday night. They put on their dress uniforms and paraded into town. They bought cigarettes and booze and hotel rooms, and everyone piled in, smoking and drinking and toasting one another until the carpet was strewn with bottles and sunlight peaked in through the blinds.

"That was a milestone," Jeff said. "So much of the stuff that happens you don't notice it happening. The way you walk, the way you talk, the way you carry yourself. It just naturally happens—you don't have time to think about it or notice it because everyone is doing it. At the time it's not real shocking, you're just part of this group."

But when the group returned to base the following evening, hungover and reflective, it had all started to sink in—the oath they swore, the duty they assumed, the daily sacrifices they had already made, and the big one that may one day await. They added up to a turning point, Jeff understood, from which there was no going back. He let the revelation hang for a moment, then took a breath and gulped it down.

WHEN MOLLY SNIDER[12] signed up for the Georgia National Guard, that kind of sacrifice was far from her mind. It was November 18, 2003, and when people brought up the war, she thought about President Bush standing on the USS Abraham Lincoln with a "Mission Accomplished" banner waving behind him.[13] It didn't occur to her that she was signing up for combat. "In my head, the National Guard was like what it used to be," she said. "Hurricanes

and floods and helping out if there was a riot. Mother Nature stuff."
In February, the twenty-two-year-old nature lover started boot camp.

That spring, however, marked a turning point in the war. After
a lull in violence, the insurgency in Iraq roared back in the first half
of 2004, with regional militias and Islamic militant groups entering the fight.[14] A series of offensives ripped through US-controlled
areas of Iraq and it became clear the mission was far from accomplished. "That's when it started hitting me that I was probably going
to be going somewhere," Molly said. By April, she had moved on
to Advanced Individual Training at Fort Sam Houston, where she
was assigned to medic school. During one of their training sessions,
a sergeant told her cohort, "Look to your left. Look to your right.
You're not all coming home."

The sergeant played an instructional video for the medics, filled
with Vietnam-era firefights. In one scene, explosions ripped through
a jungle, and soldiers immediately began running toward a clearing
where friendly helicopters were waiting to evacuate them. A lone
person was charging back *into* the jungle, toward the explosions. The
drill sergeant pointed at the screen.

"That person is you."

A few people in the room snickered but not Molly. "I was at
the beginning of my brainwashing journey," she said. "I was taking
it all in."

As service members advance through the levels of military training, they are guided through increasingly complex exercises designed
to solidify their professional identities, bolster their confidence, and
strengthen bonds with their fellow soldiers.[15] "I was happy, surrounded by my really close friends," Molly said. "We went through
a lot of hard stuff together and just got along really well." She added,
"I had this real respect for following the rules. I just wanted to be the
best that I could be."[16]

Photos from her training and deployment days show a spirited
young woman, often surrounded by friends, beaming from ear to
ear. In one picture, she had recently been named her medic school's

Junior Leader of the Week. A photographer had been sent to take her picture for the local newspaper, and she stood over a mock patient in full uniform, pretending to be in the middle of treatment. She meant to look serious and focused. A wide grin gave her away.

Her distinction came with a medal, and that night, the girls in her barrack decided to celebrate. They bypassed personal hygiene, skipped getting ready for bed, and threw Molly an impromptu fashion show. Their wardrobes were hardly designed for the runway but if there was one thing the combat medics had learned, it was how to be resourceful. Everyone was soon scrambling and trading, piecing together whatever they had available. Molly stepped into her MOPP gear, a military-style hazmat suit with a gas mask, chemical gloves, and boots, and donned her civilian beanie. With her new medal dangling around her neck, she strutted through the barracks with her best impression of Liberace.

Cameras flashed. Cheers erupted. Wolf whistles rang through the halls. The girls of the 232nd Medical Battalion modeled their most audacious catwalks and struck their most fabulous poses, laughing and twirling late into the night.

Then the sergeants showed up. Everyone got busted and it wasn't so pretty after that. The girls were marched outside and ordered to do exercises until they had all collapsed on the ground, writhing and throwing up. Was it worth it? "Totally worth it," Molly says, remembering the night. After a few days, their muscles had no longer felt like pudding, yet memories of their giddy fashion show and the bonding between them remained.

Molly was always what her teammates called a "very high-speed soldier." Their exercises were grueling, but she was the first one ready to go; whatever their challenges, she always felt equipped to overcome them. Military service is full of stressors but the majority of veterans describe their experience as a positive one. According to the Pew Research Center, 93 percent of post-9/11 vets say they matured during their time in service, while nine out of ten vets say that the military improved their self-confidence and taught them valuable lessons about collaboration.[17] "Man, I ate it up," Molly said. "I didn't question why I was there or anything else. I was taught to do something, and I believed in it wholeheartedly at the time."

After graduating AIT in August, she applied for an interstate transfer from Georgia to North Carolina. But even with her medical training, few job opportunities were available. "In the military, I could have done anything," she said. "In the civilian world, I could only drive an ambulance." She considered working as a county EMT but the pay was terrible. Eventually she found work at a Planned Parenthood office in Greensboro. She enrolled in night school to finish her degree.

On October 10, she was sitting in the office when a colleague called for her. "Hey Molly, a Master Sergeant Green is on the phone."

Master Sergeant Green was her unit master sergeant in Asheville. She picked up the receiver and suddenly felt her body snap into position, free hand sliding down to parade rest behind her back, as if she were a puppet and someone was pulling the strings.

"You will receive orders," Master Sergeant Green told her. "And you will meet with your unit in-country."

Molly said yes to everything through a haze. "I was wearing scrubs, but I was talking to this guy like he could see me," she remembered. When she hung up, her face was pale. Everyone in the office was staring at her. "I need to take a walk," she said. When she stepped outside, the chilly fall air pricked her skin and the moment started to sink in. She had received her thirty-day notice.

At the Planned Parenthood clinic, Molly's office had become like a second home. When her colleagues heard the news, they were aghast. "Everyone who worked with me—you know, being around all these pregnant women—they said, 'We can get you some fake urine.' I was like, 'Don't be ridiculous!' I signed up for this. I knew it was a possibility," Molly said.

She sent her two chocolate Labradors to her dad's house in Florida, and told her college advisor she would be going on military leave. In November, she flew to Fort Bliss in Texas, where she looked over her will, signed up for life insurance, and received her desert uniforms. The day after Thanksgiving, she flew from El Paso to Baltimore for a layover, Baltimore to Germany to refuel, then Germany to Kuwait's Camp Doha.

Soon she was receiving her "battle rattle"—her helmet, body armor, web vest, ballistic plates, and other equipment. Her unit arrived to pick her up and they went over the rules of engagement. Before she knew it, they were crossing the Kuwaiti border. As they approached Camp Bucca, a sprawling ring-fenced detention center in Iraq, Molly gazed upon it with anticipation and wonder. Her sergeant motioned them forward.

"We're taking you home," he said.

Molly arrived at Camp Bucca at the end of 2004, placing her among 135,000 US Army troops stationed in Iraq as the new year began. In 2005, 40 percent of US troops in Iraq served in units whose primary mission was combat operations—the military's "tooth"—while the majority served in the non-combat "tail" component. The addition of fifty-eight thousand contractors during the Iraq War pushed the Army's tooth-to-tail ratio down to 25 percent.[18]

While Molly's job would play an integral part in the overall war effort, it would bear little resemblance to popular and captivating war stories that exude such a natural appeal in the media. Movies such as *Black Hawk Down* (2001), *The Hurt Locker* (2008), *Lone Survivor* (2013), and *American Sniper* (2014) are reliably box office hits, typically featuring elite soldiers in harrowing combat situations, showcasing their bravery and endurance. *Lone Survivor* exemplifies the genre. The image of the lone Navy SEAL crouched in the mountains of northeast Afghanistan, surrounded by dozens of Taliban fighters, leaves a striking impression. Yet while Marcus Luttrell's survival and escape were undeniably heroic—upon his return, he received the nation's second highest award for valor, the Navy Cross—his story is hardly typical.

Despite their prevalence, these sensational stories present a wildly skewed image of military service that distorts what most soldiers go through. They contribute to a misleading narrative that all soldiers are heroic, and that military service is uniformly arduous and laudatory. The reality is far more mundane: the vast majority of service members serve in military functions directly comparable to occupations in civilian life. Though they are certainly critical to mission success, the heavy equipment operators, instrument technicians, weather specialists, mechanics, and clerks in the armed forces will rarely find their experiences reflected in our stories about war. And as narratives of violence and trauma command ever-greater attention in mainstream culture, the American public develops increasingly inaccurate ideas of military service. Among the most common misconceptions is that the typical enlisted soldier or officer will even encounter the enemy in battle. In fact, most will never find themselves within range of enemy fire.[19]

According to a 2010 Pentagon report, 40 percent of the military's active-duty personnel had never deployed once, while almost a quarter of the overall force was dedicated to "commercial activities" that any civilian could perform.[20] Experiences varied widely between soldiers fighting in combat and those serving in support—a fact that has been consistently documented by America's most enduring scribes of war.

"Division headquarters is miles—miles—behind the line where soldiers experience terror and madness. Indeed, unless they actually encountered the enemy during the war, most 'soldiers' have very little idea what 'combat' was like," observed the scholar and critic Paul Fussell, who served as an infantryman in France during World War II. Biographer William Manchester, a veteran of the Pacific Theater, wrote, "All who wore uniforms are called veterans, but more than 90 percent of them are as uninformed about the killing zones as those on the home front." His fellow Marine, the author E.B. Sledge, recounted in his 1981 memoir *With the Old Breed*, "To the non-combatants and those on the periphery of action, the war meant only boredom or occasional excitement, but to those who entered the meat grinder itself the war was a netherworld of horror from which escape seemed less and less likely."[21]

The nineteenth century Prussian general Carl von Clausewitz once remarked, "The end for which a soldier is recruited, clothed, armed, and trained—the whole object of his sleeping, eating, drinking, and marching—is simply that he should fight at the right place and the right time."[22] But the evolution of modern warfare has created new expectations for the soldier, and nations today register entirely novel modes of fighting. Innovations in weaponry and mobility create the need for different tactics, and the mechanization of large-scale military operations requires more recruits to be trained in support functions rather than combat. Soldiers are increasingly assigned to no less valuable roles in the military's administrative, logistics, and life support units, rarely needing to leave the security of their base. [23]

The expansion of military bases in both scale and scope began during America's involvement in Vietnam. Base camps were built out to resemble American cities, complete with all the consumer luxuries troops were accustomed to back home. As Meredith Lair writes in *Armed with Abundance: Consumerism and Soldiering in the Vietnam War*, "A legion of butchers, bakers, and ice cream makers fed the troops. Librarians shelved books in base libraries, entertainment specialists planned morale-boosting field trips and talent shows, craft-shop attendants minded the kilns and darkrooms, and lifeguards kept watch at the pools. Military-run retail outlets and bars employed even more personnel to stock the shelves, pour the drinks, book the bands, and count the slugs in the slot machines. On rear bases, an army of plumbers, electricians, and refrigerator repairmen kept the water running, the lights on, and the drinks ice cold." [24]

The largest of the bases, Long Binh Post, located twenty miles north of Saigon, covered a geographic area bigger than Cleveland. Among the facilities offered on-site were eighty-one basketball courts, sixty-four volleyball courts, twelve swimming pools, eight softball fields, six tennis courts, five craft shops, three football fields, three miniature golf courses, a golf driving range, a skeet range, an archery range, salons, barbecue pits, an amphitheater for movies and live shows, and even a go-cart track, complete with a starting stand, public-address system, and a pit for on-the-spot repairs. Joked one colonel, "If we ever really got attacked, the V.C. would have to use the scheduled bus service to get around the base."

Rear-base support troops and the soldiers sent into battle had little in common; they "may have served on the same side," writes Lair, "but they did not serve in the same war." Some new arrivals, self-conscious of their inactivity, distressed their uniforms and scuffed their boots to give the appearance of having survived multiple patrols. Arthur Wiknik Jr., an infantry squad leader during the bloody assault on Hamburger Hill, ridiculed the leisurely lifestyle of the rear soldier. "As near as I could tell, the only danger [he] faced was from catching gonorrhea or being run down by a drunken truck driver. And the biggest hardship [he] contended with was when a generator went down and his beer got warm or there was no movie that night." Upon returning home, a soldier who had deployed to a resting station at Vung Tàu told his mother, "Most of the time you didn't know you were in a war."

Some embraced humor to cope with the dissonance. Dean Muehlberg, a clerk-typist during his 1969 tour, admitted to being so far from battle that his rifle grew mold idling in its rack. Recognizing they would never earn a medal for valor, clerks from the Twenty-Fifth Infantry Division decided to invent their own: The Silver Paper Clip. They bestowed the inaugural honor in a profuse celebration, citing:

"Specialist Howard distinguished himself with conspicuous gallantry and intrepidity at the risk of his life when he single-handedly answered over 200 telephone calls and processed in fifteen new men, exposing himself to a hail of questions. He moved from the relative safety of his desk to the P.X. where he repeatedly bought cases of soda. Ignoring the personnel NCO, he cleaned his typewriter, picked up the mail, petted four dogs, ran off three stencils and took his malaria pill."

The extravagance of Long Binh Post and mock grandeur of the Silver Paper Clip may now be artifacts, but the structural composition of America's war machine abroad remains. In 2014, the Army's chief logistician reported that over 55 percent of fuel consumption by US forces in Afghanistan went to generating power for base facilities like hospitals, living quarters, shopping markets, gyms, and barber shops. He sounded a warning to commanders who were allocating more fuel toward 'quality of life' ends than powering vehicles and aircraft for combat missions. "Increasingly," reported *The New York Times*, "the encampments are the way many Americans experience the war." [25]

In 2005, as Molly was on her first tour in Iraq, the Army's Combat Studies Institute estimated that only 11 percent of deployed American soldiers were performing true combat operations. As the wars in the Middle East dragged on, forward operating bases multiplied and expanded to accommodate the growing number of soldiers attached to headquarters or support units. At the height of the war in Iraq, more than three hundred F.O.B.s were operating in the country. The rear-base culture of the Vietnam War was making a comeback. A new term, 'Fobbit,' gained popularity as a way of describing soldiers who rarely, or never, ventured beyond the wire. "Safe inside these massive bases, soldiers could go an entire 'combat' tour without ever knowing that there was a war going on," wrote one Army officer. Recounting his time at Bagram Air Base in Afghanistan, the officer said: "I rarely left the wire, except on occasional logistics convoys to another base or via a flight to another base. I too ate steak and lobster on Fridays at the dining facility. As infantrymen and Special Forces units waged close combat with a determined enemy, I battled ever-growing non-combat related requirements with a battery of PowerPoint slides." [26]

EVEN IN "TOOTH" UNITS like the Eighty-Second Airborne, experiences can vary based on positions and experience. Yet no matter who you are in the military, or what job you have, it is always the new guy who gets picked on. When Matt showed up to Fort Bragg in the summer of 2006, he knew he was the new guy, and tried his best to lie low. One day he was standing outside, about to light a cigarette, when a deep-voiced private asked him for a smoke. Matt, who hadn't start smoking until he joined the military, had a pack of Newports. The other private carried Camels. Instead of bumming, he offered to trade. His name was Jeff Kisbert and he was also a new guy.

The company that Matt and Jeff joined had just returned from their first deployment, and the recent combat exposure, still fresh, gave the hazing an extra edge. "These nineteen-year-olds were always giving us shit, telling us how hard their deployment was," Jeff said. Staying idle meant being a target for pointless orders to clean or do push-ups, and the company's two new privates found themselves taking smoke breaks as often as they could. "It was one-third to smoke," said Jeff, "two thirds not to deal with what was going on." Empty cartons collected under their bunks, but it felt good having a partner to stand on the other side of Bullshit Fence with.

Matt was the first to deploy, departing for southern Afghanistan's Kandahar Airfield in January 2007. In the middle of the night, his battalion flew out on UH-60 Black Hawk helicopters, touching down in faraway poppy fields. Fanning out into nearby towns and villages, they spilled through the streets, kicking down doors and securing the area. The missions occurred in short, tough bursts, and Matt soon found a groove in the tempo. His movements felt crisp, his instincts sharp. He was running as a member of the pack and his training took over: land, kick, secure. Land, kick, secure.

When the unit returned from deployment, Matt's company commander tapped him to be master driver, in charge of leading vehicle training. It became his job to coach new soldiers, thirty at a time, through everything they needed to know about Humvees, cargo trucks, multipurpose carriers—the unit's entire lineup of combat vehicles. It was a duty he took seriously. Instead of teaching from the Army's "check-the-box crap," he designed his lessons to simulate the company's actual deployments. "I was able to shape the training the way that I wanted," he said. "I tried to make it as realistic as possible." This meant that his soldiers didn't just put on a helmet, they practiced in full kit, even with night vision goggles. And when Matt cut the lights, they drilled through the controls in the dark, toggling between their assigned vehicle's headlights, running lights, and infrared lights until everything became muscle memory and they knew exactly how their hands should move without looking.

Intense as it was, his training also had its benefits. Matt saved the classroom portion for the very end. Though he could have rushed through all the material in a single afternoon, he booked an air-conditioned room down in the barracks basement and stretched out the PowerPoint slides for several days. He found an old projector, pulled in a few couches, and even prepared snacks. Between the required content, he added dozens of funny video clips on drunk driving. In the 100-degree heat of North Carolina in July, his classes became an oasis.

"We got a good thing going on," Matt would tell his students, but "you got to pay attention and know this stuff because I am [still] going to give you a test." And if they ever heard the door crack open, they knew to perk up and appear like they were taking notes. If it was someone important observing, they knew that Matt might even cold call, so they had better come prepared with something smart to say. Before Matt's second deployment, he was promoted, once more, to sergeant.

The new responsibilities also required him to attend the company's weekly advanced echelon, or ADVON, meetings, where he saw that Jeff, too, often came. They began to spend more time together. For Matt, it started as a simple process of elimination. "I'm not about to go hang out with the lieutenant," he said. "Or the supply guy because he's kind of weird. And the other guy was way too motivated, and I wasn't down with that." He began to see Jeff everywhere—briefings, health check-ups, lunch meetings—and the two kept discovering they had more and more in common. They both smoked like chimneys, and they both drank too much Red Bull just to get through the day. They both liked to kill an hour off with the same video games, but most of all, they found in each other a similar sense of humor—built on brazen, relentless sarcasm—particularly when it came to the daily mishaps of the Army's bumbling bureaucracy. "We had a great appreciation for how silly it was," Jeff said. "The left hand never knew what the right hand was doing."

For example, there was the time in Afghanistan when a half dozen of them were sent out for "ballistics training," and ballistics training turned out to be firing an anti-tank rocket launcher, pre-loaded with single-use shells, into the open range. The rockets supposedly cost $50,000 apiece and each time someone fired one, they all piped up, "Yup, there goes another grunt's salary." In fifteen minutes, they had flushed through half a million dollars of the nation's arms budget and the jokes came nonstop about explaining that one to the taxpayer. Soon no one was sure anymore if they were chuckling from amusement, guilt, or disgust.

Then there was the time when a civilian driving course requested eight guys, but the communication had gotten botched and all six battalions ended up sending eight guys each. So nearly fifty uniformed soldiers arrived for an eight-man job and everyone who wasn't needed had three free days to screw around. "We took our jobs seriously, but we didn't take the Army seriously because of all the ridiculous stuff we had to do," Matt said. "Some people are like, 'The Army is life. This is it.' [Jeff] and I are like, 'Yup, I have 274 days. You have 221 days.' We're not going to be shit-bags but if we get time to chill out in the AC, we're going to do it."

Their leadership positions on the ADVON party often came in handy. If the company commander or first sergeant was in a bad mood, orders might suddenly come down for everyone to scrub the walls or clean the bathrooms, simply because someone had been caught spitting on the sidewalk or committing some other minor infraction. As master driver, Matt had a special card to play. He would remind the commander or first sergeant that the company's next trip to the range was approaching and offer his services. "I just want to make sure everything's good and the trucks are squared away," he would say, and the commander would reply, "Alright yeah, go do that, make sure we're good to go." Released from duty, Matt would flee to the motor pool as quickly as he could, free to "go down there and hang out for two hours and wait for the bullshit to end." Jeff thought this was genius.

Soon they chanced upon another kind of shelter. The winters at Fort Bragg were especially brutal, adding one more affliction to the exhausting outdoor drills and long nights in the barracks. One night before an outdoor drill, it had snowed close to six inches— unusual for North Carolina. "You're shaving at five a.m. with a cold bottle of water and no shaving cream," said Matt. "Then we get out there and we're all laying on the ground and crawling around, doing infantry stuff. We were just nasty and cold. It was miserable." Then Jeff shared that he had recently been picked up as the commander's Humvee driver. "He would get it ready to go so when the commander stepped into it, it was already a nice and warm truck." Matt, the master driver, decided the commander's Humvee could probably use an inspection before starting, and the commander's driver was inclined to agree. It was a tag-team effort. "I might lift up the hood or check the fluid," Matt said, "but eventually I'd make my way inside and try to stay there as long as possible." The two best friends kept up the routine as long as they could, joking around in their toasty morning oasis, savoring a few more minutes before getting swallowed again by Army life and the freezing, unkind winter.

CHAPTER 3
AFTER THE PEAK

THEY KNEW the bombs were there. Earlier in the day, a raid camera had filmed four suspected Taliban fighters sitting in a trench beside a cemetery. In the footage, one of the combatants walked out into the open road and took a knee. After a few minutes, he returned to his position.

Tyson Quink's field artillery platoon had been trained on the enemy's tactics. The Taliban had great patience. They liked to plant IEDs in the ground, then find cover nearby. They liked to sit and wait, for hours if they had to, until they saw American soldiers approaching. That's when they attached the battery, when the trigger hit the charge, when things went boom.

Tyson was in charge of the third platoon. His guys had already gone out that day, a breezy morning patrol in which they went to a local village and interviewed some locals about nearby drug routes and enemy activity. While second platoon went out to interdict the enemy team, third platoon kept watch and later moved to establish a blocking position down the road.

Second platoon didn't find the enemy team; in typical fashion the enemy had fled immediately. But they had uncovered three IEDs. Better yet, they had detained two suspected combatants and now they needed replacements so they could bring the captives in. Tyson and his platoon geared up for their second mission of the day, moving to relieve second platoon.

It was June 2011, the third month in Tyson's first deployment to Afghanistan. He had graduated from West Point two years earlier.

Growing up in the San Francisco Bay Area, he had never heard of the legendary United States Military Academy, or ever considered joining the armed forces. Then one day during his senior year, he got a phone call. It was a college football coach on the line with a question: Did he want to keep playing football?

"Yes," Tyson said. Ever since he was little, tossing a football around with the neighborhood kids, the sport had been the one constant in his life.

The coach went on: Did he want to keep competing, keep pushing himself mentally and physically beyond his own limits?

"Yes," Tyson said.

Finally, the coach asked: Was he willing to come out east?

"Yes," Tyson said.

He soon took to the turf as an Army Black Knight.

Four seasons later he had six months left of school and sixty pounds to shed from his playing weight in order to graduate. Offensive linemen aren't usually worried about cutting down. They're wired to bulk up. But just as Tyson knew to hit the books for his final exams, he hit the cardio room to slim down, and while his full-dress gray still felt a little tight on commencement day, he strode across the stage and received his diploma, beaming.

Life at West Point had been a nonstop juggle between academics and football, with little energy left to consider what came next. Reminders of the sacred duty that awaited, however, were everywhere. "You're surrounded by it," Tyson said. "Most of your teachers are military. All your leadership have combat deployments. Their job is to train you so you can leave." Reminders also came in the form of casualty rolls reported on TV, or news of the latest military operations devised inside the halls of Washington. They came as announcements through the mess hall loudspeakers, names of West Point grads killed or wounded in combat read out as cadets were spooning down their cereal during breakfast. Usually, Tyson didn't recognize the names. Sometimes, he did. After the roll there was always a moment of silence, and after the silence there was always the mood that followed, often trailing him into the evening, occasionally lingering for several days or more. But eventually, Tyson had to get back to studying and training, back to the balancing act of Division I student athletics. During the season, the other stuff was easier to compartmentalize. The other stuff happened to soldiers, people who went to war. He was there to win football games.

Eventually, all of that changed. As soon as he graduated, Tyson knew he was no longer a student. He knew he was no longer a Black Knight, no longer stationed at the edge of the O-line, his job to flank the guards and shield the quarterback. Soon he was at Basic Officer Leadership Course, getting pushed beyond anything he had known on what General Douglas MacArthur once called "the fields of friendly strife." Then he was meeting his platoon at Fort Drum, getting to know the men he would lead, and not long after that, he was sitting with them inside a transport aircraft, getting dropped off in Afghanistan. Now he was strapping on his gear in Kandahar, about to lead twenty-six soldiers into the cold, dark night.

They arrived at a vineyard; blankets of twisting leaves spread across dirt-packed mounds. Someone gave a shout. Two guys from the second platoon had discovered another IED. Tyson made his way over and someone from his platoon joined him. Then they stopped. A path cut out in front of them, a little too clean not to be suspicious. Tyson decided to send someone down with a metal detector.

It was nine in the evening, no moon in the sky. Flashlight beams swiveled through the air like swords. Tyson propped his night vision goggles over his helmet, then took one step back to give the order. He heard something click beneath his foot. "Shit," he said in a whisper, and the partial darkness turned into complete, infinite black.

Tyson didn't feel the blast because he didn't feel anything—in an instant he had lost all sensation in his body. He couldn't see, couldn't hear, couldn't feel. Somewhere in the infinite blackness, he heard his own voice. "What the fuck?"

Then he heard himself say, "I'm fucking dead."

The thought played on loop.

"I'm fucking dead. I'm fucking dead. I can't believe I'm fucking dead."

A moment later, he thought: "Man, you can talk to yourself for eternity? This fucking sucks."

Eternity lasted for about three seconds. Then his vision came back, the world returned, and he was back in the vineyard again, lying flat on his back. Debris was falling everywhere.

Tyson lifted his head and saw that his right foot was gone. He could only see the jagged edge, bone white as milk. His left leg lay hidden from his view beneath a shredded pant leg. But the sensation in his body had returned. "It felt like I was standing in a fire," he remembered.

He yelled. No one came.

He yelled again and still nothing, and after a few breaths, it occurred to him why. Surely there were still more IEDs in the ground, still more buried parcels of shells and shrapnel waiting to cut him and his men into still smaller pieces. It would do no good for anyone to come charging in and set off another. Once Tyson understood this, a feeling of calm washed over him. He had a team of soldiers behind him and they had been expressly trained for situations like this. They would know what to do.

Tyson unbuckled his helmet. He removed his eyewear and took off his gloves. He put the items in his helmet and put his hands on his chest. And then he waited.

Eventually, one of Tyson's squad leaders crawled up next to him. He tried to put a tourniquet on Tyson's legs but couldn't; moments ago, the explosion had thrown him against a wall and his brain was still rattling. Two other soldiers had been wounded. One was knocked out cold; the other suffered a severed ear and wounds to both arms.

After clearing the area, the medics began tending to them. When the medevac helicopter arrived, Tyson, who had caught the worst of the blast, was carried onboard. Inside the Black Hawk, he saw the wounded men around him huddling with their heads in their hands, as if to keep their brains from shaking.

Even in the air the medics kept working on Tyson's legs. He was conscious for every second of it, the pain so intense he thought he was becoming delirious. When the helicopter touched back down at Kandahar Airfield, he was lifted onto a stretcher and rushed inside the hospital. Suddenly a doctor's face was hovering over him, blocking out the ceiling lights. The doctor's mouth was moving, asking where it hurt and what he could feel, while Tyson tried to stay engaged, stay alive. Then halfway down the hallway, he blinked, and his body shut down.

ONE WAY OR ANOTHER, all soldiers eventually leave the military. Rarely are their separations set off by an IED blast; in fact, experiences like Tyson's are shared by only a slim fraction of post-9/11 service members. Yet, news outlets fixate on casualty figures, and portrayals of veterans in the media typically amplify cases of injury. The actual numbers tell a different story: The wars in Afghanistan and Iraq have been among the safest in American history.

From 2001 to 2015, roughly 2.8 million soldiers served more than five million individual deployments to combat zones.[1] As of March 2021, roughly fifty-three thousand soldiers have been wounded in action and just over 5,400 have been killed in action.[2] Commentators often attribute the unprecedented survival rates to improved body armor and enhanced battlefield care, but service members today are less likely to encounter harm to begin with. From a high of 4.2 percent during World War II, the wounded-in-action rate fell to 3.5 percent during the Vietnam War, and less than two percent for service members in the post-9/11 era.[3] The most serious injuries are even more rare: there have been fewer than 2,000 major-limb amputees and a few hundred battle-incurred spinal cord injuries since the operations in Afghanistan and Iraq began, while other serious cases, including severe burn injuries and incidents of complete blindness, number in the hundreds.[4] According to the Department of Defense, less than 14 percent of active duty separations in 2015 were caused by medical or disability-related purposes.[5]

The frequency of fatalities has also fallen. After a decade of the US occupation in Afghanistan and Iraq, the combined annual death rate was 0.0027—270 fatalities for every 100,000 military personnel serving in the two war zones. During the Vietnam War, American soldiers died 2.5 times more frequently—670 deaths for every 100,000 personnel; their predecessors in World War II were killed at almost ten times the rate—2,500 out of every 100,000. Over time, wars have unquestionably become less deadly for their U.S military participants.[6]

Though combat injuries comprise just a tiny fraction of all veteran disabilities diagnosed by the VA, the number of benefits recipients has soared. In 2016 alone, eighty-seven thousand post-9/11 veterans began receiving disability compensation. This single-year figure was fifty-five times the number of amputees, sixteen times the number of killed in action, and more than one and a half times the total number wounded from the *entire fifteen-year span since the wars began.* Most disability recipients are granted compensation benefits for ailments unlikely to have a significant impact on their ways of life. In 2016, the two most common disabilities were tinnitus and diminished hearing. A study comparing VA-diagnosed conditions with a more commonly accepted measure of disability, published in the same year, found that most "disabled vets" experienced no substantial functional limitations.[7]

For the majority of military service members—people like Jeff, Matt, Marco, and Molly—the transition from healthy, active service to veteran status is undertaken as a voluntary life change. Terms of service vary in length, but, at some point, the commitment to the military reaches a peak. During this time, individuals might catch a glimpse of the terrain that lies beyond. As they approach the day when their oath to the country ends, their attachment to the mission and lifestyle of the soldier recedes, while the alternative path in front of them sharpens in focus and appeal. In one military-wide exit survey, soldiers said their top three reasons for separating were to seek higher pay, pursue another career, and go back to school.[8] Another reported that more than half of respondents wished to pursue a career different from their military specialty.[9] Yet even as most soldiers eagerly anticipate their post-service future, their time in the military will forever remain a momentous period in their lives, bookended by two especially unforgettable moments.

Everyone has a story about when they joined. And everyone has a story about when they left.

MARCO VASQUEZ had joined the Army to pay for college, but the plan changed on him as dusk set on the evening of September 11, 2001. Marco returned to his barracks in a daze. He felt like he had gotten dropped into a war movie, but he didn't know his part. For the first time since he enlisted, everyone was issued live ammunition, and the thought of it made Marco's skin crawl. They were suddenly carrying weapons and enough bullets to wipe out a small city.

It seemed at first that Marco's unit would be sticking around. At the end of the year, they were even allowed to go home for the holidays. Their platoon leader was a man whose last name was Commender, and at first all the guys had gotten a kick out of saying Lieutenant Commender this, Lieutenant Commender that, but none of them were joking when they got back from leave and Lieutenant Commender called a meeting to deliver the news. They were going to Iraq.

Marco's first thought was *not me*. It was a few weeks shy of the one-year mark from when he enlisted—when he would be off the hook and headed back to school. He said, "I'm sitting there and I'm like, '*You guys* are going to war.' I got my Green to Gold packet." He was already thinking about his textbooks.

Lieutenant Commender shut him down: "That's not going to happen. We're all deploying. You're going." Marco took it up the chain of command, all the way up to his company's first sergeant. Green to Gold packages had been voided, Marco was told. Everyone was deploying; there would be no one around to even put in his leave orders. After a stop in the Midwest, his company flew to Kuwait at the beginning of 2003. A few weeks later, the US officially launched Operation Iraqi Freedom.

The Third Infantry Division led the assault, spearheading coalition forces across the border into Iraq. From day one, Marco's unit followed right behind, providing support, clearing bypassed enemy strongpoints, trying to keep up. His squad battled toward Baghdad on a rotation. Each time they pushed forward, he and his teammates switched between gunner, driver, and the truck commander manning the radio. "We're talking about the first three nights of the invasion," Marco said. "I don't think anyone really slept. It was just constant going in, driving, reacting to contact."

There was contact everywhere. Enemy combatants crouched in tiny foxholes lining the dirt roads and whenever coalition vehicles roared by, they popped out, firing small arms and rocket-propelled grenades at whoever was passing through. Marco lost a friend that way, a buddy on lookout atop a rolling tank—an easy target for the enemy. But this was a shock and awe campaign, in which overwhelming force was used to paralyze the enemy; casualties were expected, and forward momentum was crucial. The unit pressed on.

They reached Baghdad in early April. The dust and debris aggravated Marco's allergies and he began plugging his nose with tissues whenever he had to go outside. Each time he replaced them, they were black. The city was black, too, as soon as night fell and they shut off the electricity and water. Within days, they had seized the capital. On April 9, American Marines charged Firdos Square and toppled the twelve-meter statue of Saddam Hussein—a dramatic, symbolic end to Saddam's twenty-four-year regime. But there was no time to celebrate; Marco's platoon had been assigned a new mission. They were headed to Mosul.

On a sweltering June day, two months after Baghdad fell, Marco was out roasting in the back of the Humvee, his turn behind the gun. He was surprised to see the First Sergeant walking up.

"Hey Vasquez, where's your M-4?"

Marco swung his carbine rifle into view.

"Come on down. The chaplain wants to see you."

Inside the mess tent, the chaplain told Marco he had a Red Cross message. Reserved for emergencies, the messages typically delivered news that a family member back home was in grave medical condition, or worse.

Marco read his message in silence. Earlier in the year, his wife had given birth to their third child, and it was immediately clear that there were complications with Shelemyah. "At around six months, she wasn't moving, she wasn't eating," Marco said. "We had a lot of issues with her." The latest exams had come in, and the doctors thought it might be cerebral palsy. Her condition was critical.

Eventually the chaplain spoke. "You're going to go back and help your family out."[10] The commander had approved Marco for leave. The chaplain added, "We're pretty good up here."

Marco walked back out into the heat. There were two gun trucks in his squad, three guys in each. They gathered around him. Two more gun trucks made up the rest of the platoon, fourteen soldiers in total, and he got everyone on the radio.

Someone broke the silence: "Man, fuck you." But when Marco looked over, his squad mate had a grin on his face. "You need to go home and take care of your family," another platoon member said, and a round of agreement followed. President Bush had just declared the end of major combat operations in Iraq and everything in the theater had begun to slow down. There was nobody on the streets, no traffic on the roads. The country felt stable. Everyone was heading home soon, they figured. "No one's reenlisting after this one. We're all leaving."

After his platoon had voiced their support, "I kind of felt okay leaving the guys," Marco said. He returned to his bunk and packed up everything he could fit into a single backpack—an Iraqi flag he had picked up, a wad of Iraqi dinar, a hygiene kit, and some socks. A few hours later, he was stepping onto the transport carrier. "Never again am I coming back to this place," he thought. Forty-eight hours later, he landed in Nashville, Tennessee.

MATT JACKSON had joined an Army at war, deliberately following in the footsteps of his older cousins and uncle. The first time he saw Uncle Dennis's 'Screaming Eagle' unit coin, he was unimpressed. "You could tell the sucker was old and worn and faded. It looked like it had been in someone's pocket for a while," he said.

The coin had been issued by the 101st Airborne Division and Matt was right: it had spent most of the seventies in Uncle Dennis's pocket, all through his uncle's service as a guardsman. Uncle Dennis later gave the coin to his eldest son, Dustin, as Dustin was about to leave for his first tour in Iraq. Then Matt's younger cousin David got the coin for his deployment, and passing it on to whoever was leaving next became their tradition. For ten years, there was always someone among the three of them serving in one combat zone or another, and Uncle Dennis never failed to hand them the coin with one important job: bring it home safe.

"And we did," Matt said. "We always brought it back to him."

In January 2007, he placed the coin in a little plastic bag, alongside his cross, and tucked the bag into his uniform's left shoulder pocket. It remained there every single day through his first tour in Afghanistan. "If anything happens to me," Matt told his platoon mates, pointing at his pocket, "make sure this gets back to my family."

After he returned in 2008 his uncle got called up to active duty with the Illinois National Guard and suddenly it was Matt's turn to do the honors. He drew out the coin. "Alright Uncle Dennis," he said. "You bring this back to me." Somehow, they had switched roles. The reversal gave Matt chills.

He thought often about a scene in *Black Hawk Down*, near the end of the film, when most of the mission forces had recovered back to base. Men had died that day, limbs were lost, spirits were broken, but the survivors were rejoicing—against all odds, they had made it back alive.

Staff Sergeant Eversmann watches, stunned, as Hoot, the Delta Force operator, begins loading magazines of ammunition back into his jacket. "You're going back in?"

Hoot doesn't hesitate. "There are still men out there."

Eversmann stares on in disbelief. Finally, Hoot turns to face him.

"When I go home, people ask me, 'Hey Hoot, why do you do it, man? Why? You some kind of war junkie?' I won't say a goddamn word. Why? They won't understand. They won't understand why we do it. They won't understand it's about the men next to you. And that's it. That's all it is."

Watching that scene, even just reading the quote, Matt finds himself getting emotional. "It's powerful," he said. "It hits me." Hoot's words articulated his truth. They explained the reason why, in the spring of 2009, he filled out his reenlistment papers and extended his term, even as he knew he would not be staying in the Army for a career.

He had made that decision by the end of his first deployment— twelve unending months, then three more tagged on when Bush's 2007 troop surge spilled beyond Iraq and everyone in Matt's battalion, already stationed in Afghanistan, got their tours extended, too. That had been hard. War was hard. "You almost die," Matt said. "You see people die. You don't just see people die, you see people die in a terrible way, in ways that only war would provide you."

Soldiers in theater typically get a mid-tour leave, a brief escape to temporarily shelter from the conflict. A mid-deployment leave is ideal in order to evenly distribute the stresses of combat, but troops begin taking leave three months in. As one of the lowest guys on the totem pole in 2007, Matt had been one of the first ones to go. He returned to their extended tour.

"I did a year straight," he said, "and I was losing my damn mind towards the end of it." At night he started having nightmares; during the day, panic attacks. Sleep became practically nonexistent. He went to see a doctor, tried taking medication, but "it would just make me so zombie the next day I would get my ass chewed out." Cigarettes went from break to compulsion to neurosis. Matt fired up three to five packs a day just to keep going.

He had never seriously considered what his long-term career

might look like, but that deployment shut the door on ever sticking it out in the Army. "I was like, 'Hell to the no!'" he said. "Why would you do it? It's like putting your hand in a meat grinder. Why would you do that? It's hell over there. Why would you ever want to go through hell again?"

Why, then? Why did he re-enlist?

As he was signing his papers, Matt had just one request. He had been promoted to sergeant earlier in the year, and, along with the new rank's three gold chevrons, he had taken responsibility for his own team—a dozen or so privates and specialists. "Don't move me," he told his commanders. "I'll do this if you just keep me here with my guys."

His request was approved. In the summer of 2009, on the very same day his uncle's deployment ended, Matt was flying back to Afghanistan for his second tour. Uncle Dennis touched down in Bangor, Maine, just a few hours before Matt was scheduled to take off from Fort Bragg in North Carolina. There was no way to pass on the coin. Matt knew it had always been a simple little token, a silly family tradition, but he still felt its absence in his empty shoulder pocket as they lifted into the air.

This time, there was one more person awaiting his return. A couple months earlier, he had been wrapping up a leadership course for recently promoted sergeants. Their graduation ceremony was on May 28, the same day as the battalion ball. The ball was the unit's biggest social event of the year. Enlisted men put on their Class A uniforms, wives and girlfriends did up their hair and picked out their best long dresses. Enticed by the open bar, all of Matt's friends were going, and at first, he planned to go, too. But the graduation tired him out and he decided last minute to stay home and relax. He had an apartment off-post and after the ball, a buddy and his girlfriend dropped by for a nightcap. His buddy's girlfriend was texting someone from back home, a girl she went to school with, and that girl was even drunker than they were. Her name was Jessica, and her messages came in roaming and wild, question marks where spaces should have been.

As a joke, Matt got her number and sent her a few messages, teasing and ribbing this stranger he had never met. The next morning, she sobered up and texted back, "Who the hell are you?" Matt introduced himself. They kept texting each other for the rest of the day and into the next. They never stopped. Before long they were instant messaging on Yahoo, then moving on to video chat. Soon Matt was counting the days to his deployment and one day he worked up the courage to ask, "Hey Jessica, do you care if I come up and visit you for a weekend?"

Matt flew into Boston and she came to pick him up. Suddenly he was meeting the whole family at their home in Salem, Massachusetts—grandparents and all. "Obviously if some random dude from the Army is just showing up, hanging out with your daughter or granddaughter for the weekend, you'd want to meet the guy," he said. Jessica showed him around town. The Puritans had landed in Salem in 1626; the Massachusetts Bay Colony was established there a few years later. Matt had never paid much attention in history class, but everyone had heard of the Salem Witch Trials, and the legacy of the region impressed him. "There was so much history right there," he said. "That's where America started for the most part." Too soon, he was on a plane back to his military post, back to his service for the flourishing nation that had grown from that fledgling colony.

He immediately wanted to see Jessica again. He held back for a few days, not wishing to appear desperate, then invited her to Fort Bragg for the weekend. At the end of her visit she asked him, "How about another week?" Matt was thrilled. They had just started watching *True Blood*.

Matt asked his commander for permission to use the extra four-day pass he had received when he reenlisted. The Army frequently offers a variety of sweeteners, usually monetary bonuses or little perks like weekend passes, to help entice soldiers to reenlist. Matt hadn't expected to use his pass when he signed, but he was glad for it now. He and Jessica drove down to Myrtle Beach. They visited the aquarium, the zip line, museums, nice but overpriced seafood restaurants. They walked along the beach, trying to avoid the subject of his impending deployment. After she went home, he missed her so much it felt like withdrawal.

"I was just thinking about her," he said. "I couldn't get her out of my mind. I wanted to spend more time with her." They had never talked about their relationship—if they were even boyfriend and girlfriend—but whatever it was, it felt serious, substantial, real. "I just really fell in love with this girl," he said. He remembered earlier conversations where she had mentioned she was the type of girl who would never get married, who would grow old and live alone with her cats. Her family had joked about it, too, and they all shared a laugh when he was visiting. At least, Matt hoped it was a joke, because now he was getting an idea that wouldn't leave him alone. *Maybe I'll propose to this chick.* The more he thought about it, the more the idea made sense to him. *I'm going to marry this girl.*

He went to the local mall with $100, about all he had in savings, and bought a ring straight off the shelf. "It had a couple hearts on it or something weird like that," he remembered. The clock was definitely ticking now, just over a week until they deployed. He called Jessica and asked for her address again. She grew suspicious. Why was he asking again now? He hadn't prepared a good answer and so he just told her the truth, that he wanted to send her something before he left, trying to keep it as vague as possible.

In truth, he hadn't prepared much at all. He thought he might Express Mail the ring to her on one of his final days, right before shipping out. Then maybe he would wait until the package arrived and propose to her on the phone or on the computer. He was still working out the details.

In fact, Jessica had a plan of her own. Two days before Matt's deployment, she borrowed money from her grandparents and bought a plane ticket back down to Fort Bragg. A mutual friend picked her up from the airport and drove her to Matt's apartment, where he had packed all his belongings into large blue storage containers. His parents had arrived from Illinois to send him off. He was just about to turn in his keys. "It's a hot July day and I was pissed off and getting ready to deploy," he said. "I was loading all these containers into my truck, and one of them I'm like, 'My god. Why is this one so heavy? What the hell is in here?' So I popped the lid open and—Pow! Lo and behold, there she was."

Her surprise secured two more days for them. Matt made a new reservation in the hotel where his parents were staying, and later that evening he stopped by their room to tell them he was going to propose. "Are you sure?" they asked him. He said he was. Then he walked down the hall where Jessica was waiting. It was July 28. "We had literally only spent two weeks with each other, physically together. And then two months, roughly, talking to each other." None of that mattered. They loved each other, and they were determined to get married.

Matt began to save up his deployment pay as soon as he got to Afghanistan. After a few months he wired the money to his parents, who helped their son pick out a "real" ring for his fiancé. In November, Matt was back for ten days on his mid-tour leave. He and Jessica got married in her grandparents' living room.

For their honeymoon, the newlyweds drove up the coast to Ogunquit, Maine, a beautiful town by the bay that Jessica had always loved as a child. It was quiet and idyllic, and Matt was the happiest he had ever been. The morning he had to fly back to Afghanistan, he woke up and considered what life had brought him. He was twenty-seven years old, married, and going back to war—never before with so much to protect.

HIS GUYS, the ones he had reenlisted for, would be on the other end of the flight. He just had to make it a few more months for them. "I had become a leader and I had been training my team to go to war," he said. "There's a level of trust you develop there that you just don't get with other people"—the kind of trust that made it possible to storm into a building and confront the enemy and yet still believe that you might somehow make it out whole.

"Everyone has their reasons for joining the military," Matt went on. There was patriotism, family tradition, desire to serve—no shortage of lofty, abstract motivations to pull men and women into the force. "But at some point, whatever you joined for doesn't matter anymore. Because you're doing it to keep the people around you alive. You develop the bond, the brotherhood, the band of brothers, the camaraderie—whatever bullshit you want to call it. You're there to keep people alive. You're there to do your job. Sure, there's your mission. 'Go here.' 'Take this town.' But it's all about being in it together. Suffering together. Doing it for each other."

Matt's team was his reason. It was exactly as Hoot described: "It's about the men next to you. And that's it. That's all it is."

His second tour was different from the first—"not more relaxed, but a slower tempo." There were no direct engagements, no shrieking firefights; Matt didn't pull the trigger on his rifle once the whole time. But, out on patrol through foreign villages, hidden IEDs lurked at all times beneath the ground and the threat of an explosion hung constantly in the air. Every night as he bunked down, he thought about his wife and how impossibly far away she was, how the final day of his deployment blinked a hazy point in the distance, disappearing every time he looked.

Then one day he looked, and it was there.

Jessica had recently finished school and moved down to Fayetteville to find an apartment for the two of them. They had talked about starting a family.

In July 2010, Matt landed back down in Fort Bragg. He was getting out.

CHAPTER 4
WARRIORS IN TRANSITION

TYSON WOKE UP in Walter Reed Army Hospital. For several days after the blast, he had drifted in and out of consciousness. Medics flew him from Kandahar to Bagram Airfield, just north of Kabul, then to Landstuhl in Germany for more treatment. Most of his waking moments blurred into a scramble, but a few snapshots lingered in his mind. On one of his flights, he woke up with an intense craving for watermelon. Other times his eyes flicked open just long enough to gauge the Sharpie marks on his blood infusion bags, the black notch sinking every hour, the red liquid flowing back into his body.

He sat up in his room and took in the scene around him. Troop levels in Afghanistan had peaked in 2011, and it was reflected in the capacity of the medical facilities back home.[1] For his first few nights at Walter Reed, Tyson had been assigned to the intensive care unit, which had filled with so many injured and wounded that the only available beds were in the hospital's wing for treating brain injuries. He had been to Walter Reed one time before, the previous October for an eye surgery before his deployment. A man had limped by on a prosthetic leg, holding a spare prosthetic in his hands. Tyson remembered thinking, "Man, that would be so terrible if it happened."

It happened. At first, all he could do was lie in bed, too exhausted to even watch television. Medical personnel filed in and out in a constant stream, cleaning out his wounds, removing dead tissue, cutting away the parts of him that were succumbing to infection. Fifteen surgeries in total—every Monday, Wednesday, Friday for three weeks. Three weeks of feeling a little bit better on Sunday, then wiped back down to nothing on Monday. Feeling better on Tuesday, wiped out on Wednesday; better Thursday, wiped again Friday.

"The first few weeks you're just exhausted," he said. "I didn't even have time or energy to process what the future was going to be."

It finally started to sink in when they brought in his wheelchair. "Man, this is absolutely miserable," Tyson thought. The chair was stiff and painful, invasive in all the wrong places. His center of gravity had shifted with the amputations and all his movements felt wrong, too much or too little, a far cry from the precision he took for granted as an athlete and soldier. Even getting through doors was a challenge; he had to depend on the medical staff for the most basic tasks. "That was the hardest part," he said. "You go from being in charge of all these people—all these life and death decisions you make—to being 100 percent dependent on everybody else."

On the Fourth of July, a hospital aide wheeled him outside to watch the fireworks. It was his first time outside since being flown into Walter Reed in critical condition. Bright flashes lit up a clear night sky. The celebratory night should have been a moment of triumph, yet Tyson felt uncomfortable, angry, lost. He was still young—only twenty-five years old. He hadn't planned on staying in the military forever, but like many young soldiers, he would have gone to hell and back for the guys around him, and his goal had been to one day make battery command.

Now he was a wounded combat vet, a double below-knee amputee. In his better moments, he was thankful to be alive. Most times, though, it was other kinds of thoughts that overwhelmed him.

How did this happen to me?

What will happen now?

What the hell is my life going to be?

One of his first hurdles would be the evaluation process for attaining disability status. A few weeks after Tyson arrived at Walter Reed, a nurse case manager sat down with him to explain the military's medical board procedure. After sustaining an injury or illness, all soldiers are given a window of time to stabilize, and to see if they can rehabilitate and return to duty.

In the wake of the 2007 Walter Reed scandal, when reporters exposed abuse and negligence inside the military's flagship hospital, ensuring proper care for soldiers became the nation's hottest flashpoint. Within weeks it had scorched the careers of top generals and provoked such fuming within the halls of Congress that a flurry of new measures was immediately pushed through. In March, President Bush appointed Bob Dole and Donna Shalala as co-chairs of a bipartisan commission to address problems in the military's health care system. "My decisions have put our kids in harm's way," the President said, "and I'm concerned about the fact that when they come back they don't get the full treatment they deserve."[2] Soon after, the Army created the nationwide Warrior Transition Unit program, dedicated to serving the complex medical needs required by recovering soldiers.[3] If the lesson from the fallout had been clear—the government wasn't doing enough—it rapidly began trying to make amends.

By the end of 2008, forty-five WTUs had opened at Army posts across the country with additional units in the other services.[4] Soldiers receiving treatment reported to a chain of command, called a cadre, just as if they had been assigned to a regular military unit. The WTUs pledged to deliver greater care by fostering collaboration between the military and medical sides. Program leadership described it as two hands coming together, clasped with interlocking fingers.[5]

After the initial rehabilitation period, typically twelve months, service members whose medical impairments continue to affect their ability to perform are referred by a physician to begin the Integrated Disability Evaluation System process.[6] Since 2007, the Department of Defense and the VA have jointly operated the IDES to facilitate the care of injured service members, and to more effectively connect them with the appropriate disability services.[7]

Before the national rollout of IDES began in November 2007, soldiers had to undergo two separate disability evaluations—one by the Department of Defense to determine their military disability rating, and then another at the VA after being discharged. This caused significant delay and confusion and was replaced by a new system designed to merge the two tracks and streamline the process. Under IDES, soldiers sit through a single disability assessment, conducted according to the VA's evaluation standards.[8]

A permanent profile[9] is created, pulling all military and medical documentation from the relevant authorities, and submitted to a Medical Evaluation Board.[10] The board's medical officers review the case file and diagnose whatever medical conditions the service member may have, as well as the severity of each.[11] Then the case is passed along to the Physical Evaluation Board (PEB), which has the ultimate say in determining whether the individual can reasonably meet the duties of their office, grade, or rank.[12] In the second half of the PEB phase, VA representatives review all medical and service records that have been attached to the case to produce a finalized disability rating.

As Tyson started making progress in rehab, chatter about the medical board and disability process became a prevalent theme in the conversations around him. Whether sitting in physical therapy or having lunch in the dining facility, discussions in the WTU invariably turned to the disability ratings system. Tyson reported, "People would say, 'Oh, you got to claim everything. When you go to meet the doctor, tell them you have these issues.'"

Part of the motivation to secure a high rating, Tyson learned, was financial. Service members determined by the PEB to no longer be fit for duty begin their separation from the military, plugging into the VA benefits system after receiving their discharge. Disability ratings are determined by the VA in increments of 10 percent, from 0 to 100, with each score corresponding to a different amount in monthly benefits. (A 100 percent disability rating equates to tax-free compensation of more than $3,000 each month.) Veterans receive an individual rating for each disability they list when filing their claims, combined at the end to calculate their total disability rating.

Inside the WTU, Tyson found tips about the easiest conditions to claim, or how best to sound convincing, to be "rampant."

He recalled, "Someone would say, 'Oh yeah, they can't really check for PTSD so put that down.' Or, 'Tell them you have hearing issues.' All the [conditions] that are more difficult to track, not the physical wounds that you can see." Claims approved for tinnitus, or ringing in the ears, could be rated up to 10 percent, while sleep apnea, another common diagnosis, with little, if any, plausible connection to military service, carried a rating of 50 percent, paying out roughly $1,000 each month, in addition to free lifetime medical care and other valuable benefits.

Tyson's initial reaction was disbelief. "I was like, 'This is crazy! Just put down what you have.'" Double-amputees presented a straightforward profile; the schedule typically considered them at 100 percent disability. It made no sense to Tyson that others would spend so much time and energy trying to exaggerate their conditions. Nor did it escape his notice that many of the patients hatching schemes had not even served in combat roles.[13]

This is a distinction long noted by soldiers at the front lines. The military historian Paul Fussell wrote of soldiers in World War II: "Those who actually fought on the line in the war, especially if they were wounded, constitute an in-group forever separate from those who did not. Praise or blame does not attach: rather, there is the accidental possession of a special empirical knowledge, a feeling of a mysterious shared ironic awareness manifesting itself in an instinctive skepticism about pretension, public enunciated truths, and the pomp of authority."

As Tyson watched many around him try to the game the system, he also encountered other types of stories that forced him to question the VA schedule's basic logic. One soldier's case became a widely cited cautionary tale. "There was a guy there who was a single below-knee amputee. He got a super low rating and tried to fight it," Tyson recounted. But the only condition that soldier had claimed was his amputation. "If you look at the schedule, he got the maximum he could for that injury." According to the VA ratings handbook, a single below-knee amputation qualifies for a 40 percent rating, scoring lower than sleep apnea.

It was clear to Tyson that some soldiers viewed their disability evaluation with a sense of entitlement, an attitude of *I need to get as much compensation as I can.* But even for those who approached the process earnestly, it could seem like one slip in the system, and you quickly got screwed. "I can see how people get frustrated," he said. One soldier loses his leg in combat and receives 40 percent disability rating, qualifying for monthly benefits of $700. Another cites a couple lines about irregular sleep and gets rated at 50 percent. Suddenly the VA is paying him a grand or more every month.

"How are those comparable?" Tyson wondered. "It just doesn't look right."

Soon Tyson's nurse case manager was urging him to start the medical board phase for himself. Alarm bells instantly went off in his head. He had heard that service members going through IDES couldn't leave their WTU until they had completed the whole procedure. Officially, IDES aimed to process soldiers through the evaluation boards in under 220 days, but the reality often fell far short of the targets. The possibility of being stuck at Walter Reed for months terrified Tyson. One guy, he heard, had been warehoused there for three years.

Tyson knew that if he was to have a shot at the kind of recovery he wished for, he had to get out of the WTU. He had to be in a place where others were pushing him to excel again, not where those around him were emphasizing their impairment, conspiring to raise their disability percentages. "I knew I didn't want to be there," he said.

He filed a petition to transfer back to West Point and requested to delay his med board phase until he had gotten out of Walter Reed. Then, like so many recovering service members anxiously anticipating their future, he waited for the bureaucracy to determine his fate.

PHILLIP BROWN did not choose his job; he was tasked with it. On June 3, 2016, he assumed command of the Warrior Transition Battalion at Fort Bragg, a post which he understood, even before starting, would be a "humbling and daunting experience."

A career Special Forces officer, Brown commissioned into the infantry in 1998, then became a Green Beret a few years later. From the moment he joined, his goal was to serve as a combat leader, to march with other Green Berets through the trials of war—that was the fuel that kept his fire burning. By 2015, he had earned on his uniform the silver oak leaf of an Army Lieutenant Colonel, and when the opportunity arose, he hoped for selection to lead a combat battalion. Instead, he was assigned to Fort Bragg's transition unit.

"I was disappointed," Brown said. "I struggled with the fact that somebody on a board basically said I'm not allowed to do that, but no one could tell you why."

It was a painful setback. But Brown had sworn a duty to serve his country, not his own career, and if the Army decided his skills were best suited away from the action, then he would swallow his pride and go where they needed him. "There's stuff that we have to do and stuff that we want to do. Then there's things you *get* to do. I get to command the Warrior Transition Battalion at Fort Bragg."

All of Brown's training had prepared him for combat, and it occurred to him that he wasn't well versed about the WTUs back home—or the particular unit at Fort Bragg he had been charged to lead. He got on his computer and ran a Google search.

The more he read, the more his stomach dropped. One after another, the results described a bungling, ineffective, sometimes overtly hostile institution, where hurting soldiers regularly endured abuse or neglect. A *New York Times* article found widespread drug abuse in the battalions, labeling them "warehouses of despair." Another article found soldiers getting disciplined for the same injuries that had caused them to transfer into the unit in the first place.[14] One Army specialist told reporters, "Being in the WTU is worse than being in Iraq."[15]

Brown let it all sink in. "I was just shocked," he said.

During his pre-command training in Kansas, his battalion's sergeant major introduced himself, then cautioned Brown not to form opinions before seeing it for himself. "I can tell you a lot about the unit," the sergeant major said. "But some of it you just have to experience."

After Brown arrived at Fort Bragg, a different picture began to emerge. The heavily publicized rollout of the WTUs, and their ensuing coverage in the media, had created a widespread perception that all soldiers assigned to them were "wounded warriors." In fact, fewer than 10 percent of soldiers in the program had been physically wounded in combat operations. More than three times as many had been referred by their commands for "various reasons."[16] The intent of the transition battalions had been to serve as sanctuaries where injured soldiers could focus on healing, but as Brown became more familiar with the reality on the ground, he came to see the unintended consequences of those lofty aims.

The problem started before the soldiers even got there. Almost immediately after the transition battalions were established, line unit commanders discovered that by filling out the paperwork and sending someone to a WTU, they could secure a replacement within days or weeks. Juggling rigorous military exercises or an impending deployment, they often faced a simple calculation: deploy with an underperforming soldier or roll the dice on someone new? The WTUs quickly became an unofficial channel for getting certain people "off the books."[17] According to an internal assessment by the Pentagon, many commanders "burdened" the WTUs "as an expedient means by which to rid their units of their 'undesirables.'"[18] As one defense columnist remarked, the transitions units were treated as "holding tanks for misfits."

Sheltered from deployment and flushed with support services typically unavailable in their regular Army units, many of these soldiers found reasons to extend their stays.[19] A 2010 Army Inspector General report identified soldiers who sought to maximize their time in the WTUs by disclosing additional illnesses and injuries at key points during the evaluation process. Even as they dragged out their stays, they continued receiving active duty pay and benefits.[20] Following an eleven-month inspection tour of WTU facilities across the country, Noel Koch, former head of the Office of Wounded Warrior Care and Transition Policy, observed, "Many tended to get quite comfortable in these units and are adept at finding ways to remain in them for months leading into years, as they dream up new complaints."[21]

Such schemes weren't conceived in isolation; often they were induced by a culture of entitlement and a network of enablers. Ubiquitous at many WTUs were the "barracks lawyers"—soldiers stationed in the unit for some time who, according to the Army Inspector General (IG) report, "either for nefarious reasons or by genuine concern, become an adjunct chain of command," freely dishing out advice to its newest members. More than two hundred cadre officers interviewed by the IG disclosed a common pattern: "New arrivals often come into the system motivated to return to duty as soon as possible. But after a few months of talking to other [transitioning soldiers], [they] change their minds and start to seek ways to prolong their stay."[22]

The change in mentality signals a broader shift as soldiers turn away from prioritizing recovery and toward "maximizing disabilities to achieve personal gains."[23] Briefings and orientations feed the impulse by highlighting the availability of disability benefits.[24]

At the center of the WTU's operation is the comprehensive transition plan, a set of individualized goals and expectations devised by every soldier alongside their chain of command. But inspectors found that senior officers frequently emphasized what the soldiers *couldn't* do rather than what they *could*, orienting them toward disability compensation rather than working for return-to-duty outcomes.[25] In 2010, less than 10 percent of soldiers entered into the Med Board process were returned to duty; 90 percent left the Army with a disability rating and entered into the VA disability system.[26]

The WTUs fostered a "noticeable sense of entitlement," concluded the Army IG, within an environment ripe for "abusing the system" and "manipulating it to maximize entitlements."[27]

Brown saw it all for himself. After taking command at Fort Bragg's WTU, he said he encountered a "significant portion of the population" who misrepresented their conditions in order to attain increased benefits. In one case, a non-compliant service member blamed his erratic behavior on post-traumatic stress disorder. After the psychologist reviewing his case confirmed that it could be manifestations of PTSD, the patient got his disability ratings back from the VA. Suddenly, "he was a new man," Brown said. "He was super compliant, loved us. He was happy to be here. It was like night and day."

Brown described a basic tension existing between the WTU's military officers and its medical experts. Physicians see their patients for a brief snapshot—one appointment every few weeks perhaps—while a commander will see them every day. The medical professionals "tend to defer to what's presented to them in that thirty, forty-five, minutes, and we see them go through their normal personalities. We just have a different perspective."

In cases like that of the non-compliant soldier whose outlook reversed overnight, Brown was incredulous: "That's the disappointing thing, like, 'Did you guys not predict that he would miraculously start doing great?' And they would say, 'Well, that just means the therapy's been working.' Okay, yeah, but he's been here for almost a year and a half. You're telling me that all of the sudden—in the last thirty days since he got his [disability decision]—that's the sudden culmination of a year and a half's worth of therapy? No. I don't think so."

Ultimately, whether a soldier is successful in their recovery or transition has "a lot to do with their mentality when they get here," Brown says. "It's the individual—their desire and their willingness to just push and be successful. If they have the mindset of 'I'm not a victim,' and 'I'm not a patient,' but 'I'm a soldier who's going through a process,' they're usually successful. "After medically retiring from the Army in 2013, Tyson completed a master's degree in Geographic Information Systems, then took on various roles in support of national security. He and his wife have had three children since his injury. Despite the daily obstacles of being an amputee, he continues to thrive. He credits his success to having a strong support team around him from day one—family and friends who never stopped pushing him to achieve what they knew he could.

Like Tyson, many soldiers have returned to positions of achievement through a combination of their own determination and the right kind of support. For Brown and his colleagues, who have dedicated themselves to helping veterans recover, it is their work's greatest privilege. Too often, however, Brown says they encounter the opposite case. "The challenge for us is the people who show up and feel like, 'I deserve this. I'm owed this money for the rest of my life.' That's what I have a problem with. No, we don't. Obviously we will help treat you and provide you care. But I don't owe you money. I don't owe you a bonus because you got hurt on a job. You volunteered. We all volunteered to serve in the military, and if we think that comes without risk or injury, I'm sorry."

Brown believes the majority of his battalion's soldiers understand this, but he also knows there are many under his command who view the process differently. "We definitely see a strong percentage of people who show up and are just very willing to [think], 'Let me get what the Army will give me,'" he said.

A FREE IPAD. That's what was being offered to Sergeant Malik.[28] All he had to do was file for PTSD.

Whether Malik actually suffered from post-traumatic stress or not, his service records could readily justify the claim. He enlisted in the Marine Corps in February 2008, a motivated 18-year-old fresh out of high school. He proved himself in training, and after graduating from infantry school, joined his regiment as an automatic rifleman and team leader.[29]

On Malik's first deployment in 2009, his regiment was assigned to Nawzad District, a mountainous strip in southern Afghanistan's southern Helmand province.[30] He was deployed for seven months. It was a long time to be in a dangerous place but by the end of his tour, Malik, who was always taking in everything around him, always crunching the inputs in his brain, concluded that it wasn't long enough.

"I think that was one of the failures of our system," he said.

The basic system didn't make sense. It took the first two months of deployment just to get to know the area, then three months after that to begin developing relationships, then the last two months was barely enough time to start outreach before the next wave of guys were coming in. The new guys might land somewhere completely different on the political spectrum, and all you could do was hope their objectives aligned with what your whole deployment had just been spent trying to achieve. And that was before you even got to the more crucial matter of the locals—did the new guys gel with them or not? Results were elusive and no wonder, Malik thought. Everyone seemed to be just marking time until the next batch came in.

Wishing to see if any of their efforts were making a difference, he returned to Afghanistan for a second tour in the spring of 2011. This time his unit was posted in Upper Gereshk Valley, not far from the town of Sangin, one of the bloodiest areas of the war. A larger coalition unit was stationed further north; Malik's group was tasked with patrolling the river and blocking combatants from advancing. On May 17, just a few weeks into his tour, his fire team went out for a routine patrol. It was routine until they hit an IED. Malik lost his right leg below the knee.

Within three days of arriving at Walter Reed's Wounded Warrior Battalion, he was being prepped on the disability payments available to him. His ranking sergeant spelled it out: "If you claim PTSD, you get a free iPad." All Malik had to do was file his claims. Get your disability, he was advised, and "you can do whatever you want with the rest of your life."

Malik was torn. On the one hand, it hadn't even occurred to him to leave the military. He understood he wouldn't be leading any more patrols again, but there were plenty of roles in which he was confident he could still serve. On the other hand, "It's never easy to turn down free money," he said, and the temptation had never been closer.

His sergeant checked in, "Hey man, thinking about getting an iPad yet?"

Malik wavered. Something was holding him back. The ubiquity of the behavior disturbed him, and for all his conditioning in the Marine Corps, he had never thought of himself as someone who blindly followed the pack. "To be honest, I think I'm a very anti-tribal animal," he said. "When it comes to disability, there's a very tribal mindset. I'd talk to wounded veterans and I knew off the bat that I didn't identify with them or their mentality of the situation."

Others in the WTUs have also rejected the callous attitude toward benefits, and the contrasting mentalities have created informal caste systems, observable within transition battalions across the country. These hierarchies often sorted according to level of combat service and injury: battle-wounded Purple Heart recipients placed at the top, followed by ill, combat-experienced soldiers, then finally non-combat service members without a serious illness or injury. According to the Army Inspector General, many WTU soldiers and cadres harbored disdain for fellow unit members seen to be "reaping the benefits" of their wounded warrior status.[31]

Yet their prevalence produced a harmful stigma. The limited number of truly combat-wounded personnel often came to resent their time in the WTUs; according to an internal Pentagon report, they expressed "concern that they may be associated with those [patients] who stay for long periods of time and 'milk the system.'"[32] Whenever possible, many requested to be sent back to heal in their regular units.[33]

At Fort Hood in Texas, leadership established a separate facility exclusively to assist combat-wounded soldiers. Brigadier General

Gary Cheek, who headed the Army's Warrior Transition Command, approved of the measure. "What I don't want to have—and what I have had—is a guy with acid reflux disease going to ring the bell at the opening of the New York Stock Exchange and portraying himself to America as a wounded warrior."[34]

For Malik, the pitfalls of embracing the wounded warrior mindset crystalized in a single moment. "I almost fell victim to it once," he said. He was sitting in a psychologist's office at the Walter Reed WTU, going over his symptoms, when the whole thing suddenly just repulsed him. He glanced over at the doctor and found himself thinking, *Who is this lady? Who is she to be telling me my limitations?* "All she'd ever done in her life was go to school. She just knew what's supposed to happen in the books. She had no life experience," he said.

He reflected on it for the next several days. "I thought it was the stupidest thing I'd ever done," he continued. "I almost felt ashamed because it did nothing for me. It felt like I almost got brainwashed into thinking I was one of the 'disabled veterans.' I almost fell into the trap of needing to get PTSD. I realized I didn't need any of that stuff."

Of course, all soldiers react differently to the adversities they encounter, and wartime service—combat service in particular—can generate deeply troubling experiences. But for Malik, the leap from minor irregularities, as likely to be caused by transition stress as anything else, to the hasty conclusion of PTSD was extreme; he felt less like he was being evaluated and more like being stamped. He refused to accept such a verdict of impairment, generated by what he viewed as an assembly line of caretakers.

"The system drives you toward a victim mentality," he said. "No one ever stops to think, 'Well, do I really need that? Do I really have PTSD?' A lot of guys get into a big cycle of coming in and [becoming] very reliant on the system. The system tells them what to do, where to go, what kind of stuff to get done. So if you want to just do it that way, it's streamlined. It's like a factory. Go here, do this. Go here, do that. A lot is just put on you. There's not a lot of free thinking involved, like, do I really need this?"

The factory's churn was non-stop; no one ever talked about the immorality of it all. For Malik, it was a devil's handshake. The lure of compensation for departing service members is seductive, but the payments don't come without a cost. "I can't really blame the guys because it's a very enticing thing. "But," he said, "for me, [I had to ask myself] what is it going to cost me? Nothing is free, so what am I giving up?"

He saw the VA as a massive, opaque apparatus sitting at the junction between the military and civilian domains, tasked with transporting service members across the formidable divide. But it wasn't a clean passage. "At the end of the day, you're giving up other things to gain that benefit. Giving up the chance to develop an identity and a profession beyond being a veteran. Your [livelihood] is because of what happened overseas. You wouldn't be anything without that. So it becomes your identity," he concluded.

Soldiers walk in, many of them still capable of meeting the military's rigorous standards of competence and conduct.

Disabled veterans walk out.

CHAPTER 5
ABLE-UNABLE

IN AUGUST 2008, Jeff was stationed at Fort Bragg between deployments. He decided to join some friends for the Eighty-Second Airborne's annual convention in St. Louis.[1] On his first night, he went out on a riverboat and started talking to one of the bartenders, a pretty woman named Bethany. He got her phone number and they made plans to see each other again a few days later.

They met in a popular district called The Loop. They walked, drank beers, smoked cigarettes, and just "kept the conversation going," Jeff recalled. When he returned to Fort Bragg, they kept the conversation going long-distance, every day for the next three weeks, until Jeff returned to St. Louis for Labor Day weekend, the first chance he got. He couldn't wait to see Bethany again. Soon he was taking days off, making the twelve-hour drive to spend time with her at least once a month.

In June 2009, Jeff deployed to Afghanistan for his second tour and the relationship went from long-distance to "super long-distance," Jeff said, "one time zone to ten." Bethany had been an English major in college, and he didn't want to disappoint her with his vocabulary. Before smartphones became ubiquitous, he typed out his messages in a Word document, often consulting a dictionary in the process, then transcribing them character by character on his flip phone's keypad. The occasional satellite phone calls were a blessing.

The battalion had been sent to Zabul, a province in southeast Afghanistan adjacent to the Pakistani border. Matt was stationed at a different base, a couple hours away, and the two friends didn't get to see each other as much. Earlier in the year, the White House had announced it was doubling the size of Afghanistan's security forces, and Jeff could already notice the effects in the camps, where Afghan soldiers soon outnumbered their American counterparts ten to one.[2]

In his spare time, Jeff was researching engagement rings for Bethany. He finally ordered one online, but when he tried to purchase the diamond in a separate transaction, his credit card was declined. He called the company and was told his card had been compromised. "You can't exactly get a replacement mailed to you in Afghanistan," he realized, so he called the jeweler, who, after hearing that Jeff was a soldier on deployment, agreed to take the payment by check.

Jeff asked around and learned a helicopter would soon be dropping off supplies from Kandahar. He explained the situation to the pilot. "And this random dude I'd never met, this Army helicopter guy, took my check and mailed it," he said. Once he received the payment, the jeweler mailed the ring to Matt's house, where Jessica looked after it while the guys were still in Afghanistan. Jeff picked it up from her as soon as they got back from tour.

A few weeks later, in July 2010, Bethany came down to Fayetteville and Jeff brought her to the Hilton Garden Inn, the nicest hotel in town. He got down on one knee and plucked the ring from his shirt pocket. A square-cut, white gold diamond flashed on the band.

Somewhere amidst their tears, she became his future wife.

FOR ALL OF US, identity is a current, fluid, always in motion. Influences, both internal and external, guide its flow and shape its course.

In the beginning, many of our currents trace similar dips and bends: idle childhood afternoons, the trials of being a teenager, developing interests through adolescence and beyond.

But when a person enlists in the military, those influences are supplemented, even overwhelmed, by a new set of forces: the sheer exhaustion of initial entry training, the enforced conformity within military units, and for a selection of soldiers, the jarring shock of combat.

Psychologists have long documented the stresses associated with such major life developments. In the clinical literature, researchers highlight the significance of *turning points*, specific occasions that reorient a person's life trajectory, and *transitions*, events marked by profound changes in external circumstances and daily life.[3] Turning points and transitions can include both positive as well as negative experiences, and cover many of the events encountered by almost all of us over the course of our lives—marriage, job moves, parenthood—but they are particularly integral to an individual's experience as a soldier. Military service in every form, whether it involves combat or not, exposes service members to especially powerful transitions and turning points, and can produce lingering effects for years to come.

Sometimes the current falters, diverted by events in its path. Other times it darts in new directions, following trajectories of least resistance. But it never stops moving. A person exiting the military is never the same one who entered. Their identity is shifting. The current is searching for a new channel.

JEFF HAD REACHED a turning point. He recalled his first months at Fort Bragg, how after a long field day, the married guys got in their cars and drove home, while the single guys dragged their tired bodies thirty yards back to the barracks. Before their first deployment, Jeff and Matt had made that wistful trek every night, pecking at cigarettes and dishing on how much they envied the married guys, the guys who had a woman to go home to. The walk became an unwanted ritual, a doleful rite of loneliness and Army bachelorhood. It was on one of these walks that they made the pledge. "If we don't ever get there, at least we'll have each other," they agreed. They would go to Montana and find a slab of rock for themselves—that would be their home. And if they could muster some electricity and internet access, they could share their lives, too, with *Call of Duty*.

By the time the summer was ending in 2010, Matt was married and Jeff was newly engaged. Kids, if not immediately, weren't far down the line. They had both started the process of separating from the Army, and their future on the rock no longer seemed as appealing. It was time to come up with a new plan.

Jeff struggled with his final stretch in the military. After making the decision to leave, soldiers reveal their intentions by declining to reenlist, or turning down their orders. At some point they notify their commanding officers, a conversation that can feel awkward at best, abrasive at worst. The high-intensity atmosphere of military life requires a constant renewal of drive and dedication; when word spreads of someone's impending departure, it can threaten to deflate the whole unit. Informal modes of social ostracism form to seal the leak. "You're kind of branded at that point," Jeff said.

After his final medical exam, Jeff was no longer allowed to participate in any physical training exercises, but he was still required to show up and check in every morning. He arrived at 5:30 a.m. like everybody else, saluted the flag like everybody else, but while everybody else stood at attention in their black Army workout clothes, he and the half dozen other guys getting out had to stand to the side, suited up in their camouflaged Army combat uniforms.

"You're immediately alienated from the first minute of the day," said Jeff. "There's the group who's still training and going to deploy and are still soldiers. And these other guys who are not."

The guys who were still soldiers took off; they had a five-mile run, or an obstacle course, or a small arms range to complete.

The other guys—the guys who were no longer seen as soldiers— seemed to loiter in a no man's land that could stretch on for weeks. Their only task was to collect the long list of stamps and signatures on their military separation checklist. Everybody else was continuing to train, staying in shape, getting ready for their next assignment. Meanwhile, "I'm standing there getting ready to smoke a cigarette and go to the library to make sure I don't have any books checked out," Jeff said.

Sometimes the soldiers running by would point and snicker, making comments under their breath. One particular staff sergeant liked to take shots at the guys who were leaving—*Why are you so special? You're no better than us. What makes you think you'll go anywhere when you get out?*—as if the world were a dead-end and post-Army careers a fantasy.

Jeff felt like he had been consumed, seemingly overnight, by an "atmosphere of toxicity." But soon he realized he had previously contributed to that atmosphere himself. In past years he had also played the role of aggressor, sniping at fellow soldiers on their way out, no different from how he was being treated now. "I was guilty, too, of partaking in that behavior," he admitted. "Everyone is—before it happens to them."

On one occasion, when he was still a private, he had been called to staff duty, a twenty-four-hour desk shift for answering phones and sorting paperwork. In walked Sergeant Harris, a non-commissioned officer Jeff looked up to. "From where I was sitting as a private, you think, man, that guy's got some rank. He's got a few junior-enlisted guys he can boss around. He doesn't have to do the same bullshit as I do," Jeff said. It came as a shock, then, when Sergeant Harris dropped a packet on Jeff's desk and announced he was leaving.

Even more surprising was how happy he looked. "I'm out of this!" he exclaimed.

As Jeff looked on, Sergeant Harris signed the clipboard, then took off his beret and threw it in the air, saying, "Woo! I'm never coming back!"

Jeff was left in a daze. "Man," he thought, "if that guy's getting out, what the hell?" For service members with a few more years on their contracts, especially for those who have an upcoming deployment, getting out can feel a lifetime away.

Inside the office, Jeff exchanged glances with the other privates on duty. Their initial surprise quickly turned to resentment. "It was like, 'Hey, *we* got a lot of work to do. *We're* going to deploy. You're not helping us. So eat shit,'" Jeff remembered. Sergeant Harris had turned his back on them, and now they would do the same. "We gave him dirty looks, like, 'F this guy.'"

At a deeper level, Jeff suspected, there was some trace of envy, some amount of wishing their own time had come. "But," he said, "none of us would say that in the moment." In the moment, they rejected the shirking sergeant, and the fact of his separation helped entrench the solidarity between those who were staying behind. "There was honor that we were the ones to do the work that needed to be done," Jeff said.

Often, this tone came from the top. Jeff returned from his first deployment in 2008, at the peak of the financial crisis. The economy was in free fall; tens of thousands of jobs were disappearing each month. One day, he was standing in formation when the first sergeant began to target specific platoon members in the process of leaving.

"I don't know what you guys think you're going to do out there," he barked. He started calling privates out by name: "Private Johnson thinks he's going to do this, Private so-and-so thinks he's going to do that," Jeff imitated.

"Well guess what?" the first sergeant spat. "The economy's in the shithole and you won't be able to do any of that. Half of you don't even understand basic math. You're going to be a failure."

The incident left a lasting impression. "This is the top dog in an infantry company, who's been deployed four or five times," Jeff said. "He's the one you go to. He's the alpha male." Such treatment can appear harsh, but commanders face a precarious challenge. They are responsible for keeping their units disciplined and vigilant, ready to complete whatever orders are served; anything that gets in the way is a distraction that must be disposed of. Eventually it was Jeff's turn, and this time the same forces closed in on him. "I felt abandoned at the end," he said.

"Imagine you work with these guys every day. Then you come back and ninety out of the 120 guys turn their backs on you. You're immediately cast as this second-class soldier. You're no longer part of the team. It changes the mentality of being part of this elite group to being part of this small group that doesn't care anymore, or can't do it anymore."

A 2018 article in the journal *Clinical Psychology Review* reported that even the most confident and capable soldiers during active service were affected by an "unexpectedly protracted and complex" process of separation. "Exiting soldiers often find themselves unprepared for the instability of the initial phases of transition, and how this period may threaten their sense of self and self-worth."[4]

After years of building an affinity for the group, a sense of unit inclusion and cohesion unlike anything matched in the civilian world, soldiers, in their final months of service, are stripped of this integral component. A suggestion of abandonment and dereliction, even impotence, is introduced, and as they move through the stages required to break free from the military, it can stifle their return to normal life.

TWELVE MILES FROM the Kuwaiti border, Molly arrived at Camp Bucca. Named after Ronald Bucca, a New York City fire marshal who died rescuing civilians from the World Trade towers on 9/11, the full-service prison facility was shuttered in 2009, then converted by developers into a hotel a few years later.[5] It would come under the spotlight again in 2014, with reports surfacing that many of the Islamic State's leaders had been imprisoned there contemporaneously, coalescing as a cell and deepening their extremism.[6] But no one was any wiser in the early weeks of 2005, as Molly settled into her new battalion.

She was quickly introduced to Sergeant Davis, who asked her to take on preventive medicine duties at the prison in addition to her regular medic job. He made it sound like Molly had a choice. "Sure," she told him. "Whatever the Army needs." Sergeant Davis had two CDs and a stack of books detailing all the different medical standards a detainee operation must uphold—requirements set by institutions ranging from the American military to the International Red Cross. Along with Sergeant Davis, Molly's responsibility was to ensure their facility was in compliance. Every week, they toured through the prison compounds, inspecting the food, checking the water for E. coli, examining all aspects of sanitation.

When the battalion was short-staffed, she pulled other assignments. One day, she was ordered to cover security detail at an off-base firing range. The job had her standing on guard for hours, baking in the heat behind a gun turret. A sergeant suddenly yelled out, "Hey Snider! You wanna shoot this thing?"

"Hell yes!"

Molly sprinted over before he could change his mind. An Mk-19 grenade launcher was mounted on a tripod atop the sergeant's Humvee; the weapon weighed close to eighty pounds. Molly had never fired one before. "What do I do?" she asked.

The sergeant laughed and gave her instructions: Center mass on the target, hold steady, push down on the butterfly trigger to fire. A short distance away the grenade exploded upon impact, spraying shrapnel and sand everywhere within a twenty-foot radius. The sergeant saw the look of exhilaration on Molly's face and let her try another. She steadied the weapon, held her breath, and pushed down on the trigger again—this time a little too hard. The force on the weapon's stock lifted the barrel skyward and three grenades quickly fired out, each aimed higher than the last. The last two rounds cleared the top of the canyon wall where the training was held.

Molly gulped. She asked the sergeant what was beyond the walls. Mostly scrub brush and sand, he replied, though they had passed by some nomadic herdsmen on previous runs. He quickly rounded up the group and they drove back to the base.

At the front gates, an Iraqi shepherd was waiting for them. As the Humvees approached, he began to wave his arms furiously, motioning toward a battered wagon behind him. Inside were the bodies of two goats—one freshly killed and the other badly wounded. A string of embittered Arabic sloshed over the soldiers. Behind a stone demeanor, Molly was ashamed. They pulled into the gates and left the fuming Iraqi man behind.

Inside the camp, all personnel in Molly's battalion had recently moved from large communal trailers into compact, two-person 'containerized housing units,' or CHUs. Molly's roommate soon got discharged and she was able to enjoy a few weeks of the CHU to herself. She turned the extra bed into a sofa and lined a wall locker on its side so that its compartments could be used as cubbies. Then she placed a portable DVD player in the middle, and stepped back to admire her new entertainment center. The two-and-a-half-inch screen was so small you could barely see, but still, "it was comforting," Molly said. She was lying in bed one night, teetering on the edge of sleep when suddenly—ZIP! BOOM!

Molly leapt up. Her training kicked in. She grabbed her rifle, flak jacket, ballistic helmet, and burst out the door. Outside everyone was running in a panic. Some of the other women, caught in the middle of showering, were wrapped in only their towels, soap suds still in their hair. The incoming alarm began to sound—WHOOP! WHOOP!

"A bit late," Molly thought.

At a nearby bunker, she met Sergeant Davis, who took accountability for the team. After things settled down, they decided to take a closer look at the damage. The mortar had torn through several of the guys' shower stalls, and blown a large hole in a refrigeration unit. Shrapnel from the blast sliced up an iron dumpster and the rocket had left an impact crater "large enough to give a small dog a proper burial," said Molly. The few guys who were showering at the time were lucky to have chosen different stalls, she thought. The only true fatalities that night were several cases of Coca-Cola and some raw chicken breasts.

The unit's Quick Reaction Force completed a report on the attack. The investigation found that four rockets had been aimed at the camp. Only one made contact, but the other three had been set to the same trajectory. Molly realized with a start that her pod was directly aligned with the male showers and refrigerator—no more than a hundred yards away. "If the other 3 hadn't been duds," she later wrote, "the 3rd rocket would have been mine."

One day in late January, an urgent announcement suddenly reverberated over the loudspeakers on base: "All medical personnel come to the theater internment facility immediately."

The theater internment facility was where Camp Bucca housed its roughly 5,300 detainees.[7] The announcement repeatedly urged medics to report for duty, while other personnel were being asked to leave the facility. "You knew something not good was happening," Molly said. She was with Sergeant Davis at the time, and he had the keys to an Army ATV.

"Come on," he said, "I'll drive us down there."

Guards at the front gate made them turn in their rifles. Molly's adrenaline was surging; she felt ready to face whatever awaited on the other side. Finally, the doors lifted. "We go in and it's pandemonium going on," she recalled.

News reports would later describe a massive, coordinated uprising that began when a group of American soldiers were conducting a search for contraband. Each of the eight compounds had its own imam, or prayer leader, and each imam had his own megaphone used for signaling their call to prayer. In the fifth compound, the Muslim cleric began inciting nearby prisoners by alleging that guards had ripped up the Qurans in their mosque. Some guards later told Molly the prisoners had ripped up the Qurans themselves. The inmates became visibly agitated. They formed into a mass and started pushing against the compound's front fence, chanting and shouting. Prisoners in four other compounds joined in.[8] Molly watched as the men took off their head scarves and wrapped them around their faces—a measure she understood as preparing for battle. Whatever ignited them initially, the riots were soon full-blown fires. "It was the end of the world is what it seemed like," Molly said.

Inmates began tearing down the barbed wire fences to form barricades against the soldiers. They made slingshots from disposable gloves and broke up the concrete foundation from their huts into stones for ammunition. One shot hit Molly's commander in the face, knocking out several of his teeth. Nails were ripped from the wooden frames of mosques; mattresses were held up as shields against the guards' rubber bullets. Some prisoners hurled plastic bags ablaze with flammable hand sanitizer.

As fires burned and violence erupted around her, Molly jumped into action. Alongside the other medics, she helped wrap wounded inmates in blankets and carried them through the smoke and chaos up to the gates. The clashes, which lasted for over an hour, would take the lives of four detainees and injure half a dozen more.

A couple months later, in March, she took her mid-tour leave and returned to North Carolina for two weeks.

One day, she went out with some friends to play basketball. Someone scored a goofy-looking layup, and Molly decided to imitate the shot. She landed wrong on her ankle, tearing the ligament in half.

At the hospital, the doctors said she needed reconstructive surgery. When Molly got in touch with her unit, they told her to report to Fort Bragg. When she got to the base, she was told she would not be returning to Iraq; they had no use for a medic who couldn't walk unassisted.

Molly was put in medical hold until June, moving around in a cast, healing slowly. She stayed at the hospital and got assigned to patient transport duty, a desk job answering phones for nurses. "It was extremely boring," she recalled.

One day, an officer called Molly into his office and informed her that her unit was finishing up in Iraq. They would return in the fall, after completing the tour without her. "I have issues, very mixed emotions, about what happened," Molly said. Worst of all, she knew, "it was just a ridiculous injury."

Under the VA's definition of disability, virtually any condition that originates, or worsens, during an individual's active duty service is considered to be service-connected, enabling them to receive compensation benefits after leaving the military.[9] As one law firm elaborated: "If you are at home on leave and hurt yourself while lifting weights, have a car accident, or slip and fall on the ice, you are eligible for disability compensation if your injuries cause a disability. In short, you are on active duty between the time you enlist and the time you are discharged or separated, regardless of whether you are on leave, on base, in combat, or in a bar."[10]

For Molly, a far greater loss than the three-month ordeal with her ankle was getting cut off from her tribe. "I feel like I let down my team," she said. "Like I deserted or something. I felt a lot of guilt for leaving my people in that situation." That hurt would stay with her for years.

AT FIRST, MOLLY was committed to staying in the National Guard. The military had filled her with purpose and direction, and if it hadn't been for that regrettable blunder on a basketball court, she knew she would still be with her unit. At the beginning of 2006, she was accepted into Officer Candidate School.

"When I went to Iraq, I saw a lot of things done improperly or that could be improved upon. I thought the best way I could make things better was to be at a higher grade. If I was an officer, maybe I could do better."

The most well-known OCS is an intensive fourteen-week course offered at Fort Benning in Georgia, but the state-run OCS offered an alternative program where candidates could commit one weekend out of every month for sixteen months, plus two two-week periods, to attain their commission.[11] Molly had heard the program was like Guard duty, but she found the workload to be far more demanding. Each week was filled with daily online meetings, a constant scramble to write operations orders, and driving all around the state to meet with her peers whenever possible. Molly was juggling a full-time job and college classes at the same time. "The stress was unreal," she said. "That was like a hundred thousand boot camps."

After thirteen months, she dropped out. OCS had recently released job assignments, and Molly, who had trained as a medic and wanted to continue serving in the Army Medical Service Corps, learned she had been placed with the Chemical Corps. Instead of staying in medicine, she would have to work with gas masks and decontamination equipment—tasks that held little appeal. "I had to decide what's more important," she said. "At the time, school was more important to me." She decided she was okay with remaining a sergeant.

In the spring of 2007, she came across a listing for a sergeant position with a medical unit in Goldsboro, North Carolina. She applied and got it. She traveled with her new unit to Hattiesburg, Mississippi, for three weeks of training. Not long after that, the unit received orders to deploy. Everyone had to go through a pre-deployment screening, where they sat for a few tests and answered routine questions about their enlistment. When Molly went in for her appointment, she "was asked if I wanted to do it. But there was heavy emphasis on would I be *able* to do it?"

For Molly, this was a loaded question. Ever since her stint in med hold at Fort Bragg two years earlier, she had been holding onto a secret. No one had said the particular words to her but during one of her checkups they had flashed across a doctor's notes and lodged immovably in her mind:

Post-traumatic stress disorder.

Was it possible? she wondered. *Had something caused her to develop PTSD?*

Though she hadn't been able to complete her combat tour, the months she spent in Iraq had been defined by a feeling of relentless, unabating insecurity. "The overall experience was being so new and not knowing anything, not knowing what to expect," she said. "That was always in the background of what was going on." Distinctions blurred and uncertainty seeped into everything. "Just convoying with normal Iraqi locals—you don't know if the person right beside you could be the enemy. They're not just wearing a uniform that says they're the enemy. You don't know who the enemy is, and yet you're around the enemy all the time." The constant vigilance ground her down.

One incident would stand out: that detention center riot. All detainees at Camp Bucca received a retina scan when they first arrived, and the deceased were required to be scanned again during their postmortem. During the riot, one of the prisoners had been hit in the head by a rubber bullet, the impact so strong it caved in his entire forehead. But they still had to scan one of his eyes. No one wanted to go near him, until Molly volunteered. "I know I did it because my sergeant actually patted me on the back. He said that I was very professional and had no issues—but I don't remember it," she said. On a few occasions over the years, the repressed memory clawed to the surface in her dreams. Otherwise, as much as she tried when she was awake, she could not recount a single detail.

Could that have been it? Parsing for the eyeball in a smush of flesh and brain, a visual so sick it had to be shelved. *Did that cause it?*

Was it true? She had PTSD?

For two years, she had kept the diagnosis to herself. "It was the stigma of PTSD and mental health at that time. I didn't want to have anything wrong with me. I wanted to stay in."

She wanted to, but sitting in her pre-deployment exam, that wasn't the question she was being asked. The officer pressed her: Would she be *able to*?

Molly realized she wasn't sure. Going on deployment this time would be different from the first; she would be in charge this time. "Whereas before, when I went to Iraq, I was a private and then a specialist. I was really good at taking orders. This time, I was going to be responsible for the success of other people." She knew that she wasn't handling stress well. Most of all, she worried that she would freeze.

Finally, she gave her answer. She told the examiner that her mind wasn't quite right, and that if there was someone else healthier and more capable, they should take her place. Even as the words came out, she knew what she was really saying. She was shutting the door on her service.

"That was a hard decision to make," Molly said. "When they realized that I was going to be nondeployable—and because of my reasons for being nondeployable—I had to be put out." She remembered how serving in the Army had once made her feel, big and bad and strong, but those days had become distant, like a footage reel of someone else. She told herself that in a unit full of medics, she wouldn't be needed as much: "There were a lot of people who could step up and do my job, so it was easier for me to step aside." She told herself that this was best for everybody, that she could have been the weak link in the chain, dragging the whole unit down. She told herself that she had made the right call.

Within days she began the med board process. She felt fragile, unfit, afraid to test her own capabilities. Once she had accepted that she wouldn't be deploying, that she had succumbed to afflictions beyond her control, "that was the beginning of the end," she said.

CHAPTER 6
YOU CAN GET PAID
FOR THESE THINGS

SINCE 2012, service members processing out have been required to participate in several days of workshops and briefings called the Transition Assistance Program (TAP), designed to support their transitions from military to civilian careers.[1] The sessions cover a mix of real-world skills, such as financial planning and technical training, along with more abstract topics like "resiliency."[2]

Many components of the program are long and dry with questionable usefulness. "It was really one of those death by PowerPoint situations," Matt said. "Someone is going through stupid slides and you just want to die instead of sitting and listening." He and Jeff rode in together each morning, and by the end of the day, they would walk out in a daze, even forgetting where Matt had parked his truck.

TAP features a series of briefings on veterans' benefits provided by the VA. Attendance is mandatory. At the same time, vocational training courses to prepare service members for civilian occupations, as well as multi-day programs on tracks like entrepreneurship and education, are listed as optional.[3]

"It was very bizarre," said Jeff. At the beginning of military service, three months of grueling combat training and infantry school smoothed everyone's disparate backgrounds into a uniform cohesion. At the end of their service, he noticed a similar leveling effect induced by the "three days of sales-pitches from the VA and National Guard." In the presentations on VA benefits, he recalled, "they basically say go and apply for benefits. Even if you don't think you're disabled, you want to apply and file your claims."

He and Matt sat next to each other at the back of the classroom, intermittently tuning in behind two dozen other guys. They were urged by the instructor, again and again, to file for disability benefits.

"Even if you don't think you are hurt, you can get paid for these things."

"Even if you had that surgery way back, and nothing bothers you now, you can get paid for these things."

"Even if you"—broke your arm, have trouble sleeping, experience fuzzy hearing—"you can get paid for these things."

According to Jeff, the message was "hammered" into them. More unsettling was how little attention the VA's other services and benefits received. Jeff had set his sights on attaining a four-year degree, an opportunity he knew he could afford with aid provided by the post-9/11 G.I. Bill. It seemed like the logical next step for many of them. "Here was a large group given the chance to get an education—not just for free but actually get paid for it since you receive a stipend." But if the VA representative said anything about it at all, the mention was brief and shallow, and she quickly moved on. "It was disappointing," Jeff said.

Until he started out-processing, Matt hadn't thought much about the VA at all. To the extent that he did, he had pictured a place for World War II veterans, Purple Heart recipients, amputees and others "who were all messed up." But he had recently started hearing of the VA's disability benefits. It sounded like everyone was applying for as many as possible, and only a fool would pass them up. Nobody ever mentioned the ethics of this behavior. "Everyone just told me to make sure I do it," Matt said. "Just one of the things people would say when they were getting out. Get it done and over with, then you don't have to worry." Soon he was hearing about all the conditions and scenarios that might qualify for service-connection, even if his military service hadn't caused them.[4] Even with Jeff rolling his eyes right beside him, Matt said, "I tried to pay attention to it."

But the massive VA system they were being introduced to

seemed to care little about therapy or rehabilitative services for the ailments they were encouraged to claim. Rather it prompted them toward securing monthly cash payments in the form of disability compensation. Originating during World War I, the modern VA disability compensation system was established to compensate veterans for lost wages due to service-caused injuries. It grew rapidly in the years following. By 1956, a commission headed by five-star General Omar Bradley stated: "Our present structure of veterans' programs is not a 'system.' It is an accretion of laws based largely on precedents built up over 150 years of piecemeal development." The government report estimated that veterans benefits spending could rise to "a level of about $6 billion annually toward the end of the century," approximately $56 billion when adjusted for inflation.[5] "We should not commit future generations to obligations that we ourselves are unwilling to shoulder," it cautioned.[6] Yet hardly anyone listened.

Those projections have far been surpassed. In recent decades, successive administrations have dramatically increased the VA's budget. By 2011, it had increased more than fourteen-fold from 1940 levels, doubling approximately every decade. Last December, Congress granted the VA a $256 billion budget for the 2021 fiscal year.[7]

New ways of plugging into the VA's disability system have proliferated alongside its swelling expenditures. A culture of entitlement at many WTUs points ailing soldiers toward pursuing financial benefits rather than individual wellness, while a remodeled TAP scheme mandates attendance at extensive benefits workshops on everyone's way out. Local, county, and state veterans offices routinely hold benefits fairs and enrollment drives.[8] Getting more vets enrolled can often bring in more cash to their districts and influence to their posts.[9] Veterans' service organizations (VSOs) like American Legion and Veterans of Foreign Wars further supply a coterie of VA-trained agents who go through applications "page by page" to help veterans claim the maximum number of disabilities;[10] many private lawyers offer the same services on commission. In one widely-circulated VSO tip sheet, departing service members were encouraged to document everything from headaches and "twinges," to hemorrhoids.[11] The document beseeched veterans to "Get Every Test You Can!!!" and described every service-connected condition as "money in the bank." It reminded vets to always state that a condition "continues to bother you"—regardless of the truth of the matter. The payoff, it counseled, was virtually guaranteed: "Pain is worth 10% even if an Xray or MRI is negative."

"They're telling everybody to claim it," said one retired Marine sergeant major. "The VA disability guy would say tendonitis, ringing ear, sleep apnea. He'd stomp his foot on the ground like a horse three times. 'Listen up! There's no test for it. Listen again! There's no test for it.'"

In 1998, the VA introduced a program called Benefits Delivery at Discharge, allowing departing service members to begin applying for disability before their separation was complete. Within ten years, more than 70 percent of service members were discharged at military bases offering BDD.[12] Hardened within a network of informal advocacy and advice, the procedure has pushed inflated claims further. Between 2000 and 2013, the average number of service-connected disabilities climbed from 2.5 to 4.1 per veteran, with younger vets driving much of the growth. Post 9/11 veterans deployed to Iraq or Afghanistan recorded an average of 6.2 disabilities, while even those who had not deployed averaged 4.7 disabilities. They were claiming far more. In 2013, BDD applicants on average filed for sixteen service-connected conditions each.[13]

Organized by service era, roughly 11 percent of living World War II veterans, 16 percent of Vietnam-era veterans, and 21 percent of veterans from the first Gulf War receive service-connected disability pay.[14] By comparison, almost 40 percent of post-9/11 vets in 2016 were VA disability compensation recipients—despite much less sustained and intense combat exposure.[15]

Veterans today are claiming more disabilities than ever because they have been "encouraged to do it," former VA Secretary James Peake said. "It has been facilitated because that's what the laws and the rules are." Some veterans, shocked by what they have personally witnessed in the VA, have put it more crudely. "Essentially what happens a lot of the time now," said one recent Iraq War vet, is that the VA "shoves the benefits down the veteran's throat."[16]

Jeff balked at the system he saw. "I was kind of disgusted by it," he said. "You hear about how the system is backed up and it takes months to get an appointment. I thought, *This is why*. You're cluttering the system with people who don't really need it." He remembered attending his VA benefits session in a classroom full of twenty-somethings. "Why would these people need to file claims?" he wondered. "Should we really be encouraging the masses of the soldiers to be filing these claims? It bothered me."

The same skepticism didn't extend to Matt, who was focused on his own concerns. "I just wanted to get my shit fixed," he said.

HIS LIST of claims was long.

Matt filed for both knees. "I'm a paratrooper with sixteen jumps. And I was an infantryman. I frequently carried over 100 pounds on my back, plus jumping in and out of trucks. I put thousands of miles on my [knees]. You're just working them to the max. [The pain] started small and hurt worse over time."

He filed for his right hand. "It was basic training, one of those 'everybody run up three flight of stairs and put this on' drills. You have thirty seconds to do it. It's an impossible task and you're supposed to fail and then you get in trouble for failing. It was our third time doing it, so the stairs were hot and sweaty and slick. I fell and tried to catch myself. I heard a crunch. My pinky and ring finger on my right hand got pushed way back. Immediate pain and swelling. It looked like a Mickey Mouse hand for two weeks."

He filed for his upper back. "When I was training in Louisiana, I had to pick up this giant hog of a man and run him to a heli-copter"—a simulated evacuation exercise. "He was a full-size, 6'3",

225-pound, combat-loaded man, and I put him on my back and ran him across a field to a real helicopter. It was as real as it could be without him actually being dead. He was living it up. He's cussing at you while you're bouncing around with him on your back." The strain on his upper back, Matt said, was his first "pretty bad injury."

He filed for hearing loss in his left ear. "When you go to the range, you're wearing your protection. But when you're in war, you don't get a time-out to put your earplugs in." Besides being caught in multiple firefights and close encounters with explosions, Matt said his hearing suffered after a particular engagement with the enemy on his first deployment. It was December 2007, the first day of fighting in what became known as the Battle of Musa Qala. Matt's team was positioned on the roof of a low building when one of them saw a group of Taliban fighters rapidly approaching. Sitting on top of a small ledge, the other soldier aimed his rocket launcher and waited for the command. Matt was standing directly behind him, communicating on the radio between the commander and lieutenant. The command came in to engage. Matt lifted his head just as his platoon mate fired. The rocket's backblast swallowed Matt's entire upper body. "I felt like I got whacked in the head with a baseball bat," he said. His hearing was never the same.

He filed for both shoulders. "Another one of those mostly wearing out [conditions]. My right one that I really hurt was on my second deployment when I was lifting weights. I was bench pressing and it just popped out of socket. I felt it go and my entire arm went numb. People in the room heard it pop. I was so mad. I could barely lift or go the gym. It just hurt for months and months."

He filed for his bladder. "We would get rigged up for our jumps for parachuting, and I can remember just sitting there for eight to ten hours, just sitting there in 100-degree heat in July. You're drinking water but you can't take a leak. It's a nightmare. Your bladder swells to the size of a basketball. Every single time you jump, the first thing you do is take your parachute off and the second thing you do is take a piss. I've seen dudes piss themselves before and they'll play it off like they landed in some water somewhere. After my last jump when I hurt my back really bad, I just had to pee all the damn time."

He filed for his lower back.Army paratroopers are required to jump every three months to stay current and continue receiving their pay. Matt's last jump came in early August 2010, right after returning from his second deployment. He was scheduled for a routine "Hollywood" jump—no rifle, no rucksack, just a man and his parachute.

"There are bleachers out there so people can go and watch. I told my wife and she's like, 'Hey, that's really cool.' It was only a five-minute drive from the airbase to where we were jumping. It took her forever to find the place. I texted her that depending on which side of the aircraft I'm in, I'm going to be either jumper eleven or twenty-two."

It was a windy day. "We stood up and hooked in. I jumped out. Everything looked good." He started counting. "One one-thousand. Two one-thousand. Three one-thousand." If they got to four one-thousand and hadn't yet felt the yank from the parachute pulling on its own, "you have to pull your reserve," Matt said, "or you're going to die."

His parachute opened without a hitch. "Everything you're doing is quick," he said. "Look left, right, down. When I was about a hundred feet off the ground, I started getting my body into position to land. You squeeze your knees and feet really tight and let your legs hang limp—otherwise you'll break them. Keep your eyes on the horizon. If you're looking at the ground, you'll want to reach for it and you'll break your hands. You know impact is imminent. The more stiff you are, the more it's going to hurt. You're basically preparing to fall, not to land."

Suddenly a big gust of wind blew by, and Matt got entangled in the parachute of the guy below him. This was among the worst things that could happen during a jump. Now it was two soldiers risking injury, possibly their lives, instead of just one. "He stole some of my lift. My chute collapsed a bit and I landed really hard. I could feel it in my lower back. Soon as I hit, I started screaming." According to Matt, it looked serious enough from the ground that some officers had already called an ambulance. Later, alone with his wife, he lifted his shirt to show her. "It was purple and bruised," Matt said. "That did it for my lower back."

Finally, and significantly, he did not file for PTSD. "From what I've been told, the Army—and the military in general—doesn't want to diagnose you with PTSD. They say that if you're diagnosed with PTSD while you're still on active duty, that puts you on a non-deployable status. So [the military] will call it different things. For me, they called it adjustment disorder. That was my issue. I'm like, 'Hey, I'm having all these problems and nightmares and anxiety,' and the doctor just wrote down adjustment disorder.'"

After leaving the military, it wouldn't take long for the VA to elevate his diagnosis to PTSD. At the time, however, Matt didn't think much of it. Five years in the Army had left him bumped and bruised, but nothing that was going to stand in the way of his return to civilian life. In Fayetteville, he and Jessica were settling into their new apartment. He had his sights on finding work with the local police department; the demands of law enforcement seemed like a natural fit for the skills he had learned. Filing his disability claims was just doing what he was told, a natural part of getting out—it's what everyone did. "I assumed that they were going to deny me on a lot of this stuff anyway," Matt said. "The way I looked at it, if I hurt it while I was in the military, then I'm just going to claim it. There was nothing to lose."

EVERY SOLDIER'S IDENTITY is a cascade of narratives and memberships. Within the military, every branch offers its own ethos, cultivated over time and closely linked with its distinct history, traditions, and role in the nation's defense. Marines, for example, "are convinced that, being few in number, they are selective, better, and, above all, different," said former commandant Victor Krulak.[17] After years of bidding recruits to "Accelerate your life," the Navy changed its slogan in 2017 to "Forged by the Sea."[18] The new tagline "captures the transformative impact the Navy and the sea has on our sailors," said Rear Admiral Pete Garvin, head of Navy Recruiting. "For more than 200 years our sailors have been tested and shaped by the sea."[19] Big aircraft carriers and other commissioned ships also have their own watchwords, from the USS Abraham Lincoln's "Shall Not Perish," to the US Naval Search and Rescue's motto, "So Others May Live."[20]

In the Army, soldiers are expected to embody what is codified in the *Army Values*, and govern their daily behavior according to the Soldier's Creed. A decade after learning it, Molly can still recite from memory the definition of leadership she had learned during Officer's Candidate School: "*Leadership* is the process of influencing people by providing purpose, direction, and motivation to accomplish the mission and improve the organization."[21]

Informal hierarchies and rivalries within each service further inform a person's self-regard. SEALs occupy the highest rung in the Navy, followed by the Naval Aviators, with carrier-launched fighters held in especially high regard. In the Army, the infantry branch is viewed as its toughest, and therefore, most prestigious, branch, while other military specialties are relied on to provide support. Even within the infantry, there are the Rangers, considered the most elite group, followed by the Airborne units comprised of paratroopers like Jeff and Matt, and then the regular—so-called "leg"—light infantry and mechanized infantry. In part, these hierarchies are sorted on true differences: the Rangers, for example, are the most rigorous cohort in both selection and training, and operate in the military's secretive Special Operations Command. Some degree of the sorting, however, must be attributed to tribalism and urban myth, and the desire in every person to be a part of something special and honorable.

Soldiers manage these overlapping cues at the same time they are forced to negotiate sometimes drastic changes in their external environments. For a service member who is leaving the military, the process can feel like an especially turbulent passage, with abrupt turns and blurring walls. One useful way to conceptualize this experience is by tracing the soldier's trajectory through three concentric spheres.

At the center is the smallest sphere, representing an active combat theater. Soldiers on deployment spend six to eighteen months at their assigned military base or operating site, where some of them are called to venture beyond the wire and into contested territory in order to complete their missions. When they return from tour, they cross the boundary from the inner sphere of combat operations to the middle sphere of "normal" military life. Stationed back on a US military base, they no longer live in proximity to the enemy; they have left the sounds of shelling and threats of attack behind. This transition is also observed as a group, eased by being around peers who have shared the same experiences and are readjusting to the same daily military routines.

Eventually, everyone who exits the military must pass through another boundary—this one marking their return into civilian society. For most, like Jeff and Matt, the crossing is planned and deliberate. But for soldiers who sustain a sudden, severe combat injury, the trauma can project them across what feel like multiple boundaries in a single leap, landing them directly in the civilian world soon after. Service members in this group must grapple with the far-reaching implications of their injury—in Tyson and Malik's cases, the sudden loss of limbs—even as they scale the psychological challenges presented by simultaneous transitions. Occasionally, members of the National Guard may encounter a similarly abrupt swing without ever suffering from a traumatic injury, when they complete their active-duty terms and demobilize, seemingly overnight, into regular reserve status—transporting from Baghdad to Fort Hood, for instance, and then straight to "Fort Living Room."

The more abrupt the transition, the more disruptive its effects can be.

A soldier making this passage is exposed to dramatic changes affecting his sense of self and purpose. Service-forged identities are twisted and roiled; the bonds built by overcoming military adversity are shed for the weaker ties of civilian life. Often it is during this period of vulnerability that systems like the VA enter the picture to help pave the way. But rather than extending ramps toward self-sufficiency and further achievement, their programs too often shuttle new veterans down the path toward stagnation and dependency.

If a soldier's identity is drawn from the honor codes and traditions of his military service, then the VA's outsized disability arm has constructed his new post-service identity in accordance with its own objectives: the veteran as an endless assemblage of afflictions and impairment. Men and women charged with defending the nation are suddenly deemed too weak, without benefits, to even survive in it upon their return.

DECEMBER 28, 2010 was Jeff's last day in the Army. He turned through the gates of Fort Bragg for the final time, then made a quick stop at Matt's apartment.

"That's it, huh," Matt said. "You're out."

Jeff pulled off his uniform and laughed, "I'm never putting this on again." Matt knew the feeling well. "Amen brother."

Soon Jeff was back on the road. He slept that night at a motel off the highway in Kentucky, then connected with Interstate 64 in the morning, taking it all the way to McLeansboro, Illinois. His fiancé was there with her family. He stayed with them for a couple nights, helping Bethany pack her things, then they were on the road again, arriving in St. Louis the day of New Year's Eve.

For Jeff, the timing felt like destiny. "I was just really, really ready to go," he said. "I couldn't wait to get to St. Louis. I was done with the Army and moving on." St Louis was where he had met Bethany, and where they had decided to start their life together. She was finishing a master's in public health administration and had already lined up a job after graduation.

"I was excited. I was optimistic," Jeff said. "I was interested in getting onto the next phase." He went on, "And I was pretty convinced it was going to go smoothly. I got this associate degree, I got this work experience in the Army, I got a great fiancé. I was looking at schools, getting ready to apply. Everybody's patriotic and so I'll have no trouble getting a job. It's going to be great."

The new year would produce some of those triumphs, but not without many more trials Jeff had not foreseen. For decades, the military has gradually untethered from civilian life, resulting in a widening chasm that all veterans must cross. In one survey, three-quarters of military personnel agreed that "the military community has little in common with the rest of the country and most civilians do not understand the military." The respondents of another survey, when asked to estimate the total number of active-duty service members, were off the mark by an average of five million.[23] In ways big and small, that gap can register as a form of culture shock.

It was unusually warm on the last day of 2010, and as night fell, a tornado whipped through St. Louis.[24] Jeff and his fiancé had just finished moving. Surrounded by stacks of boxes inside their modest second-floor unit, they allowed themselves a break to admire their new home. Jeff glanced at the window, where thick raindrops were flattening against the glass. "Let's go check it out," he said.

They stepped onto the balcony. Heavy winds were snapping at the telephone wires, branches cracking and falling. In the distance they could hear sirens screeching toward the next emergency. For a minute, they sat on the balcony and took it all in.

A minute was enough. "Let's get back in the house," Jeff said, leading the way. They celebrated the arrival of the New Year inside.

PART II:

COMPENSATION

CHAPTER 7
KABUKI THEATER

ONCE NOTHING MORE than stray farmhouses and tobacco barns near the eastern coast of North Carolina, Camp Lejeune operates today as one of the country's premier military facilities. Home to the 2nd Marine Division, the Marine Corps base has expanded to include hundreds of tactical landing zones, dozens of live-fire ranges, and a world-class facility for land and sea training operations.

Twenty miles north sits Jacksonville, North Carolina—recently identified as the youngest city in America, largely thanks to the camp's presence and proximity.[1] "It's a total Marine town," said Graham, a Jacksonville resident and former Marine sergeant major. "That's why it's so in-my-face frustrating."

Graham retired from the Marine Corps in 2009, wrapping up thirty years of service, and moved on to a sales job in Jacksonville. What quickly became so in-his-face frustrating was the abundance of disabled vets he encountered daily in his new home. Most Americans, Graham said—residing far from military bases and disconnected from military lives—are stuck with a selective view of the veteran community. "All they see is, 'Oh, a disabled vet, let's help them.' But they don't see this. What happens in the rush to take care of those in need is everybody else floods the gate," he said.

From his perch, it seemed the gates were overflowing. Veterans paraded their disability awards everywhere he went. None of it made sense to him. "The average disabled vet in this town looks like a healthy person who could go to Gold's Gym every day," he went on. Sometimes he approached them to ask about their afflictions; frequently they confirmed his worst suspicions. "The fraud," Graham said, "is everywhere."

At the local bar, he had gotten to know the bouncer, a young vet who was receiving 100 percent disability partially for a bad back. Yet Graham soon discovered that the bouncer in his spare time trained as a bodybuilder. At the post office, he met an Army vet who also claimed 100 percent disability rating from the VA. Graham watched him in the warehouse loading packages and moving heavy boxes. Later, he happened to meet the man's mother-in-law. He asked what had happened to her son-in-law. Her answer: "He broke his leg drunk in the backyard," Graham recalled. Another time his brother told him about a veteran who was rated at 90 percent for PTSD. The vet applied for an increase to 100 percent and heard from some Army buddies to soil himself at his VA appointment. He went in, soiled himself, and got the 100 percent he was seeking.

Graham came to understand that in the pursuit of VA benefits, a veteran's presentation had a funny habit of contorting itself. He related another case from when he was still active duty at Camp Lejeune. A girl he knew was a musician in the Marine Band, and one day she was caught sleeping with her husband in the barracks. Her commander gave her a non-judicial punishment, letting her off easy. Years later, as she was processing out of the military, she applied for disability benefits. "She went to the VA first about her hearing and they didn't give her money," Graham said. "So then she tried to claim she was assaulted in the barracks, and because of that assault she was depressed. It was the same case she was punished for! She ended up getting 50 percent."

The VA, meanwhile, appeared clueless, at best, deliberately obtuse at worst. For years Graham was a subscriber to the *Marine Corps Times*, and began noticing headlines reporting dramatic spikes, one after the other, in a litany of medical conditions: "PTSD up, tendonitis up, ringing ear—they're all up!" He could only shake his head. He was certain of one factor that was contributing to the rising disability rates: "it's the free money," he vented, but no one was willing to talk about it. He almost couldn't blame them; many of his own family members and close friends, hardly disabled and working full-time jobs just as he was, were also lining their pockets with benefits. He had come to know better than to speak his mind around them. "It's a sore point. If the government says that people should [be getting] this, I guess I can't blame them for taking it. They don't want to turn off the treasure trove," he said.

Once he started looking, the headlines were everywhere.

Across the state in Raleigh, North Carolina, federal investigators picked up a guy who was collecting $7,000 in monthly compensation from the VA and other government agencies. Enlisted in the US Army from 1996 to 2005, Anthony Patrick Stanford had been assigned to laundry detail shortly after completing his basic training. A few years into his service, he began to suffer pain in his wrists and ankles and underwent a number of minor surgeries for relief. After leaving the military, he met with a VA physician. Stanford told the doctor he suffered from severe joint pain and required assistance for daily activities like feeding and dressing himself. The VA granted him a 100 percent disability rating for his upper and lower extremities.

In 2011, he went in for another VA evaluation to maintain his benefits. He told the doctor that he needed assistance for basic tasks like bathing and using the toilet. At another evaluation, he said he was unable to lift objects greater than two pounds by himself. Court documents from a subsequent investigation showed these statements to be false. Stanford had no trouble walking, driving, performing "meaningful physical labor," and engaging in other manners of work and play. On one occasion, he took an unassisted trip to Disney World, paid for with his disability benefits.[2] When special agents interrogated him a few weeks later, Stanford confessed to the scheme.

In Hawaii, thirty-two-year-old Cody Joslin received over $48,000 in disability benefits by falsely claiming PTSD and other conditions from multiple combat tours in Iraq and Afghanistan. He fed the VA stories of fabricated firefights, witnessing friends die in combat, and sustaining injuries from rocket-propelled grenades.

Records showed he had served in the Army for approximately nine months, and never deployed overseas. To support his false accounts, he had purchased counterfeit military certifications online and submitted them alongside his benefits claims.[3]

Accruing over decades, the payoff can be huge. Richard Klaffka, a New York resident in his fifties, told the VA that a service-connected injury in 1978 had left him confined to a wheelchair, but federal investigators observed him pitching iron horseshoes, cutting trees with a chainsaw, and, among other activities, riding a stationary bike for forty-four minutes while on a cruise ship. For years, he had been so pleased with the easy benefits he even bragged about the "skits" he put on to get them. Before his conviction in 2017, Klaffka had received monthly benefits totaling $922,137 from the VA.[4]

Some vets kept up the ruse no matter what. Dennis Paulsen retired from the Navy in 1993 after serving for two years, claiming chest pains and loss of feeling in his face. VA doctors determined he likely had multiple sclerosis and evaluated him at 30 percent disability. Paulsen arrived for his subsequent VA appointments in a wheelchair, and eventually raised his disability rating to 100 percent for permanent and total loss of use in both of his hands and feet. He received compensation for almost twenty-five years, even as photos he posted online showed him bungee jumping, batting .300 in a local baseball league, and even competing in a Marine Corps Tough Mudder race. Despite all the evidence demonstrating his physical capabilities, Paulsen insisted that he was a disabled vet. When confronted by a local news crew, he replied, "Every job that I try, I couldn't do, but I would look healthy enough to do it. I'd go out and work at Lawn Doctor and try to open up the fertilizer bags, and the things would slip out of my hands. We wouldn't even be discussing this if I went to Iraq or Afghanistan and got my legs blown off. But I get looked at like a fraud because you can't see the disease."[5]

Other acts were so brazen, they verged on recklessness, or stupidity. In 2012, former Army specialist Justin Perez-Gorda told interviewers that he could no longer move his legs after he was caught near an IED blast in Afghanistan.[6] His wife told the non-profit Homes for Our Troops that Perez-Gorda had "permanent loss of both extremities," and was "paralyzed from the belly button down." In 2013, the non-profit raised donations to build a wheelchair-accessible house for the couple in Dripping Springs, Texas. But neighbors soon saw the veteran walking around the property. Homes for Our Troops sent an employee to assess the situation, but when he arrived at the property, Perez-Gorda refused to come out. Investigators later caught footage of him unloading lumber in the garage.[7]

Often the abuse smacked of irony. Phillip Brown, the Fort Bragg WTU commander, remembered working with a former legal assistant who had one deployment to Iraq: "She may have been around burning trash at some point, but not nearly as much as the infantry guy who is out on a remote site burning their own poop." When the woman returned from tour, she claimed lung problems that caused her to have coughing fits and made appointments with nearly every pulmonary specialist on base. Brown continued, "They all basically said, 'You're clear. There's nothing wrong with you.'" But the woman was adamant. She eventually consulted an out-of-state university physician who was studying post-combat lung sickness, and acquired the diagnosis she was looking for. "Even though the Army had basically determined she was fit for duty, [the professor] said that there may be some things that indicate [a lung condition]. So ultimately, she was allowed to pursue a full medical retirement," said Brown, who became commander of the Womack Army Medical Center's Warrior Transition Battalion in 2018.

The kick came later when the woman began working in her new civilian field. In the military, "she was claiming she couldn't be in the company areas because the paint and cleaning products were too upsetting for her. And yet, her profession [now] is working fiber arts." For a veteran with alleged lung problems, Brown could hardly imagine a space with more invasive particles and fibers in the environment. "She expected us to not get the irony that she could work in a facility that has constant air disturbances and be okay, but not be okay working in the unit," he said. "It was just mind-boggling. She's gonna get 70 percent disability the rest of her life."

The more time Graham spent in Jacksonville, the more he began to feel claustrophobic. Veterans faking disability couldn't possibly be the norm, but ever since he left the military, it was rare for him to see otherwise. Recently he had enrolled in classes at the local community college, but even that was no escape. "You want to talk about every disabled parking spot being taken—taken by these jacked up four-wheel drives," Graham said. He traced the problem back to the VA, which he blamed for pumping the town full of disabled vets—some genuine, but many suspicious. "Everyone is reaching for it now. It's too easy. They all sit around and talk about what to say when they get out," he observed. "I see thousands of Disabled Vet plates—they're all over the place. My neighborhood, my town, every bar, every Walmart that I go to."

Somewhere along the way, his perception of disabled veterans shifted. "When I see another one of those plates these days, I used to think of someone struggling," Graham said. "Now I just think of money."

CHRISTOPHER FRUEH knew that if there was ever a true accounting of the country's misappropriated disability payments for veterans, the total sum would be staggering—billions siphoned from the American taxpayer. After working at the VA for fifteen years, he wished he still felt outrage, but fraudulent accounts of disability no longer surprised him. Inside the VA, he said, "We'd see a lot of acting in order to get the desired diagnoses." It was so common that it became routine.

Frueh (pronounced FREE) began his career in 1992 as a staff psychologist at the VA Medical Center in Charleston, South Carolina. He had just wrapped up his doctoral studies—focusing on veterans with PTSD—and his placement at the Charleston VA hospital was a natural fit. His passion for working with veterans sprang from early influences. His father was an Air Force physician who had served in

Vietnam, and his great-grandfather, who lived to the age of nine-ty-nine, was a veteran of the Spanish-American War. When Frueh was a child, "both of them talked quite a bit about their experiences and what they saw," he said. "I remember [their stories] strongly."

In an interesting juxtaposition with his military heritage, Frueh came of age in a Quaker household that taught conscientious objec-tion as the moral choice. This choice was pitted against US law that required young men to register for the selective service when they turned eighteen. As the decisive birthday approached, he met with elders in the community for advice. They emphasized the Quakers' commitment to peace and their long heritage of resisting war efforts. His father, a career military physician, was discouraging in a differ-ent way. War is "dirty, ugly, nasty business," he told his son. "You don't want to be in it." In the end, though, Frueh couldn't shake his sense of duty. "If there was a draft and I took conscientious objector [status], then someone else would have to go in my place," he rea-soned. "So I did register." Frueh never got called up to serve—there would never be another draft—but the experience helped to orient his purpose: he decided he would devote his life to "taking care of our veterans who *had* served."

His great-grandfather's story illustrates how far the evolution of veterans' care has progressed in the US. Born near the end of the nineteenth century, he had started his service lying about his age in order to join the American militia. A scrappy sixteen-year-old, he shipped off to Cuba and took up arms in the Battle for San Juan Hill. It was a short, decisive battle in a short, brutal war. Six weeks later, Spain sued for peace and America's forces were sent home. "His whole unit was basically dropped off at the docks in New York City," Frueh said. "They were mustered out right then and there."

The port filled with malnourished, ailing men, freshly returned from fighting in the war. Many had dysentery, fevers, or worse. Frueh's great-grandfather was lucky. Shortly after he landed, a local woman and her butler pulled up in a horse-drawn carriage. She grabbed half a dozen guys off the docks and brought them to her house, where she fed and nursed them for several months. When they were healthy enough to travel, she helped them get back home. "This was immediately after the war was finished. There was no VA system. This was a civilian woman who said, 'I want to do something for the men who served,' and she took it upon herself to do it," Frueh said. His great-grandfather never forgot that woman, and neither would he.

Nearly a century later, Frueh's job at the VA was to help rehabilitate veterans with mental health disorders, but he soon found his work inextricably linked with the administration's massive compensation division. Though most outsiders perceive it as a single entity, the Department of Veterans Affairs is divided into three separate departments: the National Cemetery Administration, the Veterans Health Administration, and the Veterans Benefits Administration.

The National Cemetery Administration—representing less than one percent of the VA's annual budget—supervises the nation's 131 VA cemeteries, where more than 3.5 million Americans are buried, including veterans from every period of service dating back to the Revolutionary War.[8]

More than nine million living veterans, along with a small number of family members, are enrolled with the Veterans Health Administration (VHA), the country's largest integrated care system, which supports a network of over 1,240 health care facilities.[9] Because its mission is to provide treatment for a wide range of medical needs, the vast majority of VA staffers, including Frueh, are employed by the VHA. In the VA's 2021 budget request, $94.5 billion of the proposed $243.3 billion total was allocated to this healthcare division.[10]

In contrast, the Veterans Benefits Administration (VBA), which oversees the administration's various compensation programs, directs a much smaller staff but a significantly higher budget. In 2021, the department is expected to administer $133 billion in benefits paid to 5.7 million beneficiaries.[11] Comprising the bulk of these payments are disability benefits made to the department's service-connected veterans. In Charleston, where Frueh often helped to assess patients seeking such disability payments, he began to encounter accounts of handicaps that seemed suspicious.

"There was this dance that the patients and clinicians played with each other," he said. Convinced that whatever the clinicians wrote could affect the success of their disability claims, patients "were really trying to show how sick they were." If Frueh recommended a treatment that might rein back their benefits, they would urge him not to record it, sometimes even threatening to file a complaint. And if their bid to increase benefits came back from the VBA denied, they would insist on transferring from outpatient appointments to inpatient hospitalization before applying again.

During his graduate work and internship, Frueh had heard about incidents of fraud and abuse, but he assumed those patients were rare, a few bad apples in the basket. "I thought it would be one or two in a hundred, and it would just jump out at you," he said. Within weeks of starting full-time, he began to realize the scale of the problem, as well as its consequences.

Clinicians who pushed back against certain claims frequently provoked animosity from their patients. In many cases, Frueh came to feel that the outbursts were part of a strategy to validate the patients' compensation attempts. Every time he documented anything to suggest a veteran's problems were not directly induced by PTSD, even the mention of an alternative diagnosis provoked a fierce response. "Diagnosing substance abuse was a no-no. Diagnosing personality disorders was a no-no. Diagnosing any type of pre-existing condition, or even asking about pre-existing conditions, became a problem," he said. It was a problem because any other diagnosis, no matter how accurate, would not be as easy to "connect" to military service and therefore would not be a ticket to a lifelong stream of compensation.

Once, after he determined that a patient suffered from depression rather than PTSD, the veteran lost his temper and began to yell, even hurling a chair across the room. The vet went on to meet with the clinic's director and was assigned to a different psychologist, who eventually granted him the PTSD diagnosis he was seeking. Such cases were not unusual. In a national survey of VA mental health professionals, the majority of clinicians believed that lying or exaggerating was a significant concern among veterans applying for PTSD compensation. Their outlooks corresponded to their experience. The longer the clinicians had been working with veterans, the more strongly they believed that symptoms were misrepresented in order to gain benefits.[12]

AT THE CHARLESTON PTSD CLINIC, Frueh worked closely with a psychiatrist and social worker as part of a three-pronged treatment team. Three or four times a week, they reserved a spacious room in the hospital, spread a dozen chairs into a circle, and hosted hour-long group therapy sessions called "rap groups." Roughly fifteen vets were assigned to each group, with more than half in attendance at any given meeting.

Almost immediately, the meetings veered off track. "We noticed a lot of times, group therapy became about the guys comparing notes and mentoring each other on how to get disability—even with us right there," Frueh said. In the same room where their clinical team was observing them, the veterans strategized over how to maximize their ratings. "Make sure you don't look good," they counseled one another. "Maybe don't bathe that day. Maybe don't sleep so well the night before." They shared tips on what terms to use, which claims advisors to go to, which doctors were the most likely to yield.

Of course, not everyone attending therapy had the same aim. After Frueh and his team wrapped up the discussions, "it was not uncommon for two to three guys to approach us outside," he recalled. The troubled parties would disclose their misgivings privately. "They would say, 'We're concerned about this or that patient because the stories he's telling about his combat don't make sense. They don't jive with what really happened.'" A suspected malingerer might mention the wrong weapon, or reference operating procedures that didn't exist. "There were all kinds of ways these guys would out somebody,"

Frueh said. Some had sharp enough memories to flag historical discrepancies: "We were not in A Shau Valley during the springtime of such and such year." However, even when everyone agreed that a member of the group was trumpeting false accounts, "there wasn't much we could do about it," Frueh said, "because the VA doesn't offer a way to fact-check."

Richard Burns, who worked as an outpatient therapist at the Gainesville VA Medical Center through the 1990s, estimated that nine out of ten patients he saw for PTSD were "wannabes." A Special Forces veteran who served two combat tours in Vietnam, he was uniquely qualified to spot fabricated accounts of combat service. Wannabes often resorted to a recognizable bag of tricks: they misused acronyms, mispronounced geographical names, claimed secret missions where all other team members—and possible corroborators—were killed, or boasted of their own "fifty confirmed kills" in combat—numbers that were impossible to verify. The VA's disability system presented them with a golden opportunity to skirt "the pesky problem of having to work," Burns said. "Wouldn't you rather be diagnosed as a hero suffering from war trauma and given $3,000 a month?"[13]

In many cases, veterans genuinely seeking to rehabilitate are the ones who take the most offense. Soon after returning from a fifteen-month combat tour in Afghanistan, Brendan O'Byrne, a former Airborne Infantry sergeant, began experiencing issues in his normal life. He checked himself into a forty-five-day inpatient treatment facility for PTSD and attended the program's daily group sessions, where an open environment was fostered for participants to share their experiences of trauma. Some relived firefights deep in the jungles of Vietnam; others recalled tense patrols gone awry in sunbaked Iraqi streets.

"But more than those traumatic stories, I heard stories that sounded a lot like a bad day rather than a traumatic moment," O'Byrne recalled during a 2017 Congressional hearing. "As weeks went by, I realized the sad truth about a portion of the veterans there. They were scammers, seeking a higher rating without a real trauma." His suspicions were confirmed when he overhead one veteran divulge to another that he was there to "pay the bills," and hoped "this in-patient was enough for a 100 percent rating."[14]

Unfortunately, securing benefits can become the most important feature in some people's post-service lives. Mark McVay, a retired teacher in Colorado, remembered introducing himself to a fellow Vietnam vet exercising at his local gym. McVay shared that he was in the 11th Armored Cavalry Regiment from 1969 to 1970, then asked the other man where he had served.

Ignoring McVay's question, the man said instead, "Are you getting your PTSD benefits yet?"

"No," McVay replied.

"Well then you ought to go over to the VA and sign up for the session," the other veteran advised. All it took, he assured McVay, was "a couple weeks of group."[15]

It was this sort of mentality that pushed Frueh and his team to eventually shut down their clinic's rap groups. If their purpose had been to move veterans away from fixating on their handicaps, the sessions appeared to be accomplishing the opposite. During the meetings, many of his patients showed little interest in recovery, diverting their energy instead to exhibiting behaviors they believed would be successful for attaining money from the VA. O'Byrne, sitting in the halls of Congress years later, would share the same lesson in his testimony to the nation's lawmakers. "When there is money to gain," he told them, "there will be fraud."[16]

FRUEH WAS TORN. He had always considered this line of work— to treat and help veterans— his calling, but what he began to see every day in the VA clinic clashed with his sense of duty as a doctor. More than that, it tarnished everything he grew up believing about the people who served. Still, he knew that the stakes were high: even the thought of dismissing a veteran who was truly in need made him queasy. He had to be sure.

Among the first and most basic measures in conducting psychiatric assessments is the structured interview. Different structured interviews exist for different disorders, but most are comprised of scaled questions designed to record both the frequency and intensity of a patient's symptoms.[17] As a core component of standard mental health evaluations, the interviews feature questions with obvious "right" and "wrong" answers, meaning a patient seeking a desired result can easily figure out the "correct" way to respond. A sample PTSD question on the VA website poses: "Have you experienced painful images or memories of combat or other trauma which you couldn't get out of your mind, even though you may have wanted to?"[18]

Given this reality, many interviewers have honed their ability to detect faking. "When you've got somebody that endorses every single item—virtually every single symptom—at the most extreme level, that always gave me room for doubt," Frueh said. Sometimes there were signs that the vets had been coached. In one of his appointments, Frueh assessed a patient who hadn't graduated high school, yet kept describing his condition using specialized terms such as "hyper vigilance."

Another strategy Frueh picked up was to prolong his structured interviews by adding a few questions of his own, such as, "When you're having symptoms, do you find that the back of your eyeballs itch?" Or, "When you have nightmares, do you dream in purple?" The questions were nonsense; they had no medical correlation to anything. Yet many of the veterans Frueh examined continued to endorse them: "Yes, doctor, yes. Everything's in purple."

Such techniques carry a long tradition. In the 1970s, a surgeon named Gordon Waddell noticed a rise in his patients who were claiming lower back pain—including perplexing, 'non-organic' symptoms which deviated from what he had always understood about the condition. Eventually he developed a series of "Waddell signs" to distinguish between anomalous and true expressions of physical pain.[19]

After seeing multiple veterans whose complaints of discomfort sounded suspicious, Danny Harris, a physical therapist in the Army, began to incorporate these Waddell signs into his own appointments. One of the signs, known as the 'distraction test,' taught examiners to perform the same test twice—once while diverting the patient's attention to something else. When veterans came to Harris with reports of knee pain, for instance, they might insist they couldn't bend their knees beyond ninety degrees. "But then," Harris said, "if I put them in a different position and say, 'Hey, I'm looking at the strength of your hip,' I'll bend their knee all the way to their butt."

Harris, who is based at Fort Drum, works primarily with active-duty service members. When many of them make appointments to see him, "it's not actually anything anatomically wrong," he said. "They won't have any pain, as long as they think that's not what I'm looking for." He estimates that at least a fifth of his daily patients are prompted by ulterior motives, such as getting out of work or documenting ailments to get VA benefits down the line. "It's what all the physical therapists complain about," he said. "We literally talk about this almost every day at lunch."

It took William McMath a year before he, too, started getting smart to the tells of a veteran's misrepresentations. After one particularly memorable instance—in which a retirement-age vet who had worked for decades in the civilian police force insisted on speaking "as if he were Dustin Hoffman's Rain Man"—McMath realized he had "become adept, not at identifying liars, but at detecting bad acting."[20]

A psychologist by training, McMath worked at the VA as a Compensation and Pension (C&P) examiner, helping to evaluate veterans who apply for disability benefits or re-apply to raise their disability rating.[21] It was a position that placed him at the nexus of the VA's massive healthcare and compensation arms; as an employee of the VHA, he conducted C&P exams, then transferred the evaluations back to the VBA. The results were picked up by a ratings specialist, who would review the evaluation's results, alongside other

records, and determine the claimant's service-connection and ultimate percentage rating.

McMath described a set of "red flag" behaviors that tipped him
off to veterans who were likely faking or exaggerating their ailments.
Often these patients would arrive at the interview in dirty or ripped
clothes, unshaven for several days. They would act excessively unso-
cial, prone to sudden outbursts, or refuse to shake his hand. Some
demonstrated anxiety by incessantly twitching throughout the exam.
Many times, McMath said, patients would try to flatter him at the
expense of their regular therapist—a common maneuver in mental health settings known as 'splitting.' Veterans would share stories
about wartime experiences that they insisted they had never told
anyone—despite sounding like "over-rehearsed narratives" featuring
"details that would only have been known to historians," McMath
said. Finally, they would ask at the end of the interview, "Well, Doc,
will I ever get better?"

Another C&P examiner, working at the Hudson Valley VA hospital in New York, learned to observe a veteran's behavior in the lobby
as part of the evaluation. He said, "I've had patients who say, 'Look,
I can't lift my arm above 90 degrees horizontal.' And when they're in
the exam room with me, that's all they can do." But later, as soon as
the appointment was over, they suddenly appear fine. "When I see
them in the lobby, walking in and out between patients, I see the
high five—'Hey Leroy! How you doing?'—slap! And I'm thinking to
myself, here's a guy with shoulder problems, clearly there's a disconnect between what he's telling me is wrong and what's really wrong."

With mental health disorders, signs of feigning were often more
subtle. "Frequently, guys would come to their appointments and
they'd look sad, or down, moving and talking slowly," Frueh said.
"Then we'd see them walking out of the hospital, standing out in
front with some of their friends, laughing, having fun, having a good
time. Nothing wrong with that except it was completely inconsistent
with the way they represented themselves when we were evaluating
them." People's moods can change, of course, and a fit of unease in

118

the morning may have passed by the afternoon. But with many of Frueh's patients, "it wouldn't be hours later, it would be fifteen minutes later," he said. "And in session they would be telling us things like, 'No, we never have fun. We never smile.'"

Patients might also spin grand tales around a single kernel of truth. During his medical exam, Gulf War veteran Felton Gray told his VA psychologist in Portland, Oregon, that he had put "hundreds of Iraqi soldiers in bags." On one mission to clear an enemy trench, he said that his best friend took a bullet in the face, and that he was spattered with "blood and chunks of head." His psychologist wrote in her evaluation: "This man has suffered severe enough traumas to qualify for a diagnosis of post-traumatic stress disorder and in fact has serious symptoms." Gray was granted 100 percent disability compensation.

A subsequent investigation by the Associated Press found that Gray's best friend, Ronald Rowe, did indeed have an M-16 fire close to his face, but the incident had occurred during a training exercise in a mock-up of an Iraqi entrenchment. Rowe left with only a scratch on his face that required no medical attention. And far from being best friends, Rowe said he barely knew Gray.[22]

People like Gray populate the VA, though it is impossible to know exactly how many. Hundreds of thousands file through the halls of the administration's 170 medical centers each year, where proud vets seeking honest care to meet genuine needs are lumped in with opportunists.[23] Those with honest intentions spend long hours in waiting areas, while inside evaluation rooms for treatment and C&P appointments, "there's a great many veterans pretending to have a fictitious condition," said McMath, "and a great many doctors pretending to treat it."

At a certain point, Frueh realized his own role in the production. Working at the VA, he said, "you're part of this Kabuki theater." His disillusionment grew and his goodwill for those in uniform, accumulated over a lifetime, began to deplete. To his horror, he noticed a common wariness creeping into the other clinicians. "All of my colleagues had a very cynical attitude about the patients," he said. "They viewed them as being there primarily for the disability benefits. It wasn't a warm, fuzzy, caring environment." What developed was a vicious cycle: dishonest vets, grabbing at compensation, stiffed their medical providers, who over time hardened against their patients, some of whom truly depended on the VA for care.

The conundrum consumed Frueh. He had confidence in his judgment, but what was he supposed to do? As his frustrations grew with the VA's inner workings, he began to rely more on his other posting—his professorship at the Medical University of South Carolina. With his clinical training and foothold in the academic world, he saw an opportunity in the methodical nature of research and the irrefutable assurances of data. Only after the difficult truth of the veterans disability system got out could people like him finally begin working to solve it. He was still young; even if it took the rest of his career, he was determined to get it right. The problem had to be exposed. If the public only knew, Frueh was convinced, surely they would not stand for it.

CHAPTER 8
BURKETT SYNDROME

JUG BURKETT was sitting in the Philadelphia airport, waiting for his flight home. It was May 1969. A few months earlier he had turned twenty-five in Vietnam, too focused on the work at hand to allow his mind to drift to his return date.[1] Now he was back on American soil, his first twenty-four hours as a new civilian.

He thumbed through his exit packet. A letter signed by General Creighton Abrams read, "A grateful nation thanks you for your service." Burkett put it away. Even before coming back, he had gleaned that may not be true. Still, he wasn't prepared for the resentment that awaited him. At the airport diner, a waitress repeatedly snubbed him as if he didn't exist. Finally, another server took his order. "Don't mind her," the second waitress said. "She's got this antiwar thing. She won't serve anybody in uniform." On the plane, a man sitting near Burkett learned that he had just returned from Vietnam and began hurling shots across the aisle. "Oh, a big war hero?" the man said loudly. "Hey, folks, we've been sitting here on the runway waiting for a big goddamn hero." He ran his mouth for the entire hour-long flight.[2]

The animosity didn't seem to end. After getting accepted to business school at the University of Tennessee, Burkett encountered teachers and classmates who made no secret of their opposition to the war, or their distaste, by proxy, of its participants. One professor outright banned any discussion of Vietnam or America's military in his class. When discussing management principles, the other students were encouraged to use case studies and lessons from their

121

previous jobs, yet despite having commanded over fifty troops, two gun-Jeeps, three separate machine gun crews, and a variety of service personnel in different roles, all of Burkett's work experience was off limits because the professor wanted nothing to do with it.[3] After graduation, he had just as much trouble looking for jobs. In one interview, the executive of an Atlanta bank ripped up his resume. "I'm not hiring any Vietnam vets," the manager said. "I'm going to get a cup of coffee, and I don't want you here when I get back."[4]

Burkett gritted his teeth through all of it. His father had been a Canadian citizen who joined the US Air Force under a special program during World War II, eventually becoming a naturalized citizen and reaching the rank of full colonel. Burkett and his siblings grew up on military bases all over the country, from Arkansas, Alabama, and Louisiana to California, and their family life revolved around the rituals of the military: flag raisings and lowerings, unit parades, the playing of "Retreat" every evening bringing the whole base to attention. Whatever they were doing, people stopped to salute the flag or put their hands over their hearts. That sense of respect and duty left a deep impression on Burkett, and the veteran pilots he encountered through his father became his heroes. And so when the war in Vietnam began heating up in 1965, he found he was secretly thrilled. "For the professional warriors of my father's generation, World War II had been the highlight of their lives," he said. "If the American military was involved in a war, I wanted to know what it was like." In the summer of 1966, a few weeks after graduating college, he joined the US Army.

But at the induction center in Little Rock, Arkansas, the doctor conducting his physical identified a heart murmur. Burkett was sent to a cardiologist for further testing. He waited nervously as the specialist squinted at the results of his electrocardiogram. Finally, the doctor asked, "Do you want to go in or don't you?"

"Excuse me?"

The doctor repeated himself. "Do you want to go in or not?"

Confusion quickly gave way to realization. Without explicitly saying it, the doctor was indicating that the heart murmur was not serious but could provide a sufficient reason to keep Burkett out of the military. "Oh, no, I *do* want to go," he hastily replied, and the doctor passed him through.[5]

His orders for Vietnam came in April 1968. At Bien Hoa, an air base near Saigon, Burkett received his assignment to be the 199th Light Infantry's material readiness expediter, making it his job to procure whatever the officers needed—through whatever means necessary. The position kept him out of bush patrols and direct combat for most of his tour, but there were a few scares with enemy fire and shelling. Jolted awake one night by mortars raining down on camp, he grabbed his clothes and dashed for his unit's assembly point in his boxer shorts. The meeting point had been set to the top of a steep hill, where a carpenter had recently started building a set of wooden steps. But Burkett did not know this. In the same instant that a brilliant flare lit up the night sky, he tripped over the planks and, with his whole platoon watching, crashed down the hill, badly tearing his knee. The medic who was later cleaning the gash told him, "Looks like you can get a Purple Heart for this one, sir."

It sounded like a joke, but the medic wasn't kidding. Burkett had technically suffered a 'wound under fire.' Stories of Purple Hearts awarded for trivial wounds were commonplace. Everyone in camp knew about one soldier who had been watching an open-air movie in Saigon when a Viet Cong grenade exploded on a street nearby. The soldier jumped in fright, cut his finger on the seat, and secured a medal. Burkett flashed to the future and saw himself telling his grandchildren what his "wounded in action" story truly amounted to—tumbling down a rocky hill in his underpants. He made up his mind. No Purple Heart for him.[6]

At business school, the other veterans Burkett met were typically three or four years older than the regular graduate students. "We didn't party. We buckled down to business," he said. After graduation, he found work as a stockbroker for a securities firm in Dallas, and his career in finance took off.[7]

Burkett was not an anomaly. A nationwide survey released in 1985 found that nearly 30 percent of Vietnam vets had some form of college education, compared to 24 percent of the overall population, an edge that contributed to higher employment levels. Three quarters of Vietnam vets reported annual household incomes exceeding $20,000—roughly $49,000 today—while more than half earned over thirty thousand a year.[8] Furthermore, 78 percent were homeowners, a higher rate than among civilians, and eight of every ten veterans were married, the majority bearing children. "Ten years after the fall of Saigon and after the trauma of returning home, most Vietnam veterans have successfully entered the mainstream of American life," the survey reported.[9]

Within a few years, Burkett was promoted to junior partner. When an old friend called in 1986, inviting him to help raise funds for a Vietnam veterans memorial in Texas, Burkett agreed to help. As soon as he began making calls, however, he ran into a brick wall.

"Why the hell are you involved in something like that?" a long-time client asked.

"What do you mean?" Burkett said.

"Why would you be involved with people like Vietnam veterans?"

"Well, I'm a Vietnam veteran."

"You're kidding me." The other man was stunned.

Another client responded in similar fashion. "Hell, I've dealt with you for years, and I never figured you were a Vietnam veteran."

At almost every office he visited, Burkett faced assumptions and stereotypes about Vietnam veterans. At one point, he called the Department of Labor and requested a statistical analysis of the much-maligned demographic. The analysis revealed that far from being jobless drifters, Vietnam vets had a lower unemployment rate than the national average every year since 1974. Burkett also found that veterans had lower rates of divorce, suicide, alcoholism, and drug addiction.[10]

Yet the negative perceptions stuck. Despite all evidence to the contrary, the majority of Americans had bought into the image of the

Vietnam vet as a loser, bum, addict, drunk, and derelict. Again and again in his fundraising efforts, Burkett ran into the same obstinate refusal: "*No, no,* and *hell no.*" The problem was not with the facts, he realized, but with a "public relations nightmare." From World War II heroes to Vietnam War vagrants, how had the narrative surrounding veterans so dramatically flipped in little more than a generation? He was determined to find out.[11]

Part of the difference can be attributed to how the public understood the two wars. Recognizing the importance of public support, President Franklin D. Roosevelt enlisted Frank Capra, the most influential filmmaker of his era, to direct a series of films promoting America's fight against fascism.[12] Upon their return home, veterans who served during World War II were embraced by a grateful nation and celebrated for their patriotism. A drastically different reception awaited the veterans of Vietnam.

Public relations for the Vietnam War played out in the hands of news media, with a special fixation on the worst reports. In March 1968, soldiers from C Company, First Battalion from the Twenty-Third American Infantry Division, led by platoon leader William Calley, marched into My Lai, a small hamlet in Son My village, on a search-and-destroy mission. Facing down a village of unarmed civilians, Calley and his men brutally murdered hundreds of women, children, and elders, piling the bodies up in ditches and along the sides of the road.

The heinous war crime would become the conflict's defining symbol. Such atrocities, of course, hardly reflected how the vast majority of soldiers served in Vietnam. "For every Calley, there were [large numbers of] young American officers who were brave and selfless and treated their men and the enemy with respect," said David Halberstam, a Pulitzer Prize-winning journalist who covered the war. Accusing American troops of vicious bloodlust even preceded the massacre: one 1967 antiwar pamphlet depicted an armed American soldier towering over a frightened Vietnamese woman. The caption read, "At a cost of 59.9 percent of our total national budget, the US fighting man is the best equipped soldier of all time. For what? For this? To make war on women and children?" After My Lai, however, assumptions that such atrocities were the norm became widespread, and the image of the Vietnam War baby-killer took hold.

Hollywood embraced the image, disseminating the portrayal of Vietnam vets as irreparably damaged and deranged to great commercial and critical success. In the 1976 film *Taxi Driver*, Robert De Niro was nominated for his first Academy Award for playing a former Vietnam Marine turned violent Manhattan cabdriver—addicted to pills, stockpiling guns, obsessed with a teenage prostitute. He assumed the role of a Vietnam soldier again in *The Deer Hunter*, a dramatic war epic depicting veterans as hollow and repressed after service, with one of the main characters committing suicide. It went on to win five Academy Awards, including the award for Best Picture. The following year, *Apocalypse Now* plunged into theaters, eventually becoming one of the top five highest-grossing films of 1979.[13] Filled with gratuitous scenes of excess and gore, it captured the senseless brutality of war, injected with a dose of glorified American supremacy. "My film is not *about* Vietnam," said director Francis Ford Coppola. "It *is* Vietnam."

Then in 1982, the release of *First Blood* pushed the Vietnam veterans narrative to the next level. John Rambo, played by a subdued, stone-faced Sylvester Stallone, wanders through life, a drifter isolated by his wartime experiences. He becomes the target of an abusive small-town sheriff's department, triggering flashbacks of torture as a Vietnam POW, and violently fights back. *First Blood* topped the box office and Rambo came to embody the "Hero as Victim" archetype—the maligned victim of a society that created, then expelled, its heroes. Sequels heightened Rambo's isolation, as well as his physical capabilities and skills in guerrilla tactics. The veteran's maladjustment problems were no longer his own fault; they were the product of the ruthless government that sent him to war. "It was *because* he is the perfect fighting machine that the Vietnam veteran can't cope with the world, *because* he is a real man," Burkett said. Vietnam vets no longer had to distance themselves from their service: association with the war now conferred status, and the more troubled they appeared, the more ample the evidence of their heroics. In this way, Rambo became "a touchstone for pretenders, a pattern to follow consciously and unconsciously," observed Burkett.

By 1987, his Texas Vietnam Veterans Memorial fund was finally within range. At an unveiling ceremony for the monument's granite tablets, Burkett was approached by a Dallas television reporter. "Let's get some comments from Vietnam veterans," she said, and Burkett was happy to oblige. He led her to a circle of Dallas businessmen dressed in suits and ties, prominent men in the community who "looked more like a gathering of business colleagues than men who had fought in the rice paddies and red clay hills of Vietnam twenty years earlier." These men had come home and "got on with the business of living," said Burkett. "The war had only been one episode in their productive lives."

But the reporter and her cameraman weren't interested in them. Instead, she pointed toward another group: "No, I mean *those* veterans."

Invited or not, the kind of veterans she was referring to made an inevitable appearance at every function relating to the Vietnam War. They wore camouflage fatigues, battered jungle boots, and an assortment of medals and patches on their disheveled military garb. They were frequently the loudest people in the room, and the most forthcoming in sharing gruesome battlefield tales or their nightmares of the war since. They were "irresistible magnets for reporters and photographers looking for a little gritty realism to add to their stories," Burkett found, and he was growing increasingly fed up with them.[14]

A few months later, another "deranged veteran" story grabbed the headlines. A Dallas police officer in a busy downtown intersection had gotten into a scuffle with a mentally ill man on the street. Somehow the man had grabbed the officer's gun and shot him in the face. When two nearby off-duty policemen heard the gunshot, they hurried to the scene and shot the man dead. The *Dallas Times Herald* identified the suspect as Vietnam veteran Carl Dudley Williams, and in an editorial a few days later, the paper's columnist, Dick Hitt, interviewed a man who attended Williams' funeral. "I'm thirty-eight and he was four years younger, but he used to be one of my heroes," the man said.

"Hell of a thing," Hitt responded. "Do you think Vietnam did that to him?"

Burkett had instant misgivings about the story, and this time decided to pursue them. He contacted a friend at the National Archives, where he knew that many basic components of a veteran's military records were available to the public. Burkett filed a request for Williams' records through the federal Freedom of Information Act. He soon learned the truth: Williams had joined the Navy on August 30, 1974—almost a year and a half after combat troops had withdrawn from Vietnam. Williams, in fact, had never set foot in Vietnam, and was released from the military five months after he entered, due to mental health problems. But when Burkett wrote to the *Times Herald* pointing out the errors, the newspaper refused to correct the story. The publisher sent back a defensive letter: "We have editorialized, we have reported, and we have done some sensitive pieces about the special problems that many veterans faced and continue to face years later."

The sensationalized headlines were a setback for Burkett's fundraising efforts; potential donors, seeing their worst suspicions confirmed in the news, were quick to clam up. "Every time we took a step forward, a story appeared in the newspaper sending us three steps back," he said.[15] Still, by the fall of 1989, construction on the monument was nearing completion, and at the memorial's official dedication on Veterans Day, Burkett gave his prepared remarks in front of thousands in attendance. "Each one of these 3,427 young men was an American doing his duty," he reflected. "Remember them, ladies and gentlemen, remember them all."

Seated next to him on the dais were President George H.W. Bush and his wife. CNN broadcast the dedication live. Following the speeches, a recital of "Taps" wafted through the air and a stream of military jets and helicopters soared overhead, rumbling and swooping against a clear blue sky. It was a beautiful ceremony. As cameras flashed, the President and First Lady shook Burkett's hand. Yet the feeling of accomplishment he had anticipated never arrived. "A true memorial is what we feel in our hearts," he thought. "And America in her heart still did not believe those who fell in Vietnam were worthy."

That evening, he tuned in to watch coverage of the event. He and the other organizers had arranged a security fence to keep the slovenly "'Nam vets" crowd in the periphery, yet all three local news stations had sought them out anyway. In one of their segments, a reporter interviewed Joe, a scraggly Vietnam vet wearing a boonie hat busy with unit patches. "This is long overdue," Joe said. "I've had posttraumatic stress for seven years and nobody gave a damn."

Something inside Burkett began to boil. Despite the best intentions of everyone involved with the memorial, their efforts had once again been drowned out by the dominant narrative victimizing veterans. He saw that the pervasive misrepresentation had created a self-feeding cycle; as he recounted in his 1998 book, *Stolen Valor*, such veterans "had learned how to be vets from the media, then in turn reinforced the image. A giant circle, with no beginning and no ending." Where did these offenders keep coming from? And what drove them to present themselves this way? Watching them dominate coverage of the state's hard-earned monument, deepening false stereotypes of Vietnam veterans to the wider public, Burkett suppressed the urge to scream.[16]

WHAT BURKETT had not yet considered was that successfully presenting the image of a tormented and down-and-out Vietnam veteran could pay off on a scale similar to winning a major damage settlement in a lawsuit. Doctors for centuries have identified the link between incident-borne sickness and various forms of compensation. The nineteenth-century French pathologist Jean-Martin

Charcot dismissed many such cases as instances of "hysteria and neurasthenia." Robert Foster Kennedy, a revered Irish-born neurologist, was no less skeptical, writing in 1946: "Compensation neurosis is a state of mind, born out of fear, kept alive by avarice, stimulated by lawyers, and cured by a verdict." [17] When money is on the line after a potentially detrimental incident, dishonest individuals have always made themselves appear more damaged than they are to obtain larger compensation awards.

Commonly cited until the mid-twentieth century, compensation neurosis took on many names: traumatic hysteria, disproportionate disability syndrome, greenback neurosis, sometimes even "justice" or "litigation" neurosis. In the nineteenth century, the condition became almost universally associated with "railway spine," a set of physical disorders that seemed to appear in otherwise completely healthy and uninjured victims of railway accidents.[18] The diagnosis exploded in popularity as the danger of railroad collisions entered mainstream consciousness, prompting many surgeons to freshly examine the link between psychological perceptions and the physical manifestation of symptoms. The steam-powered rail engine, symbolizing the breakneck pace of the era's technological transformations, became an "agent of traumatic experience" for a society newly "threatened and vulnerable," observed the historian Ralph Harrington. "Though conceptions of 'railway spine' had begun with shaken spines," Harrington wrote, "they had ended with splintered minds."[19]

References to compensation neurosis still appear occasionally in psychology manuals, but the term has effectively faded from medical literature over the last fifty years.[20] Within the military and veterans community, among the first people to ever document feigned or exaggerated medical symptoms was a clinical psychologist named Loren Pankratz.

Fresh out of graduate school, with long hair framing his youthful face, Pankratz began working at the Portland, Oregon, VA Medical Center in 1969. Young veterans like Burkett were coming home from Vietnam, many of them just starting to dribble into the VA system. Generational differences leapt to the surface, often creating an antagonistic relationship between the edgy, skeptical patients and their older, more conservative doctors. The sentiment was codified by a popular adage, widely embraced by the younger vets: "Don't trust anybody over thirty."

Pankratz was one of the few VA doctors whom patients opened up to. Negative stereotypes of the returning vets were beginning to fill broadsheets and airwaves, but in talking to the young men in his office, Pankratz found that most hardly fit the media's image. "These guys were all in their twenties, and they were now trying to get integrated back into the mainstream—to get jobs, buy a pickup, get married," he said.

Some, though, seemed bent on acting out the Hollywood stereotype. When a physician colleague asked for his help examining a particularly unruly patient, Pankratz, like Burkett, took it upon himself to verify the veteran's service records. The patient had frequently burst into long tirades about being captured and tortured by the Viet Cong, describing in great detail how the enemy had jabbed him with bamboo sticks covered in feces. Yet in consulting the government's prisoner of war records, Pankratz discovered the veteran had never been held captive in Vietnam. As he dug further, he found the patient had in fact never gone to Vietnam, nor even served in the military.

Clerks at VA hospitals rarely verified a veteran's eligibility status as they should, and Pankratz soon developed a habit of checking the service records himself. "A lot of times I'm the one who finds these patients are not veterans," he said. Whenever he encountered a patient claiming something that sounded suspicious, he immediately requested to look through their "C-file"—an administrative file that includes the veteran's personal, educational, and financial information, medical treatment history, previous attempts at filing for benefits, and crucially, their DD-214, a comprehensive record of their military service. A pattern quickly emerged. "It was not unusual to discover that an individual had recently requested an increase in benefits for his service-connected disability," Pankratz said. In other words, the patient was trying to gain an increase in the monthly cash payment amount received from the VA. This one element, Pankratz found, usually held the key "piece of the assessment puzzle."

In 1978, Pankratz teamed up with a psychiatrist named John Lipkin and published a paper titled "The Transient Patient in a Psychiatric Ward: Summering in Oregon." The authors described fourteen patients who traveled to Oregon during the summer months and demanded VA care with little intention of actually getting better. One patient used his 100 percent service-connected disability compensation to pay for travel around the country, staying in fine hotels near VA facilities. As soon as he was admitted into the VA hospital, his psychotic symptoms vanished. Another man drove cross-country from Florida. A few days after he gained admittance into the hospital, Pankratz went to interview him and found he had gone on a fishing trip off the coast.

In all the patients, Pankratz found characteristics of Munchausen's Syndrome. Named after an eighteenth-century German baron who became notorious in his time for spinning wild, fictitious tales about his service in the Russian Army, the term "Munchausen Syndrome" was first used in 1951 to describe patients who similarly falsified illnesses in order to trick doctors and procure medical care. In a different paper, Pankratz had documented the misadventures of "Major Munchausen," a Korean-era veteran who impersonated a casting call of wartime roles—from prisoner of war to fighter pilot to nuclear physicist—and feigned a variety of illnesses to gain entry into one hospital after another. Convinced that the major suffered from kidney failure, surgeons at one clinic performed an emergency operation only to find his kidney had already been removed. By the time of his death in 1983, twenty-five years after his discharge from the Army, Major Munchausen had accumulated more than three hundred hospital admissions from around the country and over $7 million in treatment expenses.

Throughout the 1970s, Pankratz became aware of more and

more veterans reporting symptoms associated with PTSD. In 1983, he published, alongside Landy Sparr, a study in the *American Journal of Psychiatry* titled "Factitious Post-traumatic Stress Disorder," describing the case histories of five men at the Portland VA Medical Center, all claiming to have been traumatized by their service in Vietnam. Three of the men said they were former prisoners of war, but upon inspection of their military records, not even one of them had actually been captured. Only one of the five men had served in Vietnam, and only two had served in the military at all. Within the group, a twenty-nine-year-old man who said he sustained a serious shoulder injury as a medic in Vietnam had actually hurt his shoulder in a motor vehicle accident in Germany. One of the men who never enlisted admitted that he had heard about the VA's disability benefits from a cellmate when he was in prison for involvement in a burglary. "Simulating is easy," Pankratz and Sparr wrote in their paper. "Patients may manufacture or exaggerate symptoms and misidentify their origin [...] especially when it is known that compensation may be available to those with a positive diagnosis." It was one of the first clinical studies ever to address counterfeit PTSD.[21] Others would follow.

THE SAN ANTONIO Vietnam War Museum opened on the Fourth of July 1989, drawing visitors from all over Texas. Launched by two purported Vietnam War vets, it featured loud sixties rock 'n' roll music, artifacts confiscated from captive Viet Cong fighters, and plentiful displays of automatic weaponry and combat equipment. Gaylord Stevens, a gaunt and bearded Vietnam Navy SEAL, was the museum's director; Kenneth Bonner, a Green Beret in the US Army Special Forces, was his assistant.

To Burkett, their museum appeared more like "a cross between a surplus store and a hobby shop," feeding the public's most reductive perceptions of Vietnam vets. As he followed news about the two founders, neither of the men struck him as having the bearings of someone who had served in the elite forces. What's more, their pairing was unusual, Burkett thought, as "getting a Navy SEAL and a Green Beret together at that time was like a duck mating with a chicken."

For their fundraising, Stevens and Bonner had been recruiting volunteers to stand on street corners and solicit money from pedestrians. Dressed in ragged military garb, the volunteers were tousled and aggressive, soon prompting the city council to pass a law limiting solicitations on San Antonio's streets. Burkett decided to look into the case. He filed FOIA requests for the two founders' service records, and quickly discovered what no one else had bothered to verify. Stevens was not a Navy SEAL but a Coast Guard member with no history of combat tours. He did have a criminal history, though, laden with multiple convictions for theft and fraud. Bonner, meanwhile, had not joined the Army until 1978, three years after the Vietnam War had ended. He certainly had never been a Green Beret. To appear old enough to have served in Vietnam, he pretended to be seven years older than his real age.

Burkett found a local reporter who agreed to run the story. After it was published, the article was picked up by *The New York Times*, circulating the episode to a national audience. Something clicked. Catching the two fraudsters was a "watershed event for me," Burkett recalled. "I realized that these phonies were not just a few 'bad apples' but a national phenomenon, a weird ripple in the American psyche."[22]

Pursuing the faker phenomenon became his calling. Whenever he saw a Vietnam vet portrayed in the media as an "image maker"— someone slotted to fit the profile of a drug addict, alcoholic, homeless person, war or civil criminal, PTSD or Agent Orange victim, alarm bells rang and Burkett dashed off a request for the person's service records. As the list of frauds he exposed grew longer, so did his contacts. "I became a sort of clearinghouse with a network of sources that stretched from Alaska to Florida," he recounted. Military buffs from all over the country sent in tips and information. At one point he was filing so many FOIA requests that an official from the National Archives called him their top client.

Burkett had stepped into a sprawling network of posturing and deceit. Many of the veterans he investigated had entirely invented their military service, exaggerated the nature of their heroics, or embellished their membership in certain elite military units. The lengths that people went to in order to substantiate their fake accounts astonished him. "They bought medals at flea markets and through catalogs. They cried on camera when talking about their dead buddies, about witnessing atrocities. Some had fooled their wives, congressmen, psychiatrists, even military commanders who had also been in Vietnam," observed Burkett.[23] The further he plunged into this pool of deception, the deeper it reached. There seemed to be no bottom.

THE 1988 RELEASE of the film *Bloodsport* conferred the Hollywood treatment upon the story of Frank Dux, a former Marine lance corporal turned international martial arts master. Billed as "the true story of the ultimate champion," the film, which minted Jean-Claude Van Damme as a leading action star, dramatized Dux's path to victory at the mysterious "Kumite" tournament, an international gathering of ninja fighters held every five years. Dux's achievements at the event were legendary: he held the record for most consecutive knockouts, fastest knockout (at 3.2 seconds), fastest recorded kick of seventy-two miles per hour, and fastest recorded punch of 0.12 seconds. But his skills as a fighter and capacity for courage preceded his martial arts career.

After enlisting in the Marine Corps in 1975, an eighteen-year-old Dux was recruited into a special operations group and sent on a covert mission into Laos. The mission went awry but Dux, as one of the few surviving members, "fought his way back into Thailand" with "bayonet wounds in the stomach and shrapnel in the back." His career in the military didn't end there; he went on to receive the Navy Cross, the Silver Star, the Bronze Star Medal, the Navy and Marine Corps Medal, the Purple Heart, and even a "secret" Medal of Honor, earned on another clandestine mission. In an excerpt from a commanding officer's diary, produced by Dux to support his claims, the commander wrote: "When we almost gave up, [Dux], by himself, charged the gun. The next thing you know, [he] was behind the gun, cutting the enemy to pieces. He must have killed a hundred gooks at least. He turned defeat into victory."

This was the Frank Dux he publicly projected. And then there was the Frank Dux from his official Marine Corps record. Dux served on active duty in California for roughly four months in 1975, before getting honorably released from active duty. (He served on reserve status until 1981.) His record contained no mention of overseas service, no decorations for valor, no training credentials for any of the clandestine missions he touted. Instead, as a private in the Marine Reserves, his insistence that he was working for intelligence prodded his superiors to refer him for psychiatric evaluation. "This individual interviewed because of some bizarre type behavior which centered @ [sic] flights of ideas and exaggerations," an examiner wrote in his file, before diagnosing him with "problems in adjustment to adult life." His only notable injury was sustained not in combat, but from falling off a truck in the motor pool while on painting duty in May 1978. Doctors indicated he suffered from "possible muscle strain." After *Bloodsport* hit theaters, a skeptical *Los Angeles Times* reporter investigated the trophy Dux claimed he won from his ninja-fighting world championship and discovered that it had been made in North Hollywood. Dux was a "bright but undistinguished young man who […] recreated himself as a superhero a decade ago," the reporter said, "painstakingly authenticating his new persona with military medals, trophies, and newspaper clippings of questionable origin."[24]

On the opposite coast, other journalists were falling for the story of Joseph Yandle. A multi-tour Vietnam vet and heroin addict, Yandle was involved in a botched liquor store robbery in June 1972, where the proprietor was shot and killed. Yandle was convicted of murder and sentenced to life in prison without possibility of parole. A few years later, with backing from various Veterans Service Organizations, his wife and lawyer began campaigning for his pardon, attributing his regretful crime to the horrific experiences he endured during service. In 1993, *The Boston Globe* joined the effort, covering Yandle's attempt to win parole in a series of articles, referring to him repeatedly as a "decorated Vietnam veteran."

Yandle claimed he had enlisted in the Marine Corps as an unhappy seventeen-year-old in 1967 and was assigned to a company nicknamed "The Walking Dead" due to the short life expectancy of its members. In early 1968, his unit was moved to Hill 861, right outside the village of Khe Sanh, where he and a fellow Marine named Dusty were standing guard. Suddenly, fire broke out. The battle of Khe Sanh would be remembered as one of the most brutal periods of fighting in the entire war, a relentless enemy siege that lasted for seventy-seven days. Amid the chaos, a blast ripped off Dusty's face. Then, as Yandle was dragging him to safety, another mortar round broke them apart. The failure to save his friend still haunted him. "I've struggled with the idea of being a coward, even though I understand there was nothing I could do," he later said.

Yandle was knocked to the ground by shrapnel and almost buried under the sea of dead and dying Marines around him. After surviving the battle, he volunteered for a second tour in Vietnam. His feats earned him two Purple Hearts and a Bronze Star Medal, but he ultimately succumbed to heroin as a way to escape the trauma. "I was scared to death," Yandle told *Boston Globe* columnist Mike Barnicle in 1994. "I still get shaky today just thinking about it." In December, Barnicle published an impassioned endorsement of Yandle's attempt to earn Christmas commutation. It was titled, "A Time to do The Right Thing."

In May 1995, Massachusetts Governor William Weld submitted to public pressure and recommended Yandle's release from prison, recognizing combat-induced PTSD as a main factor behind his crimes. "While the crime can never be excused, Joseph Yandle went to serve his country in Vietnam," an aide told the *Boston Globe*. "He returned a scarred man."

Yandle was released that fall.

But there was one hitch: he had never served in Vietnam. None of the writers and reporters who covered the story ever checked his claims of combat. Burkett did.

Yandle's military record showed he had not gone overseas until September 1968—six months *after* the battle of Khe Sanh had ended. Assigned to the Ninth Marine Amphibious Brigade as a supply administration clerk, his unit had deployed not to Vietnam but Okinawa, where he eventually worked his way up to administrative manager. Contributing to the war effort by performing paperwork duty over 1,500 miles from the fighting, Yandle had served overseas for one year before returning to Kansas City, Missouri.[25]

The same lack of basic due diligence plagued even big documentary productions. In 1988, CBS aired its highly anticipated program "The Wall Within," a searing look at the young Americans who were "haunted by their deeds" in Vietnam. In the feature's opening minutes, Dan Rather introduced viewers to Steve, a middle-aged man with a thick mustache and hidden troubles. "I think I was one of the highest trained, underpaid, eighteen-cent-an-hour assassins ever put together by a team of people who knew exactly what they were looking for, and who [was] used to the maximum and then dumped back on society to take care of," Steve said. The hour-long television special, fourteen months in the making, was hailed as the "rebirth of the TV documentary." One critic called it an "extraordinarily powerful" story of Vietnam vets, who "wrestle with demons they cannot drive out."

Rather and his producers, Paul and Holly Fine, profiled six "outcasts, broken spirits" from Washington State, all of whom had allegedly served in grueling Vietnam combat operations. Steve revealed on camera that, as a Navy SEAL, he had been ordered to massacre Vietnamese civilians, then litter their bodies with communist literature to pin the war crimes on the enemy. When he returned, he quickly fell under the grasp of PTSD, once almost strangling his own mother after mistaking her for a Viet Cong combatant. Narrating the program, Rather's voice sounded grave and urgent.

"Steve knew he was sick. He knew combat had made him different. He asked for help. That's unusual. Many vets don't. They hold back until they explode."

All six veterans in the program described with anguished faces the flashbacks, nightmares, abusive tendencies, and addictions they suffered since coming back from war. "These are American sons and daughters who went into a green jungle hell and came out with nightmares that won't go away," Rather told the *Chicago Tribune*. "I won't kid anyone. This is not happy-time viewing. This is real. But if you want to know how it was and how it is, watch this program."

The most horrific story belonged to Terry Bradley, a visibly disoriented former "fighting sergeant." Bradley described one mission in which he skinned alive as many as fifty Vietnamese men, women, and children, before heaping their mutilated corpses into a large pile. "Could you do this for one hour of your life? You stack up every way a body could be mangled—an arm, a tit, an eyeball, a soldier that, turned over, don't have no face, guts, maggots, because they have been there more than a day, whatever, and the stink and the smell and stuff like this. Imagine us over there for a year and doing it intensely," he told the stunned newsman.

"You've got to be angry about it," Rather said.

"I'm suicidal about it," Bradley replied.

The segments infuriated Burkett and spurred him into action. "How had they chosen the veterans?" he wanted to ask. More importantly, he wondered, "Were their stories true?"

Most of the six men had gone to VA facilities in or around Tacoma and Spokane. Burkett pulled out a road atlas and drew circles around the two points, then began calling every county courthouse and motor-vehicle office in the area, asking for public records on the six names listed in the CBS transcript. He learned that Terry Bradley had been assigned to be an ammunition handler in the Twenty-Fifth Infantry Division, but nothing in his records indicated performing the level of atrocities he claimed to have committed during his tour. In fact, in Bradley's three and a half years of service, he had spent three hundred days either AWOL or in the stockade. After the CBS documentary aired, a columnist for Spokane's *Spokesman-Review* interviewed Bradley and discovered the veteran had suffered severe emotional problems long before he ever joined the military. Both of Bradley's parents had been heavy drinkers, the columnist found, and he had dropped out from school in his freshman year to join the Army and flee a broken home life. After he returned from tour, doctors had diagnosed him with paranoid schizophrenia, but he refused to take his medication.

The claims made by Steve, the Navy SEAL, were initially hard to corroborate because CBS withheld his last name. However, a local newspaper published another interview with him a few days after the program aired, disclosing that his last name was Barbe and he lived in Jefferson County. Burkett picked up the trail, contacting the county courthouse and locating a divorce record, which provided the full name and address of Barbe's ex-wife. Burkett then found her number listed in the phonebook. When he called, she explained that Steve had changed his last name to Barbe—his mother's maiden name—after leaving the military, and that his birth name was Steve Southards. A FOIA request for Southards' military records revealed that he had not served in Vietnam as a SEAL, but as an "internal communications repairman," who spent most of his tour on a rear base far from the fighting. And rather than the elite exercises that would have drilled into the "eighteen-cent-an-hour assassin" he claimed to be, the only specialized training Southards ever received was from a "motion picture operation course (16mm)" held at Subic Bay in the Philippines. His record also showed that after transferring to the Philippines, Southards had spent several months in his ship's military prison for multiple AWOL violations.[26] Though uncovering these realities required an extra layer of fact-checking and diligence, all of the information could have been found in the veterans' service records, available to anyone in the public through a FOIA request. Yet in every veteran's sensational story, broadcast to millions in "The Wall Within," Burkett unearthed fabrications and exaggerations that undermined their accounts.

What made it worse was that these skewed, and ultimately inaccurate, portrayals did not simply represent a bungled yet sincere effort to uncover the truth; they were the whole premise from the beginning. The program's producers had initially decided on the idea of shooting a story for CBS about "trip-wire" vets— a term for antisocial Vietnam veterans living in remote areas borrowed from the wires used to trigger booby traps. Their initial plan had been to call veterans' therapists across Washington State, hoping to find access to disorderly vets camped out in the wilderness. When this tactic failed, the producers contacted regional veterans centers, where counselors put out a call that CBS journalists wanted to interview veterans suffering from PTSD. Dozens of vets answered the call, even as locals bristled at the crew's tactics. "I got the distinct feeling that CBS had a story they had decided on before they left New York," said Sarah Pilley, who managed a local restaurant where the CBS team frequently dined. "They came out here and filled the bill for what they wanted by talking to those people who would fit in best with their script." The producers had initially asked to talk with Pilley's husband, a retired Marine lieutenant colonel from Vietnam, but they lost interest after learning he had transitioned into a stable, successful career after service. Out of the eighty-seven Vietnam veterans the crew interviewed, CBS ultimately chose the "four or five saddest cases to put on film," said Mrs. Pilley. "The factual part of it didn't seem to matter as long as they captured the high drama and emotion that these few individuals offered."[27]

Ever since Burkett embarked on his crusade to expose phony vets, he had always made sure to contact the media's producers, correcting their inaccuracies and offering them a copy of their subject's military record—or proof that it didn't exist. Whether the journalists worked for the local press or the most wide-reaching national outlets, rarely did they ever corroborate a veteran's account with the official service records. Many didn't even know the records were available to begin with. While the journalistic profession espoused the rhetoric of integrity and truth-telling, Burkett had too many times bumped into a more cynical reality presiding over how things really worked: the truth was secondary to the story. Even after presenting many reporters with the facts, he recounted, "few wanted to acknowledge that they had been fooled."

IN THE NORTHWEST CORNER of the National Mall in Washington, D.C, two reflective black-granite walls ascend from the ground, creating a quiet, protected space to consider some of America's most precious displays of service and sacrifice.[28] Dedicated in 1982, the Memorial Wall—one partition pointing east at the Washington Monument, the other west toward the Lincoln Memorial—features the engraved names of the 58,272 soldiers who died serving in Vietnam, presenting an open, chronological record of the war's irreversible toll. Over the years, the Wall has become a site for tributes and reflection, a place where former comrades, grieving family members, and an indebted public find occasion to honor the fallen.

Yet not everyone arrives with honorable intentions. Almost as soon as it opened, the memorial became the grounds for a thriving commercial market, as merchandise stands and vendor booths sprang up hawking posters, books, T-shirts, baseball caps, bandanas, bracelets, dog tags, coins, clocks, decanters, small blocks of black granite engraved with whatever name the customer cared to ask for. Often, the products amplified existing stereotypes of the war's veterans, exploiting the monument's symbolism for commercial gain. Bumper stickers were placed on display next to mock unit patches and replica medals; printed across one set of glass containers was the message: "A POW never has a good day."[29] One group called "Freedom Birds" sold T-shirts with the image of the Three Soldiers statue for $8 each, though none of the proceeds made it to the Vietnam Veterans Memorial Foundation, the organization they claimed association with. "These guys came to D.C., used the copyright and sold sixty thousand [shirts], and we never got one red penny," said the foundation's president, Jan Scruggs. The naked opportunism disturbed Burkett, who equated the flock of quick-buck vendors to "money-changers in the temple."[30]

Worse, among the opportunists lurked the inevitable imposters, and as always, that was where most of the attention went. A striking photograph featured in the 1993 *Life* book, "The Wall: A Day at the Vietnam Veterans Memorial," showed a weeping man in jungle fatigues, overwhelmed with emotion during a group-therapy trip to the memorial. Pinned onto his outfit was a bouquet of medals and decorations: the Silver Star, the Soldier's Medal, master jump wings, an Air Assault badge, plus an assortment of further distinctions from the Army, Navy *and* Marines. "A clear phony," Burkett immediately saw, in this case without even needing to check the man's records. On the imposter's attire was displayed a "V," granted for valor in combat, worn on a Meritorious Service Medal, a decoration awarded only for non-combat service.[31]

On Memorial Day, 1996, *The Dallas Morning News* splashed across its front page a prominent color photograph of Roni DeJoseph, a long-haired man in a boonie hat and military jacket, his face pressed against the reflective black surface of a Memorial Wall replica. DeJoseph's eyes were closed, his mouth twisted in anguish, cheeks wet with tears. Supplied by the Associated Press, the image was printed in newspapers across the country with the caption, "Marine veteran who fought in Vietnam, pays honor to a friend." But an astute reader soon pointed out the many inconsistencies in the photograph: DeJoseph's camouflage jacket was issued for the first time in 1983, eight years after the Vietnam War had ended; the full-color Third Marine Division patch on his shoulder had been discontinued since 1947; and the shoulder patch was contradicted by a pin on the man's hat belonging to the First Reconnaissance Battalion, which was part of the First Marine Division, not the Third. A search through the records confirmed it: DeJoseph had never served in the Marine Corps, nor any other military branch. The Memorial Wall had been used to stage another manipulative performance.[32]

It wasn't until several years after the Wall opened that Burkett finally paid a visit himself. He had felt no "burning desire" to see it, but on a trip to D.C., finding himself only blocks from the National Mall, he decided he would go, if for no other reason than to placate his sense of duty. He recognized its significance in honoring the Vietnam generation, but he rued its unintended capacity to typecast and perpetuate the broken veteran narrative. The memorial attracted as many as five million visitors a year[33], and on the spring day that Burkett arrived, a thin crowd was moving slowly through the concourse under a bright blue sky. Burkett took note of the people around him. A young girl, supported by a man in uniform, held up a piece of paper to an engraved name and rubbed a pencil across its surface. In front of another black panel, an elderly woman knelt in grief; not far from her, an older man stood with hunched shoulders, sobbing quietly to himself. Burkett fidgeted in place. The whole scene felt wrong, he thought; their reactions missed the mark. The grave silence was observed out of respect yet it produced the opposite result, reducing the names on the wall to little more than the war's unlucky victims. Once again, he felt an urge rising.

"Victims!? These men and women weren't victims. They were the best and brightest of my generation. They were warriors, patriots. Some of them were heroes!" he wanted to shout.

He wanted to seize his fellow Americans by the shoulders and shake them until they saw what he saw.

"You see that name right there? That's Bobby Stryker. When his Army unit was ambushed, he threw himself on a mine just as it detonated, saving six of his wounded friends.

"And this one? This is Jimmy Cruse, a corpsman who ran under enemy fire to give aid to two wounded Marines.

"Here! Tiago Reis. He died while repeatedly dragging his wounded buddies to safety.

"Victims? Heroes, ladies and gentlemen, heroes! These men wouldn't want our pity. They would want our respect."

But he reigned in the impulse, and the moment passed. Burkett silently considered the sad reality of a world "in which sometimes black is white, falsehood is truth, and cowardice is courage." The true heroes passed on in anonymity, whether in life or death, while "thousands of liars and phonies, celebrated in the media, have stolen [their] valor to claim as their own."[34] He followed the crowd a little while longer, drifting along with their ritual procession. Then he made for the exit and walked away.

IN 1998, after investigating thousands of cases, Burkett published his military tome, *Stolen Valor: How the Vietnam Generation Was Robbed of Its Heroes and Its History*, with the journalist Glenna Whitley. It was part memoir, part social criticism, and an extensive, dramatic registry of the veteran "phonies" he had uncovered in the decade since he began. But when he tried making contacts in the publishing world, the response he received was overwhelmingly negative. Publishers rushed to judgment: "Why in the world would we publish a book called *Stolen Valor*?"[35]

Burkett reflected on the irony of the situation. For the past several years, he realized his mission had been to recast the image of Vietnam veterans in the popular culture, to sand down its excesses for a more accurate portrait. Back in the civilian world, veterans were more than just former soldiers. Burkett believed this to his core, not just as a matter of self-definition but as a statement of truth, evidenced by the facts. After the war, "I assumed my other identities," he wrote, "[college] graduate, golfer, stockbroker, husband, father." It was the same course, with all its joys and trials, embarked on by countless others who had served.[36] Yet so many others, both real veterans and imposters, had chosen instead to embrace a caricature, slipping into the disputed role of victim. Burkett had stumbled into his second calling to right this wrong. Though he had prided himself on carving out his new identities after service, this adopted enterprise, in the end, pulled him right back into the heart of American veterans life.

He tried hard to understand what drove the imposters, even as he knew their reasons could not redeem them. "Why the deceivers lie probably emerges from deep feelings of inadequacy, the need to be seen as a man's man, bigger than life," he said. "For some, belonging to a group defined as 'warriors' is irresistible."[37] *Fake Warriors*, another book on the subject published by the attorneys Henry and Erika Holzer in 2002, detailed the various legal mechanisms through which veteran pretenders could be identified and punished, and expanded on the motivations behind their behavior.

People concoct false stories to fuel ambition, relieve loneliness, achieve fame, embellish otherwise undistinguished personal backgrounds, defuse envy of others, benefit from prominent associations—reasons that were endlessly "varied and encompass a wide range of human psychology," the Holzers wrote.[38] They cited Charles Ford, a notable academic and expert in the psychology of lying. Imposters exhibit a much more "pathological and pervasive form" of deceit than everyday liars, explained Ford, often "in an attempt to achieve a sense of identity and confidence."[39] The more people believe such deceptions, the more the culprit is able to cohere his identity. In this way, the Holzers concluded, "the imposter attempts to fool himself that his life is not a lie."[40]

Burkett came to realize that nearly all the schemes he uncovered were driven by the promise, in some form, of secondary gains. For disability fakers, this was often the availability of financial rewards, yet he understood that the gain could also take other forms, feeding a veteran's desire for recognition, acceptance, and stature.[41] More than the demons which enabled these misdeeds, however, Burkett was occupied by how the actions reverberated through society. In one of the first cases he had ever investigated, he met Timothy Honsinger, a former Army private first class who had lost an arm in combat, then fully rehabilitated and worked for years as a radio dispatcher, then police lieutenant. "Honsinger, a genuine hero, had not boasted or sought acclaim," Burkett noted. Yet in perpetrating their scams, "pretenders had stolen something Honsinger and others had earned with their courage, pain, and tenacity, devaluing what real men of valor had done for their country."[42] One day, while contemplating the repercussions of this injustice, the phrase "stolen valor" popped into Burkett's head. He knew immediately it would be the title for his book, a project he had already been considering for some time.

Due to the reluctance he encountered with traditional publishers, Burkett self-financed the book's first print run in 1998. Its reception quickly proved his detractors short-sighted. The book established his legend. In its aftermath, Burkett has received praise, awards, and more invitations than he could manage to lecture at government agencies, think tanks, and universities around the country. Magazine profiles toasted him as a "one-man truth squad" and a "self-appointed watchdog for the reputation of Vietnam vets."[43] In 2002, he met with George W. Bush and personally delivered to the president a signed copy of his book. The following year, he received the US Army's highest award for civilians. At the ceremony, he was honored for "almost single-handedly set[ting] the record straight on Vietnam veterans."

But an even more significant boon came in December 2006, when President Bush signed into law the Stolen Valor Act, making it a federal misdemeanor for anyone to falsely represent any US military decorations or medals, and expanding the domain of fraud to include attempts of purchase, sale, shipment, production, or exchange of military distinctions.[44] The following year, a US Attorney from Washington State launched Operation Stolen Valor, a year-long effort by the Justice Department to investigate and prosecute fake veterans.[45] Burkett estimates that in over three-plus decades of pursuing the truth behind veteran claims, he has looked into approximately three thousand cases, of which "roughly 2,500 were bogus in one fashion or another."[46]

These days, he still receives calls to purchase his book—stray requests that come in every few weeks from schools, community groups, and veteran centers. He is quick to point out that the fraud's ubiquity has not waned. "There are millions of Americans doing this after every war. It's happened through history," he said.[47] Still, he allows himself to take some credit for advancing a more truthful depiction of veterans, and for launching the term *stolen valor* into the public's consciousness. In his head, sometimes, he calls the regrettable phenomenon by another name, a nod to its first crusader. He refers to it as Burkett Syndrome.

CHAPTER 9
PAID TRAUMA

CHRIS FRUEH continued to see patients at the VA during the day, but carved out time whenever he could to consider the bigger picture. He discovered a large body of pre-existing research documenting the prevalence of veterans malingering—an observation first mentioned in the appendix of the original *Diagnostic and Statistical Manual of Mental Disorders (DSM)*, the standard reference for many mental health facilities, including the VA, then expanded upon since the release of the *DSM*'s third edition in 1980.[1]

The Uniform Code of Military Justice defined malingering as the crime of feigning personal incapacity in order to shirk duty or service.[2] Incidents of malingering within active-duty populations were relatively rare, Frueh learned; unit cohesion and the active social expectations borne by soldiers create strong impediments to committing the offense.

The psychological literature, however, recognized a broader spectrum of motivations, regarding the condition as any "purposeful production" of false or exaggerated medical complaints with the goal of receiving a reward.[3] The behavior varies in purpose and intensity: pure malingering occurs when an individual completely fabricates a non-existing disorder, while partial malingering, the more common occurrence, describes a patient who exhibits genuine symptoms but consciously exaggerates them.[4] Stated plainly, malingering is the act of faking illness, injury, or impairment to get something in return.

Experts have long warned against the warping effects of financial gain in assessing psychiatric disorders. In the *Clinical Assessment of Malingering and Deception*, the foremost text on the subject, the implication is spelled out clearly: "Malingering should be considered in all referrals seeking compensation." The connection has grown clearer over time. In the ten years after the *DSM*'s third edition began to feature PTSD, personal injury lawsuits in federal court increased by more than 50 percent. Worker's compensation claims for mental stress-related disorders rose to become the fastest growing type of claim, while insurance costs for mental stress disorders soon overtook the costs of physical injury claims.[5] In the 1990s, a consensus of top mental health specialists advised that patients seeking money in the form of disability benefits should be excluded from clinical trials for PTSD, noting that pursuing compensation may affect results.[6] In a survey of clinicians, probable malingering was reported in nearly a third of all disability cases.[7]

One reason for this prevalence is that psychological symptoms are easy to fake and nearly impossible to verify. PTSD diagnoses are based almost entirely on what patients tell their doctors, and patients can easily look up the diagnostic criteria in print and online.[8] Researchers have also noted the "leading nature" of many PTSD symptom evaluations. In one study, 94 percent of participants with little prior knowledge of PTSD fulfilled the condition's diagnostic criteria simply by "symptom guessing."[9] As Graham, the former Marine in Jacksonville put it: "It's stuff that can't be disproved by a doctor. If you say you have bad thoughts, nobody can disprove that."

Suspicious cases may also be the product of outside help. "Evaluators should be aware that disreputable attorneys may coach their clients about psychological symptoms," warned the *Clinical Assessment of Malingering and Deception*.[10] In a study of 158 car crash victims, researchers found that the single biggest predictor of who later received a PTSD diagnosis was whether the individual had been in contact with a lawyer.[11]

When it came to malingering among veterans, Frueh was astonished by the breadth of evidence collected by previous doctors and scholars. He discovered Dr. Loren Pankratz's landmark 1983 paper, detailing the gaudy fabrications manufactured by members of the Vietnam generation. Another doctor, he found, had recorded similar observations in 1944, identifying notable jumps in "the simulation of psychosis" during wartime.

Frueh soon began adding to the literature himself, researching and publishing his own articles on the detection of malingering among veterans. Many studies in the field utilized psychometric testing, a broad category of assessment tools that applied scientific methodologies to gauge a subject's mental or behavioral fitness.[12] Among the most rigorous and widely used psychometric exams is the Minnesota Multiphasic Personality Inventory, or MMPI, which measures complaints related to a variety of conditions, including depression, paranoia, and schizophrenia. Whereas many psychological evaluations elicit responses that can easily be manipulated to achieve a particular diagnosis, the MMPI presents subjects with hundreds of true/false questions to statements like, "My friends think I'm talkative," or "I read the editorial page every day"—statements with no clear association to known disorders.

Crucially, the MMPI also features four types of validity scales, designed to root out people intentionally over-reporting certain symptoms, as an eager job applicant might be tempted to do, or under-reporting particular capabilities, as in the case of veterans who wish to appear more handicapped than they really are.[13] In one 1985 study, researchers conducted MMPI evaluations of fifteen Vietnam vets with genuine symptoms of PTSD, then compared them to the results of two groups trained to fake PTSD—one, a batch of fifteen well-adjusted Vietnam vets, and the other fifteen mental health professionals. The MMPI successfully determined the true profiles for over 90 percent of the subjects.[14]

In 1999, Frueh and psychologist Paul Gold released the results from a study that analyzed MMPI-2 results for 119 veterans at their outpatient PTSD clinic. Using two different MMPI validity indicators, 22 percent of the participants logged scores unusual enough to be classified as "extreme exaggerators" with one validity measure, and 14 percent registered as "extreme exaggerators" on a second. The flagged exaggerators had lower rates of PTSD diagnoses than members from the non-exaggerating group, but they scored much higher on self-reported measures of various psychological symptoms. There was one other important correlation: exaggerators were much more likely to have filed claims for disability compensation.[15]

AROUND THE SAME TIME, Frueh learned a career development grant he had written was approved for funding by the National Institute of Mental Health. It offered to pay 75 percent of his salary, plus an additional $50,000 of expenses, for him to pursue his own research. After seven years at the VA as a full-time clinician, he had been looking at opportunities to branch into other related domains. "I had my eye on working with community mental health center populations, with prisoners, doing some other kinds of things," he said. With the grant, the idea came to him to compose a comprehensive review paper on malingering—the subject he had been studying for so many years. It would be his parting gift to the field, a way to consolidate all that he had learned and at the same time present a useful resource for his erstwhile colleagues. The review paper would be "my valediction to the VA and veterans work," he determined.

In 2000, he and several colleagues published "Apparent Symptom Overreporting in Combat Veterans Evaluated for PTSD," a sweeping survey of the veterans symptom-overreporting "phenomenon" spanning more than a half-century of medical literature. Compiled all in one place, the evidence was formidable. The authors of one paper, for example, had analyzed the MMPI-2 results of veterans within the VA's PTSD outpatient clinics, and from the distribution of validity scale scores, estimated the base rate of malingering at roughly 20 percent.[16]

Introducing disability benefits tipped the scales further. Frueh cited some of his own contributions to the canon, including a 1996 study in which he and colleagues divided veterans into two groups— those who were seeking disability payments and those who weren't.

The compensation-seeking vets were found to produce significantly higher pathological scores on every psychological measure—including MMPI validity scales and other measures of severity for PTSD, depression, and dissociative experiences—even though both groups exhibited the same frequency of actual PTSD diagnoses.[17] Their results suggested that veterans concerned with the monetary consequences of their diagnosis were more likely to exaggerate the symptoms they report.

Another study, published the following year, asked 165 combat veterans evaluated for PTSD to complete a variety of self-report mental health inventories. Participants seeking compensation were found to endorse dramatically higher levels of psychopathology across a range of testing than those who weren't. The compensation-seeking vets also produced sharply elevated validity readings, indicating that they were intentionally underperforming in order to appear more disabled. "The availability of VA disability compensation for combat-related PTSD impedes accurate initial assessment of veterans," the authors concluded.[18]

The research Frueh reviewed approached the subject from all different angles, employing a wide spectrum of assessment tools with various methods and controls. Yet almost all the findings converged on a single point: the results "cast serious doubt as to the response validity of a substantial percentage of this population," Frueh wrote.[19] In other words, there was a lot of faking going on.

Even in the customarily dry language of academia, these findings were a bombshell. Among the most consequential implications was how it affected the field's understanding of veterans' treatment and recovery. In the mid-nineties, a team of four researchers followed 164 combat veterans over the course of an inpatient PTSD treatment program. They examined each individual's MMPI-2 scores when they entered and exited the program, and found that veterans who were not seeking a change in disability payments progressed normally through the treatment course, showing signs of improvement so that their measurements gradually aligned more closely with those expected from the general population.[20] Compensation-seeking veterans, however, continued to report distress at abnormally high levels.[21] They weren't getting better, the researchers concluded, or else they weren't admitting that they were getting better. The finding dovetailed with what Frueh himself had learned from conducting a survey of VA mental health workers a few years earlier, just as his own education in the VA's illogical incentives was accelerating. Respondents to his survey had identified veterans' pursuit of disability compensation as "one of the most serious obstacles to successful treatment."[22]

DAVID DIETZ, a Compensation and Pension examiner from Ohio, came to view the issue as one of the central contradictions in his profession. He had joined the VA full-time in 2012, after beginning his career in the mental health division at Walter Reed. Later at Fort Carson, he had worked with soldiers as a staff psychologist, then moved on to stints in consulting and private practice. Working with members of the military community again at the VA, his job quickly settled into a routine. "I have about sixty to seventy questions that I ask, three times a day, day in, day out," he said.

From the routine emerged certain patterns. In one recent appointment, a veteran in his twenties arrived for an evaluation to increase his benefits. Dietz saw that the patient already had a 30 percent rating for depression and anxiety. "What brings you in now?" he asked.

"Well, I'm having more problems," the young vet replied. "That's why I'm here."

"You know this isn't treatment?" Dietz said.

"Yeah, I know."

"Have you made an appointment, or tried to make an appointment for treatment?"

"No, I don't want to do that."

At first, such exchanges had baffled Dietz. "I know when something's wrong with me, and I think it's getting worse, I call the doctor," he said. "I try to go and get treatment." And yet, so many of his patients didn't think that way. "For some reason, they think money is going to solve all their problems."

Two other veterans he saw recently had come in for appointments just a few weeks apart. Both were under the age of thirty, and both had appeared singularly concerned with attaining 100 percent disability. Dietz saw from their records that neither had fought in direct combat, but served in support roles with limited, if any, exposure to fighting. The worst part was that neither of them had shown any interest in improving their conditions. Such an attitude was common among the vets Dietz assessed in his disability evaluations. "In my experience, half the people that apply aren't interested in getting treatment," he said. "They have no desire to participate in treatment, no desire to get better. They come in and they want an increase in their benefits."

Military doctors and therapists working with active-duty military members describe a similar dynamic, like running into the same brick wall from the other side. "As a physical therapist, it makes our job difficult," said Scott Carow, who at the time oversaw the physical therapy and rehab services at Fort Bliss in Texas. A 1997 graduate of West Point, Carow earned a PhD from the Army-Baylor University physical therapy program, and then a second doctorate in Sports Medicine-Physical Therapy. Even with the two advanced degrees, however, he was unprepared for some of the distortions within the field. "This might be a failing of physical therapy education in general, but you go through school assuming that your patients are going to be compliant, and that they're going to be willing participants who want to get better," he said. "Then you get out to the clinic and realize that that's not always the case. Patients have other interests and other goals that may not have anything to do with getting better." Within the structure of the veteran's disability system, he found, a patient's goals are often pitted against one another.

Carow continued, "They know that if they get better, they will either have to go to work or potentially decrease their disability ratings. A question I hear frequently is, 'I don't know if I should get surgery because it might decrease my disability rating.'" For him, such tradeoffs should be a no-brainer. He told his patients, "Well, it may or may not decrease your disability rating, but your shoulder will work again." And yet, "that doesn't seem to be the motivation in a lot of people that we talk to."

One day he encountered a senior non-commissioned officer claiming back aches, debilitating shoulder pain, and various other physical ailments. She shared that she was retiring from the military and was checking off the requirements to get medically evaluated and processed out. "She said that if she did not receive at least 90 percent disability, she would march on Washington—that's what she told us," Carow recalled. He was incredulous. "If her stated goal is to get at least a 90 percent disability rating, then she's really not likely to be motivated to work hard and make her back or knees feel better." Two weeks later, the NCO returned for a routine follow-up appointment. Carow recalled, "She sat down in the chair and lifted her arms overhead. She's doing the raise-the-roof thing, and literally singing, 'I got 100 percent!'"

In Carow's mind, it was the perfect expression of the system's contradictions: a supposedly handicapped patient, celebrating her 100 percent impairment with a triumphant dance that her diagnosis technically ruled her incapable of. "That's been the most egregious case I've seen lately, but she's not an extreme outlier," he said. A flawed process inevitably produces faulty outcomes.

The problems escalate in the field of mental health, where diagnoses are murkier and the path to recovery more unpredictable. In a 2005 sample of 92 veterans with PTSD, the VA's Office of the Inspector General found a drop in mental health visits in nearly half of the patients after their disability ratings had been raised to 100 percent. The average decline in visits was 82 percent; some veterans stopped showing up to their appointments altogether. The report concluded: "The compensation program has a built-in disincentive to get well."[23]

The disincentives also prevent many recovery programs from achieving their intended results. Phillip Brown, the Warrior Transition Battalion commander, once had the idea to implement an adaptive reconditioning course with promising alternative treatments to assist hurting soldiers. He had watched new placements arrive at the battalion saddled by physical limitations diagnosed by well-meaning doctors, and the course was designed to work around that. "You can't do push-ups, you can't do sit-ups, you can't run, whatever it is—we take that, and we say okay. But you can do swimming. Or you can do archery. You can do yoga," Brown said. Adaptive reconditioning offered soldiers a customized program to promote healing through activity, and to get them moving again after injury.

But the program's leaders soon confronted a lack of interest. One officer recounted a soldier telling him in confidence, "I'd love to go swimming, but the truth is, I'm waiting on this [evaluation] that's going to determine my ratings. Maybe after all that stuff is done, maybe then I'll start doing adaptive [sports]." Brown found his efforts to emphasize the long-term merits of rehabilitation floundering next to the monetary appeal of disability benefits. "It's a constant struggle to get people to participate," he said. "Folks don't want to get better while they're here. Their fear is that if they improve, it will affect their ratings. So they don't do it."

Recovering from any illness or injury is an arduous journey. Success requires a combination of factors, not least a relentless desire to improve that must come from within. Yet when service members and veterans face uncertainties in determining their well-beings and futures, the easier decision can also seem like the rational one: pursue a VA disability rating—the higher the better.

Carow, the Fort Bliss physical therapist, wracked his brain over how to reorient soldiers toward prioritizing future health over possible compensation, but the solutions evaded him. "The incentives are all there to maximize [the soldiers'] disability," he said.

"Part of the problem is it's hard to appeal to anything other than, I think, their pride. You can appeal to their pride and their decency and their self-respect, and say, 'Is this *really* who you want to be? Are you the kind of guy that wants to sit on the couch and earn a government paycheck? Or do you want to go out and provide for your family and have dignity and pride?' But in terms of reasoning—the reasoning is on the side of maximizing disability, unfortunately."

Carow came to see it as the structural flaw at the center of the veterans disability system, an underlying mechanism calibrated to produce the exact wrong results. "We've incentivized the wrong things. The incentive toward illness and injury outweighs the incentive toward good health. Patients are not motivated to get better," he said. "The disability system runs counter to good patient care."

The reality of these contradictions wore Dietz down. When he first started conducting C&P exams for disability claims, he tried to edge his patients toward more productive treatments. "Part of the psychologist in me would be saying, 'Hey, nothing's permanent. With help, you can get better. Your goals should not be focused on these benefits your whole life, your goal is to get *away* from them." Over time, however, he found he was no match for the VA's siren song of "big monetary benefits. "Among doctors tasked with evaluating patients with compensation claims, frustration and burnout are common.[24] "The professional in me struggles," said Dietz. "My level of empathy has gone down. Part of that is eroding in me." He sighed. "I try to encourage people but it just doesn't... It is what it is."

These days, he said, "I see myself more and more as just an information gatherer. I get the information and I let the VBA decide what they're going to do with it." A veteran himself who served in the late-nineties, Dietz has stopped wearing his Army sweaters. At the local high school football games, when the announcer asks for current and former service members to stand, he prefers to remain sitting. "I don't like to advertise it. I don't talk about it anymore," he said. Three times a day, day in, day out, the procession of benefits-seeking patients he encounters has poisoned his understanding of what it means to be a veteran and neutered his sense of purpose in the medical profession. "I'm a psychologist. I'm supposed to be helping people," he said. Yet at the VA, "I don't feel like I do anything worthwhile. My cynicism over the last few years has increased greatly."

AT FORT BLISS, Scott Carow preached judiciousness with the rehabilitation center's limited resources. "We have a finite amount of personnel and time available to us," he told their doctoral interns. "There are a number of people who actually do want to get better, and we want to have clinic availability for them."

Ironically, it was the least affected who frequently requested the most appointments—distant disciples of Major Munchausen, demanding ever more MRIs and testing for their back, their neck, their knees, their shoulders, their everything. "These kinds of people will clog up the system," Carow said. "People who actually have injuries wind up having to come in three, four, five weeks [later], or come in at the middle of the night, because we're performing needless imaging on people that don't even want to get better in the first place."

The most upsetting cases, even in a physical therapy environment, involved PTSD claimants. "I encounter so many patients that come in with PTSD diagnoses that I think are total crap," Carow said. In one case, a guy he had served with came back from deployment and immediately made it known he suffered from crippling PTSD. "He was a cook who didn't leave the FOB once for an entire year," according to Carow. Such bad actors did more than occupy the clinic slots meant for others coping with true trauma; Carow was convinced their misdeeds reverberated into the wider world. "Guys like that cheapen the PTSD diagnosis for people who actually have it," he said. "I don't doubt that PTSD is a very real thing, but it is being abused badly."

Psychiatry manuals warn clinicians to be on the lookout for signs of malingering, involving guilty parties who "emphasize how their problems are a direct result of alleged war experiences."[25] Jill Wilschke believes the reality can be more complicated. "I don't think [the soldiers] are being untruthful," she said. Given the individual's particular context, she suggests that such signs may be part of their natural response. A former therapist at Camp Lejeune, Wilschke worked primarily with infantry Marines who were experiencing problems after deployment. The unexpected return of their symptoms, triggered by a forthcoming examination or the judgment of some perceived authority, was an occurrence she observed commonly. "These people I had known for one or two years, who in their evaluations things are going well, when it comes time to actually write pen-to-paper what their symptoms are currently—all of a sudden they're having nightmares and seeing things, or reporting flashbacks." The abrupt regressions initially left Wilschke deflated and confused. "I was like, 'Wait, I thought things were going really well. I thought we were doing good work,'" she said.

But after forming deeper connections with some of her patients, she began to unpack what was happening. One Marine she was treating had appeared firmly set on the road to recovery. "He hadn't for months and months been talking about nightmares and sleep issues," she said. Yet as soon as he was scheduled for review by the medical board, confronted with the impending call to leave the military, he was a mess again. "Now, all of a sudden, he was saying he was having nightmares more nights than not, being vigilant, patrolling his house." Wilschke began to realize the immense pressures that vets like her patient felt squeezed by. All of a sudden, "he's now facing, 'I don't have a job, I thought this was going to be my career and now it's over'—so of course [his] anxiety is going to increase."

She continued, "In context, it makes a whole lot of sense. If somebody were to tell me next month that I don't get to be a therapist anymore, and I have to find a whole new job, and I have a child and wife—of course my anxiety's going to shoot through the roof."

For some veterans, Wilschke believed the promise of the VA's disability benefits represents a lifeline of sorts, however desperate, in a civilian world that looms unfamiliar and uninviting. "Again, I think, in context, it makes sense," she went on, "this sense of feeling betrayed that the service you have done for fifteen years wasn't going to pan out anymore." Questions arise—*Who can I turn to? What else can I offer? How will I support my family?*—translating into a panic that can cause psychological responses to swell. "That's not a direct reflection of combat exposure. I think it more speaks to this idea of, all of a sudden, I have no plan, I have no future forward. So what am I going to do?" For these veterans, benefits projected stability—*this is the path, this is how I make it happen*—even though it was a path that eroded their capacity to advance on their own.

Other experts contend that to a well-trained doctor, the contrast between malingerers and the truly needy can be glaring. According to psychiatrist PJ Resnick's *Clinical Assessment of Malingering and Deception*, "Veterans with genuine PTSD are [...] generally hesitant to blame their problems directly on their combat experience and often seek help as a result of the insistence of family members."[26] In many instances, the veterans who are most qualified to receive care, or most deserving of compensation, aren't the ones who seek money from the VA. Mark Worthen, a long-time C&P examiner, observed the paradox often at the VA. "The guys that really got badly injured are the ones that need the benefits," he said. "But the VA doesn't see the veterans who say to themselves, "Yeah, it was tough, but I'm dealing with it.'"

When Worthen did meet such patients, their stories often reflected an independent, even defiant, outlook. "They're really pushed and urged by their wife, or their buddy, [until] they finally give in and say, 'Okay, I'll file a claim.' When they come to see us, they say, 'Look, I don't really have this PTSD thing. I told my wife I'd do it. Here's what happened. Here's what I'm experiencing now,'" Worthen said. Veterans in this category intentionally minimize the effects of their combat experience, and the stressors that their evaluations turn up. "Yes, they did go through trauma, but they've coped relatively well. They may still have nightmares occasionally, or this or that symptom, but they'll tell you, 'Yeah, it sucked. It was bad, but other guys had it a lot worse, and I don't think I'm disabled.'"

Such cases inspired Worthen, exemplifying the spirit of service and reminding him of the importance of his work at the VA. But they were the exception, he said. Frequently the PTSD claims he examined were barely disguised attempts at securing monetary gains, evoking the opposite reaction.

Von King, a VA psychologist in North Dakota, began conducting C&P exams in 2010, shortly after the VA's requirements for PTSD service-connection were loosened. Many of the patients she initially evaluated were older veterans who had lived independent lives, unfamiliar with the services the VA offered. "Most of them were farmers who had no money, no access to mental health[care]. It was very rewarding for me to meet with them and give them an answer for why they had been suffering for thirty, forty years. Then also, on the side, they would get a little bit of compensation for that," she said.

These former service members were polar opposites from another class of veterans, she said, "the guys who say to me—and it's not infrequent—'I was in Afghanistan,' or 'I was in Vietnam, so the government owes me.' They look at it as an instant paycheck." The paychecks frequently appeared to amplify afflictions. A 2008 study found that veterans filing for PTSD benefits recorded "small but significant increases" in their symptoms right before an upcoming disability examination. The changes correlated with the financial health of the claimants; veterans who were unemployed or had lower incomes exhibited more substantial cases of the claimed condition.[27]

In another research study, 109 veterans with PTSD claims were given two examinations—the first when they were first applying for disability benefits, and again when they went in for their evaluations. PTSD symptoms and functional impairment were found to be significantly worse for the participants right before their compensation exams, with unemployed veterans indicating far more severe declines in their condition than veterans with employment.[28]

"Those are the ones I get suspicious of," said Jay Phillippi, a C&P examiner at the VA Medical Center in Fargo, North Dakota.

In his appointments with veterans seeking disability benefits, it was usually the patients who showed great initial improvement that later displayed signs of malingering. "It's the ones that look like they're doing great. Their [meetings] with their therapists are fewer and farther between, and their clinical notes indicate that they've improved. And then they get the notification that they're up for review again. It was like they transformed overnight into a different person. They go to the emergency room a week before they come in, or they have a breakdown and now suddenly their symptoms have [returned]. They end up in the inpatient unit or they're suicidal. All these things happen," Phillippi said. "Then I get suspicious."

From the veteran point of view though, the VA has spelled out the consequences and rewards in a perverse Catch-22.

Be well and get nothing. Be impaired and get paid.

CHAPTER 10
MAGIC 8-BALL

IN THE POPULAR IMAGINATION, America's disabled veterans are casualties of the worst aspects of war. The myth is that they have all become disabled through combat and that their disabilities include amputations, spinal and head injuries, blindness, burns, and crippling psychological traumas.

In reality, the vast majority of disabilities processed by the VA are conditions commonly encountered in normal life and have nothing to do with combat. They result predominantly from aging, genetic, and lifestyle factors. While the *total* number of combat-wounded soldiers from Iraq and Afghanistan remains steady at about 55,000 through nearly twenty years of war, this group is dwarfed by the 300,000 veterans—and rising—who become new compensation payment recipients in the VA disability system *each year.*[1]

In his two decades since leaving the Navy, Alex Montelongo has been a frontline witness to the VA's burgeoning multitude of dependents and the rapid inflation in their claimed disabilities. As a medical examiner trained to assess these conditions, he knows that the vets themselves can play a central role in manufacturing the infirmities. "It's like candy in a jar, man. We're having people with no proper documentation, just claiming stuff out of a hat," he said.

Montelongo began working at the El Paso, Texas VA medical center in 2013, hired as a physician assistant in the VA's special exams unit, a department under Integrated Disability Evaluation System (IDES). His job was to evaluate the disabling conditions claimed by soldiers processing through med boards. "Initially I thought, 'This is great, I can help some veterans get their funding from the system,'" he said. As with many in the VA's rank and file, however, he quickly ran up against the confounding logic driving how many claims are initiated. "It didn't take me a long time to start figuring out—well, at least for most people that I've seen—this was more of an incentive to make money than get the disability that they actually deserve."

The way he saw things working on the ground clashed with what he had understood to be the VA's mission—to properly provide care for deserving veterans. Disappointment and regret crept into his work, a sentiment he discovered many of his colleagues shared. "After they figure out what's going on, everybody gets upset as to what they're seeing. But of course, it's a job. We've got to do it," he said. Recently, Montelongo assessed a sergeant first class who claimed over sixty disabling conditions, "of which maybe five were legitimate." He bristled at what he considered a waste of four days, but other cases stretched the limits even further. "We get [claimed conditions in] the sixties, the seventies, the eighties. We have people with up to a hundred and some conditions."

James Morales[2], a physician assistant at Fort Bliss, refers to them as "frequent flyers"—the significant percentage of service members he treats who clearly have ulterior motives. "The majority of patients I see don't have a true mechanism of injury," Morales said. "No catastrophic falls, no deployment injuries. They're just here and they start developing, you name it—knee pain, back pain, shoulder pain—whatever it may be."

In the civilian world, insurance policies approve rehabilitating patients for a select number of physical therapy sessions and require the doctor's permission before covering additional appointments. Within the military, however, "there's no insurance factor where [service members] have a cap on how many visits they can get from physical therapy," Morales said. What results is a pattern of over-treatment. "These guys are just being seen over and over. Not only are they getting paid to get sick, they're getting out of work to go to medical appointments for months and months and months. Who wouldn't love to get paid to go to physical therapy, get paid to go work out, get paid to be away from work?" He believes that over a third of his patients are responding to the draw of such secondary gains.

In the years since Frueh published his review paper in 2000, new research has shed greater light on patient malingering and symptom validity. One analysis found that from 1985 to 2015, the number of articles published on the subject in two leading neuropsychology journals blossomed from under 10 percent to one quarter.[3] With respect to the veterans population, a 2008 study led by Thomas Freeman from the Central Arkansas Veterans Healthcare System was the first to examine symptom validity utilizing multiple differ-ent best-practice instruments—including the MMPI-2, the wide-ly-used Clinician Administered PTSD Scale (CAPS), a consistent and reliable self-report questionnaire called the Structured Inventory of Malingered Symptomatology (SIMS), and, most notably, the Structured Interview of Reported Symptoms (SIRS). Among the most comprehensive evaluation tools available at the time, SIRS fea-tured eight scales specifically designed to differentiate between gen-uine and malingered pathologies. The study focused on a sample of seventy-four veterans, mostly from the Vietnam War, who had been previously diagnosed with chronic PTSD. Among them, thirty-nine subjects scored results that met "categorical SIRS criteria for clear symptom exaggeration." As Freeman wrote, "Over half our veteran subjects demonstrated clear and significant symptom exaggeration."[4]

Another prominent study addressed the "signature wound" of the current era. Traumatic brain injury—defined as "an alteration in brain function caused by an external force"—has become syn-onymous with the conflicts in Iraq and Afghanistan, where new modes of fighting have exposed combat soldiers to enemy IEDs, mortars, and rocket-propelled grenades. From being a little-known affliction when the wars began, incidents of TBI have skyrocketed. In 2017, nearly 120,000 veterans received service-connected dis-ability for TBI, compared to under a thousand receiving treatment for its symptoms a decade earlier.[5] Given the condition's explosive growth, a recent paper in the *Applied Neuropsychology* journal sought to uncover the extent of exaggerated TBI claims. Two highly accurate performance validity measures, the Test of Memory Malingering and the Medical Symptom Validity Test, were selected to evaluate seventy-four veterans who had completed C&P exams for TBI. The results were conclusive: 52 percent of the participants failed at least one performance validity test, while 33 percent failed both. In other words, at least one third to one half of the sample was found to be malingering TBI-related cognitive deficits.[6]

This kind of behavior was not unique to veterans. Various studies over the years have examined disability claimants in all contexts—accident victims coached by profit-hungry attorneys, criminal offenders wishing to avoid prosecution, disgruntled employees pursuing workers' compensation—reporting malingering base rates between 7.5 and 33 percent.[7] A 2009 study published in the *Psychological Injury and Law* journal asked sixty-one adult patients who claimed PTSD in independent medical examinations to sit for three symptom validity tests. Seventy percent of the patients produced scores suggesting they were over-reporting cognitive deficiencies on at least one of the tests, a quarter of them in all three.[8]

One review paper crunched the findings from eighteen different studies, covering 2,353 subjects of closed-head trauma, and found "more abnormality and disability in patients with financial incentives, despite less severe injuries."[9] The desire to obtain greater payments led all types of people to magnify and manufacture their impairments. The title of the review was: "Money Matters."

THE GAP BETWEEN Montelongo's perception of service and what he witnessed among the younger cohort of veterans, in particular, seemed to crystallize with every patient. One claimant had come in complaining of negligent providers, and yet after a quick review of his records, Montelongo saw "the guy was in sick call like every other day, if not every week for the whole time." The brazen entitlement infuriated him. "How do you have time to get injured when 90 percent of your time is spent going to sick call? I'm like, 'Guy, you didn't have time to get out there and get hurt.'"

If the Vietnam generation came back victimized and beleaguered by the national media and popular opinion, then veterans as a block have since rebounded in reception and stature. A new attitude has metastasized and within the VA, staffers and medical professionals like Montelongo—some former military members themselves—have been the first to observe a younger generation of vets who push the pursuit of VA spoils to new extremes.

"Let me tell you something. As a veteran, I don't feel anybody owes me anything, and I shouldn't be catered to," Montelongo said. "I volunteered for service because I wanted to serve. I didn't expect anybody to think more or less of me for that." Signing his enlistment papers at eighteen, he had understood the nature of his commitment, accepted the risks of getting deployed, getting hurt, even getting killed. "But people here—most of the veterans I've seen—these people go into the military wanting to get something back from it that they don't deserve." As a veteran, Montelongo felt the integrity of his own service was sullied by others who treated the passage as a cash cow. As a taxpayer and citizen, he felt swindled, "because my taxes are paying these people's income that are not sick."

According to the 2017 study on TBI, as much as a quarter billion in nationwide disability payments are made out each year to potential malingerers.[10] Whether it was TBI or some other disability, plenty of veterans "are getting 50, 60, 70 percent for nothing," Montelongo said. "I don't like it at all."

Among older veterans, the edge of resentment is not uncommon. Graham, the former Marine sergeant major said, "I spent my life in the Marine Corps. You work hard and you play hard. I was proud. You don't go to sick bay." When he received his promotion to sergeant major, an orderly reviewed his medical records and was surprised to find how thin the file was.

Growing up in the Midwest in the 1970s, he remembered how

rare it was to see a disabled veteran plate on the road. These days, Graham sees them filling up parking lots all around town. "It's usually a Cadillac SUV, and some guy jumps out in a Gold's Gym uniform and jogs around," he winced.

Treating veterans in the El Paso area, Montelongo arrived at a similar conclusion. "Most of these guys—they don't have anything wrong with them. They're out there splurging the money that they're getting and they're having a great time." It wasn't just the veterans; Montelongo read news reports about rising fraud in Social Security and worker's compensation claims and sensed a growing entitlement among the younger generation writ large. "You're talking about a generation that's different from before. A generation that wants to be given everything, even if they don't deserve it," he said. "Most of the veterans that I've seen—they eat it up because they know that they can get away with it. Everybody just placates them."

From 1960 to 1999—a forty-year span beginning before the Vietnam War and ending after the first Gulf War—the percentage of veterans receiving disability benefits hovered around a steady 8 percent. From 2000 to 2014, the proportion more than doubled to 18 percent. Average payments more than doubled across the same period, from $6,400 in yearly awards to $13,500. Together, the twin spikes have contributed to the disability system more than quadrupling its total expenditure—from $22 billion in 2000 to $110 billion by 2020. [11] "The most recent fifteen-year period shows a fundamental change in participation in the [VA's] disability compensation program," said the Institute for Defense Analyses in a 2016 report. [12]

Younger veterans disproportionately account for this jump in participation. Iraq and Afghanistan vets from the post-9/11 era receive compensation, on average, for 7.613 service-connected disabilities, compared to between two and three disabilities for World War II and Korean War veterans, and under four for vets who served in Vietnam. [13] One review found that combat veterans and prisoners of war from World War II and the Korean War did not exhibit the same markers of symptom-malingering found in the veterans of later conflicts.[14] Morales, the military physician, described the younger cohort's pervasive attitude as: "Throw everything against the wall and see what sticks."

In recent years, the most commonly claimed VA disability has been tinnitus. Characterized by the perception of external noise that's not actually there—whether ringing, buzzing, whistling, hissing, or swooshing—the condition added 183,000 new veterans onto the VA's disability payroll in 2019. Rather than service-related stressors, VA doctors have commonly attributed the excess of diagnoses to loose standards and ease of approval. "Everybody claims it and there's no test for it," said one former C&P examiner. "It's a subjective symptom and the only distinguisher we used within the VA is, 'Is it mildly bothersome?'"

The unchecked proliferation of another commonly cited condition, sleep apnea, spurred one veteran to contact his congressman. In a 2013 letter to Jeff Miller, the chairman of the House Armed Services Committee, former naval aviator Michael Webster described observing "widespread abuse" in the VA's disability compensation system, particularly in the exploitation of sleep apnea.[15] Webster, a practicing family law attorney from Florida, wrote, "Virtually every single case I have handled involving military members during the past three years has had the military retiree receiving a VA 'disability' based upon sleep apnea."

First recognized as a service-connected disability in 1996, sleep apnea is a disorder characterized by irregular breathing during rest. Patients who receive even a mild diagnosis are recommended the use of a CPAP machine, designed to assist with their airflow, which automatically approves them for a 50 percent disability rating according to the VA's rating schedule. Nine hundred and eighty-three veterans were granted service-connected disability for sleep apnea in 2001, the first year of the War on Terror. By 2019, 1.3 million veterans had a sleep apnea diagnosis. The VA's internal watchdog found that roughly a fifth of them used a device meant to help manage the condition less than half the time.[16] From a rarely considered diagnosis a generation ago, hundreds of thousands of veterans today are compensated for the affliction, qualifying them for at least $855 in monthly disability benefits, even though with a CPAP machine they are able to sleep and function on a daily basis without impairment.[17]

The trend is a disservice to veterans with "real disabilities," said Webster, whose father had lost his arm to a gun mount explosion as a twenty-one-year-old Marine. Despite the significant handicap, Webster recalls that his father remained active in raising the family and fixing up the house, so much so that after he passed, the family even carved his signature catchphrase onto his tombstone, the letters HHT—"Here, hold this." The idea of his father, an amputee capable of anything, beside a younger veteran "debilitated" by sleep apnea, made Webster furious. "By God, if somebody is disabled, compensate them," he said. "But this is a sham and it rankles me to the core."

Every day in his corner of Texas, Montelongo says he reviews claims that he considers to be sham. Often the claimants have been coached, including during the pre-separation TAP briefings, where soon-to-be veterans are told to "list everything" on their VA forms. Montelongo estimates that the average veteran he sees applies for between twenty and twenty-five conditions. "They list everything. A fallen toenail, they'll list. It's amazing what these people will do," he said. No one pays any mind to the moral questions around claiming "disability" for conditions only obliquely caused or worsened by military service. Two decades after leaving the military, he feels like he is living in a new era with its own caricature of the disabled veteran. At the VA, he encounters a long line of them, exploiting their positions for gain without scruples.

THE EXISTING SYSTEM of veterans' disability originated over a century ago to distribute benefits among veterans of the First World War. Since then, the system has multiplied in complexity, spreading into new areas of coverage and adopting layers of procedural bureaucracy—even as it has withstood major reforms to match a fundamentally transformed society.

Designed in 1917, the aim of the original benefits system was simple: to compensate returning soldiers for loss of income, arising from wounds sustained in service. Rating decisions at the time were made by temporary panels of local adjudicators, with the expectation that they would disband after all the claims had been processed.

Compared to standards today, medical practice in the early twentieth century was rudimentary at best. Hospitals were rare and specialists virtually nonexistent; most doctors worked as general practitioners and saw their patients during house calls.[18] Meanwhile, medical education was inconsistent and often insufficient. It wouldn't be until after the Great Depression that a science-based model would become the basis for all medical schools. Diagnostic testing, already limited in what it could uncover, was rarely used; to arrive at their rating decisions, benefits adjudicators exclusively considered symptoms that had manifested during or immediately after the claimant's service. The veteran's condition at the time of evaluation was frequently the main factor in determining their rating.[19]

The world today looks vastly different. In "A Benefits System for the Information Age," James Ridgway, a law professor at George Washington University, breaks down the VA's stalled evolution amidst a century of medical and societal progress that has "completely changed our understandings of disease, injury, and medical causation." Conditions once attributed to personal deficiencies, bad luck, or even superstition, are now understood to be the expression of countless factors—genetics, diet, environment, lifestyle, and more. Doctors no longer sling a bag of instruments from home to home but work in massive hospital facilities replete with state-of-the-art technologies and devices designed for even the most specialized functions. Diagnostic criteria have become more accurate, medical records more reliable, treatments more effective. The continual progress of modern medicine has expanded recovery far beyond what was once thought possible. Healthcare today accounts for roughly a fifth of the national GDP.[20]

In this new era, the boundaries of disability are not fixed. With advances in technology and societal accommodations, the range of what is possible is continually expanding. In light of the changing landscape, two major models have developed for understanding disability, ultimately presenting two radically different paths for a veteran.[21]

The "medical model" posits that impairment or diagnosis equates to disability. In this philosophy, the amputee is immutably disabled by virtue of his amputation, whether or not a prosthetic device can replace or even enhance his function; a cancer patient is disabled, even if his cancer is in remission; someone who is shortsighted is disabled by vision impairment, even with corrective lenses. This model does have some utility. For instance, the Americans with Disabilities Act of 1990 was eventually enhanced by the 2008 ADA Restoration Act, which protected people against discrimination based on disabilities that were controlled by medication or devices (eyeglasses, prosthetics, etc.)

But where the medical model fails—and fails badly—is in allocating benefits, the function of the VA disability compensation system. Virtually anything that can go wrong with the human body gets categorized as a disability: instead of recognizing the age-related degeneration of the knees and back as a normal part of the human condition, for instance, such conditions are interpreted as disabilities—in fact, they are two of the most commonly claimed disabilities in the VA. Under this medical model, the purpose of the disability system is reduced to providing benefits, rather than facilitating a return to functionality.

A more adaptive approach to disability is the broader "social model," which assumes that a physical ailment is only one component of determining whether a person is truly "disabled." In addition to the physical diagnosis, the social model also considers environmental and personal factors. A wheelchair user, for example, will be much more limited in an environment where his movement is constrained by obstacles—curbs, stairs, etc.—than in an environment where he can get around using elevators and ramps. This model also considers personal factors, which often have profound effects on an individual's experience of their disability. Many families find that they can achieve a "new normal" after one of their members becomes disabled. Yet, not all do. Similarly, there are individuals who are able to display great resiliency in the face of daunting challenges. Others crumble. The social model acknowledges these differences.

From its inception, the VA's statutory requirement has been to compensate for disabilities based on "average loss of earnings"—a measure of disability principally understood by its effect on income. In 1917, as the VA's disability benefits were first being disbursed, farming and industry were the pillars of the American economy. A person's livelihood often depended on his capacity for manual labor; physical injuries could consign a returning soldier to a life of impoverishment.

In the twenty-first century, information and service-driven sectors power the economy, and the traditional relationship between military-borne injuries and post-military earning potential has been upended. A combat amputee may have no trouble operating a computer; wounds and strains can have little effect on a veteran's ability to manage a team. As a whole, the country has moved beyond the medical model of disability and gravitated toward the social model. The passage of the Americans with Disabilities Act in 1990 eliminated many physical barriers to wheelchair mobility and mandated reasonable accommodation of disabilities in the workplace. Expanding public awareness has changed attitudes, while medical, prosthetic, and drug advancements have cracked open new possibilities. These days, amputees race down ski slopes; children with disabilities keep up in mainstream classrooms; adults with disabilities flourish in many kinds of jobs. Serious conditions by themselves no longer equate to permanent disablement and resignation. Far more people with disabilities today—even serious ones—are able to hold meaningful, sustainable work.

The VA has categorically failed to adapt to these positive developments. As a *National Review* article articulated, "The VA's disability system remains fixed in amber, organized around an outmoded model that equates physical impairment with inability to work."[22] Indeed, despite dramatic improvements in medicine, a mature economy, and deep shifts in the average American way of life, a veteran's disability rating remains fixed to an antiquated loss-of-income table from a bygone era. The VA's compensatory scheme continues to ignore the unique life conditions of real veterans—personal qualities, family support, educational potential—factors that are far more relevant and impactful to the degree in which an injury results in true disablement.

Yet what has evolved within the VA system is the rationale for determining a disability's "service connection." When a condition is rated as "service-connected," it becomes part of the calculation for a veteran's monthly disability payments, which can often last for life. Even as the VA mistakenly equates impairment to disability, the list of conditions covered by the scope of service-connection has broadened beyond what the program's founders could have imagined at its inception. According to the VA, disability compensation is intended for "an injury or illness that was incurred or aggravated during active military service." But an injury incurred *during* service is not the same as one *caused by* military service.

Under the current system, benefits flow from a bureaucratic abstraction—a fundamentally flawed black-and-white diagnosis—rather than what that diagnosis actually means in the real world. Are Paralympic athletes sprinting on the track or competing in the pool disabled? What about wounded veterans working profitably in Wall Street banks? In his essay, Ridgway continues this line of inquiry: "Is a veteran whose disease is fully controlled by medication or other treatment disabled? Is an amputee entitled to no compensation if a prosthetic is available that is as good as (or better) than the lost appendage?"

The VA as it exists today is ill-equipped to address these questions. Disabled veterans move through a remade and dynamic world, but, as Ridgway writes, "the system has yet to embrace a coherent new vision of what is to be compensated."[23]

THE RESULT IS a chaotic institution, capable of confounding and even bizarre outcomes. VA diagnostic code 7823 rates vitiligo, a condition that causes the skin to lose its natural color (most commonly associated with Michael Jackson), at 10 percent service-connection for "exposed areas affected," despite the American Academy of Dermatology recognizing the condition has no known cause.[24] Code 7617 grants a woman undergoing a complete hysterectomy— the removal of the uterus and both ovaries, either as a required or elective surgery—with a 50 percent disability rating. A hysterectomy is surely a serious operation, bearing potentially lifelong consequences, but the need to have one is unlikely to be generated by a soldier's military service. Even in cases where a direct service-connected link exists, it is difficult to imagine how the surgery justifies a veteran's "loss of earnings." The same puzzlement can be found in the VA's disability awards for the loss of half or more of a man's penis, an injury which certainly affects his self-image and capacity for intimacy but only in rare circumstances might correlate with his earning potential.[25]

Such perplexity is caused in part by the interaction between a piece of legislation and its implementing regulations. The VA's authorizing legislation, Title 38 of the US Code, relies strictly upon loss of average earning capacity, with no consideration of payments for detriments to quality of life. Nevertheless, the rule-making procedure that executes the VA's legislation, which assigns disability codes and their corresponding compensation levels, does account for such concerns—including, for example, the effects wrought by losing sexual organs—by enshrining them in the order of compensable disabilities, even as they bear no connection with a person's ability to perform income-generating work.

Another factor complicating the mix is the natural human tendency to deflect blame rather than accept responsibility. This habit of "misattribution" is particularly common in disabilities that may be related to lifestyle choices or genetics rather than military service. For instance, while it is perhaps possible for soldiers to develop sleep apnea from the rigors of barracks life, obstructive sleep apnea, the most pervasive form of the condition, is related primarily to excess weight, large neck circumference, being male, and natural aging.[26] According to the American Academy of Sleep Medicine, sleep apnea is a growing problem among all Americans, affecting roughly a quarter of the population between thirty and seventy years of age, and rising in tandem with obesity rates.[27] Yet veterans who are all too willing to blame their military service have pushed the disability into becoming one of the fastest growing conditions granted compensation benefits by the VA. When this is combined with the fact that a CPAP machine makes individuals with sleep apnea able to function normally, the outcome is even more baffling.

Similarly, mental health conditions are common in society, where one in six Americans have been found to take antidepressants.[28] These conditions can be caused or worsened by trauma, but may also be caused or worsened by genetics and lifestyle choices. When interviewed, the wife of one veteran was quick to attribute her husband's crippling PTSD to his combat trauma, despite acknowledging many other contributing factors: "Most likely he was already predisposed because his dad was a schizophrenic. After he got back from combat, he did drugs, he snorted meth, which damaged his brain. Everything together, it just snapped something."

Unfortunately, such cases are common, with veterans frequently attributing their physical and mental health conditions to military service instead of more likely causes like genetics, lifestyle, or just the normal ravages of time. In addition to disability compensation, creating such a causal link allows the veteran to escape responsibility for their manifesting health issues; in fact, they may even be honored for having them. Beyond the significant financial incentives, an alluring social cachet exists in the presentation of a "wounded warrior."

As a group, disabled veterans may appear beyond criticism and reproach, but its messy reality becomes visible on the ground, eliciting a different conclusion from those who see it. Phillip Brown, the former Warrior Transition Battalion commander, recalled one service member who was approved for service-connected disability after a boating accident—a non-duty incident that occurred while the claimant was on leave. In another case, a soldier suffered a traumatic brain injury from jumping out of a moving vehicle—while high on cocaine. Despite not being in the line of duty, and the obvious lapse in discipline, the soldier was able to medically retire and receive compensation for the incident. "I'd say I struggled with that one the most," Brown said.

What alarmed him equally, from a different angle, was learning about doctors who use a catch-all "conversion disorder." He first heard about the disorder when a young officer told doctors he had occasional problems walking and talking. "The medical professionals couldn't quite determine what's going on," Brown said. "There's a physical problem, but biologically there's nothing wrong. Other times, when you could tell he was focused, he was phenomenal. So they just gave him a blanket diagnosis called conversion disorder." Soon the officer was granted 100 percent disability by both the Army and the VA.

In many cases involving mental health disorders, Brown questions the frequency of sympathetic diagnoses pegged to military service when family history and previous traumas may be just as much at fault. "Once folks spend that first twenty-four hours in the Army, the Army's philosophy is that you're in the Army, we'll take care of you," he said. "In some ways, that's really encouraging, but I think there probably should be a little bit of common sense." Brown went on, "I have folks in the unit that are very young—first-term officers and soldiers—who have some serious mental health issues. They haven't been in long enough, or deployed at all, for the Army to have caused those conditions. And yet, from a medical standpoint, they'll say, 'That's alright, we'll still compensate you for the rest of your life.' To put something like paranoid schizophrenia on a twenty-two-year-old person, first time in the military, literally hasn't really even been in a unit—we'll pay them for the rest of their life for that."

Von King, the VA C&P examiner from North Dakota, noticed

that even her patients who appeared to be exaggerating their afflictions for benefits were usually less on guard when she asked about their personal backgrounds. The number of veterans bringing up past traumas surprised her. "They don't stop to think how their past might affect how they may or may not be traumatized," she said. "'Dad beat me,' or 'Mom kept me in the closet'—believe me, I get a lot, a lot, a lot of those people. It's obvious that kind of vulnerability can set somebody up for mental health issues later."

Applying the appropriate linkage between mental health and military service is not a problem unique to the United States. Ian Palmer, a former senior psychiatrist for the British military, said, "Within society there seems to be an almost reflex desire to link health problems in veterans with their military service. Just because someone has served, it does not mean that their mental health problem is related to their service." Yet in order to justify its assessments, the VA can flout basic common sense. For example, one thirty-two-year-old man received 100 percent service-connection for bipolar disorder after serving just six months in the Army. His mental condition had been disclosed to the recruiter at the time of his induction, and yet during his medical evaluation for benefits, his claims examiner concluded, "As likely as not, the veteran's pre-existing bipolar was exacerbated because of the structure and high expectations of military service."

When a service-connected disability is determined to have caused or aggravated other health issues, the VA will also rate the secondary conditions for service-connection, opening the opportunity to claim benefits for ailments arising long after an individual's military service has ended. While the rule rightly qualifies many veterans for greater support, it also compounds the potential for abuse. An active veteran's "medical consulting" company described a hypothetical case on its website: As a twenty-six-year-old service member, "Joe Veteran" injured his right knee jumping out of airplanes in the military. He received a 20 percent disability rating from the VA and began to collect $3,157 in benefits each year. In the ensuing decades, he stops exercising and gains weight, gets divorced and loses his family, and over time, gradually develops a litany of additional problems: low back pain, chronic pain disorder, type 2 diabetes, high blood pressure, sleep apnea, peripheral neuropathy, and kidney disease. With the right counsel, the veterans advocacy firm insisted that all of these conditions can be traced back to Joe Veteran's original knee injury. "Joe doesn't know that he's left an additional three quarters of a million dollars in tax-free VA benefits on the table," the website reveals. In fact, the company promises, "we often uncover *more value* in secondary conditions than the primary conditions."[29]

Behind these suspect practices is an archaic bureaucracy without a coherent vision. Independent reviews of VA rating decisions routinely reveal significant lapses in decision quality, while veterans with comparable circumstances frequently receive varied outcomes. The Government Accountability Office has consistently identified the VA disability program as a 'high-risk' federal program, primarily due to its outdated definitions of disability, slow claims processing, and rapid growth.[30] Yet, instead of simplifying its codes and streamlining their execution, the VA has only ever moved in the opposite direction.

A baffling system spins new protrusions after its own image, bulging into an ever-greater procedural nightmare. In the 2016 edition of the Veterans Benefits Manual, published by the National Veterans Legal Services Program, the applicable laws and guidance expanded to nearly 2,200 pages.[31] As new rules are written to administer a growing system, the number of interactions between the rules increases exponentially. An already complex process grows into a monster. As one veteran's advocate rued, the claims adjudication process is less like a straight-forward equation—"three plus two always equals five"—and more like "adding two irrational numbers, pi plus the square root of two."[32]

Untangling the mind-numbing math usually falls upon the shoulders of VA employees. For many of the VA's clinical psychologists, an online discussion forum has become a popular place to vent frustrations. Paul, a clinician from North Carolina, blasted colleagues who diagnose patients exclusively off their self-reported symptoms, ignoring the conflicting information. "If you're going to disregard test results showing exaggeration/simulation of symptoms, why even bother giving the test?" he posted.[33] On the same topic, Susan, a VA psychologist in Kentucky, admitted to having doubts in conducting some of her own evaluations. "I am not sure that my approach is the right one," she wrote, wondering if sometimes she granted disability diagnoses because of her own internal biases. "I tell myself that what I am doing is trying my best to reconcile different pieces of evidence, some of which contradict each other. But, of course, I question myself."[34]

Another C&P examiner, Ruth, wondered how to handle a case where the veteran had been diagnosed with service-connected dyslexia. How joining the military could have induced dyslexia "has me baffled," she wrote. Another psychologist picked up on the thread: "During my time in service, I saw several disorders like this which were 'discovered' once the person got through basic training. Many times the 'diagnosis' was based on self-report."[35]

With an endless list of statutes and a limitless universe of subjective interpretations, sometimes it felt like the results of an evaluation were no more accurate than if they had simply been left up to chance. Rather than aspiring to diligence, one contributor suggested a wry alternative: "I'm going to market one of those Magic 8 Balls with the plastic floaty thing inside having diagnoses from the [ratings manual]."[36]

CHAPTER 11
100 COMBAT VETS

IN WHAT FRUEH had thought would be his final months at the VA, he received a message from a young doctoral student, requesting to work at the Charleston VA for his psychology internship. The student's name was Jon Elhai. "He wanted to work with me as his mentor," Frueh said. "He showed up and had a lot of energy."

Elhai was especially curious about Frueh's main research interest: the relationship between veterans' disability compensation and malingering. He brought many fresh ideas to the inquiry, constantly brainstorming new research questions and the methods to probe them. Frueh found himself delaying his plans to leave the VA, then found himself delaying them again. "It was like in Godfather III," he said. "Just when I thought I was out, I got pulled back in."

In one of the first big studies that Frueh and Elhai collaborated on, they drew archival data for 320 male combat veterans who had received PTSD treatment from the VA between 1995 and 1999. They divided the veterans into a compensation-seeking group and a non-compensation-seeking group, then analyzed the clinical and self-report evaluations available for their subjects. The results, published in the *Psychiatric Services* journal in 2003, showed that compensation-seeking veterans recorded significantly higher pathology scores on a range of self-report assessments, including measures for depression, dissociation, and PTSD symptom severity. MMPI-2 primary validity scales were also elevated for the compensation-seeking veterans, indicating a much greater likelihood that they were over-reporting or exaggerating their symptoms. "These data suggest that current VA disability policies have problematic implications for the delivery of clinical care, evaluation of treatment outcome, and rehabilitation efforts within the VA," they concluded.[1] In short, their study reinforced previous findings on the link between money and malingering.

Around the same time, Frueh and Elhai both came across Burkett's book, *Stolen Valor*. The brazen accounts of fraud stunned them, but their shock quickly became a form of inspiration, adding fuel to their work ethic. "We should do a study on this," the two VA psychologists decided. "Let's take Burkett's methods and apply them in a systematic fashion to our patients and see what we get."

Frueh found Burkett's phone number and called the author, who by then had become a prominent name in the military research community. Burkett agreed to help, and they began to design the parameters of a new study together. They identified a VA medical center in the southeastern United States, then chose one hundred consecutive subjects registered at the hospital's combat-related PTSD outpatient clinic. The participants were all men, age eighteen and older, who had checked into the clinic as Vietnam combat veterans between November 1997 and November 1999. Of the sample, 94 percent had been diagnosed with PTSD and 62 percent reported having applied, or were intending to apply, for VA disability benefits. Frueh and his research team then submitted FOIAs for all the subjects' military service records.

Some records took as long as eight months to arrive, and in a few cases, a second FOIA request had to be filed. As soon as all the responses came in, the analysis began. "[Burkett] coached me through all of it," Frueh recalled.

What does this ribbon mean?

What do these dates signify?

What's supposed to show up here that doesn't?

Over dozens of phone calls and months of analysis, every record in the participants' personnel files was unpacked and reviewed. When the results were finally tallied, they knew they had stumbled upon something explosive.

Only 41 percent of the sample had served in Vietnam and been exposed to combat—even as the entire sample was pulled from files at the *combat-related* PTSD outpatient clinic. Another 20 percent had served in Vietnam but had no objective evidence of combat exposure in their files.Generally, their records indicated completion of combat training, or designation of a military occupational specialty, but lacked badges, medals, or any further corroboration expected of their "combat" service. 2 percent of the sample had served in the military but had no evidence of having been in Vietnam, 3 percent had records showing that they were definitely *not* in Vietnam, and 2 percent had no evidence of any military service at all.

The remaining veterans, comprising 32 percent of the sample, were by far the most curious. Though their files showed they had served in Vietnam, they had been assigned to support roles that would have normally kept them on large bases far away from combat. They were "cooks, supply clerks, truck drivers—all the people who support a large Army in a war zone," Frueh said. Base soldiers might certainly still be exposed to stressful, trauma-inducing events—the terror of mortar fire, for instance, or the grief from a friend landing on the casualty list—yet many of these subjects had given detailed theatrical accounts of enemy firefights and reconnaissance patrols, extensive combat tales that were entirely inconsistent with the duties described in their records.

Several from the group claimed to have been wounded in combat, though none had a Purple Heart from their military service. Five had told their therapists they were involved in 'classified' combat activities in Vietnam, Cambodia, or Laos, despite having no documented evidence of such activity (and even though all such classified operations have long since been declassified). Two individuals recounted periods of captivity as Vietnam prisoners of war, yet neither had any reference of this in their records nor did they appear on any accepted registries of repatriated POWs. Most perplexing of all, the vets who had not served in combat were more than twice as likely to describe witnessing or committing battlefield atrocities, compared to the veterans with real Vietnam combat exposure. A colleague of Frueh's, with a clinician's characteristic understatement, summed it up: "That's weird."[2]

The findings were jaw-dropping. Burkett's book had been largely driven by anecdotes and scandals out in the real world, but the study showed that fakery and exaggeration were commonplace within clinical settings as well. Veterans and imposters were faking combat distinction right under the noses of VA professionals and getting away with it, sadly even outnumbering those with genuine experience.

As the implications of their results were becoming clear, Frueh pulled Elhai said. "You know, I'm funded now, and I'm not planning to have a career necessarily in the VA at this point," he told his junior colleague. If there's heat from this, I don't mind that." He had seen and heard stories of what could happen to staffers who raised controversial points and felt the obligation to warn his protege and partner. He made sure he was understood. "If you're going to have a long-term career in the VA system, this might not be, politically, the best paper for you to co-author."

Elhai didn't hesitate. "I don't care. It's an important study. We're doing it."

Frueh nodded. He wouldn't mention it again.

FRUEH AND BURKETT'S RESEARCH had focused on fraud among Vietnam-era veterans, but since the new millennium a new cohort of veterans and imposters have been treading the same path. As the Fourth of July approaches each year, Americans across the country get ready for picnics, barbecues, gatherings with their family and friends. In 2014, Shawn Gourley had prepared for the celebration by purchasing a thousand yard signs. Her husband, Justin Gourley, had served in the Navy from 2000 to 2004, and returned a changed man. After he was diagnosed with PTSD in 2009, Shawn created a Facebook group for veterans and their loved ones, which she eventually launched into a nonprofit called Military with PTSD.

One day, a member of the group posted a photo of a sign he had made, cautioning neighbors that fireworks may trigger his PTSD. Shawn liked the idea. After asking the original creator for permission, she began distributing the 18-by-24-inch yard signs herself. They read: "Combat Veteran Lives Here / Please Be Courteous with Fireworks."

By Independence Day the following year, more than five thousand people had requested a sign.[3] News outlets picked up on the story and the demand grew from there, the cautionary message making appearances in front lawns around the country. Not all vets, though, welcomed the representation. "I don't like the insinuation that every combat vet can't handle fireworks. As a vet, I love fireworks," read one online post.[4] Other reactions were less diplomatic. A popular veterans' blog blasted the signs as "pathetic, self-defeating crap."[5]

The saga of the divisive fireworks sign took a further twist when it was revealed that Justin Gourley's military service was hardly the intensive, trauma-riddled experience his wife had portrayed in a 2011 book, *The War at Home*. In one incident, she wrote that Justin had been aboard the USS George Washington when it was called to assist a fishing vessel that had caught fire. Most of the passengers were evacuated safely, but Justin was tasked with recovering the body of a fisherman who had died. "That was the first dead body Justin handled," his wife wrote. When a skeptical veterans website checked the USS George Washington's logs, the ship was found to have been anchored at the Norfolk Naval Shipyard in Portsmouth, Virginia— nowhere near the fishing vessel rescue that allegedly occurred.[6]

Justin also described attending an anti-terrorism course where, after running countless drills, "We stopped hesitating and acting on emotion when it came to everyone. Everything I thought I knew about people changed then. No one could be trusted. My view on life now was simple, everyone is the enemy." Justin "talked about his weapon qualifications and how well he'd done on the sniper test," his wife recounted. "Sitting there talking to him gave me the chills. There was no emotion in his voice and his eyes were black as the night. The fun-loving Justin I knew my whole life had been transformed into a well-trained, highly skilled machine that could kill without thinking twice."[7]

Yet when other skeptical combat vets retrieved Justin's DD-214, they found no records of any sniper or terrorism training. Other discrepancies included Justin's accounts of a botched plane landing, and the death of an airman when equipment malfunctioned in his ship's hangar bay. In fact, Justin had served as an Operations Specialist, a radarman and technician who spent the majority of his time below deck in the bowels of the ship.

At their core, the Gourleys' embellished claims, as well as the breakout popularity of their fireworks sign among a segment of veterans, are expressions of a powerful and universal human need to be recognized. They are driven by the same motivations—a mix of financial gain and desire for attention, personal concessions to the self and ego—that can induce vets to amplify or even completely falsify their military experience.

In another case, on the opposite coast, a Seattle man presented himself as a decorated Marine captain and former chaplain, despite having served just two years in the Army and never seeing combat. Before he was exposed and convicted, Reggie Buddle had officiated at service members' baptisms, weddings, and funerals, and even delivered the opening prayer at the Washington State Senate's opening ceremony.[8]

Investigations over the years have uncovered evidence to suggest a systemic problem. In 2009, the *Associated Press* found large mismatches between the official record of surviving prisoners of war and the number of VA-recognized POWs collecting disability compensation. For veterans of the first Gulf War, the Department of Defense recognized twenty-one living POWs, even as the VA was paying out benefits to 286 recipients who had claimed enemy imprisonment during the conflict. Among Vietnam-era service members, 996 purported POWs were enrolled in the VA disability system, while, according to Defense records, only 661 POWs had returned from the war alive, of whom about one hundred had since passed away.[9]

Usually, it is other veterans who take the most offense at these discrepancies, enraged by their peers who would stoop to such misrepresentations. One popular VA blogger wrote, "Some of you will always aspire to feel you were in danger and you will manufacture the requisite emotions to convince yourselves and others. I see it frequently. The mind is an interesting playground of emotions and some can sway your vision of reality to fit your desires."[10] When another prominent veterans website featured a post titled "How & Where To Report VA Abuse And Fraud," the comments section quickly transformed into an unofficial hotline, serving up more than seven hundred complaints of fraudulent disabled vets.[11] A commenter named Richard wrote:

I worked with a guy who was in the air force [sic]. He likes to brag about how he faked a shoulder injury with the med board and was medically discharged and now gets his free monthly check. Not sure how many steroid shots he gets each month but on top of this he lifts waits [sic] for competition and he looks like the incredible hulk. Talk about fraud he should be made to pay every cent back to the VA.

In witnessing others receiving unjustified benefits, many vets drew comparisons to their own conditions. One man, posting under the name Bud, shared the story of his brother-in-law who had served in the military for two years:

...never near the front lines in Vietnam, mentions agent orange [sic] to his case worker, wears diapers to the visits, blames every damn problem he's ever had on his service time. Gets full disability while I work my arse off, never complaining once about many more serious injuries that might actually have been a result of my 4+ years in another branch of service (prefer to remain anonymous). He continues to work a contracting business along-side a lucrative part-time job harvesting shellfish bent at the waist for 5-6 hours at a time (considered to be at least as demanding physically as any job on earth). He buys and sells vehicles with his windfall while I drive my one 20-year-old jalopy to my full-time job 50 miles away so that I can barely make ends meet. If there is karma, he will drive one of those Dodge Hemis into a bridge abutment.

Though Bud felt resentful toward his brother-in-law, he understood that it represented only one case among many produced by the larger structure in place. "Is it his fault that our VA allows this sort of fraud?" he wrote. "One has to wonder how we arrived at this place."

In some ways, such cases are expressions of a natural psychological impulse. In 2003, social scientists Sarah Brosnan and Frans de Waal carried out an experiment by pairing brown capuchin monkeys in a cage, then giving them each tokens to be exchanged for food.[12] Capuchin monkeys typically prefer grapes over cucumbers, though when isolated, the monkeys enjoyed both, happily eating whatever they were given—grape or cucumber. The researchers found that when one monkey was handed a cucumber for her token, she was perfectly content with it. Yet if she observed that her partner had received a grape for the exact same token, she suddenly reacted in anger. Some of the aggrieved monkeys discarded their cucumbers or hurled them from the cage. Such a reaction is known as disadvantageous-inequity aversion. Primates, as well as people, hate feeling like they're getting the short end of the stick.[13]

The VA's disability apparatus can perpetuate a similar dynamic. Given the compensation system's maze of perplexing principles and irregularities, veterans inevitably receive disability ratings that can appear lopsided and unjust. One former C&P examiner refers to it as a "contagion effect," elaborating: "Say you were in combat, and you're having some problems now. You have a buddy who wasn't ever in combat—maybe he had a Scud missile in the Gulf War fly overhead. He says he's got PTSD, and suddenly he's got 70 percent [service-connected disability]. It's natural to feel like, 'Well, wait a minute. That's not fair. I should get some of that too.' One of the big effects is the feeling that everyone else is getting these benefits—so why shouldn't I?"

A perceived sense of injustice can warp behavior. A VA psychologist on the West Coast said, "Picture somebody who has had a lot happen to them. They hear that somebody else is getting 100 percent, getting $4,000 a month tax-free for the rest of their life doing nothing."[14] These interactions may occur in therapy rap groups, VA waiting room conversations, the local watering hole, or online chatrooms and comment sections. The typical veteran may respond in one of two ways: they either "get so disgusted they abandon the process entirely," or they decide they'll fight back and try to get as much as they can from a flawed system, the VA psychologist said. What arises is "a social comparison process that makes everybody feel bad and invalidated." After working with hundreds of veterans, she estimates that three quarters of her VA patients encounter this environment and become galvanized to increase their rating. "They recalibrate their internal understanding of [the benefits system] and they say, I'm more impaired than that guy, so I'm going to refile and push and push and push until my last dying breath to get what's 'owed to me'."

An unreliable system breeds ill will, and as the ill will spreads, it hastens further erosion. How pervasive, truly, is this cynicism and misbehavior among the VA's millions of disability recipients? Jug Burkett, informed by his decades of vigilante work exposing veteran fakers and exaggerators, has longed to get to the bottom of it. He says all you would need to do is perform a simple test. "Audit one VA hospital. Just one. Don't announce it, just pick one and quietly check everyone's records, and that will be a good indication of what's happening in every VA hospital across the country," he said.

He has little doubt what the results will testify. "You'll find so much fraud you'll be shocked."[15]

IN THE SPRING OF 2004, Frueh and his team were finalizing their study, preparing to release its findings. To his surprise, he recalled, "the excitement started before it was published." They had recently submitted the paper to the *American Journal of Psychiatry*, the most widely read psychiatry journal in the world[16], when one day soon after, Frueh received a call from Terry Keane.

Keane was the director of the VA's National Center for PTSD. With more than thirty years of experience, he was one of the most distinguished and highly respected figures in the field.[17] After receiving his grant from the National Institute of Mental Health, Frueh had been able to work with Keane and the two had developed a warm, professional relationship. On numerous occasions Keane had invited Frueh to his office in Boston, always going out of his way to introduce him to friends and colleagues, and Frueh had come to see him as a mentor figure. But on this particular day, the voice on the other end of the line carried none of its usual warmth.

"Chris, Terry Keane here. I'm calling from the undersecretary of the VA's office in Washington. We're both looking at this paper you submitted to the *American Journal of Psychiatry*." [18]

Frueh immediately knew something was wrong. Submitting work to a peer-reviewed journal was supposed to be a confidential process, an integral element to the publication's integrity. If one of the journal's reviewers had shared it with Keane, it would have been an ethical violation. Frueh tried not to jump to conclusions. It was possible that Keane was a reviewer himself, or one of Frueh's own co-authors had sent it to him, but Keane never explained how he got it. Instead, he had quickly moved on to express concern with what the study's conclusions suggested.

"We have a Congressional hearing tomorrow to discuss the federal VA budget for PTSD," he said. "A paper like this could be extremely damaging to our ability to fund programs for veterans with PTSD." He asked Frueh not to publish it.

Frueh was shocked by how explicit the request was. He took a moment to gather himself, then replied, "Terry, I'm not going to pull it. It's just data. The data are what they are." It felt strange having to defend himself in this way to his own mentor. "I'm a scientist," Frueh went on. "You're a scientist. I think we serve veterans the best in the long haul by doing the best science and sharing the data no matter what comes out of it."

Keane kept pressing. "Malingering is not the problem," he

insisted. "You really are doing harm by overemphasizing it in this population. There's a bigger problem with veterans needing care who don't get care." The two of them had clashed on this issue before— long discussions buttressed with medical citations that skirted to the edge of civility before always ending at an impasse. They were not likely to suddenly agree this time. As if recognizing this, Keane suddenly switched to a different tack, remarking that the study's sample size had been too small, listing various hypotheticals that may have invalidated the data, and finally stating that the paper was simply "not a great research study, anyway."

Frueh knew that hundreds of studies were published each year with a sample size of fewer than one hundred participants. He told himself not to get defensive. "Well, I agree that it's not the perfect study," he replied. "But as an unfunded pilot study, it sure raises some important questions that are worthy of getting out there." He didn't want his paper to be the final say; rather, he wished that the findings might open new avenues for conducting research that others may not have considered before. The more concern and attention the topic received, the better outcome ultimately, Frueh believed, for all veterans.

There was silence from the other end of the line. Finally, Keane said, "This is politically a hot potato. I'm not going to personally throw you under the bus, but if I'm standing in front of Congress tomorrow and they bring up this study..." He trailed off, then sounding resigned, added, "I'm not going to be able to defend you."

The next day, Frueh listened to the Congressional testimony from a web stream. Keane was never asked to take the stand, and neither Frueh nor his study were ever mentioned, yet things between him and his mentor would never recover.

Not long after, Frueh and his co-authors learned that their paper had been rejected by the *American Journal of Psychiatry*. The results came as a surprise; even worse, there was no reasonable explanation for the decision in the review team's feedback. "The rejection just said this study can't possibly be valid or meaningful, because if it is, it would undermine everything we think we know about PTSD," said Frueh. Such a curt message was extremely unusual; papers that reach a publication's review stage typically elicit a comprehensive response that argues for acceptance or rejection on a scientific basis. This time there was none of that. The rejection "did not critique [the results] on scientific grounds," Frueh recalled. "It just said this can't possibly be true. It would upset the order too much."

Convinced that their findings were still worth publishing, Frueh and his team submitted the study to the *British Journal of Psychiatry* in May 2004, figuring a respected publication abroad would have "none of the politics of America, or the American VA." In their paper's analysis, they had been careful not to overstep their bounds. "These results should not be interpreted to deny that many combat veterans do suffer from severe and debilitating symptoms of PTSD," they cautioned. At the same time, they made sure that nothing diluted their core insight. For any patient maneuvering within the VA's disability system, "the financial incentive to present as psychiatrically disabled [...] is significant." A better system for determining disability benefits was necessary to ensure the VA's integrity. The authors concluded: "Ultimately it is hoped that the Department of Veterans Affairs will take steps to ensure that its scarce resources are directed towards people who are both deserving and in need. Such efforts are essential to guard the legacy of actual combat veterans from being trivialized."

Their paper was accepted in September. With some minor revisions, it was published the following summer.[19] More excitement was on the way.

CHAPTER 12
PERMANENT DISORDER

WHEN WILLIAM MCMATH came across the VA job opening in the newspaper classifieds, he was ready to leave the education world behind. It was 1999, and since earning his graduate degree in psychology a decade earlier, he had worked at a New York private school for developmentally disabled children, rising through the academy's ranks to become the psychology department's supervisor.

For many years, he had found the work rewarding. "The school did an awful lot of good things for an awful lot of children," he said. With the approach of the new millennium, however, national trends were reshaping the perception and treatment of children in his field. McMath watched as the number of autism diagnoses exploded throughout the nineties; kids everywhere across the country, it seemed, were suddenly being tagged with symptoms related to various developmental disorders, landing huge new numbers on the autism spectrum. He consulted about the influx with his colleagues, many of whom suspected the diagnoses were being inflated. They discussed a largely overlooked factor they believed were pivotal in driving the spikes: the afflicted children's parents.

In many high-expectation families, parents with kids who were shy, or behaved oddly, or had trouble making friends, were finding relief in a plausible new explanation for their children's inability to fit in. McMath and his colleagues saw that attaining an autism diagnosis for their kids, in its own way, provided a kind of absolution. The child's struggles were no longer the fault of the parents, or even the fault of the child—the responsibility could be placed squarely on the shoulders of an external disorder. "It was counterintuitive, but I understood their motivation in a way," McMath said.

The more parents pushed him to diagnose their children, however, "the stranger my position seemed to me," he said. "I wasn't seeing their children as autistic, but it was a diagnosis that a lot of people wanted to see." He felt he couldn't continue affixing labels to cases he didn't believe were the right fit and soured on his position at the school. Soon he was looking for other opportunities. After interviewing for the role of C&P examiner at the Northport VA Medical Center on Long Island, he was offered the job and decided to accept. He had spent almost his entire career working in children's mental health, but he felt excited to apply his skills in a new environment, assessing a new kind of patient.

In his first few days at the VA, McMath observed three C&P exams conducted by two different psychiatrists at the hospital. That was the entirety of his training. One of the psychiatrists told McMath he rarely conducted evaluations lasting more than half an hour. McMath saw that the psychiatrist dictated his assessments in a "stream of consciousness," which assistants later transcribed into a coherent report. McMath was surprised to find that this psychiatrist was considered one of the hospital's most competent C&P examiners.

With his lackluster training completed, McMath was quickly assigned to a small office in the Northport VA's outpatient mental health clinic. Because the hospital was short-staffed, McMath was expected to perform additional duties beyond conducting his regular C&P exams, such as seeing patients from the clinic's outpatient psychotherapy program. "It was during that period of time that I began to question the criteria being used to diagnose PTSD," he said.

In graduate school, McMath had studied Freud and psychodynamic theory. Later during his years in education, he was exposed to a broad range of psychological conditions and mental impairments. Yet when he first started at the VA, he admitted to only a tenuous grasp of PTSD, particularly as it afflicted the military community. The vague notions he did have had come mostly from Hollywood dramas and sensational newspaper stories, which often presented jarring portraits of a terrible disease that plagued unhinged and unhappy Vietnam vets.

A far different picture came into focus as soon as he began interacting directly with veterans. In one of his first cases at the VA's outpatient clinic, an Army vet who had never served in combat insisted he was traumatized from once feeling the concussion of an artillery shell during training, and then from getting into an argument with his superior officer which resulted in a general—rather than honorable—discharge. The patient was adamant that McMath record these events into his files, and even demanded to review them himself after each psychotherapy appointment. Such attention to detail was not uncommon, McMath found. He saw many of his patients trying to maximize the appearance of trauma in their evaluations, believing that such indicators would help them secure service-connection when they later applied for PTSD disability.

To supplement his knowledge, McMath began studying PTSD on his own. He was surprised to learn that the fundamental elements of its diagnosis, indeed the very nature of the disorder, were under contention. Within the mainstream discourse, in news articles and even much of the scholarship, PTSD was typically presented as a rigid diagnostic box with firm edges and clear boundaries. In reality, McMath realized that pathologies of the mind did not work that way. Mental disorders were fluid constructions, defined by overlapping symptom sets and a heavy reliance on subjective inputs. Unlike infections, for example, there was no laboratory test that could eliminate the doctor's own judgment. There would always be the presence of subjectivity and the possibility of human error.

FROM THE BEGINNING, the definition and application of post-traumatic stress disorder as a diagnosis has been dogged by fierce political winds, complicating public discourse and making it nearly impossible to consider the condition through an objective, scientific lens. Military psychiatrists have long recognized that acute stress symptoms can arise in previously well-adjusted individuals, originating from their proximity and participation in war's horrific events. Such reactions, however, were understood to subside as soldiers left the battlefield behind.

In the wake of the Vietnam War, a cohort of impassioned antiwar psychiatrists, led by the influential scholar Robert Jay Lifton, adopted a new outlook. They insisted that many veterans never improved after leaving the service but continued to suffer severe psychological stress, frequently in silence. At the same time, they found other vets—even those appearing to have adapted successfully into civilian life—who they said were actually prone to developing delayed stress symptoms months, or even years, after settling back home. Allying with veterans' advocacy groups, this vocal band of psychiatrists and activists lobbied for an official "post-Vietnam syndrome" to chronicle what they insisted were widespread instances of chronic and delayed stress. Though there was never a scientific consensus over these claims, this faction of the psychiatric community was effective in leveraging their clout and connections to sway public opinion. In 1980, their campaigning resulted in the watershed publication of the first clinical definition for PTSD in the field's definitive *Diagnostic and Statistical Manual of Mental Disorders*—at the time, the volume's third edition, or *DSM-III*.[1]

Since its conception, the qualifying feature that differentiates PTSD from most other psychiatric disorders is the existence of an external traumatizing event—a stressor. Exposure to a stressor is crucial in the diagnostic process. Though the architects of the *DSM-III* had in mind directly life-threatening events such as military combat, earthquakes, rape, and other experiences of possible mortal danger, revisions made in the mid-nineties for the *DSM-IV* significantly broadened what qualified as traumatic exposure.

New language in the *DSM-IV* multiplied the avenues from which PTSD might arise. Previously, only people who had experienced a traumatic event themselves, or directly witnessed the event as it occurred to someone else, had the basis to claim a stressor.

With the entry's updated criteria, a third, more derivative form of exposure was established: any patient who "experienced, witnessed, or was confronted with an event or events that involved actual or threatened death or serious injury" could now be susceptible to the disorder as well. A 2003 *Annual Review of Psychology* paper called attention to this diagnostic expansion, warning against a phenomenon known amongst psychologists as "bracket creep." The authors of the paper surmised, "No longer must one be the direct (or even vicarious) recipient of trauma; merely being horrified by what happened to others now counts as a PTSD-qualifying event."[2]

The brackets have continued to expand. Published in 2013, the fifth and most recent edition of the *DSM* stretched PTSD's qualifications further, consolidating a new cluster of symptoms while identifying three additional individual symptoms, bringing the total list of recognized symptoms to twenty. The latest entry also created a fourth type of exposure, articulated by the experience of encountering, on more than one occasion, "distressing details of an event, such as a police officer repeatedly hearing details about child sexual abuse."[3] After decades of wrangling and revision, a condition initially conceived, amid controversy, as a possible outcome from direct exposure to acute trauma has swelled to such proportion that anyone ever encountering the details of an unhappy circumstance may now be afflicted. As a pathology's aperture widens, its gravity dilutes. And as dilution becomes more commonplace, modern practitioners can lose sight of the original principles holding the diagnosis together.

The true frequency of combat-induced stress has been the subject of ongoing debate since the end of World War I. Not long after PTSD was codified, Congress mandated a study to determine its prevalence among veterans of the Vietnam War. The 1990 National Vietnam Veterans Readjustment Study (NVVRS), a survey of more than a thousand male Vietnam vets, found that 30.9 percent had developed PTSD at some point in their lives and 15.2 percent were still suffering from it. The findings immediately triggered objections—historians observed, for instance, that the lifetime rate was twice as high as the 15 percent of Vietnam vets who had served in combat roles—yet the figures were popularly disseminated and became the standard reference.

Another major study, issued by the Center for Disease Control at around the same time, produced significantly different estimates, finding that the lifetime PTSD rate among Vietnam vets was actually 14.7 percent—less than half what the NVVRS projected—while only 2.2 percent still had PTSD when the data was collected.[4] Some critics of the CDC study have argued that the study under-reported PTSD symptoms, though subsequent research has found that symptoms persisting beyond the first month after trauma are uncommon, appearing in less than 15 percent of cases.[5] Even so, McMath recalls many of his patients claiming a limitless longevity to the effects of their trauma. At the VA, he was also encountering veterans who claimed the sudden and debilitating onset of PTSD. He noticed that many of them had already spent decades in the workforce, and were just approaching retirement, or coincidentally, in the process of filing for increased disability benefits. "After forty years, to say that you are having increased symptoms of exposure to trauma—it just doesn't fit the facts," he said. "I was looking at that research and I was interviewing a lot of veterans. They were telling me stories that didn't make sense in terms of how human memory and human reactions to trauma work."

At the heart of diagnosing PTSD is the external stressor from which all symptoms manifest. That is also where the problems begin. Examiners can never actually assess the traumatizing event itself, only the afflicted individual's memory of it. At the time of PTSD's original formulation in 1980, memories of trauma were generally viewed as reliable indicators of true events. However, new findings in the decades since have demonstrated the fallibility and malleability of human memory, and the trouble with basing clinical evaluations on a subject's personal testimony.

In a landmark 1995 study on the formation of false memories, subjects were presented with a fabricated account of how they got lost in a shopping mall as a child. One out of four adults claimed to remember the episode.[6] When asked to elaborate on the event, some professed to remember it with even greater clarity. Others insisted the account had occurred, even after they were debriefed on the nature of the experiment.

Another study, published in the *American Journal of Psychiatry*, tracked a group of fifty-nine Operation Desert Storm vets in the aftermath of the war.[7] A team led by Steven Southwick, a psychiatrist at Yale University, interviewed the veterans at two different times—one month after they returned, and again two years later. At both intervals, the subjects were asked to complete a nineteen-item questionnaire, referring specifically to traumatic events during their deployments—including watching their close friends die, witnessing the gross disfigurement of others, near-fatal missile attacks, and other extreme threats to their safety.

Two years out from their wartime service, nearly 90 percent of the veterans changed at least one item in their response. Seventy percent recalled at least one incident that they had not reported during their one-month assessment; almost a quarter recounted three or more.[8] At the same time, almost half the subjects did not recount an incident at the two-year mark that they had previously endorsed after one month.

As greater probes are made into the science of memory, a growing body of work has documented the power and prevalence of what researchers call the "misinformation effect."[9] When subjects who have witnessed a particular event are introduced to misleading facts about it afterward, they consistently integrate the new information into their accounts. Also known as interference theory, the phenomenon has led subjects to recall nonexistent objects, misidentify salient features in others, and fabricate the structure of entire buildings. As one memory scholar wrote, "new information invades us, like a Trojan horse, precisely because we do not detect its influence."[10]

In the study of the Gulf War veterans, the participants who reported the most "new" events after two years were also found to score highest for PTSD, indicating that their memories of trauma had amplified over time.[11] Southwick and his colleagues considered several scenarios that may have produced this result. They acknowledged that some participants may have genuinely forgotten, denied, or suppressed certain experiences at one month, which subsequently surfaced two years later. Reflecting the field's better grasp of modified recall, they also suggested that the subjects may have distorted or exaggerated their memories after hearing stories from other traumatized vets, or from repeatedly retelling the same events, with slight alterations accruing over time. Such retroactive interference helped explain why some individuals no longer recalled adverse experiences they had initially reported. As mainstream media accounts trumpeted the success of Desert Storm, simultaneously diminishing its tolls, some vets may have been primed to follow suit, minimizing their memories of the traumatic event.

For the veterans whose new memories manifested in more intense nightmares, flashbacks, and other intrusive symptoms, Southwick proposed a similar revision working in reverse: "It may be that individuals who became increasingly symptomatic over time unknowingly exaggerated their memory for traumatic events as a way to understand or explain their emerging psychopathology." Narratives form in hindsight and present conditions can color old memories with new significance, leading to imprecise diagnoses of delayed onset PTSD.

A 2007 study further illustrated the tenuous connection between a PTSD diagnosis and true trauma. Psychiatrists at Harvard's McLean Hospital examined ninety clinically depressed patients, screening them separately for PTSD and trauma. Given the conventionally understood link between the two, traumatized patients were expected to score higher on their PTSD scales, while patients exhibiting the most severe PTSD symptoms were assumed to have traumatic histories. Instead, researchers found no correlation: the PTSD rate among patients had no relationship at all to their trauma rate.

The finding exposed the limits of a clear-cut symptom profile for PTSD and plunged a dagger into the idea that developing stress reactions from a traumatic episode necessarily meant that someone will also have PTSD. What frequently gets conflated as PTSD, the authors wrote, is actually "a non-specific group of symptoms, widely observed in patients with mood and anxiety disorders—regardless of trauma history."

By the end of his third year at the VA, McMath no longer accepted patients' statements about their disabilities at face value, and had developed a set of red flags to parse out the genuine claims from problematic ones. "I was no longer willing just to give a blanket diagnosis of PTSD," he said. In his own research process, he had come across the work of Richard McNally, a clinical psychologist at Harvard University. For years, McNally had been one of the most outspoken voices championing a "network perspective" on PTSD, a view that treats mental disorders as clusters of interacting symptoms rather than discrete clinical illnesses. In one widely discussed article, he told *Scientific American* that PTSD "has become so flabby and overstretched, so much a part of the culture, that we are almost certainly mistaking other problems for PTSD."[12]

As McMath became more versed in the fallibility of PTSD's commonly associated indicators, he began to view the VA's whole diagnostic process as ill-conceived and reductive, simplifying a complex mental phenomenon into a replicable, yet ultimately misleading, checklist for C&P examiners like himself. Within the VA, "one doctor's diagnosis of PTSD might be another doctor's diagnosis of depression due to alcohol abuse and yet another doctor's diagnosis of personality disorder," he said. "That checklist has rendered the diagnosis essentially meaningless."

Emerging as the most common denominator, PTSD has assumed the role of a diagnostic safety net, pulled out to catch a broad and diverse range of distress signals. But it was not simply an issue of mislabeling a case or putting someone into the wrong bucket. McMath worried that a mistaken diagnosis could mean channeling patients down the wrong path, pushing them into the wrong treatment, and consigning them to counterproductive—sometimes even dangerous—outcomes.

AS MCMATH MET with more patients at the VA, something else began to gnaw at him. It was the way he noticed many veterans talking about PTSD, how they seemed to conflate their own identities with the diagnosis. All at once, it struck him: it was the echo of a dynamic he had seen before.

In the early nineties, the American Psychiatric Association had expanded the diagnostic criteria for autism, triggering a dramatic rise in the number of the country's autism cases.[13] Working with disabled children as a school counselor at the time, McMath noticed that when students who were genuinely struggling were given the diagnosis, their parents typically reacted hotly—with anger and denial and desperation to find a "cure." On the other hand, in cases where the children were "just a little delayed," hardly deserving of placement on the spectrum in the first place, their parents often welcomed the diagnosis, even appearing glad to receive the news.[14]

McMath recognized the same sense of relief, the same swell of validation, in the veterans who passed through his office. "The PTSD diagnosis was a confirmation of their heroic, or at least honorable, service to the country," he said. It functioned as a badge of honor, a sign of membership into the club, and an outlet into which other miseries were frequently deflected.[16] For many vets, these symbolic reasons could be powerful drivers in their pursuit of PTSD benefits. McMath came to see that a high disability rating from the VA was interpreted as a "formal, belated recognition by the United States government of the individual's sacrifices."[15]

The rationale manifested in peculiar ways. "If you tell somebody you don't have cancer, usually they breathe a deep sigh of relief," said David Maxey, a C&P examiner from Oklahoma City. "This is one of those rare jobs where, as a health professional, you tell somebody, 'You don't have PTSD,' and you get a very different reaction." When

Maxey was first hired by the VA, it made no sense to him: why would anyone get *upset* when they learned they were healthy? But as he talked to more veterans, getting to hear their journeys and trying to place himself in their shoes, he began to parse the different strands of their motivation.

Some vets faced precarious financial constraints, struggling to support themselves or their families. Whether they were truly impaired or not, the disability compensation offered a means to help alleviate that pressure. But many others, Maxey found, cared more about simply getting *an answer*. "They want to attribute the emotional stuff they're going through to something that happened to them in the military," he said. "Seeking out a diagnosis like PTSD helps them feel better. They think, 'Okay, this is fine now. I know what it is.'"

The Vietnam generation had come home to a hostile environment, prompting many to evade reconciling with what they had gone through. Maxey believes the more recent cohort of veterans, returning from Afghanistan and Iraq, are folded back into a culture that relentlessly projects trauma onto their experiences, casting all vets as permanently damaged. He sees younger vets who are more willing, consciously or not, to pin life's routine adversities on a damaged psyche, wrought by their military service. "Everybody has a time in their life where they have a boss that they don't like," he said. "Sometimes they might get into an argument with their boss and get fired—I don't think that's uncommon. But some people will go, 'Well, that must have been my anger problems because of my PTSD.' It becomes a piece of evidence toward them having PTSD as opposed to, well, something that happens to a certain percentage of young men between the ages of twenty and thirty."

Maxey also came to observe that when compensation payments are on the line, motives get tangled and the picture becomes messier. Among the veterans surveyed in one 2004 study, only half who were seeking PTSD compensation were also seeking any kind of treatment to get better.[17] Frequently, at the end of Maxey's evaluations, veterans turned to him and asked, "What do you think, doc? Do I have PTSD? Am I going to get compensated?"

For Maxey, such questions were missing the point. "I say to them, 'You're a person who has told me about the problems in your relationships, your problems with your kids, your problems with your job.' Who cares what I say? Who cares what the VA says? If you've got problems about these things, the better question is, 'What can I do about it?'" Shared widely, albeit discreetly, among the disability division's rank and file, the view is also held by some of the administration's highest officials. Jim Nicholson, VA secretary under George W. Bush, has acknowledged, "the VA's benevolent benefits system is making permanent victims out of young Americans in the prime of their lives."[18]

Benevolent intent during the Obama administration drove a major update to how the VA determined PTSD service-connection for granting disability benefits. Eliminating the requirement for specific enemy contact or a similar stressor to form the basis of a PTSD claim, a new VA rule in 2010 stated that any *fear* of hostile military or terrorist action would be sufficient for meeting PTSD's criteria.

The change heralded a clear inflection in the prevalence of veterans deemed to be PTSD-disabled. Eroding diagnostic boundaries, combined with the lowering of VA requirements for determining service-connection, have lifted the floodgates for any veteran with intent to attain a PTSD diagnosis. Soon after the new policy, PTSD claims jumped by 60 percent, while approval rates rose from 55 to 74 percent.[19] The trend has hardly faded: in the decade since, PTSD disability recipients have nearly tripled.[20] As of 2019, 1.1 million veterans are service-connected for PTSD.[21]

Faced with the deluge, C&P examiners around the country have sought counsel from one another through their online listserv. Recently, a VA psychologist in Ohio brought the forum's attention to the case of a veteran stationed at a stateside military hospital, placed in medical hold for a non-service-connected condition. The veteran, who was seeking PTSD compensation, claimed he had been traumatized after "sitting with severely injured soldiers," from simply hearing their distress.

Another psychologist, working at a VA Medical Center in the Southwest, encountered a veteran who had applied for PTSD benefits claiming military sexual trauma. The patient, she posted, "was intoxicated, went willing to the other person's home, engaged in foreplay, disrobed without complaint, engaged in intercourse more than once without threat or coercion, spent the night, and didn't report the incident. He states only that he was confused afterward, no fear, but guilt and shame." The psychologist consulted her colleagues: "How do you separate post-sex regret from a criterion-A stressor?"

As vets purporting trauma have flooded the VA's disability payroll, they have not escaped the ire of others in the military community. On popular websites and online groups, veterans ridicule the illegitimate compensation recipients they personally know. They joke about watching out for the "PTSD fairy," and warn each other to stand guard. In these new times, they caution, everyone is at perpetual risk of suddenly "catching the PTSD."

BY THE TIME THE VA eliminated its stressor requirement for PTSD, McMath had worked as a C&P examiner for nearly a decade. He had seen enough PTSD cases of every stripe and color to understand exactly how the system was stacked. In his own assessments, he insisted on observing the higher standards set forth by the medical literature and his own ethical compass, but staying true to those principles had become harder, often putting him at odds with the VA's overbearing culture.

At the Long Island VA, McMath regularly interacted with the inpatient PTSD program's head psychiatrist, an impressionable man who never failed to portray his patients as utterly unemployable, saddled with chronic and crippling PTSD. Miraculously, their symptoms would remain essentially unchanged even after months of intensive treatment, psychiatric medication, and regular group therapy. Lengthy emails to McMath frequently recommended raising patients' disability ratings for higher compensation. Once the psychiatrist was scheduled to give a presentation on PTSD to a room full of veterans. He opened his address with the remark: "You all have PTSD."[22]

On some level, McMath understood that the psychiatrist's outlook came from a place of empathy. But by treating all veterans as "damaged beyond repair," McMath believed his colleague was "robbing them of their autonomy and self-worth"—ultimately doing more harm than good.

IN 2000, not long before America's new wars would launch PTSD into the national consciousness, Richard McNally was in the middle of writing his second book. This was the aspect of academia, and his chosen field of trauma, that he loved the most: poring over volumes of data and literature, attempting to chronicle how trauma victims remember their experiences. He was deep into his research when he stumbled upon a citation that piqued his interest.

The reference was a self-published book unlike any of the academic tomes McNally was used to. Titled *Stolen Valor*, and written by a Vietnam veteran named Jug Burkett, the book detailed a litany of fakes and fraudsters pretending to be combat veterans for various ulterior motives. McNally found the work to be groundbreaking. "It stunned me," he said. "It absolutely stunned me."

Much of his own research had centered on patients diagnosed with PTSD, a group that had increasingly become associated with the veterans population. After finishing Burkett's book, McNally realized there was an important piece to understanding the whole picture that he had never paid much attention to: the VA system.

Soon after PTSD was codified in the *DSM*, the VA began to recognize it in determining it as a condition eligible for service-connected benefits.[23] Between 1999 and 2004, the number of Vietnam vets approved for PTSD disability benefits nearly doubled, alongside an 80 percent increase in the overall number of PTSD cases.[24]

Disability payments for the disorder tripled across the same period to $4.3 billion. Burkett was the first person McNally had encountered who dared to pin a significant portion of PTSD's rise on compensation-seeking veterans who were acting in response to the VA's convoluted disability program. It was an instantly provocative claim, and McNally found its implications jarring.

As a city clinician in Chicago during the late eighties, he had been a member of the team that collected data for the original 1990 NVVRS. Dashing through Chicago's neighborhoods and nearby suburbs, he tracked down veterans from the Vietnam War and recorded their experiences. Yet like others in the scientific community, he was surprised when the study reported that almost a third of vets nationally had developed PTSD.

McNally later sat on the committee that revised PTSD's guidelines for the *DSM-IV* published in 1994. After the 9/11 attacks in New York City, he watched as a wave of traumatologists argued in favor of diagnosing PTSD among people who had merely watched the events on television. He realized that PTSD's looser diagnostic measures in the *DSM-IV* contributed to the inflating assessments. Through his research and publications, he began to serve as an outspoken voice against further expansion of the disorder's scope. But rather than correcting for the problem, the momentum within the trauma field was pushing the criteria in the other direction, becoming even more lenient.

PTSD had been conceived as a disorder afflicting survivors of truly life-threatening incidents—traumatizing experiences faced during military combat, torture, concentration camps, or horrific natural disasters—yet McNally watched over the years as diagnoses piled up for far less serious incidents—fender benders, minor accidents, even verbal disagreements. In one study, patients reported PTSD symptoms after simply getting their wisdom teeth removed. McNally worried that a well-meaning public, suffocated by skewed accounts from the media and veteran advocates, risked losing sight of facts indisputable within the trauma field: PTSD is a *rare* condition, known to subside over time, and proven to *improve* with treatment.

"The vast majority of people who have survived a traumatic event do not have PTSD," said Charles Figley, the founding editor of the *Journal of Traumatic Stress* and a leading expert in disaster and resilience. Crucially, he adds, in the minority of cases where people do develop symptoms, "there is every reason to believe that they can overcome the negative consequences and negative memories."

After serving in the Marines during the Vietnam War, Figley became an active member of the anti-war movement back home. Participating in numerous demonstrations as a civilian, he witnessed firsthand the mental health tolls that his fellow vets had suffered from combat, yet also saw the additional damage inflicted by casting normal transition pains as permanent pathologies. "There were a lot of us in a fog the first five or six years after getting out of the military," he said. "That fog should not be translated into a mental disorder."

A particularly memorable experience of protesting alongside other vets on the National Mall "woke me up," Figley recalls, and he embarked on a career to explore the various ways in which trauma can be healed. Today, after almost four decades in the field, he stands behind a more constructive view of trauma as an *injury*, correctable through rehabilitation, rather than an *illness* to be endured, too often through endless medication.

"To think that [a traumatic] experience will automatically lead to a mental disorder—without much that we can do—is not only dishonest, it's inconsistent with what kind of hope we want to impart for the patient," Figley said. Studies have shown that even the most distressful responses to a traumatizing event fade over time, while patients truly afflicted by PTSD stand to benefit from treatment no matter how much time has elapsed.[25] Figley compares it to a far more quotidian scenario: when an active runner suffers a sprain, he doesn't give up running forever. He slows down, tends to the injury, and gives it time to heal. "It's the same way when we're exposed to a traumatic event. It forces us to address questions, and when we're able to answer those questions, then we move on," Figley said.

And yet, despite everything that—in Figley's words—"we as therapists and human service professionals know to be true," veterans diagnosed with PTSD do not show the same levels of improvement. Treatment methods reliably proven to benefit victims of rape or assault do not have the same effect on the veteran population. In one study, 67 percent of civilians in a PTSD psychotherapy program were able to minimize their symptoms below the level of diagnosis, yet the program produced virtually no benefits among veteran samples. "You don't have this with many other disorders," McNally said. "If someone has panic disorder or obsessive-compulsive disorder or agoraphobia, you can take them at face value when they complain about those symptoms. There's no incentive structure to exaggerate or fabricate these things."

Yet the intersection of PTSD and veterans seemed to defy all norms, occurring in its own laboratory of suspended reality. Burkett's book, *Stolen Valor*, helped shift McNally's focus to a key component he had overlooked. Within the VA's compensation system, more than 90 percent of vets receiving mental health treatment are concurrently seeking PTSD disability benefits.[26] The fault is in the design, flawed from the start. People of all traits and backgrounds will respond to the incentives in front of them: when economic benefits are pegged to disability status, veterans are incentivized to resist rehabilitation, thereby achieving significantly worse results.

Between 2005 and 2013, the number of VA patients treated for mental health issues grew more than three times as fast as the number of overall VA users.[27] Taxed by heavier workloads, an already constrained VA risks burying the truly sick under patients whose motivations are financial, rather than medical. "The clinical services are limited, so we want to make sure we're targeting the people that actually have the condition," McNally said. "Of course, if they get better, they can put their benefits in peril." As one widely cited medical journal put it: "If you have to prove you are ill, you can't get well."[28]

Within the VA, well-meaning actors, even without realizing it, can become role players in the production of a singular, extreme outcome: PTSD-diagnosed veterans who rarely get better. McMath noticed a tendency among many of the VA professionals he worked with to offer the diagnosis as a form of absolution. Whatever had gone poorly in their patients' lives, they would hang on the hardships of PTSD. "These were veterans who may have failed in their marriages or in the workforce or were going to retire from jobs they hadn't especially liked," McMath said. "They felt like something had to explain why they had been so unhappy for twenty or thirty or forty years. VA psychologists and psychiatrists were telling them, 'Oh yeah, you absolutely have PTSD, and that's why things are so bad for you, why you're so unhappy.'"

A colleague once passed along the files for a PTSD-diagnosed veteran who had recently completed a three-month inpatient program at the hospital's mental health clinic. The colleague, a social worker, ran a counseling group for vets after they had completed the program; in that particular patient's files, she noted that he had successfully "graduated" from the treatment, yet recommended an increase in his disability rating.

"I thought we should polish his PTSD service-connection and bump him up to 50 percent," she told McMath, expecting him to support her opinion by documenting that the patient's symptoms had "progressively worsened."

McMath reflected on the dissonance: "It did not occur to her that such a report would imply that all of the veteran's treatment had been worse than useless."[29]

An inclination to declare the worst outcome can be found throughout the VA. "If all you have is a hammer, everything looks like a nail," said Jay Phillippi, the C&P examiner from North Dakota. Among many of his colleagues, he said, the overriding assumption is "that every veteran is mentally ill."

The first few months after military service are crucial for veterans as they attempt to construct a new personal narrative. Yet when the very infrastructure built to support them during this period is too preoccupied with their infirmities, too eager to harden temporary setbacks into permanent labels of impairment, a promising transition from soldier to civilian is hijacked and diverted down an alternative track: warrior to patient, veteran to victim. The VA ensnares patients into what mental health experts have called a "downward spiral of invalidism."

"I would *expect* people to have nightmares for a while when they came back," said Matt Stevens, a former Army captain who served in Iraq.[30] After returning from his tour in 2006, Stevens watched as the members of his unit were folded into a culture, within the VA and the country at large, eager to interpret any rough patch as an undisputed sign of PTSD. The cavalier connection disturbed him. "Clinicians aren't separating the few who really have PTSD from those who are experiencing things like depression or anxiety or social and reintegration problems or who are just taking some time getting over it," he said.

Compounded by politicized rhetoric and the spread of misinformation, these hastily applied PTSD diagnoses often carry the finality of a lifetime sentence. One former VA psychiatrist compared the practice to "telling someone with a spinal injury that he'll never walk again—before he has had surgery and physical therapy."

In case after case, McMath witnessed the damage inflicted by this cycle of learned helplessness. "The VA has been doing a disservice to millions of veterans by telling them that they're disabled because of psychiatric symptoms that will go away," he said. He found the misperceptions infuriating. "In almost no case that I know of do a veteran's symptoms truly result in a permanent disability. It results in a need for treatment, a need for recuperation, a need for rehabilitation psychiatrically. But it does not result in a permanent disability—unless they have been told to *believe* that it is a permanent disability."

From McNally's vantage point, balancing a career steeped in the scholarship of trauma with enough distance from the VA to objectively consider its effects, all forces led back to the same source: the veterans disability system. From this one nexus, normal distress responses from participating in war get recast into markers of pathology. Pathways to recovery are underemphasized or dismissed, distorting a treatable condition into a lifelong curse. Finally, monetary benefits are introduced, incentivizing disability status and hampering motivations for improvement. "It's a perfect storm," he said.

CHAPTER 13
SCIENCE VERSUS ADVOCACY

LATE ONE EVENING, not long after Frueh's paper appeared in the *British Journal of Psychiatry*, his home phone rang. It was almost nine at night—well past working hours. Frueh answered to the voice of his immediate supervisor, George Arana. Frueh got along well with Arana, a studious psychiatrist who led the Charleston VA's mental health practice, and Arana had even contributed to the research effort behind the 2005 study, which credited him among the co-authors. Published in June, the paper had brought alarming questions about the validity of veterans' combat and disability claims to the forefront of the scientific community. On the phone, his voice was spiked with alarm.

"Chris, have you read your email?"

Frueh replied that he hadn't. He had just cleaned up after dinner and was preparing to unwind with some reading before bed. Arana sounded spooked.

"You need to get on your email right now."

Frueh logged onto his computer and found an unread message in his inbox. Though it was addressed to him, a number of other recipients had been copied, including Arana. It said the VA Central Office was requesting a meeting at seven the next morning—a full hour before Frueh's regular reporting time. The message included a list of written questions, all relating to his *British Journal of Psychiatry* paper. Frueh should be ready to present answers in front of a panel of VA research directors, the email informed him, then field additional questions from a conference line of VA Central Office officials. And he was to bring all his files and documentation from conducting the study.

Arana didn't bother to hide his uneasiness. Both men knew how unusual this query was; neither of them had ever heard of anything like it. Their work was occasionally subject to audits by the Institutional Review Board, but that process was randomized, and researchers were given as much as a month of notice in advance. This was something else entirely. Frueh was confused, then agitated. "It was notable to me that I was given virtually no time to prepare. They were acting as though this was an extreme emergency. It felt like a midnight witch-hunt," he said.

He worked late into the night. The questions in the email carried the tone of an interrogation: *Why did you conduct this study? Who paid for it? Who approved it? Were you authorized by the IRB?*

"It felt like they were fishing for something that I had done wrong in the process of conducting this study," Frueh said. Worst of all, there was no attempt whatsoever to explain why he had suddenly become the subject of so much scrutiny.

It was almost two in the morning when he pulled everything together and submitted his responses. Even when he got into bed, however, sleep evaded him. His mind went recalling another encounter he had, just as strange, with the VA's opaque central leadership.

Earlier in the year, after his phone call with Terry Keane but before the paper had come out, Frueh accepted an invitation from the House Committee on Veterans' Affairs to testify before Congress. The day-long hearing had nothing to do with PTSD or disabled veterans; its subject was telemedicine— another of Frueh's research specialties and a procedural matter with far less baggage. The VA approved Frueh for the testimony and even offered to cover his travel to Washington—with a catch. Several weeks before the hearing, Frueh was to submit his remarks to the VA's Central Office for vetting. He understood that the VA would review his speech and reserved the right to make adjustments. But when he got his statement back, it no longer resembled anything he wrote. "They literally took my remarks and rewrote them," he said. It struck him as a scene out of George Orwell's *1984*.

More puzzling was that his remarks had already been remarkably tame: he had simply addressed some of the recent developments within the telemedicine field, explained that the research was ongoing, and that further evaluations were needed to better understand the full scope of the technology's benefits and challenges. Even so, the VA insisted on their own text—a "VA is wonderful and we're doing all these incredible things for veterans rah-rah kind of speech," Frueh said. The administration's key concern seemed to be less about advancing public knowledge, or avoiding controversy, or even presenting its work accurately. It was about control, Frueh thought. More than anything else, the VA wished to maintain complete authority over its employees and messaging.

Frueh had packed his finest suit and flown to Washington, D.C. He was restless; the idea of playing the part of the VA's designated mouthpiece bothered him. When he heard his name called in the hearing room, he took a deep breath and realized he couldn't bring himself to recite the agency's script. He delivered his original remarks. As soon as he left the chamber, he braced himself for the repercussions.

None came. "No one ever said a word," Frueh recalled. The other VA staffers at the testimony—both the medical professionals like himself and the representatives from Central Office—were all friendly and gracious, their behavior toward him unchanged from before. Frueh thought he was breaking out in defiance, and he had been prepared to face the consequences. Instead it was as if no one had even noticed. He was left scratching his head.

The incident replayed in his mind as he arrived at the VA the next morning. This time the stakes felt much higher. The substance and integrity of his research on veterans—the main through-line of his professional career—was being called into question, and he already knew from his call with Terry Keane that the VA did not approve of his findings.

Shortly before seven, he was met by two of the hospital's top research heads in the director's office. They assured Frueh that they were on his side and would help defend his work if necessary. Together they went through the papers Frueh had retrieved. The call began.

"To this day I don't know who was on the other end of the line," Frueh says. "It was never clear to me why I was being interviewed or by who."

Yet regardless of who sat on the other end asking questions, Frueh had diligently prepared his responses. *Yes, that form is here. Yes, we have the signatures. Yes, the IRB approved it.* After about an hour, the interviewers signaled the end of the meeting. Just like that, the call was over.

Frueh looked at his two colleagues in the room. "Now what?"

They shrugged.

"And that was it," Frueh said. "We never heard another word about it. We never got a response later, never got an explanation, never got anything."

A STRIKE was launched, and Frueh had successfully parried. It was soon followed by a censor. Frueh's article had started attracting attention—first from the academic and mental health communities, then among mainstream media outlets. VA employees were not permitted to grant interviews without express approval from the agency's public relations department, and Frueh was promptly assigned a media handler named Tanya.

Every time Frueh received an interview request, he was required to forward the reporter's contact to Tanya, who cross-checked the details of the interview with the article's intended purpose. She then submitted the proposal for clearance from the VA's Central Office. The procedure could take a week or more. Facing deadlines, some reporters dropped out, while on other occasions the requests were denied—as was the case with a BBC journalist—without any explanation.

Approved media requests carried the condition that Tanya would be present. If the interview was conducted in person, Tanya was right there sitting by Frueh's side; if it was a phone interview, Tanya was also there listening from another line. She was never shy about cutting Frueh off mid-sentence: "Don't answer that. That's outside the scope of the approved interview." Other times she would address the reporter directly: "Strike that from the record. The response is outside the scope of his expertise." Frueh found her presence smothering. He felt as if he was being treated like a child, or someone stifled under authoritarian rule—"like I was living in a communist country where my words and thoughts were being dictated to me," he said.

Still, as time passed, the study's findings, and their implications, spread to a bigger and bigger audience. Within the VA, Frueh's reputation grew—though not always in the most complimentary ways. Some colleagues viewed him as a troublemaker, intentionally out to be provocative. Others admired the courage it took to publish such controversial research. Broad support from the scientific community helped Frueh offset the psychological toll from receiving hate mail—sometimes even threats of violence—from members of the public. Anonymous emails landed in his inbox accusing him of being a "war profiteer," or of being motivated by the wish to cut veterans spending. Nothing made Frueh feel more misunderstood. "I *work* for veterans. What I want to do is see a better, more healthy, and more effective allocation of resources for them," he said. His co-workers in Charleston helped to reassure him that his work was meaningful—though that didn't spare him from the occasional teasing. "Hey Chris," they asked in the mornings, "when you walked in, did your eyes scan the rooflines for snipers?"

Among the most high-profile interviews Frueh gave was with National Public Radio, as part of an ongoing series called "The Impact of War." Producers from NPR had reached out and scheduled a phone call, with Tanya, as usual, listening in. The segment broadcast in May 2006. At the time, recent data released by the VA showed that the number of veterans receiving PTSD disability compensation had increased seven times as fast as recipients for any other disorder, and the interview highlighted Frueh's research as one of the possible factors explaining the dramatic surge. Featured in the same segment was another expert in the trauma field, someone Frueh had admired for a long time: Richard McNally.

The pair had met in person for the first time the previous year, though they had known of one another's work for longer and even cited some of each other's research. On a trip to Boston visiting relatives, Frueh had reached out, and the two psychologists met for a burger in Harvard Square. They discovered a shared attitude toward asking the tough questions. McNally "doesn't judge people on their titles, or academic affiliations, or how much money they have," Frueh said. "He looks at the ideas they bring, and he didn't like to see a fellow scientist get bullied." For his part, McNally was full of praise for Frueh's research. Advancements in trauma research frequently led into a dangerous minefield—"there's always some brouhaha going on," McNally says—but that made it all the more important to get to the truth. "The best way to serve victims of war is to find out what the truth actually is about post-traumatic stress disorder," McNally had said to NPR. "Avoiding trying to find out what the truth of the matter is, is no way to serve anyone."

Yet this belief in the power of ideas and the infallibility of data also exposed him to attack. In the summer of 2006, Columbia University epidemiologist Bruce Dohrenwend published a breakthrough analysis in *Science* magazine, revisiting the landmark 1988 National Vietnam Veterans Readjustment Study and aiming to resolve the lingering debate over its results. Dohrenwend and his team had devised more precise measurements for determining trauma exposure, then used them to recalculate all the numbers from the original sample. In the end, they found that there was little evidence to suggest wide-scale fraud among the respondents, but concluded that the NVVRS had indeed overestimated the prevalence of PTSD.[1] While the original survey reported almost a third of Vietnam vets developing PTSD after the war, the new estimates were far more modest. Dohrenwend found that 18.7 percent of Vietnam vets developed war-related PTSD at some point in their lives, with 9.1 percent still afflicted roughly a decade after the war.[2]

The revised figures were widely admired for their rigor, and McNally joined his colleagues in praise. He then built upon them by conducting his own calculations. McNally believed that Dohrenwend's results might still have been inflated because his team had counted in the PTSD group veterans showing mild "sub-diagnostic" symptoms—people who McNally considered as "generally functioning pretty well." By distinguishing between minor life issues and issues that warranted genuine clinical treatment, McNally ran the analysis again counting only veterans who had exhibited "clinically significant impairment"—the same standard set by most insurance companies for compensation. The rates fell again: 11 percent lifetime and only 5.4 percent in 1988, the year the original survey had been conducted.

These figures were much closer to what one would expect given the broader scientific literature, yet when McNally presented his methodology at an annual trauma symposium a few months later, his findings provoked derision and outrage. Three commentators who followed his presentation described the work as "misleading," "immoderate," full of "spin," and issued a call for more "responsible" research, stopping just short of outright accusing McNally of lying. "What I would like to do is to swear Rich and other critics in under oath to tell the truth, the whole truth, and nothing but the truth," said one prominent trauma specialist. "If that were done, you would have seen an entirely different presentation, I think."

McNally was unprepared for how sharp, and how personal, the animus would become. One audience member wondered aloud, "Is Rich McNally the anti-Christ?" Peals of derisive laughter scattered through the crowd. Another attendant later reflected that the whole affair revealed "traumatology to be a field in crisis."

The experience was unsettling. "It was like a lynch mob," McNally recalled. "Self-censorship was the order of the day." But it was not his first time in the line of fire. In the wake of the 9/11 World Trade Center attacks, he had watched as a swell of well-intentioned grief and crisis professionals traveled to New York to provide intervention treatments believed to help mitigate the onset of PTSD and other psychological distress.[3] Alongside two colleagues from the U.K., McNally published a controversial article detailing how these psychological debriefings in fact had little effect on patients' recovery, and in some cases might have caused more harm than good. "We caught all kinds of flak for that initially," he recalled. "But then the whole field turned around. We changed the opinion there."

He stepped into a bigger squabble with the 2003 publication of his book, *Remembering Trauma,* which re-ignited decades of discord among traumatologists over the proper approach to repressed memories of child abuse. Throughout the decades, "when scientific data are perceived as clashing with efforts on behalf of victims, there have been ugly scenes," observed the psychiatrist Sally Satel, a resident scholar at the American Enterprise Institute.[4] Elizabeth Loftus, a cognitive psychologist known for her groundbreaking research on how easily memories can be manipulated, was accused of sympathizing with child molesters after she presented her research as expert testimony at criminal trials. In another case, a study on the modern epidemics of hysteria drew death threats to its author, the literary scholar Elaine Showalter. Yet McNally had also seen that "good arguments in the trauma field can sometimes change things." Even on the explosive issue of repressed childhood trauma, he was eventually able to "shift the whole dialogue and put the controversy to rest," he said. With some more time and understanding, he had cause to believe that the lightning rod of veterans' PTSD, too, might lose its charge.

FRUEH FOLLOWED THE COMMOTION from Hawaii. In 2007, he left the VA to take a faculty position at the University of Hawaii-Hilo. He had been promoted to director of the Charleston VA's PTSD clinic a few years earlier, but although he got along well with his local leadership, the suspicion and bureaucracy from the VA's central office were becoming too much to bear. Still, the Medical University of South Carolina, his local VA's affiliate institution, housed one of the best psychiatric programs in the country, and some colleagues, including McNally, were baffled by his choice to leave.

"Rich actually had the best reaction," Frueh recalled. "He told me it was like going from the New York Yankees—the major leagues—to a Double-A club team." Nevertheless, Frueh and his wife were excited to make a big change. His last day at the VA, after fourteen years on the inside, was uneventful. His confrontations with the administration's entrenched interests, though, were far from over.

When he heard about the trouble that embroiled McNally at the trauma conference, he knew exactly what his friend was going through. For standing by research that dared to question assumptions the established veterans community held dear, their work was systematically marginalized within the VA. To an extent, they were also personally targeted, cast out as pariahs. "I had junior colleagues at the National Center for PTSD who would tell me, 'Oh yeah, when you and Rich's names come up, people start to say, *Those are bad guys and we need to watch out for them*,'" said Frueh. "Rich and I probably formed a bit of an alliance by being identified as the enemies of PTSD by the in-crowd. Of course, neither one of us is an enemy at all. We just want the data to reflect what's really going on there." As McNally liked to say, the problem, too often, was the "advocacy tail wagging the scientific dog."

One mysterious incident gave Frueh some hope. In his final months before departing the VA, amidst his disintegrating relationship with the central office, he received a phone call at his office. An unfamiliar voice on the other line introduced himself as Mike. Mike revealed he was calling from Washington, D.C., where he was in charge of helping direct veterans policy at the VA headquarters. "I know you're getting some heat from within the VA right now," Mike said, "but I just want you to know that you've got some friends up here too. You've got some people up here who appreciate what you're doing."

Before Frueh could think of how to respond, Mike went on. "I'm not just talking for myself," he said, mentioning that Jim Nicholson—the Secretary of the VA at the time—was a close personal friend. Over pizza recently, Mike said they discussed the surge in disabled veterans, particularly those diagnosed with PTSD, and Frueh's research had come up. Mike was familiar with all the latest trend lines.[5] From 1999 to 2004, veterans receiving PTSD disability benefits rose by 80 percent, compared to a 12 percent increase in vets with other disabilities. The VA's total PTSD payments rose by 150 percent over the same period, almost quadruple the 42 percent rise in payments for other disability categories. He also cited a 2005 Office of the Inspector General's report that found a quarter of disability claims had been approved without sufficient evidence of combat exposure.

The figures deeply concerned him. "He believed that we were turning the VA into not a healthcare organization, but an organization that's there to provide disability and little else," Frueh recalled. Before hanging up, Mike reiterated his support. In the ensuing years, Frueh thought back to that phone call often, even as the worrisome trends deepened and the atmosphere intensified. Many of the disability claimants to flood the VA in the first years after 9/11 had been older veterans from the Vietnam era, filing for compensation as they approached or entered retirement age. But as the wars in Iraq and Afghanistan matured, a younger generation of service members were sinking into the disability system at much higher rates, and with longer lists of recorded impairments.

Frueh watched the VA struggle to keep up with its burgeoning disability crisis. As a young man, he had taken a factory job during his summers away from college; tireless and driven, he had been hungry to make extra cash to help pay his way through school. His co-workers at the factory took notice of his initiative, and they weren't happy about it. Frueh remembered, "Their concern was I was upping the benchmark for what they should be expected to produce. I was making them look bad. They would tap me on the shoulder, 'Hey bud, what's the rush? You're working pretty hard, maybe you ought to pace yourself a little bit.' And that's what I saw at the VA."

While the rest of the country saw a mass of broken soldiers coming home, saddled with unfixable mental disorders, Frueh saw a malfunctioning system inflating diagnoses and undermining recovery. And he saw the embedded bureaucrats who gained from the widespread decline. "Pick any large bureaucracy and you've got people who are on the inside tracks. Career officials in the VA or the DOD—people who've based their entire professional lives on veterans and PTSD and injury, who want to keep their power and their funding base," he said. These folks perhaps believed they were acting in the best interest of veterans, Frueh thought, but the truth was that their power and influence hinged on the established narrative of sick veterans *only ever getting sicker.* Any alternative was a threat to their stature.

The bureaucracy ignored statistics that Frueh could not. One study found that 94 percent of veterans seeking mental health treatment at the VA concurrently applied for PTSD disability benefits; meanwhile, only half of those applying for PTSD benefits also sought out psychiatric care for their conditions. "They will explain away all of the potential evidence," Frueh said—of malingering, of benefits-seeking, of financial inducements impeding treatment and rehabilitation. Frueh said, "I've been told in private to just lay off. They'll say, 'Don't mess with these issues. It's politically explosive. We don't want veterans to lose their services.' But ultimately, it's not about the veterans. It's about them. It's about preserving their position and their funding."

The VA held a "virtual monopoly" on behavioral science research relating to veterans, Frueh went on. "In a lot of ways, this puts clinicians in a bind. Nobody was willing to study it, to talk about it on the record. Most people would shrug their shoulders and say, 'the VA doesn't want to hear it.'" As he began attracting more attention and pushback from the central office, some of his own colleagues began ducking him in the halls, avoiding assignments with him, concerned that they might become collateral damage by association. What they told him in private was a different matter: "Chris, I know you're right. The VA system is driving me crazy, the disability is harmful to veterans, but I need the job. The pay here is good and I have lifetime job security as a federal employee. So don't rock the boat."

The attitude remains in place today. A regular speaker at universities and conferences on veterans' mental health, Frueh encounters new people at every event who share his views and support his work. "It's very common that they'll come up to me after and say, 'Hey, I really admire what you did, good for you for speaking out about it. I work at the VA now and I see it's a real problem.' I get that kind of thing a lot over the years. It's an open secret across disciplines," Frueh said.

As the years have passed and the conditions have degraded further, the more unlikely his phone call with Mike has seemed. Secret meetings, confidential pledges of support—it all seemed to Frueh like something out of a John le Carré spy novel, not the life of an academic psychologist. The only way to make sense of it was to consider that, perhaps, there had been a moment when the prospect of real change appeared possible.

"There's a fragmentation that exists in any large organization," Frueh reflected. "There were factions in the VA at the time. Certain people were saying, 'We must attend to this issue. There is a problem of veterans either gaming the system or buying into the disability narrative, which in itself can be harmful to them.' My guess is there were people within the VA who were looking at this and who wanted to change it at the time." Buoyed by the sentiments, his voice had sounded confident when he told NPR in 2006 that the field was heading toward an inflection point: "People are starting to wonder about these things more. It's gathered a lot of momentum." But that moment, he conceded, had passed. The inflection point never came. And his optimism, brief as it was, has faded.

CHAPTER 14
COLLUSION

FRUEH'S 2005 STUDY remains one of the best-known in his career—a bright spot in a small but ongoing effort to properly care for veterans passing through the VA. Yet at many of the administration's hospitals around the country, claimed disabilities are blindly accepted as fact, while the professional judgments of many clinicians are institutionally sidelined or suppressed. The steep rise in recipients on the VA's disability payroll represents both cause and symptom of this permissive, and ultimately dangerous, attitude.

At the center of the VA's procedure for determining disability compensation is the C&P exam, which establishes a link between a veteran's military service and his claimed conditions, and designates the level of impairment involved. C&P exams are forensic in nature, meaning they are designed to answer legal questions arising directly from US statutes, regulations, and case law—not medical questions. The practice of forensic psychology is governed by an exacting set of standards; whether such forensic exams are employed to assess witness credibility for court, evaluate child custody in divorce, or help design correctional programs, they demand a high level of rigor from the certified psychologists who conduct them.[1]

Yet in conducting these exams, particularly for mental health disorders, the VA often operates according to its own set of rules, divorced from common benchmarks observed in the rest of the field. "When I got to the VA, I was shocked," said Mark Worthen, who was hired in 2010 to conduct C&P exams for the VA in Shreveport, Louisiana. A seasoned practitioner of mental health evaluations,

Worthen joined the VA with twenty years of experience in clinical psychology, having previously worked on cases ranging from workplace violence to juvenile court. He noticed immediate differences in how disability evaluations were conducted in his new environment, and became alarmed by "how much lower the standards were."

Among the first things Worthen noticed was the scarcity of any scholarly literature on the VA's evaluation methods. While the forensic psychology field boasted thousands of peer-reviewed articles on everything from personal injury and employment discrimination to a subject's mental status at the time of a violent offense, there was hardly any published research looking at C&P exams. Worse, Worthen discovered that a structural tension often dictated the dynamics between C&P examiners and their supervisors. The year he was hired, the VA had already begun to feel the increased weight from mounting caseloads. The agency's response had been to emphasize the speedy processing of claims, frequently at the expense of accuracy, a top-down pressure that would only amplify during Worthen's tenure.

In 2011, Worthen transferred to the VA medical center in Asheville, North Carolina, where he joined a C&P staff continually driven to "increase productivity," he said. By then, he had become familiar with the name Christopher Frueh, having read much of the prolific clinician's work from the previous decade—particularly Frueh's scholarship on the prevalence of PTSD malingering among veterans, as well as the symptom validity measures necessary to detect it. Researching in his own spare time, Worthen discovered that the VA had published its own "best practice manual" for PTSD C&P exams in 2002, overseen by the National Center for PTSD and even listing Dr. Terry Keane as a contributor. The comprehensive manual stated plainly that the exams required "up to three hours to complete, [while] complex cases may demand additional time."[2] It provided a detailed breakdown of the necessary components in a proper evaluation:

- Records review (30 minutes)
- Orientation to interview, review military history, and conduct trauma assessment (20 minutes)
- PTSD symptom assessment and diagnosis (40 minutes)
- Mental status examination and multiaxial DSM-IV diagnoses (20 minutes)
- Psychosocial history and assessment of change in social and occupational functioning (30 minutes)
- Report preparation (50 minutes)
- Psychometric assessment (additional time required, if administered)

Worthen realized that guidelines for how to properly conduct veterans' disability exams did exist—they were composed, in fact, by the VA's own panel of PTSD experts. So why didn't the VA take them seriously? "I was reading all these reports and guidelines and saying to myself, 'Wait a minute, we have these [resources] that are well-written and well-referenced and consistent with the professional standards in psychiatry and psychology.' And yet none of these things were being followed by the VA." When Worthen and his colleagues took the necessary time to conduct a rigorous evaluation, "we found ourselves having to defend ourselves to the C&P clinic director," he said.

The imperative to meet certain targets was crowding out the ethical obligation Worthen felt to conduct his cases with diligence. He had joined the VA at a time when disability claims were growing almost five times faster than the administration's ability to process them.[3] "When you don't have enough providers and you get inundated with these numbers, you don't have time to think, you don't even have time to complain," said Alex Montelongo, the claims examiner from El Paso, Texas. One VA employee, given orders to complete an unrealistic number of claims, likened his supervisor to "the type of person who thinks they can get a baby in one month by getting nine women pregnant."

As their caseloads continued to rise, some VA doctors took to working weekends in order to avoid compromising on the quality of their exams.[4] Others took the easier route, simply allowing their standards to lapse. A 2014 Government Accountability Office investigation found examiners who sped through their evaluations in fifteen minutes or less.

When Montelongo approached his managers to request more time for his appointments, they offered him a different solution. "What they started telling me was, 'Don't ask these questions because the veterans are going to answer yes, and then you've got to check it.' They were basically telling me what not to do, what not to ask, what not to check. And they were saying, 'If the veterans tell you this or that, well, just give it to them, it's okay.'" An internal VA statement from December 2012 prohibited C&P examiners from considering "personal information about a veteran or service member found on the Internet or through social media" in completing their evaluations.[5] In other words, clear inconsistencies between a veteran's clinical presentation or claims of impairment and evidence of social functioning found easily with a Facebook search were barred from use in exams.

Under the pressures of these top-down quotas, rules are skirted and corners are cut. In 2010, the VA introduced its Disability Benefits Questionnaires, standardized evaluation forms used in determining a veteran's disability rating that aimed to simplify a complex procedure.[6] But VA claims workers have complained that the DBQs place undue weight on a veteran's self-reported ailments, neglecting consideration of their military records, medical histories, and other important evidence. The result is a dismantled, performative process: "moving checked boxes from one place to another," as one claims processor put it, so mindless that "a monkey could do it."[7]

At the Shreveport VA where Worthen had been first hired, he benefited from several weeks of comprehensive training and was able to shadow his colleagues to learn from their C&P appointments. His hospital's lead psychologist, who also conducted the evaluations, was sympathetic to how challenging they could be. As best he could, he had buffered his team against the time pressures imposed from above and fought to maintain a caseload of ten thorough examinations per week.

After moving to Asheville, Worthen began to realize how the VA operated in other parts of the country. Colleagues shared stories of VA hospitals where C&P examiners needed to complete fifteen, twenty, twenty-five cases a week. One job posting at a Northeast VA site stated that psychologists would be expected to complete as many as six face-to-face appointments with patients a day. Worthen was stunned. "All you've got to do is read the ethical standards as a psychologist and it's pretty obvious. If you're doing thirty of these evaluations a week, there's no way you're doing an ethical job," he said.

Worthen came from a long line of public servants. His grandfather had served as a judge and his father worked as a military physician. Worthen still remembers watching his dad come home each evening in his immaculate Navy uniform. "We were always brought up to respect men and women in the military," he said, making the broken practices he witnessed at the VA that much harder to swallow. "It became apparent that this was not a reliable system. It was so unfair to veterans and veterans' families—and also to the taxpayers." One day, he heard about an online listserv where C&P examiners around the country could reach one another and discuss their experiences. He quickly became one of the group's most active members, regularly posting new research and interesting articles, as well as ideas for how to improve their evaluation process.

Dispersed around the country, C&P examiners have turned to the listserv as a space for refuge and counsel. "For me, it's the most valuable thing we have because the training the VA gives us is laughable," said one C&P psychologist from the Midwest. "It's where I've learned the most about how to do my job."

Among his colleagues online, Worthen soon developed a welcomed reputation as an outsized personality, vocal about his opinions while generous with his time and advice. It was a role he happily filled. "The main advantage of the listserv is the peer consultation," he said. "There's really no other way for C&P psychologists to advance their education, training, and experience for conducting such complex forensic examinations, other than this listserv."

And it was through this listserv that he first got in touch with a colleague from the VA medical center in Tampa, Florida, a fellow C&P psychologist by the name of Robert Moering.

EIGHT EXAMS A DAY. That's what Robert Moering was told at his job interview for an open C&P position at the Tampa VA in the fall of 2007. By then in his career, Moering had already conducted thousands of disability evaluations for Social Security claims—relatively straightforward assessments that he had managed to drill down to forty-five minutes per appointment. The VA's expectations, he thought at the time, seemed reasonable. "At that point, I didn't know anything about the process," he recalled. "They were saying these are basic disability evaluations, that they could easily be done within an hour." He took the job.

By the end of his first week, Moering was certain that to fulfill the VA's expectations, to actually complete eight exams a day, would amount to malpractice. "It was just not possible," he said. "You can't do it. Or at least, you can't do it ethically." His Social Security evaluations had been relatively lean assessments of a claimant's present symptoms and capacity to function in the workplace. But the VA's C&P exams, he found, were "a far more in-depth assessment than what I was initially led to believe." They required the medical practitioner to analyze the subject's military, medical, employment and social histories, constructing elaborate portraits of the veteran before and after their service in order to determine whether specific conditions could be proven connected to, or aggravated by, the military. "I can't tell you whether their [disability] is related to their service or not without knowing all their background and all these details. It's not just a matter of what their current social life or current symptomology is like, but understanding that through their lifespan,"

Moering said. Compared to Social Security exams, it was like putting a grade-school worksheet next to the SATs.

When he raised the issue with his VA's hospital directors, their
first response was skepticism: *What's changed? Why can't you perform
when you said you could?* Moering explained how the two types
of evaluations were incomparable and requested a more manageable caseload. Soon his required evaluations were scaled back to
six exams a day, and then a few weeks later, to five. "It was still
nowhere near the amount of time" necessary for a thorough evaluation, Moering said, but as a fresh hire, he appreciated that his
supervisors had at least heard him out and reduced his workload,
if only by a little.

By the end of the month, his attention had moved on to another
pernicious issue: "It became very clear that there were people who
were just exaggerating." This was before Moering knew about Frueh
and the deep well of research on veterans' malingering; his intro-
duction to the problem came from basic common sense. One of
his early appointments was with a Vietnam veteran claiming PTSD
for disability benefits. "He's telling me one of his symptoms was
an extreme severe problem with startled response. Any little noise
makes him jump to the ground and roll around, happens multiple
times a day with him," Moering recounted. At the time, his office
was in a section of trailers outside the main VA facility that had
recently been converted into office space. They were located beside
the parking lot. As Moering proceeded with his clinical interview, a
motorcycle right below his window suddenly revved its engine. The
sound was deafening. "Even I was jumping out of my skin at the
sound of it," Moering said. And yet with his patient—nothing.

"He had absolutely no reaction whatsoever to this loud sudden noise. I know he doesn't have a hearing problem because we're
talking in a normal level. He's going through his story about all his
trauma, how many people were getting shot at and killed. In my
mind I'm like, 'Wait a minute, you're telling me one thing but you're
showing me something different.' We have this serious inconsistency.

Very quickly I'm getting to realize that if I just put down on paper, 'Veteran reports extreme problems with startled response,' that's not the whole story."

Moering began to encounter other cases, many of them, where he suspected the patients were presenting crude and false signals, picked up perhaps from a website or some other questionable source. "You see posts that say, 'Make sure when you go in you haven't had a bath in three days,' or 'Don't change your clothes in a week,' or 'Present yourself at your absolute worst.'" Among the most cited triggers, he found, was the sound of a car backfiring, a trope that agitated Moering to no end.

"Well north of 50 percent of people claiming PTSD will give an example of startled response as hearing a car backfire. I can tell you one time in the past seven years I've heard a vehicle backfire, and that was a school bus. So are the 50 percent-plus of these people truly hearing this frequent number of cars backfiring, or are they getting this information somewhere and sharing it? Seriously, when was the last time you heard a car backfire?"

Usually the difference between a malingered, or exaggerated, account and a genuine one was impossible to miss. When veterans spoke truthfully about their experiences, the stories rang with a specificity that was striking. One veteran, in talking about the one instance he had been provoked by a noise, said that he had been traveling with some friends in a small van. After getting out, someone went to slide the van's door shut, and the whirring skid of the sliding door, for an instant, suddenly conjured the sound of an RPG zooming by his head. The veteran said his body reacted on its own, tensing up and getting ready to dive, but in the next instant, he saw that the sound had come from the van's door, and he was able to quickly settle down.

Another time, Moering evaluated a veteran who shared that he had walked past a metal trash container just as someone tossed in an empty Coke can. The veteran jumped; the hollow ricochet of the tumbling Coke had sounded exactly like a bullet's ricochet. Such stories "fit," Moering said. "They're giving me situations that are unique, not something you can go and read about it." Though such genuine accounts did happen, they were not the norm.

As a veteran himself who had served for a decade in the Marine Corps until 1998, Moering knew that his military background granted him a certain status with his patients that most civilian examiners did not receive: "It gave me an instant credibility and rapport with every veteran that came into my office," he said. Patients would notice the Marine Corps lanyard around his collar or the magnets on his filing cabinet; they sure wouldn't miss the massive eagle, globe, and anchor cutout in front of his office window. These signs usually put his patients at ease, assuring them that they were being evaluated by one of their own.

Outside his work, Moering encountered plenty of vets at gatherings and veterans' halls who didn't bother to hide their feelings about what they were due. "They owe us," and "We deserve everything we can get" were commonly overheard refrains. He noticed a similar stance from many of the vets who came into his office for compensation claims, a sense of entitlement that was felt as much as said. *They owe us. You're a veteran too, you get that. You understand that we should be getting everything we can.* Moering was careful not to extrapolate too much; nobody from his appointments ever came right out with it, but their tone was difficult to ignore. His suspicions prompted him to take more care with his evaluations, in order to weed out the opportunists and usurpers and ensure that he got it right.

Unlike typical forensic mental health examinations, including the disability claims Moering used to evaluate for Social Security, the VA's C&P exams are governed by their own set of rules. Most forensic psychologists and psychiatrists are expected to treat their patients from a professional distance, and to exercise a standard known as "beyond a reasonable doubt," or "preponderance of the evidence," in which a diagnosis must be supported by the majority of the available evidence before the determination can be made. The VA, meanwhile, requires C&P examiners to be uniquely "pro-claimant," blurring the line between objectivity and advocacy. They are instructed to apply an "equipoise" standard to evaluations, a lower measure of proof in which a diagnosis is rendered when there is evidence to show the claim is "at least as likely as not" to be true. None of this should prevent C&P examiners from diligently performing their duties, but many at the VA have found the unconventional customs cited in blocking efforts to root out possible malingerers.

Federal oversight agencies have long raised concerns over rising incidents of fraud and abuse within the VA's disability compensation system.[8] In 2005, an Office of Inspector General report highlighted the "increased risk of not identifying fraudulent claims"—particularly in PTSD claims, which the OIG had singled out for investigation due to their greater vulnerability to fraud.[9] The report's finding prompted a committee review by the Institute of Medicine (IOM) into how it was diagnosing PTSD.

After a series of hearings, the IOM committee in 2006 endorsed the existing diagnostic standards from the *DSM-IV*. But concerns that healthy claimants were simply seeking financial gain drew a renewed commitment to more rigorous testing and ensuring the accuracy of C&P diagnoses. Committee member Darrel Regier, executive director of the American Psychiatric Institute for Research and Education, stressed that VA psychologists should avail themselves of all ready assessment tools in order to help detect malingering; even then, he insisted, there could be no substitute for their own medical experience and expertise. "Part of the reason for asking that clinically well-trained people evaluate patients is to avoid over-diagnosing people faking PTSD," he said.[10]

In 2007, the Institute of Medicine released two additional reports to clarify the purpose and best practice for the VA's C&P evaluations. Among veterans seeking or receiving disability benefits, the reports reiterated the large body of empirical research chronicling the prevalence of "symptom elevation," "over-reporting," "exaggeration," and "extreme exaggeration."[11] Another paper, published in a prominent psychiatry journal not long after, was titled: "Posttraumatic Stress Disorder Can Easily Be Faked, But Faking Can Be Detected in Most Cases."[12]

In early 2008, a few months into the job, Moering called for another meeting with his supervisors. By then he had evaluated too many veterans not to notice the pattern. "It became very clear that there were people who were just exaggerating," he said. "Just doing a simple clinical interview was not going to be enough to capture what was going on. We needed to do testing with it." His supervisors pushed back on his request: "It's never been done before so why should we do it now? Do we really need to?"

For Gail Poyner, there was no doubt the answer was yes. A licensed psychologist in private practice, Poyner was contracted by the VA to evaluate veterans applying for PTSD and TBI compensation benefits. As she started conducting the VA's C&P exams, she became "increasingly disturbed" by the "astonishingly large number" of patients for whom "the finding of symptom feigning [was] simply unavoidable." Poyner approached her evaluations the way she had been trained: for each patient, she performed a clinical interview, a review of background and collateral materials, and some structured testing. She soon learned that her process made her the exception, not the rule. She reviewed more than one hundred diagnostic and follow-up disability evaluations, and found only one occasion in which a malingering screen had been conducted by another VA practitioner.

Before long, Poyner was directly prohibited by the VA from using "malingering" as a diagnosis, no matter how many red flags the veteran she was evaluating raised.

In a 2010 *Psychological Injury and Law* article, she wrote that the VA's "underlying political climate influences what are otherwise supposed to be objective and professional assessments of psychiatric disability claims. After two years of conducting C&P exams, her contract was cancelled by the VA. Because she used assessment tools designed to detect malingering—the same instruments advocated for in many of the field's best practice guidelines, including by the

VA itself—she was accused of presuming all veterans to be malingerers. The testing measures she used were unfair, Poyner was told,
because they "do not give the veteran the benefit of the doubt."[13]
Her previous cases, where she had determined that the claimants did
not meet the requirements for a PTSD diagnosis, were scheduled for
reexamination by other psychologists.

Internally, the VA has also demonstrated a preference for approving higher disability levels. David Dietz, the C&P examiner from
Ohio, found that his judgment frequently came under fire whenever
he determined that a veteran did not qualify for the disabilities they
were seeking. "When we don't give a diagnosis because [the veterans]
have invalidated the assessment instruction, our supervisors give us
blowback," he said. In cases where the veteran has been granted a
more severe diagnosis by clinicians from the treatment side, the questions from his managers can be especially patronizing: *Why aren't we
using the clinical judgement? Why aren't we taking the treatment provider's diagnosis as being true?* Dietz has found the additional labor of
defending his proper practices exhausting. "Treatment and forensic
examinations have two different sets of guidelines," he said. "I can't
just take people at their word. I've got to get more verification."

On the treatment side, meanwhile, many clinicians and care
providers confront a headache of their own: patients who just want
to be rated sick. "We document clearly, in their medical records,
that their stated goal is to increase their disability rating," said Scott
Carow, the former head of rehab at Fort Bliss. Carow knew that
such cases were a waste of everyone's time, but what do you do with
them? When a veteran has expressly stated their wish to *raise* their
disability levels—that they wish to be considered *more* impaired, not
less—how are they supposed to improve from physical therapy, or
from any of the other recovery services Carow tried to provide?

Often, the easiest thing to do was shuffle these cases through,
clearing out the individuals who simply wished to cash in so that
treatment could better be portioned to others who actually wanted
it. "That's the path that gets them out of your clinic because that's

what they are wanting—for you to inflate their disability ratings," said Carow. "Then there's less room or need for these guys to appeal. That's the path of least resistance."

And the path of least resistance, duplicated across a broken system, leads to a proliferation of bad outcomes. "I feel somewhat powerless to do anything about it," Carow said. Despite all his qualifications and experience—two doctorate degrees and more than twenty years in the military—despite the resources and personnel granted to his rehabilitation outpost, often he feels like one small log, failing to staunch the powerful flow of a big, wide river.

IT TOOK SIX MONTHS before Moering and his C&P colleagues were granted permission to use the additional assessment tools. They had prepared a presentation to make their case, informing their supervisors that to conduct exams without the available veracity testing would amount to shirking their professional ethics codes. Still, "we were just sitting in limbo for them to decide," Moering said. A 2011 survey of C&P mental health examiners revealed that 59 percent "rarely or never used" any additional testing in assessing their patients, while less than 10 percent regularly used any type of standardized diagnostic interview at all in their evaluations.[14]

When his team's request was finally approved in the summer of 2008, Moering said the effects were immediate. Before, "we didn't have the means, the resources, or the time" to ensure high-quality assessments, and often relied on a veteran's self-report alone. But after receiving permission to use instruments like the MMPI-2, "we were able to say, 'Look, we have this objective data. We can point to specific results to show that this person is saying one thing, but it may not be completely accurate.' The competence level definitely went up."

So, too, did the number of complaints filed against their C&P clinic. Moering says he had never received a single complaint before his department began using testing, but after the shift, their team of a half-dozen full and part-time C&P examiners began to receive one or more a month. The letters came from veterans who had been denied the diagnosis they were seeking, and accused their examiners of being rude and unprofessional, of barely asking questions and rushing them through.

"Nothing was further from the truth," Moering said. His appointments typically lasted at least two hours, frequently longer—time he had fought to get from his supervisors. He typed direct quotations into his reports whenever possible, often filling the forms with a hundred or more lines exactly as the patient had said. This material came in handy later, when Moering and his colleagues had to respond to each individual complaint; their previous notes supplied the evidence they needed to properly defend themselves.

But many C&P examiners, conducting disability evaluations at VA sites across the country, fell short of such rigor. When University of Minnesota researchers conducted a review of PTSD C&P exam reports, they found that even when measures like the MMPI were used, many of the vets who recorded a high likelihood of malingering or symptom-exaggeration still received the same service-connected disability ratings as those determined to be entirely honest and forthright.[15] Moering regularly encountered shoddy appraisals in the cases he reviewed. Often the veteran's treating psychiatrist had failed to test for the validity of their symptoms and simply endorsed whatever conditions the patient had claimed. In one particularly egregious example, he reviewed the files of a vet whose psychiatrist had replicated the same treatment notes after every appointment going back five years. "The same misspellings, the same punctuation errors, the same word and character counts. The notes didn't change," Moering said. "Is that guy providing an accurate assessment then? You tell me." In another case, he met with a PTSD patient who had nothing to support the diagnosis in his psychiatrist's treatment notes. "There was not even a single symptom in there. It was just a diagnosis and an opinion on the diagnosis with zero justification."

Moering aired his frustrations in the listserv for mental health C&P examiners, where he found common cause with other conscientious psychologists. Like Mark Worthen, he soon established himself as one of the most prominent voices in the group, frequently responding to queries and drawing attention to flaws he witnessed in the VA's procedures. In 2010, Worthen introduced Moering to Barton Evans, a VA psychologist who was editing a special issue for the *Psychology Injury and Law* journal devoted entirely to VA mental health exams.[16] Evans had invited Worthen to submit an article for the issue, and Worthen asked Moering to collaborate. Together, they stitched together a deeply sourced, peer-reviewed "how-to" manual for all practitioners in their line of work.

Noting Moering's military experience, Evans also commissioned a separate article from him, aimed at helping civilian C&P examiners more accurately review service personnel records. Moering was glad to accept. A joke he once heard had lodged in his mind, striking a little too close to the truth: "There were about 500 SEALs that operated in Vietnam and I've met all 20,000 of them."[17] He viewed the assignment as an opportunity to encourage a more discerning eye in his colleagues all around the country. Titled "Military Service Records: Searching for the Truth," his article was published in the December 2011 issue of *Psychology Injury and Law*, alongside his joint paper with Worthen, "A Practical Guide to Conducting VA Compensation and Pension Exams for PTSD and Other Mental Disorders."

Reactions to both pieces were overwhelmingly positive. "From my C&P colleagues at the VA, from other psychologists and psychiatrists, from people on the ground actually doing the work, there was really good response across the board," Moering said. He received emails and letters of gratitude, as well as warm notes from C&P directors pledging to make the papers required reading for their teams. To his surprise, even his local VA leadership had some kind words to say, and later granted their office additional evaluation time for more complex conditions.

But the goodwill didn't last long. At the VA, Moering continued to assess veterans whose behavior raised his suspicions. But even when he expressly cited the MMPI-2 and other testing results, showing high probability of symptom-exaggeration or malingering, the claimants kept qualifying for inflated rewards. No matter how much evidence Moering backed up his diagnosis with, or how much he pushed back on unjustified benefits, nothing seemed to curb the growth in disability payments.

Quite the opposite, the VA was presiding over a systematic campaign to expunge any suggestion of veterans' foul play from its disability operations. In its 2002 best practice guidelines for conducting PTSD exams, psychometric assessments had been deemed critical in evaluating cases with "findings of questionable validity." Yet updated guidelines released in 2010 erased any mention of symptom validity or malingering. Additionally, VA disability assessment training prior to 2010 had educated clinicians on the possibility of malingering among veterans, obligating C&P examiners to report all "misrepresentation of facts" whenever such instances were "detected or suspected." But in new training modules rolled out since, the terms "malingering" and "misrepresentation of facts" have no longer appeared.[18] Even after Moering and Worthen's guide to conducting mental health exams was released to widespread praise among practitioners, the VA declined to promote or recommend it. Meanwhile, the administration's own internal training continued to be "really inadequate," said Worthen. "It's four hours of online video, then you take this online test and you have to get 80 percent of the answers right. It's not enough."

Doctors who stick to their field's professional standards and continue to consult validity measures have faced pushback from their superiors. One former VA chief psychologist emailed explicit prohibitions to his staff: "Please do not use the diagnosis of malingering. If the testing shows suboptimal performance, please defer the diagnosis. Also, we need to focus ONLY on the test materials and not make any comments that appear to question patients' reports of trauma." Other administrators have blown further past the line, reviewing patient records and modifying them directly. In one case, a veteran's "malingering" diagnosis was removed from his evaluation report, as well as pages of the C&P examiner's assessment notes because, according to the administration, they had "put the patient in a bad light."[19]

Yet denying the problems and censoring them did not make them disappear. Posting recently in the national C&P listserv, a VA clinician who had previously worked in the private sector wrote she was "not prepared for the extent of exaggeration and fabrication I see in the VA population."

She continued, "It has made me question at times whether I am truly providing a useful service. There may be [other doctors] who rejoice in bestowing a 'malingering' diagnosis, but the majority probably feel the way I do. I am disappointed and discouraged." The VA, she proposed, should be moving toward greater transparency and more support for fairness and accuracy, not in the opposite direction. "If I am going to document validity concerns/malingering, I feel more comfortable doing so in a way that is well studied and agreed upon by fellow colleagues in the field. If we really want to decrease and dismantle the malingering and exaggerated epidemic in the VA, we need to be good psychologists," the clinician wrote. "We need to look carefully at the system that is creating it and reinforcing it."

Every organization develops its own culture, and over time, becomes wedded to it. It is that culture which governs behavior and shapes what its members do and say—and what they don't. In the winter of 2014, Moering received a call from a *Los Angeles Times* reporter who was working to expose the pitfalls of the VA's PTSD claims process. Moering decided that he would publicly say what he knew many around him had long been afraid to: that the VA's disability system was badly broken, beset by deluded procedures and perverse incentives, and was perhaps precipitating more harmful outcomes than good ones. The reporter asked if he was willing to go on the record. "I had to think about it for all of ten seconds," Moering said. "Absolutely," he told the reporter. "Use my name. Quote me." He had nothing to hide.

The *Los Angeles Times* investigation was published in early August of 2014, while Moering was away for vacation. Citing a diverse network of mental health providers, researchers, and therapists, it laid out a damaging case against the VA's handling of its rising PTSD caseload. "This is the dilemma we face," Moering was quoted, describing a system of deterrents that prevented employees from successfully challenging bad diagnoses. The article was a striking departure from the dominant media coverage of victimizing veterans, and quickly got a lot of attention from inside the VA.

On the day Moering returned to work, he was summoned to his C&P director's office. He was informed that an investigation had been launched into his contact with the press, and that he would be suspended from interacting with veterans until further notice. But he was still required to come in. "For weeks, I would go into work, get there at seven, and then leave at the end of ten-hour days. I would've done absolutely nothing," he recalled. On December 28, Moering received a letter from his VA's hospital chief calling for his termination. The previous several months had been a long string of tense meetings and coded threats. An effort to degrade his end-of-year performance review had left him feeling betrayed and exhausted. Moering knew that all of it could be traced back to his decision to candidly speak about his experience of working at the VA. Yet even during the worst of it, he had no regrets.

"If you're speaking the truth and you believe what you're saying is important, then you should put your name behind it," he said. On the same day he received the letter, the VA confiscated his employee ID card and barred him from accessing his computer. He was asked to leave the premises. "After more than twenty years of federal service, I have found myself in a position where I appear to have no other option than to resign my position," he wrote in an official resignation notice. "I thank the VA for the opportunity to work with some of the finest professionals as well as the opportunity to serve veterans in a unique capacity."

In his final minutes at the office, as he cleared his desk and packed his belongings into a box, an administrator appeared in the doorway. She didn't say much but stood by, watching. Her eyes, Moering recalled, tracked his movements, following him until he had carried everything to his car, until he had started up the engine, until he had finally driven off the lot. Good riddance, he thought, as he left the VA behind.

IN NEW YORK, WILLIAM MCMATH had also come under fire. His director at the Northport VA hospital was receiving letters from Disabled American Veterans, a national VSO with a prominent local chapter, and on a Friday afternoon in the summer of 2014, McMath was called into his supervisor's office. He was told that numerous complaints, specifically targeting him, had been coming in from vets unhappy with the results of his C&P exams.

McMath was dismayed but not surprised. He had known for years that the availability of compensation could affect how patients presented their conditions. In the extensive literature on the problem, documented over decades by the likes of Frueh and others, such monetary benefits were referred to as "secondary gains," but McMath had begun to develop a more discerning view. "For many veterans, compensation is really the *primary* gain," he believed. Treatment and rehabilitation—the pillars that should have been at the center of what the VA offered—had instead become secondary.

In the preceding months, he and his colleagues at Northport had been called into mandatory meetings to discuss how they might improve the "veteran experience." It wasn't difficult to read between the lines. McMath understood that for all the pleasing rhetoric, the VA's concern for the "veteran experience" amounted to a binary: granting more benefits ensured a positive experience, while denying compensation, however justified the decision, meant a negative one—in which case the examiner invariably exposed himself to attacks.

By insisting on conducting what he viewed as ethical and principled mental health evaluations, McMath realized that he had developed a reputation for "being a hard ass"—not only among veterans but with some of his peers as well. He came to see that the VA produced a bifurcation among its ranks, where many clinicians and disability examiners, whether they knew it or not, sorted into one of two camps.

Most employees conformed to the VA's overarching philosophy, smoothing the way for their patients to receive ever-higher disability ratings and benefits. In group therapies at his VA's mental health clinic, McMath watched as the same rituals played on repeat. "The ultimate goal was to 'get 100 percent' and/or to be declared 'unemployable' because of PTSD symptoms," he reflected in an anonymous blog that he had begun to write. "It did not occur to [the veterans] or to the social workers who ran the groups that treatment was supposed to make them better, not worse, and that 'getting 100 percent' meant their VA group therapists and psychiatrists had failed them completely. In fact, since the increased percentages were supposed to be connected to worsening symptoms, those increases suggested that treatment may have actually worsened their illnesses."

A PTSD diagnosis seemed to assert its own gravity, crowding out everything else. Once, McMath and a colleague from the clinic interviewed a Navy veteran who said he was suffering from PTSD. The veteran described his symptoms as hearing voices and occasionally seeing things that weren't there—certain signs of schizophrenia—while nothing he divulged indicated he was having stress reactions to trauma. Yet as soon as the interview concluded, the psychiatrist turned to McMath. "Well, that was a classic case of PTSD," he said. "I think we can ignore the voices—they don't matter really."

Sometimes, even the veteran's own family members can face rebuke for questioning such assumptions. In one case, a veteran suffering painful skin and breathing problems had sought help from his local VA in Albuquerque. Though the symptoms were later attributed to constrictive bronchiolitis by a pulmonary specialist, his doctor at the VA insisted it was PTSD. When the veteran's wife questioned the diagnosis—"PTSD doesn't cause tumors," she told her husband's doctor, "it doesn't cause coughing up blood"—she was accused of being in denial. "It's wives like you that cause soldiers to commit suicide," a VA staffer told her. "Because you won't admit they have PTSD."[20]

In the other camp, a minority of VA employees, alarmed by the agency's culture and refusing to partake, find themselves on a precarious and isolating path. McMath began to field accusations of "lacking empathy" and being "anti-veteran," the noise against him rising anytime he adjudicated claims with "anything less than a diagnosis of 'severe PTSD,'" he said. Echoes of his experience populated the online listserv. "I dread discussing the results (clinically)," wrote one C&P clinician. "I most certainly dread documenting the results in a system that allows the veteran to immediately see what I have written word for word. In some cases, this makes me concerned for my safety."

Rather than embrace measures to support a more accurate assessment, internal VA policies compel staffers to look the other way. A 2012 memo directly prohibited disability examiners from considering any information found outside a veteran's claims file and records, and instructed them to use only the information the vets themselves provide. "Please do not go beyond these sources," warned the memo. "Use of personal information about a Veteran or Servicemember found on the internet or through social media is not responsive to the Veteran-centric policy of VA."

McMath found this reductive form of veteran-centrism dominating the entire bureaucracy. In every department and at every level—among the psychiatrists and psychologists, physicians and therapists, social workers and nurse practitioners—the prevailing attitude seemed to be that all veterans are unquestionably sick, and that the main job of VA employees was to bend to their patients' demands. "The quality of an individual clinician's care was seen by VA management as the inverse of the number of complaints veterans made about him or her," he wrote on his blog. The agency's veteran-centric model, in practice, ensured that "the best 'doc' was the one who always did what his patients wanted."[21]

And in this manner, the whole operation proceeded on bad information and clouded judgment, a perverse machine lurching forward on broken rails. In September, bowing to pressure from outside veterans groups, his boss transferred McMath into a different role, preventing him from performing any more C&P exams. The move came just a few months after a new article was published in the *Psychological Injury and Law* journal, presenting one of the most forceful condemnations of the VA's internal culture yet. "Systemic issues are endemic to VA," declared Arthur Russo, a VA psychologist in Brooklyn. "When rationalized as giving veterans the 'benefit of the doubt,' this blinds a knowing eye from the facts that some veterans feign injury for compensation, and that all VA staff are obligated to report fraud."

Russo cited the anthropologist Frederick Bailey's landmark study of deception: "Collusive lying occurs when two parties, knowing full well that what they are saying or doing is false, collude in ignoring the falsity. They hold it between them as open secrets. They may do so voluntarily or because one party compels the other to go along with the pretense." The VA's many administrative policies and prohibitions, Russo stated, "are forms of collusive lying."[22]

McMath had never met with Russo, but he had arrived at the same conclusion. In his last blog post, he wrote, "It wouldn't do for me to collect a taxpayer-provided salary for what I had come to see as collusion with a corrupt process." When the opportunity arose, he took early retirement. Though he had tried to maintain his integrity through his job's grating demands, he knew that one man's efforts could never be enough to challenge the deep-rooted status quo. Filing through any of the VA's halls and examination rooms to this day, he believes, are "a great many veterans pretending to have fictitious conditions. And a great many doctors pretending to treat them."

PART III:

HOME

CHAPTER 15
LOST TRIBE

MATT JACKSON basked in the comfort of never having to deploy again, in the warmth of Jessica's doting attention, in the thrill of his new freedoms without the military's rigid structure. The possibilities felt endless. He could go anywhere he wanted, any time he felt like it, or just stay inside the house all day, if that was the mood that struck. He had an apartment in Fayetteville, just outside of Fort Bragg, a beautiful wife, and after the first few days of lounging, a jumpy readiness to begin his next act.

The plan was to get into police work. Law enforcement in the civilian world seemed the natural outlet for skills he had honed through years as an infantryman: wariness and alertness, being part of a team, and a capacity for decisive action if the situation were to ever turn south. The field also represented an opportunity to extend his service into a new form. He would no longer be protecting America's interests in the far reaches of the globe, but he could still tend to its needs back at home. The work would be rewarding and exciting, a new challenge.

But the challenge, it turned out, was getting into the police force. Fort Bragg was not only the largest military base in the nation by population, it also housed the headquarters of the US Army's special operations units, supplying a constant stream of Green Berets and top-tier soldiers.[1] The Fayetteville police had few positions to offer, Matt learned, and a wealth of qualified candidates. "I'm not the only guy that has the idea of getting out and staying in the area, getting into law enforcement. They get the cream of the crop when it comes to veterans applying there. They kinda beat me out," he said.

Soon, his apartment lease was coming due. Jessica had moved down from Massachusetts the previous year to be closer to him, arriving a week before he got back from his last deployment. The year had flown by. Their apartment had become a kind of landing zone for Matt's infantry buddies who were also separating during that time, a way station as they maneuvered out into the "real" world. For some of them, like his best friend Jeff, it had been their first stop after leaving the base. Others stayed with Matt and his wife for a few weeks as they figured out what to do next. "Our place was like a transitional area while they got their stuff done so they could move on. It was pretty cool. We had fun," Matt said.

But with no luck finding work, Matt and his wife had to give up the apartment. It was a bitter pill to swallow, the first instance of perceived injustice. "I kinda felt like [the local police departments] were prejudiced against me because I wasn't from that area," Matt said. "They almost had the mentality that I was an outsider. I was a northerner."

Matt was troubled, a little embarrassed, but not deflated. As he and Jessica packed up their things, he came up with a new plan. They would move back to his hometown in Marion, where he would have a better chance at getting his foot in the door with the police force. The plan had other upsides. They would be closer to Matt's family, and he could work part-time at his father's construction company. He had done his research: "Let's say hypothetically I was hired by the police department. The local sheriff's department schedule is you work four ten-hour shifts, then you're off for three days. I could've helped with my dad's business then as a part-time thing." It was the summer of 2011. He had left Marion more than five years earlier, to take on the most demanding profession he could imagine. He had completed two tours in Afghanistan, and returned tested and true. What could possibly be harder than that?

IN THE BEGINNING, America defined a clear path for its citizen-soldier. Matt had risen to the challenges of battle and his return to civilian life followed a path traveled by many generations who came before—all the way back to the Revolutionary War. In George Washington's Farewell Orders to the Continental Army, the storied commander made an appeal "to all the troops […] that they should prove themselves not less virtuous and useful as citizens, than they have been persevering and victorious as soldiers."[2] The Americans he commanded had taken up the cause of national defense, transforming into soldiers, and Washington believed they must now rejoin society again as citizens. Touring the United States nearly half a century later, Alexis de Tocqueville recorded the same observation. Most sons of the nation "bow to their military duties," he wrote, "but their souls remain attached to the interests and desires they were filled with in civil life."[3]

Subsequent eras have eroded the citizen identity to the identity of soldier. During the Civil War—which engulfed and ravaged a generation of Americans on an unprecedented scale—combat became viewed less as an event than a metamorphosis akin to religious passage—"touched by fire," in the words of Oliver Wendell Holmes, who fought in the Union Army. Those who survived increasingly viewed themselves as members of a closed order, having more in common with one another than civilians who remained forever oblivious to the experience of the battlefields.

The attitude deepened through successive conflicts, consolidating by the time Ernest Hemingway, T.S. Eliot, and other members of the "Lost Generation" imprinted the profound shocks of World War I onto their chapter of American history. But at least the World Wars drew much higher levels of participation: 4.6 and 11.6 percent of the Americans served, respectively, while 4.4 percent served in Vietnam. The proportion of the country to have experienced military life has fallen dramatically since, accelerated by the draft's abolition in 1973. The result is an armed forces on the fringe of today's national mainstream—what the historian Andrew Bacevich, whose son was killed in action in Iraq, has called "the 1 percent Army."

The gap between America's armed forces and the society they

serve continues to widen today. While establishing an all-volunteer force produced a military that is more competent and professional than ever before—people who *choose* to serve are better, unsurprisingly, at serving—other trends have become more apparent over time. Those who serve are increasingly concentrated in the socio-economic middle class, the geographic South and Midwest, and the political center-right. Now, almost three generations after the all-volunteer force was created, the military has moved toward becoming a "family business." More than ever before, those who serve and those who do not view the other through a disinterested, suspicious, and sometimes even antagonistic, lens.

THE SETBACKS FOLLOWED, one after the other, like waves crashing down on shore. Back in Marion, Matt made it through the first rounds of hiring at the local police department, but after the final interview the position was given to someone else. Matt took it in stride—"a better candidate beat me out"—but the blow would sting for months.

He and Jessica moved in with his parents until they were able to find a cheap place of their own. Matt began working at his dad's construction business. It was full-time manual labor of the most grueling kind: pouring concrete, laying bricks, enduring heavy loads and long days under a hot sun. Matt had hours to contemplate all the places he would rather be, all the ways in which life was turning sour.

"It was tough to go back and have to live with my family," Matt said. "I was depressed after I couldn't get the jobs I wanted. My dream jobs weren't panning out for me. Working for my father was always a fallback plan. Of course, I'm glad I did have my dad to help me. I grew up working for him, but I couldn't do it like I used to. I started to crash after the tremendous high you get from being released from service."

Pain in his knees and back, which Matt traced to his duties as a paratrooper and infantryman, resurfaced like angry hornets. The demands of his job aggravated the injuries until they were impossible to ignore. While building a set of steps one day, he picked up a brick and suddenly felt a hot knife slice through his lower back. It was a pinched nerve. He was out for a month. As the condition worsened, his range of motion narrowed. One afternoon he was outside the house, tending to the lawn, when a fiery pang smacked his back again—in the exact same place. Jessica was out of town and he laid on the couch for four straight days until everything had disappeared from the fridge and his mom finally dragged him to the hospital.

"It was a combination of everything holding me back," Matt said. His physical ailments were preventing him from taking on a leadership role in his father's company, and he felt himself withdrawing from family and friends, isolating himself further from the network of people that could have best supported him. Insomnia ravaged his nights; difficulty concentrating pestered his days. His handle on basic tasks deteriorated, and he found his mind wandering to the IED that once exploded just yards away, the firefights that engulfed his platoon, the bullets spraying by. Neighbors sometimes shot off their guns in their backyards or in the woods nearby, and Matt's breathing would stop, his chest starting to seize. He felt saddled by circumstance more limiting than any flak jacket the Army had ever issued, and he began to wonder if maybe it was for the best that he didn't end up in law enforcement, that he never got the jobs he was aiming for. "An employer might be able to accommodate me for one or two disabilities, but no one can put up with everything," he said.[4]

"It seems like the mental stuff took a while to unravel completely," he went on. "In the military, everyone is going through the same thing. But now I didn't have my military friends around that I could lean on. Not having the glue that the military gives you, by myself, I just started to unravel."

The glue that binds young men together in small-unit warfare predates the modern era. From Greek city-states to Native American tribal bands, warriors have developed complex rituals to ease their transitions home after battle. Yet the modern American military features no such rituals, snapping a vital passage between the two domains and trapping many veterans in the perilous zone in between.

Entering the military, every soldier's journey begins with a high-pressure transformation, designed to simultaneously strip him of his previous identity and condition him for actions unimaginable in the civilian sphere. After enlisting, a new recruit is "sworn in" by taking an oath that places him in direct subordination within an unquestionable structure of authority.[5] At boot camp, his hair is shorn off (cropped short for women), civilian clothing is swapped for indistinguishable uniforms, and daily language is replaced by military-specific jargon. The bathroom becomes the "latrine;" calling someone "an individual" becomes a slur; weapons become extensions of the body. In the Marine Corps, recruits are instructed to yell "Kill!" with every movement during drills; in the Navy, they are told to internalize the branch's core values: the "ship" comes before the "shipmate," the "shipmate" comes before the "self." As one former officer put it, "You are not the hero of this movie."[6]

After graduation from basic training, each soldier is assigned to a unit, a collective that formally subsumes the individual. Warfare acts as the cement, fortifying their connections and activating qualities like loyalty, cooperation, inter-group reliance—"ancient human behaviors," writes the author and journalist Sebastian Junger, not "easily found in modern society." Nor are the behaviors limited to combat. Civilians facing extreme circumstances have engendered the same deep emotions of closeness and understanding, prompting Londoners pummeled by the Blitz of World War II, survivors of the AIDS epidemic, and members of other trauma groups, to subsequently discover that they "miss those days" under siege. But this kind of affinity can be particularly intense among soldiers, whose combat platoons, numbering between thirty and fifty, operate in nearly the same structure as their ancestors in hunter-gatherer bands.

Humans, like many animals, prioritize group affiliation and cooperation. Throughout the evolution of our species, group behavior has been crucial for helping the individual survive. It triggers the release of dopamine and oxytocin, chemicals and hormones that act as rewards in the body, reinforcing each member's loyalty to the group. A soldier in the military is virtually never alone, embedded at all times within his pack. "You eat together, sleep together, laugh together, suffer together," Junger writes, through patrols and exercises, achieved objectives and buried dead, until day after day, month after month, a new dynamic is forged—a shared attachment, an undeniable glue. "I don't know if there's a way I can accurately describe this glue," said Matt. "You know that the people around you would die for you. It's the kind of bond that you can't get anywhere else. The camaraderie, the brotherhood, the bond—it's like when you play on a sports team, but like a million times playing on a sports team."

Then, in stark contrast to the structured, socialized process of joining, separating from the military is solely an individual effort. The soon-to-be veteran is given papers with a set of tasks to check off and a list of signatures to gather. During this procedure, the soldier is still emotionally attached to his unit; he continues to see his fellow unit members every day, but he is no longer part of the team. The change is jarring with every step. Suddenly the departing service member is being viewed with remove, envy, even disdain. A painful distance rends what had once been an unmatched closeness.

When the gates open and the veteran walks out, he becomes a civilian again, on paper, yet his internal reality is far messier. He has completed a ceremonial conversion, one designation swapped for another, yet he has not yet embarked on the arduous work of reshaping his identity back to a productive civilian one. A military-shaped hole is punctured in his psyche, a hole that little in the civilian world can readily fill. "The problem doesn't seem to be trauma on the battlefield so much as re-entry into society," Junger writes.[7]

"Regardless of what your service was, regardless of what branch you were in, regardless of what your job was—whether it included deployments or not—there is something uniquely painful about transitioning out of the military and back into the civilian world," said Jill Wilschke, the Camp Lejeune veterans counselor. "Even though you were a civilian before, now that you have become a veteran, it's different."

MATT FELT THE ABSENCE of his military bonds deeply, while at the same time his civilian bonds seemed to be fraying with little effort. The social ties he was seeking remained elusive. As the holidays approached, so did his first VA compensation payments.

Sitting through the military's Transition Assistance Program during his separation, he had followed the VA representative's urging to claim anything he could think of. "You can get paid for these things," the rep had told them, and Matt had figured, why not. "There was nothing to lose," he said. He mulled over his five years in the Army and filled out disability claims for everything.

In December 2011, he was approved for compensation related to a dozen conditions, stemming from what he experienced in the military. He received a 30 percent disability rating for PTSD; 30 percent for migraine headaches; 10 percent for his right shoulder strain; 10 percent for intervertebral disc syndrome and thoracic spine strain; 10 percent for sciatic nerve damage; 10 percent for cervical spine strain; 10 percent for bilateral recurrent tinnitus; 10 percent for chondromalacia in his right knee; 10 percent for his left knee as well; 10 percent for a left shoulder strain; 10 percent for tenosynovitis in his right hand; and though his disability claim for tenosynovitis in his left hand was also approved, he received a 0 percent rating for the condition. "I couldn't tell you what that means," said Matt's wife Jessica. His combined disability rating was 80 percent.

The VA's system for rating and combining multiple disabilities is often a source of confusion for veterans and their families. Each rating increment is intended to account for the percentage decrease in earnings that an average veteran would experience with that disability. A 10 percent disability rating, for example, means that the veteran retains 90 percent of his capacity for work.[8] Each subsequent disability is then subtracted from the remaining capacity—not from

100 percent.[9] Ratings of 0 percent, which Matt received for an inflammation in his left hand, are fairly rare; the VA assigns them to conditions that are service-connected but determined not sufficiently severe so as to be disabling.[10] The rating does carry important implications, however, including serving as a placeholder for future claims to increase the rating if the condition worsens.[11]

Matt's benefits package from the VA helped him scale back at his job. Winters in southern Illinois are wet, freezing, and miserable; by then most construction work had already slowed. Matt halved his hours down to twenty a week.

The natural athlete who had conquered his fear of heights to excel as an airborne soldier, who had returned to his hometown as a proven combat veteran full of dreams and vitality, had become a disabled man one year later. With an 80 percent rating, the VA had stamped Matt four out of five parts disabled. He began to believe he really was.

CHAPTER 16
I DESERVE IT

MARCO VASQUEZ found himself standing outside baggage claim in the Nashville airport, surrounded by his wife and children. It was June 2003. He had been in Mosul only two days earlier, the dust still settling from America's invasion of Iraq. After receiving a Red Cross message from his wife, he had rushed to take the next flight home, stopping only at the base exchange to charge a fresh set of civilian clothes to his credit card.

Marco hadn't known what to expect when he saw them again, but he wasn't expecting this. His wife had rushed to embrace him, his kids—Zoe, little Marco, Shelemyah—lighting up as his figure appeared at the gate. But he wasn't the one hugging them back. It felt as if his mind had left his body and he was observing the scene from above—watching as his face burrowed into his wife's hair, as his arms lifted his young son into the air. It was like briefly stepping into the twilight zone, more disorienting than distressing. The moment passed. "Everything's cool," Marco told himself. They had more urgent matters to attend to.

He checked in with his battalion at Fort Campbell, sixty miles north of Nashville. His first sergeant told him to go and take care of his family. The next morning they took Shelemyah—"Sheme," as the family liked to call her—to Vanderbilt Hospital. Marco and his wife stayed at the hospital's Ronald McDonald House, while Sheme endured a week of testing. The doctors found that she had developed cerebral palsy, and there was scarring in the part of her brain controlling basic motor functions. She wasn't paralyzed but she would never be able to walk, and she would likely be legally blind.

The news hit Marco like a bullet. "This sucks," he kept thinking. "I just fought a war and now I'm going to have a daughter with disabilities." He couldn't keep that terrible thought away. "This really fucking sucks."

He reached out to an old friend who owned a ranch in North Carolina's Smoky Mountains. Marco packed the car and drove out with his wife and kids. They stayed at his friend's ranch for a month, reassembling as a family, hardly making any contact with the outside world. When he finally reported back to Fort Campbell, his first sergeant unleashed a string of curses: "Where the fuck were you? I was about to count your ass AWOL!" But in the end, he sympathized with Marco's situation and pursued no disciplinary action.

Soon Marco's platoon mates were returning from Iraq. Their mission had ended. Marco passed the days at Fort Campbell, pulling guard and CQ—charge of quarters. The holidays were approaching. Aside from taking a week off in the fall of 2001, Marco realized he hadn't gone on formal leave in almost two years. He had ninety days saved up. He used them right after Thanksgiving, carrying him through the remaining days in his contract.

He and his wife had talked about returning to Texas, but because of Sheme, they knew they had to live near a good hospital. They settled on Round Rock, a twenty-minute drive to the Dell Children's Medical Center in Austin. In February 2004, almost exactly three years after enlisting, Marco separated from the Army with an honorable discharge. He was done.

It didn't take long to find a job. A car dealership in Round Rock hired him to sell Toyotas and Hondas, and Marco, raised in a bilingual household, sold like he had been born for the task. He was named salesman of the month. With commission, he was making more than $10,000 a month. In June of 2007, he managed to bring in $12,168.38 topped off with a big bonus—a company record.

But the fast talking and big checks cloaked a cyclone brewing beneath the surface. Marco had started self-medicating. "I was like,

'Yeah my back is sore, so I'll take some Vicodin. My shoulder is sore, I'll drink after work.' I could afford it. I never made so much money in my life. I got my wife the house she wanted, the cars, everything." Money was coming in and for a time, that was enough. "I was that guy who functioned a bit too well—a functioning alcoholic. But every day I was either smoking, or getting high on something, or at lunch I was having a drink. And then I would go sell cars. And I would sell a lot of them." As soon as he got home, the facade fell apart. He fell apart on his wife, instigating massive arguments over nothing. He fell apart on his kids, until he became a presence in the room they would shrink from. It occurred to him how much damage he was bringing into the house, how he was slowly ruining the lives of his loved ones like a tumor. But he couldn't stop. When the economy crashed in 2009, Marco crashed right along with it.

He had been promoted to a management role not long before, tasked with overseeing the financial division for some of the dealership's most profitable lines. But when the market capsized, everything froze—no lending, no sales, no transactions of any kind. Marco could no longer afford his habits. He could barely afford his bills. He quickly cracked. One day an altercation with a colleague escalated to a physical brawl. Marco was forced to resign. With no job and no income, there was no longer anything to keep the storm's darkest clouds at bay. The market had bottomed out, but he had further to go.

HE CRASHED THROUGH thirteen jobs in four years. He got a job as an electrician, but kept mixing up the wiring. He got a job as an air conditioning technician, but the fiberglass irritated his breathing while spending all day in attics drove him mad. He worked as a manager at a corner store, at a Pep Boys service station, and even tried selling cars again at an Acura dealership, but nothing lasted more than a few months. "I went everywhere," Marco said. "But I couldn't hold it together."

His set of vices expanded. He began smoking marijuana. He

started using opiates. His use was bound only by his access. "If I could get it, I knew things were better. But then I couldn't get it because I couldn't afford it—I wasn't making ten grand anymore," he said. Signs of trouble, previously masked by his constant spending and his daily self-medicating, rose to a boil. "I was that loud guy in the room. I was always angry. Narcissistic, probably, too. For me, it was straight out of fear, but I showed it in anger. I tried to coat all my fear with anger. You know when someone walks into the room and you know they're mad, even before they've said anything? That was me. But I was oblivious. I thought that I was okay."

Without steady income, the whole family downsized, selling the cars and barely managing to keep the house. Sheme's condition had stabilized; despite the cerebral palsy, she was walking and talking now, growing up and becoming a little firecracker. But none of Marco's children listened to him. The language between them had become rigid and foreboding. The worse things got, the less control Marco felt he had. "It was the complete opposite of who I was in the military," he said. "I felt left behind. Disregarded. Ashamed. Totally confused. No security. Like the omega rather than the alpha."

He had first applied for VA disability compensation in 2005, the year after he left the Army. He was having nightmares and, after talking to his wife, he submitted a claim for PTSD. His claim was denied. He tried again the following year but got the same result. By that point things were picking up at work, and with good money coming in, he didn't think about benefits again until 2009, when he lost his job. Without much else to do, "I really had time to fight the VA," he said. He called and secured an appointment at the nearby VA hospital in Temple. When he arrived, the hospital was under construction. To Marco, the racket from the drilling and hammering sounded like "pounding bullets." He felt disoriented and he let it show during his disability exam. "I had a fit. I was like, 'This is fucking crazy.'" His agitation was convincing. "Right there, they discovered that I had 50 percent PTSD from that meeting."

Soon after, he connected with agents from the Wounded Warrior

Project, a veterans service organization, who helped him file for a benefits increase. He was approved for 70 percent PTSD in 2011. Marco's growing substance abuse had landed him on the VA conveyor belt that produces diagnoses of PTSD for nearly every signal of mental distress raised by a veteran. Without any requirement to stay in treatment, the VBA applied the catch-all bandage of more cash. The VA payments added another line of income for Marco's family—nearly $2,000 a month—but they did nothing to fix the heart of the problem, nothing to stop his sinking. His drinking and drug use continued, only now they were subsidized by the VA.

In 2013, he applied for another benefits increase to take him the rest of the way—100 percent disability. Yet with the problem of substance abuse still festering and unaddressed, the bottom continued to drop.

One day in the spring of 2014, he was driving on the highway when another car cut him off. Marco honked. The driver ignored him, while a guy in the passenger seat raised his middle finger. Marco felt something inside him release. When the car turned off to exit, Marco followed. They ended up in the West Campus neighborhood, near the University of Texas at Austin. The two guys were college students, "just goofing off in the car, probably stoned or something," Marco later said. But in the heat of the moment, he rammed into the other vehicle's door.

Marco got out and walked over to the other car's passenger side. He dragged the kid out. Even as his arm cocked back, he could see how terrified the kid was. Marco couldn't believe how hard he hit him, and suddenly, he was the one who was terrified. He reached down and flipped open the kid's wallet. He read the name and address, then told the driver, with as much malice as he could muster, "Man, I know who you are so don't fuck with me."

He stepped back into his car and sped away from the scene. He was shaking. He threw up across the dashboard. He called his VA therapist, and realized he was only a few miles from the hospital. "Come on in," she said. When he arrived, his wife was there waiting for him.

"Marco, I can't do this anymore," his wife said. Marco nodded. *Who could?* Who could put up with what he had become, year after year, the moods, the tantrums, the aggression, the lost jobs, the drug-fueled binges? He knew this was his last chance. "I took it seriously," he said. "I wanted to get sober."

After checking into a nearby VA inpatient facility for two weeks, he flew out to CLARE Foundation, a rehabilitation center in Santa Monica built around the twelve-step program developed by Alcoholics Anonymous.[1] Wounded Warrior Project helped pay for his flight.

Marco's priority was to get sober. The first step was to admit his decline and confront his failings.[2] "It took me a long time," he said. The meetings initially filled him with dread. He couldn't bear to sit through the other people's stories, cringing at the depravities of their addiction and the depths of their plunge. After a while, he was allowed to leave the clinic and receive treatment at the nearby VA hospital in Los Angeles, where he attended targeted sessions of EMDR (Eye Movement Desensitization and Reprocessing) therapy, biofeedback, and cognitive behavioral therapy. The combination of treatments began to take effect. In April, he turned thirty-six. He couldn't remember the last birthday he had without getting smashed. His twelve-step sponsor encouraged him to take on new challenges, starting with the most trivial tasks, small rituals and habits that he would have never previously entertained. "You have to use the other side of your brain," his sponsor said. "You're doing everything for the first time again because you're doing it sober now."

The mindset sounded silly to Marco but he went along. He went along during his birthday celebration at the clinic, when he was told it was his first birthday again now that he was sober, and he tried to believe it was true. He went along first thing the next morning, picking up his toothbrush and brushing with his left hand instead of right. And when his sponsor asked, "Have you ever thought about meditation?" he went along with that, too—though not before clawing back his instinct to sneer at the whole endeavor. He had been among the first wave of soldiers into Baghdad during the invasion and now he was going to sit on a pillow, breathe, be silent—"and that's going to help me?" he wondered. "Right."

The first few tries he fell asleep. Then he visited a studio run by Matthew Preece, a celebrity stylist who had lived a past life as a yogi in India. Marco took off his shoes and stepped into a candlelit space, lined with mats, and with the bells and whistles and chants of a Mother Divine track chiming in the background. It was hardly the aesthetic he would have found ordinarily appealing, and yet something about the ambience—and something about Preece—struck a chord.

Preece became his guru. One evening, he brought Marco to the beach, where a large bonfire was burning. Preece told Marco to close his eyes and imagine himself inside a teepee. *Through the tent folds, anger comes in.* Marco felt his anger enter. The emotion took the form of fiery pillar, fifteen feet tall, spinning closer until it stopped right beside him. Preece told him not to panic. *Next, let anxiety come in.* Anxiety appeared as a column of ice, approaching Marco and stopping at his other side. He suddenly felt cold until he heard Preece's words cut through, wrapping around him like a blanket. *Your anger and your anxiety kept you alive in Iraq. They need to be recognized. Stop trying to resist them. Stop trying to hide them.*

Marco broke down in tears.

MEDITATION BECAME HIS SALVE. Marco dived into his mindfulness practice and a new outlook began to set in. "Those two guys—anger and anxiety—that's what kept me alive in Iraq," he said. "They kept me on guard, they kept me on point, they kept me on the gun. I can't do without them. But when I got back to the states, I thought I couldn't show people that I'm angry. So I numbed myself with alcohol and drugs and all this shit. That's what created the addictive behavior. But with my practice, I've been able to control it. I tell it, 'I see you.' I physically say, 'I see you.' Because you don't want these things to control you." Like so many broken-veteran depictions, Marco curated a narrative in which his anger and

265

anxiety revolved around his military service, minimizing the potential that other factors like his substance abuse might also be at work in his story.

Little by little, Preece convinced Marco to let go of his shame. "Before I would let shame dominate, but now, when I get angry and anxiety comes, I don't shame myself," Marco said. "My guru kept telling me, 'You can't work with shame. You can work with guilt, you can ask for forgiveness. You can work with resentment to relieve it. But you can't work with shame. Shame is what keeps the prostitute a prostitute, the drug dealer a drug dealer.'"

The key to keeping his darker impulses at bay, Marco eventually realized, was sobriety. In his second month of rehab, he felt himself elevating during a meditation session, as if something were lifting his body off the ground. The sensation marked a turning point. Marco doubled down on his twelve-step work. "Nothing was interfering," he said. "I was in rehab, going to meetings, eating, going back to meetings, sleeping." Three sessions in the morning, two in the afternoon, 120 days of re-committing to sober-living and fortifying his resolve. At the end of the summer, Marco returned to Texas, determined not to regress into old vices.

He fought to incorporate the positive new rituals into his life, while shedding harmful old ones. He rolled out an exercise mat next to his side of the bed, so that he could begin each morning with yoga. "I don't even stand up. I just fall out of bed and I'll do a couple of poses right there that I know are uplifting," he said. He got into tai chi and mountain biking, tried out equine therapy, and retooled his diet to eat healthier. "When you lay a foundation, you can build upon it," he said. He stopped hanging around his former circles, and in particular, with other vets. He no longer met with his former drinking buddies at the bar for Sunday football. Without drinking, so much of what had tied them together fell away. Before long, he could hardly stand the smell of beer. "Everyone liked to get loaded. Once I stopped doing that, I started noticing how loud and obnoxious these people really were. I was like that, too, so I didn't even care. But I was changing," he said. He found he no longer had to be the center of attention, the loudest man in the room. He credits marriage counseling for saving his relationship with his wife.

After Marco started making healthier choices, he gained more clarity about his years of destructive choices. What he believed were the tendrils of Army-induced trauma had been mixed and amplified by his addictions. Were the nightmares caused by a repressed past or his drug-hazed present? Was that ceaseless, gnawing sense of dread the product of experienced military trauma, or from drowning his diminished prospects in the bottle? Where did PTSD begin and his drug abuse end?

For years, Marco had been trapped under his own shame, afraid to seek help, believing that his conditions were permanent. He credits Preece for helping him break through. "He taught me that you have to treat all these feelings as visitors, because they're always going to come and go. Anger's going to come and then it's going to leave. Even happiness—guess what, enjoy the present moment because it's also going to leave." The twelve steps had helped Marco to re-center himself, while meditation kept him from backsliding. He was finally accepting that it was possible to create a new man from the old.

During this transformation, Marco received a notice from the VA. He had applied for a disability rating increase from 70 to 100 percent almost two years earlier, when his collapse had yet to find its bottom. With generous support—personal, spiritual, and financial—he had clawed his way out. Then in 2015, the VA informed him his request had been approved. His disability was 100 percent permanent and total.

PERMANENT AND TOTAL DISABILITY is a VA designation assigned to veterans whose disabling conditions are rated at 100 percent (total) and determined to have zero—or close to zero—chance of improvement (permanent).[3] At the same time that Marco was discovering his demons could be overcome—as Preece often said to him: *you have to treat all these feelings as visitors*—he embraced the

VA's label of disability and began receiving increased monthly benefits for his "permanent and total" PTSD.

While permanent and total ratings may be an appropriate designation for veterans with disabilities that are truly static and unlikely to improve—amputations, spinal cord injuries, etc.—they are misapplied to mental health disorders like PTSD, which have been repeatedly demonstrated to improve with effective therapies like those Marco utilized in his own recovery.[4] Even so, permanent and total determinations have proliferated as many C&P examiners confront the pressure to grant higher ratings. Veterans who don't receive their desired disability status have multiple avenues to pursue: they can continually submit new claims to increase their ratings percentage, contact their elected officials or powerful veterans groups, and file grievances with licensing boards against the medical professionals whom they believe have wronged them. Faced with these pressures, it is far easier for the VA's C&P examiners and rating specialists to capitulate. But every capitulation adds up, contributing to the VA's ever-growing budget.

In the post-9/11 discourse, one constant critique of the VA relates to its chronic underfunding. Journalists have largely substantiated this claim; in a 2014 article in *The Nation*, Katrina vanden Heuvel argued that members of Congress have neglected the VA because they're afraid to place the burden where it rightly belongs—on "the political and economic elite."[5] The gap between the nation's military and its elites has indeed widened, but funding for the VA has also swelled. According to a 2012 report by the Congressional Research Service, the VA's budget multiplied more than fourteen-fold in inflation-adjusted dollars since 1940.[6] And the growth is accelerating. For fiscal year 2021, the VA requested $243.3 billion, an increase of 350 percent from its annual expenditure twenty years earlier.[7] This rise is even more striking in the context of a shrinking veteran population: over the same period, the number of living veterans declined from twenty-six million to roughly eighteen million in 2021.

One factor contributing to this rapid and sustained growth is the VA's liberalizing standards for issues such as adult-onset diabetes, burn-pit exposure, and traumatic-stress-related conditions. While expanding the table of qualifications has affected many veterans who wouldn't have otherwise been affected, the cause-and-effect link between many claimed conditions and military service is far from conclusive. A formal study addressing the nexus between type 2 diabetes and Vietnam-era vets exposed to Agent Orange found only "limited or suggestive evidence" of the herbicide as a causative agent.[8] And a 2017 paper found that diabetes among veterans aged twenty and older from 2005 to 2014 is "primarily attributable to the high prevalence of obesity."[9] Other debates have sparked over whether issues like willful substance abuse can be blamed on military service.

On a perfectly still day, you can toss a stone into a pond and easily track the ripples it creates. But when the wind is blowing, when people are jumping in, when a group of ducks is swimming nearby, where the ripples are coming from becomes much harder to define. Yet when it comes to establishing service connection, the VA tends to treat a veteran's service as a lone stone tossed into a still pond—even as the ducks are flapping, winds are blowing, and kids are cannonballing into the water from the dock. Kenneth Toone, to take one example, is an Iraq War vet who was featured prominently in the 2016 documentary film *Thank You For Your Service*.[8] Since returning from deployment, combat exposure has been blamed for his mental health problems, yet many psychological disorders have a strong genetic link and can be triggered or worsened by drug use. Toone's wife, Angie, recognizes the other factors. "Most likely he was already predisposed [to PTSD] because his dad was a schizophrenic," she said. "And then after he got back from combat, he did drugs and he snorted meth, which damaged his brain. Everything together—it just snapped something."[11]

Through successful rehabilitation, Marco eventually understood that substance addiction can be just as derailing as any amount of combat trauma, but like so many other veterans, he had much to gain materially from a high disability rating. Rated at 100 percent, Marco receives over $3,000 in monthly disability benefits.[12] The GI Bill, Vocational Rehabilitation, and other grants cover tuition costs for both him and his wife as they pursue higher education. Marco has also been receiving Social Security Disability Insurance (SSDI), which pays another $1,600 each month. Under a relatively new VA program, his wife has also been approved as a "caretaker," adding $600 to their monthly income from the VA. All these payments are tax-free; in addition, Marco is qualified for a break on his property tax as a veteran.

MARCO KNOWS EXACTLY how much personal effort, strength, and willpower it took to stitch his life back together. He tries to take none of it for granted. He also recognizes that he could not have turned things around on his own. In addition to all the support from his family and guru, the VA's monthly disability benefits created the space for him to focus exclusively on his recovery, providing a safety net that was crucial to his ultimate success. "With that income," he said, "I was able to get healthy and stay where I'm at."

This has been the intended purpose of the VA all along: to provide effective medical care for mental and physical ailments incurred during service, and to tender a financial cushion for assisting veterans as they retire their warrior mentality and reintegrate into society as capable, productive citizens. This, however, is also where the gears get stuck. Marco was diagnosed with PTSD—a condition known by clinicians to be entirely treatable—yet the VA has promoted an understanding of disability that views such conditions as life sentences, while attaching monetary incentives that incentivize vets to never report their improvements.

"My PTSD is permanent," Marco said. "And my [disability payments] are not. Technically I could work a little bit, I just can't make more than twelve grand. As soon as I hit twelve grand, it shuts you down." He recounts the financial uncertainty his family had endured when he lost job after job; those memories serve as a reminder to hold onto his disability pay as long as he is able. "We went through heartache for years. Losing that money is a big thing," he said. Benefits became Marco's main link to the VA. After a while, he scaled back on his weekly therapy appointments, and while he had tried to keep up with AA for a while, dropping into a meeting at least once a month, it was an hour-long drive to Austin and the commute just as often kept him away.

All former addicts know that the long slide to the bottom is, in fact, not so long at all. Sometimes it is only one bottle away. Meditation, mindfulness, mountain biking, tai chi, equine therapy—these are the pursuits that now fill Marco's life, hobbies and activities that keep him too busy for alcohol and drugs. Without all his benefits from the VA, he is convinced, "I'm not able to recover." Occasionally, a dissonance washes over him, particularly when someone, perhaps making small talk, asks about his profession. "I'm military-retired," Marco replies, but he admits, "It feels empty to say I'm not doing anything." He tries to reframe his unemployment. "I am healing," he says, and he tells himself that is as demanding a job as any.

He believes that he has earned his compensation payments. "I'm grateful but it was a long road. It's sad that we have to fight for it, first of all. I talk to my other buddies and they don't want to mess with it at all. They just suck it up. They just stay with their jobs."

The overwhelming majority of Americans are unquestioningly generous to their men and women in uniform. But a culture of flag-waving and hero worship has slowly become pervasive since at least the first Gulf War, resulting in an air of entitlement pervasive among segments of the veteran population. Often it is other vets who take the most offense. In a recent blog post on the website of the successful veteran-owned T-shirt company Ranger Up, one vet wrote: "We have created a strange new culture within the Veteran [sic] community...honestly it offends me. How did we get from being men and women of honor to a subclass of entitled...whiny, wussified leeches?"[13] The comments section exploded. Many accused the author of disrespecting veterans with PTSD. But many others defended his point.

In his recent book *Paid Patriotism*, the political economist James Bennett catalogs the extensive growth of new veteran benefits and programs to have spawned from Congressional provisions. The ever-growing network has created a book genre all its own. Wrote Bennett, "These works typically apply the veneer of patriotism to a grab-all-you-can-get entitlement mentality."[14]

What do the American people owe their veterans?

"Not a damn thing," Marco said. Yet his actions indicate otherwise. He considers his disability to be both a life sentence and a lifelong pass for benefits.

Marco entered the military as the textbook case of a positive response to the benefits package the Army offered for his enlistment. He knew a good thing when he saw it. The Army was his ticket out of El Paso and a means to provide for his family. But his three years of service would eventually pay off far more. Even after landing a successful job in the civilian workforce, he would try for getting on the VA's disability payroll; years later, the VA would pluck him from the gutter of substance abuse, pinning his poor choices on the military, and allow him to pursue tai chi, meditation, and mountain biking for his remaining days. The only catch is that he must maintain the narrative. And he does.

"I know, psychologically, I'm mentally ill," he said. "And I know it's not going to be healed. I didn't ask for it. Yes, I wanted to serve. But I wanted the college money. I wanted to come out with my degree. I didn't have that opportunity. War scared the fuck out of me. The first time that Kiowa [helicopter] went over me, the first time I heard all those shells land on my truck, I flipped, man. We're all kinds of messed up. There's no going back on that. And there was a lot of sorrow and pain for many years. So I really think that's the deserving part."

It's a view that represents what many veterans believe. "I deserve this because…I deserve it," Marco said.

CHAPTER 17
DRIFTING APART

LESS THAN FIVE MINUTES into his first class, Jeff Kisbert felt his grip on college slipping. The professor had gone over the course syllabus quickly; when there were no questions, she launched into the lesson. "Get out your graphing calculators," she said, and the class complied. "Solve this binomial," she said, and everyone went right to work.

Jeff stared at the unfamiliar machine in his hand. *Shit*, he thought. The keys might as well have been Egyptian hieroglyphs.

Things weren't supposed to go like this. When Jeff received his acceptance letter to Saint Louis University in the spring of 2011, it had all been part of the plan. With financial assistance from the post-9/11 GI Bill, his tuition would be covered when he started school in the fall, and he would receive an accommodating stipend each month.[1] He thought he had everything he would need to pursue his degree in physics, not least a lifelong fascination with the hard sciences. As a soldier, he had always been hungry to learn about ballistics—how bullets cut through the air, how rockets launched toward their targets—and on one of his deployments, he even worked his way through a dense Stephen Hawking volume on space and time. After two tours and five years of service, he viewed college as his reward, his haven to explore these interests.

"I had an associate degree. I had been to combat. I had been the captain's right-hand man—the guy who took over radio and operations, who signed for over a million dollars of Army equipment, who was responsible for all kinds of things. Surely I could handle college,"

Jeff had thought at the time. What could possibly go wrong?

His first class on a balmy late August morning, Calculus I, mocked him with the answer. He had sailed through a survey calculus course in community college, but that had been almost a decade ago. Jeff was thirty-one years old, and a chilling thought suddenly passed through him: *I'm in class with people who were in high school just four months ago.* It had been years since he had last sat in a classroom, and even then, he was among working adults, most of them squeezing in time for a night class or two. These kids next to him came from a different breed. They were dialed in, textbook-trained, craning to answer the professor's questions in a language he could hardly understand. *These sharp nineteen-year-olds are blowing me out of the water*, he thought. He wished he could disappear into his seat.

Things didn't get better on day two. In General Chemistry, another requirement for Jeff's major, the professor was going through the lab's routine safety procedures. He asked everyone to put on their lab goggles. It was hot in the classroom and Jeff was nervous. His goggles started to fog. The professor continued from the front of the class, explaining the instructions for using the Bunsen burner. Jeff moved to retrieve something from his backpack, and accidentally bumped into a glass beaker at the edge of his table. It shattered on the floor. The room instantly turned to stare. He could sense everyone's judgement, aimed at him through thirty pairs of plastic goggles.

It was a battering entry back into student life, but things looked a little brighter when the weekend finally arrived. After a hard and humbling first week, Jeff and Bethany got married on Saturday. Immediately following the ceremony, the couple was off on their honeymoon, a cruise out of New York City, through Boston, then up the eastern coast of Canada. Jeff packed a couple textbooks and even managed a few hours of study, but he framed the trip as a kind of reset, one that he badly needed. *I'll take a breather, then come back and catch up*, he thought. *Everything's cool.*

But things were not cool. When he returned to his classes, he felt more out of place than ever. "It might as well have been a two-*month* honeymoon," he said. "I was too far behind. I was lost in the sauce. I was done."

THE ONLY THING Jeff could think to do was keep showing up. At least he could get attendance points, he told himself, if nothing else. As the semester rolled on, the gap between him and the other students grew wider. One day in his English class, the professor asked everyone to write a short response describing a problem on campus. A classmate volunteered to share her answer. "The elevators in my dorm are too slow," she began, and as she went on, Jeff suddenly felt something stir inside him. The classroom started to feel hot again. He told himself to breathe, just breathe, but the temperature inside him kept rising. He flashed back to the worst day in his life: a patrol during his second deployment when his Humvee hit an IED. The blast threw him off the vehicle. He suffered a concussion, a broken nose, and cuts all over his body, but that wasn't the worst of it. The other guys in his platoon had gone out for another patrol and hit a second IED on the same day. This one was deadlier. His captain was killed in the explosion.

"What the fuck are you talking about?" he suddenly wanted to scream at the girl in his class. "That's your problem on campus? The elevators are slow? I just spent a year in a place with no running water. People died. And that's the problem in your life?" Jeff barely managed to bite back the outburst. But by the end of class, his anger had turned into a kind of sadness. As he walked out of the classroom, he felt more isolated than ever. Despite all the people streaming by him in the hall, he felt he could not have been more removed from the place, as if he had not a single thing in common with any of them.

It had been nothing like this in the Army. In the Army, twenty-four hours a day, seven days a week, he had been embedded in a tight mesh of soldiers whose defining experience was exactly what they were living through, together, moment by moment in real time.

They all carried rifles, and they all had Jeff's back; at any time of the day, they would have given him the shirt they were wearing; hell, they would have jumped in front of a bullet for him, and he would have done the same for any of them. He might not have always agreed with everyone, and certainly there were scuffles and tension now and again, but twenty-four hours a day, seven days a week, he was understood, and he was safe. Even within range of the Taliban, with his guys around him, it was the safest he had ever felt.

On campus, Jeff hardly ever felt safe. He was surrounded by frat boys who thought he was a loser, by stoners who didn't give a shit about him, by Muslim students who still gave him pause, by a student population more likely to know every word of a Katy Perry song than a single fact about their country's war in Afghanistan. He knew better than to get worked up, but his body sometimes didn't. Breathe, he was always telling himself, just breathe. In the Army, every tiny detail of his days was mapped out, every foray on deployment preceded by a thorough briefing. Jeff could still hear his commander's staccato bark: "Okay, we're gonna have twenty guys get in five trucks, we're gonna drive eight miles at top speed, Jeff you're gonna be in the second truck, if we engage with the enemies we're gonna call a helicopter that's patrolling two miles away." There was always a plan, and the plan covered everything.

College, by comparison, was chaos. Sometimes you did everything right—completed your homework, prepared for lecture, arrived in class five minutes early—just to find a notice on the door that class had been cancelled. The military had trained him to scan the environment and evaluate every scenario; he couldn't just shut it off. Strolling through the quad, he would notice the maintenance man cutting grass, pushing back and forth a screaming hulk that hid whirring razor blades powerful enough to sever limbs. What would he do if there was an injury? His mind flipped through CPR techniques, jumped to the location of the nearest hospital, sorted through all the campus facilities which might carry a tourniquet. No one else around him thought like that, he knew. Why should they, he knew. But the fact of it still made Jeff uncomfortable, isolating him further. "If there's some situation, I know I can't depend on any of them," he said.

Civilian life required a different modus operandi and new forms of vigilance. Financial literacy had been low among Jeff's peers in the Army—especially young soldiers, usually in their late teens and early twenties, who were often getting their first real paychecks.[2] When Jeff returned to Fort Bragg after his first deployment, he went out with his friends almost every night. After one late outing, passed in a blur at some nearby casinos, Jeff had overdrawn his bank account so much that his entire next paycheck hadn't been enough to cover it. It was two brutal months of overdraft fees: a $5 carton of cigarettes became $35 as his bank kept slapping him with extra charges. He eventually managed to claw out of the hole, in part because the military was covering all his basic needs. "No matter what I do in the Army, I know I can go to the chow hall," he said. "Even if you blow all your money, you'll still eat. You'll still have the barracks. You don't have to worry about any of that." In his new life, he had to watch his money like never before.

After leaving the military, Jeff had collected a couple months of unemployment before finding work at a bicycle repair shop. He had learned his lesson never to slide back into debt. In addition to the post-9/11 GI Bill, he was also able to secure a transfer scholarship of $10,000 for scoring high marks in community college. When his first university bill arrived, he looked upon the zero balance with immense relief. He was struggling in every class, his grades in free fall, but at least he wasn't in debt. As long as he remained enrolled in a minimum number of credits, the GI Bill supplied him with a stipend of roughly $1,200 each month. At least his horrible experience was getting subsidized.

He tumbled through the rest of the semester, never able to get a firm footing. He passed two out of his five classes, his GPA barely scraping above 1.0. "It was awful. I was super anxious. I had failed at everything, more or less," he said. All he could do was tell himself that it wasn't over yet, that he would get another chance when the second semester began. Then, as classes were starting back up after winter break, he received a letter from the university.

Jeff had always assumed the GI Bill would cover his full tuition, but the outstanding five-figure charge on his statement was suddenly telling him otherwise. When he brought the letter to the VA rep on campus, he was told his education benefits only took him part of the way. If he wanted to remain at the university, he had to pay the rest of the balance himself. Jeff's stomach lurched. That's a wrap, he thought. He didn't feel he had any other choice. He withdrew from his courses that week.

MATT WAS LOOKING for his own turnaround and hoped that the VA might provide it. In the winter of 2012, the week following a quiet but tender Valentine's Day with his wife, they received another letter from the VA benefits office. In his original notice a few months earlier, two of his claims had been deferred. With the pair now granted, both deemed secondary to his back condition, Matt's combined disability rating was raised to 90 percent.

Matt soon stopped working for his dad. "It beat me down too much and I just couldn't do it," he said. "I have other adult responsibilities—I'm married, I have a house to take care of, all kinds of other stuff. I can't injure myself every two weeks and fricking lay around for a week." It was a tough decision. The men in Matt's family had been working construction for six generations; there had been an expectation that he would take over the family business. His father took the news hard. He had always been the strong, silent type; Matt had only seen him cry once, when Matt's grandmother passed away. "I could tell it hurt him," Matt said, when he announced he would no longer be working. "He was disappointed—not in me but at the situation." Stepping away from the business was "one of the hardest things I had to do in my life," Matt said. But it felt like a decision he had to make. It felt, ultimately, like a decision that his body had made, not him.

It was around the same time that he finally turned to the VA for treatment. The VA's relative lack of emphasis on treatment, as opposed to benefits, has long perplexed many in the healthcare field. In Matt's case, he had been counseled and urged to file for disability compensation before he was even fully out of the Army—a full year before he would decide, with no prompting or guidance from the VA, to pursue healthcare. His case is not unique. Since the 2012 rollout of the military's Transition Assistance Program, the VA has actively served up its menu of available benefits to departing service members, with hardly the same level of attention given to rehabilitation and recovery services. "It's an outrage in my view to put people in a disability pipeline before they've ever been treated," said Sally Satel, an expert on mental health policy and former VA staff psychiatrist. "In the VA, that happens."

Satel believes the VA's confounding approach to disability and healthcare denies many veterans even a chance at viability. Imagine getting into a car crash, she said, and the system that takes you in immediately tells you, "Here's your wheelchair. This is what you're going to be in for the rest of your life." The patient would rightly respond in bewilderment. "You're thinking, 'Where's my physical therapy? Where's my surgery? What the heck!'" Yet at the VA, severe clinical designations are quickly attached to veterans, impeding what is purportedly the organization's central mission. Satel laments how far the agency has strayed from its mark. "To say someone is disabled, in the clinical realm, that's a prognosis," she said. "That means for the foreseeable future you're not going to be functional. Now it could be that in the immediate future—even a year or two—you're going to have a lot of problems. But we are going to work like hell to make you as functional as possible. That [should be] the goal."[3]

AT SAINT LOUIS UNIVERSITY, Jeff had found a guidance counselor genuinely committed to that goal. He started seeing her early in his first semester, as his grasp on school was rapidly slipping beyond his control. In his new terrain of private higher education, full of uncertainties and its own indigenous customs, she became a bulwark. Though her specialty was in sexual trauma, she helped Jeff to understand that much of what he experienced—the constant hypervigilance, his problems with trust—were consistent with civilian trauma cases like sexual assault, and far from unusual given his background in the military. Crucially, she impressed upon him that his symptoms did *not* consign him to failure, and that none of it prevented him from thriving in college. Hearing this from a medical authority allowed Jeff to retain his sense of agency, at a time when he needed it most. His twice-a-week appointments came to feel like a lifeline.

But the meetings, like everything, were suddenly disrupted when he received the nasty shock of his tuition bill. Not only was he forced to suspend his classes, but his counselor could no longer officially see him; their sessions had been covered by a student insurance policy he no longer had. She still tried to help him as she could, though it now had to be off the books. They maintained a correspondence through email; during Jeff's more trying periods, she was always reachable by phone. In the meantime, Jeff learned through a campus VA rep that Saint Louis University was a member of the Yellow Ribbon consortium, a national program in which participating schools agree to provide additional funding for veterans who meet certain requirements. Saint Louis had a limited number of Yellow Ribbon slots, all of them already filled, but several of the veterans were graduating in the spring. Stick around, the VA rep advised Jeff, and he would be a strong candidate for the program when the next academic year began. Suddenly, Jeff felt he had hope again, something to work toward. He would have another chance.

While enrolled in school full-time, he had scaled down his hours at the bike shop where he worked. But taking leave from Saint Louis also meant he would stop receiving his monthly GI Bill stipend. He requested extra hours at the Touring Cyclist, but business was slow during the winter. Jeff and his wife resolved to get through it. They tightened their belts and cut back on all unnecessary expenses. Jeff used the time for reflection. "I thought about my failures," he said. "Physics just wasn't working. I couldn't go to these labs. The math was too much. So I thought, *How am I going to graduate reasonably quickly, get a job, and move on?*" He sat down and reviewed all the eligible transfer credits from his associate's degree, then matched them against the different departments at Saint Louis University. One offering jumped out—a degree in business administration with an information-technology focus. He liked the sound of it; his parents had run a small delivery business and he had always been interested in how companies operated. He did more research and saw that the degree leaned more toward management than computer science. That suited him just fine.

When the fall of 2012 arrived, Jeff steeled himself for what was to come. *Take two*, he thought. But this time, he knew what to expect. Due to his dismal first semester, he had been placed on academic probation, preventing him from transferring to the university's business school. Nevertheless, he enrolled in a full course load of business classes and was determined to dig his way out. The change in discipline provided a more settling environment. There were older adults in his courses, many who had worked before, and a few of the department's professors had also served in the military. On the first day of his public speaking class, Jeff noticed a classmate about his age. He looked closer and saw that some of the man's fingers were missing. They found each other after class and sure enough, the other man had also served in the Army, deployed to Iraq around the same time that Jeff was fighting in Afghanistan. Having a new friend on campus felt like a salve. Jeff now had someone who could pick up on his references, who could share in his humor and bewilderment at the rest of the school, whom Jeff knew he could trust to act in the right way if there was ever an emergency. It made a big difference. Jeff's nerves gradually relaxed, and he was able to attend more to his schoolwork. Meetings with his counselor, on their regular schedule again, fortified his new ethos.

"I would go into her office and say, 'Hey, I had a really hard time yesterday. I was breathing really hard and I was sweating because the classroom was closed, and I wasn't prepared for that and it just threw me off.' It was still that infantry mindset of, 'We're going to plan out the whole day and we're going to follow steps A, B, C, D.' Now all of a sudden, I get to Step D and it's not there, class is cancelled or whatever, and I have nowhere to go. Not a big deal in the scheme of life but it's the sort of thing that can go throw someone off who's used to a very regimented life, where you can depend on everybody. So a lot of the counseling went into working through those things and getting to a point where I either planned for those things or was able to just accept them. Able to say, 'Hey, that's okay. I'll go to the library. Or go to the Chick Fil-A. Or call it a day and just go home and have a beer.' Just getting to the point where the environment and the changes and the uncertainty was no longer so upsetting and difficult."

By the end of his second semester, Jeff had raised his grades enough to shed academic probation. His transfer to the business school was approved. He had drawn a map of the credits he needed to graduate in just over two years, and with the first semester successfully completed, he was on his way. *I'm on track here*, he thought. *This is going to be a thing that I can do.* He gave himself a moment to consider the achievement. One year ago, he had been crashing through the floor at college, unsure if he had even reached the bottom. Getting into the Yellow Ribbon program, which covered his tuition and allowed him to stay in school, had stabilized him. Working with a counselor who understood his challenges, without letting him make excuses for them, had pushed him forward. He stared down the path toward graduation and knew that he could make it.

MATT KEPT DELAYING his first visit to the VA's healthcare branch in part due to a misguided attitude shared by many vets. He still carried ideas of the VA as a treatment facility for amputees and other maimed victims of war—an antiquated notion that had made him feel undeserving by comparison. He admitted that he was also, for a while, in denial. "I knew I had some physical aches and pains, but I was still trying to be John Wayne through it all. I knew there were people out there worse off than me and I didn't want to take up appointments. I felt like I [might be] taking something away from people who needed it more than me."

Once he started, though, his experience reflected another sentiment found just as common in the veterans' community: utter frustration. First, there were the long wait times just to get an appointment. Compared to the week or two that it takes to see a civilian specialist, "at the VA you gotta wait three months in order to get in," Matt said. One of his first VA treatment appointments was with an orthopedic surgeon, an aging doctor "probably ten years older than God," Matt recalled. After a few cursory questions about Matt's knee pain, the doctor noticed Matt's tattoos and the consultation veered into a lecture about "how unprofessional tattoos were." Matt was put off by the encounter. "It's an American flag! How unprofessional is that? And besides, what am I here for, dude? Fix my knees! I don't care what your feelings are about my tattoos."

Matt was told to get X-Rays and MRIs. He was passed from one department to the next, referred from this specialist to that radiologist to that physical therapist. Spaced weeks to months apart, he lost track of how many appointments he had been to, everything fuzzing out into an ineffectual blur. He was told his kneecaps were "tilted." On WebMD, he learned the misalignment was typically caused by overuse and blunt trauma. "Well, that's my whole Army career right there," he thought.

Eventually Matt gave up on his knees. They weren't feeling better, but they weren't getting worse, while his back had been getting much, much worse. He was pinching it more frequently in the middle of the most mundane tasks, and the pain could get so bad he could barely dress himself or use the bathroom without his wife's assistance. The VA took more X-Rays. They assigned him more physical therapy. Nothing was working. His therapist said he wasn't doing the stretches. Matt said he was. He was referred to someone else. The constant shuffling irritated him, while his back continued to feel like it was "getting stabbed by a hot poker." No one seemed able to help; no one seemed able even to explain what was causing the pain. "You should just do more stretches," he was told. "You should quit smoking," he was told, "because nicotine constricts your blood flow." Matt's frustration turned to disbelief. Of course smoking was a bad habit, but it wasn't the kind of bad habit that continually pinched nerves in your back and caused you to double down in pain. "Get off my smoking," he wanted to say. "You people are the reason I am smoking."

Matt had tried to get better, but none of it was going the way he had hoped. "I felt dismissed so many times," he said. Without getting the results he sought from the VA's healthcare, without finding a path to become "as functional as possible" again, he turned away from treatment altogether. At least the VA's disability system was delivering what it promised. At least he was getting his payments every month.

IN CELEBRATION OF VETERANS DAY, some restaurants in St. Louis invited vets and their families to come in and dine on the house. Jeff was not the type to pass up a free meal. He and Bethany went out to Applebee's one year, to the local casino's buffet another, and once to a fancy seafood spot where they feasted on crab legs. The restaurants, of course, asked veterans to show something as a proof of service. Most vets simply flashed their VA cards, but Jeff had never gotten one. Since leaving the Army, he had made it a point to avoid the VA. The transition classes he was required to sit through during separation had been enough. He had listened uncomfortably to the VA agent's sweeping rhetoric about all the disabilities he and his fellow soldiers weren't even aware of and had felt repulsed by how quickly the others around him flocked to claim their benefits.

Jeff shook off the collective stampede toward disability payments. He had done his research; all he wanted from the VA was his education stipend and tuition assistance through the post-9/11

GI Bill, which he was able to sort out with the VA liaison on campus. Everything else—his service records, medical paperwork, empty claims packet—he had dumped into a trunk in the corner of his apartment. To validate his veteran status for his Veterans Day meals, he retrieved his DD-214 each year, folding the official document until it was the size of a business card and cramming the thick stack into his wallet. Every year he received confused looks from the waitstaff, and every year he endured the awkward exchange of trying to convince them that he had legitimately served—all to receive his complimentary meal. As Veterans Day approached again in the fall of 2014, Jeff had successfully adjusted to school and finished most of his credits to graduate. He decided it couldn't hurt to just stomach an appointment and finally get his ID card from the VA.

He braced himself for an ordeal. Though he had successfully stayed away from the VA for more than three years, he had skimmed the headlines of the organization's many scandals and heard nightmarish anecdotes from his friends. His wife Bethany took the day off from work to accompany him. They arrived at the John Cochrane VA Medical Center in St. Louis on a cool morning in October. They took a number at the reception desk; an attendant told them to expect a wait time of over an hour. The lobby was mostly filled with older vets. One man noticed the Eighty-Second Airborne badge on Jeff's messenger bag and shared that he had served in the same division during the Persian Gulf War. "Get your benefits, man!" he told Jeff. "You deserve it!"

When Jeff's number was finally called, he was handed a pile of papers. The only way to receive an ID card, the attendant told him, was to enroll in the VA's health benefits system. Jeff was happy with the healthcare coverage he was receiving through his university, but he went ahead and filled out the forms, only to be told that his household's joint income was too high to qualify. The only other option, the VA attendant said, was to submit a disability claim.

Jeff was shepherded to a VSO office on the second floor. But the VSO representative had already gone out to lunch. He and

Bethany waited for another hour in the lobby as vets from Vietnam and previous generations kept trying to engage him, kept wanting to commiserate over disabilities and their shared hardships as veterans. Jeff wondered if an ID card was worth all the hassle. With his class schedule and his wife's job, the best time to visit the VA had somehow landed on his birthday. He had thought the process would be just like getting your picture taken at the DMV, but it was dragging on and on, and now he was turning thirty-five surrounded by a crowd that was making him feel sixty-five. Worse, he was just a couple months away from completing all his course requirements—on the doorstep of graduating with a university degree—and yet he was now being funneled into the claws of the VA's disability system. *I don't want to be a part of this culture*, he thought. When the VSO office reopened in the afternoon, a representative from the American Veterans told Jeff he couldn't file a claim on his own, and had to sign over power of attorney, so that his application could be managed by AmVets. "He kinda cornered me into it until I said fine," Jeff said.

The AmVets agent continued to press. Jeff had brought a folder with all his medical records from the Army; he had broken his leg during stateside training and required a metal plate and a couple screws to support his ankle. "Do you have pain?" the VSO agent asked.

"Every once in a while," said Jeff.

"You probably have a lot of pain," the agent said as he filled out Jeff's paperwork. "Do you have hearing loss?"

Jeff replied that he had jumped out of airplanes and worked with artillery. His hearing wasn't as sharp as it used to be, but he didn't think it was hearing loss.

"It's probably worse than you think," the agent said. "You don't know it but you're reading lips."

"He was really just feeding me lines," Jeff recalled. "He was really encouraging, like, 'Oh, you got this disability. What about that disability? We'll just put this in there.' He definitely suggested that the problems were more severe and kept pushing me further and further.

He was saying, 'These are benefits you need. These are conditions you may have and not know it.' He was saying that I wasn't the same out of the Army as when I went in."

The interview lasted almost two hours. Jeff never got to see his own claim; the AmVets agent filled out the whole thing. "Good," the agent said, finally ending their meeting. "We'll get you some appointments."

MONTHS WENT BY without a word from AmVets or the VA, and then in the winter of 2015, Jeff received three letters in quick succession, notifying him of three separate VA appointments in the ensuing weeks.

His first appointment was with a VA physician who evaluated his leg and ankle. A second C&P examiner evaluated Jeff's hearing, and the third appointment paired him with a VA psychologist for a mental health evaluation. They sat and talked for more than two hours, the psychologist running through a long list of topics from her questionnaire. Jeff hadn't expected to open up, but once he started, he couldn't stop. He told her about all the major incidents from his deployments, about the brief counseling sessions he had attended after his first tour and during his second; he told her about the intensity and bliss of the group cohesion he experienced as an Army infantryman, about his feelings of abandonment during his final weeks; he told her about crashing through his first semester of college, the spears of anxiety that had torn him down, and the steady ways he was picking himself back up. Through it all, the psychologist kept emphasizing the occasions Jeff had felt the most debilitated—how often he had nightmares, how frequently he felt insecure, vulnerable, exposed. She kept insisting on getting numbers, and she recorded all of them down.

At the end of the evaluation, Jeff asked the VA doctor what mental health services were available to him. She replied that she had no role in that, and that there were no obligations for him to attend any follow-up treatment. Jeff was startled. "So you're going to tell me I have these issues, and you're going to give me money for them, but not require me to attend any follow-up services?" he asked. "Correct," the VA psychologist said. Jeff was momentarily speechless. He wanted to ask, "What kind of a system would do that—spend hours poring over a patient's ailments, diagnosing the patient, and then have nothing to offer when it comes to fixing the patient's problems?" He kept the questions to himself. That system, it sank in, was called the Veterans Benefits Administration. He left the evaluation room in disbelief.

His disability payments arrived soon after. In May 2015, Jeff opened his mailbox to find a letter and a check from the VA. By then, with tireless support from his wife and university counselor, he had finished all his degree requirements and graduated from Saint Louis University in December 2014. He had taken a little time off then picked up his hours again at the bike shop, while throwing himself into the job hunt for better opportunities. The notice from the VA paid no mind to his achievements and progress; after reviewing his records and evaluation reports, the VA had assigned Jeff 10 percent disability for his ankle, 30 percent for PTSD, while acknowledging TBI and hearing loss—for a combined disability rating of 40 percent.

Holy shit, Jeff thought, standing with the letter in his hand. *I'm disabled.*

Was he? He thought back to the previous fall, when he had first visited the VA and initiated the disability benefits process without even intending to. Nothing about that person, he thought, was 40 percent disabled. "I went in there as someone who was graduating college and entering the workforce," he said. "I thought of myself as fairly successful in those terms. I was moving on with my life and things were going well. And now you're telling me that essentially I can only do 60 percent of what I should be able to do?"

He hated his 30 percent PTSD rating in particular. He hated that percentage, hated the diagnosis, hated its connotations, even hated the term. "I would never label myself that way," Jeff said.

"People think you're afraid of fireworks or won't go to a baseball game. 'Oh, he has PTSD—he doesn't like crowds, be careful around him.' I hate all that shit." Once, attending a Fourth of July party at his sister-in-law's house, he heard some of her friends bring up the scheduled fireworks. "They have a bus that takes the veterans down to a place that's not so noisy," one of her neighbors said. "It's for their PTSD." Jeff had to bite back a retort. "I was just sitting there wanting to be like, 'Shut the hell up! You don't know anything!'" He had joined the Army almost a decade earlier to become a better man, never expecting that after leaving, he would rejoin a world so eager to believe that he was irreparably damaged, that his time in service had caused more harm than good.

Publicly, he dressed the diagnosis in a veil of humor. At work the next day, he announced to his colleagues at the bike shop, "Guess what everybody? I'm disabled!" At home, he pretended he was too disabled to do the household chores. Once, when his wife snapped at him, he defused the situation with a joke: "Would you yell at a disabled person?" Privately, though, the prospect spooked him. "It's instantly like a lifelong label," he said. "Most other medical conditions, whether it's mental or physical, a doctor diagnoses you and then you do some rehab or take some pills and then you move on with your life. Doctors don't just say, 'Well, you're 30 percent messed up. See ya.'"

While the VA typically schedules a review exam after eighteen to thirty months to update a veteran's disability profile, the process virtually never results in reducing a patient's disability rating[4]—in effect signifying that veterans, once deemed disabled by the VA, never got better. More than anything else, Jeff found this fact to be baffling.

"It's something that can be overcome," he said. "Certainly I struggled with anxiety and paranoia and nervousness at times, but it's a temporary thing." After leaving the military and moving in with Bethany, he had slept with a loaded pistol next to him on the nightstand for years. Every night, he had to check to make sure his firearm was right there, within arm's reach, or else he couldn't fall asleep. "That was just the level of comfort that I needed," he said. But not forever. The feelings of alarm and compulsive contingency planning faded, until eventually, they disappeared altogether. He got rid of his guns. His sleeping improved. "I won't say everything's 100 percent perfect but that stuff that interfered with my daily activities went away," he said. "I went to therapy and worked through it. It's not a lifelong crippling thing, it's just a difficult transition from lifestyle A to lifestyle B and that's very hard to do for a lot of folks."

He resolved never to set foot in the VA again. His one trip had resulted in a *disabled* designation he never wanted, even as he was graduating from college and entering the workforce. He didn't want to be like the other vets he saw who embraced their ratings, who slid right into an identity of brokenness. The VA, he came to see, was doubly complicit—both prompting that narrative among veterans and reaffirming it. "You're giving them this label forever and making them feel like they're handicapped or disabled or crippled in some way, like they can't contribute to society," he said. "It's fucking silly."

He still hadn't received his ID card.

CHAPTER 18
OUT OF THE NEST

MOLLY SNIDER wouldn't allow herself to stop working. She had always been a high achiever. Even before leaving the North Carolina National Guard in the fall of 2008, she had been hired as a health center assistant at Planned Parenthood. For years she juggled the National Guard, her job, and college courses at the same time. She expected a lot from herself. In the spring of 2008, she graduated *summa cum laude*, but didn't get to walk at commencement because she had already gone down to Mississippi for training with her unit. Things happened quickly. After her unit received orders for deployment, she had met with her first sergeant. She revealed that she felt she might have been experiencing symptoms of PTSD—a disclosure she knew could likely end her military service. She was right. "After we talked, [the first sergeant] was like, 'We'll put in your med board. You don't have to return for drill. You're free to go, basically.' And that was it," she said.

Molly had already received her first VA disability service-connection in March 2007—a 10 percent rating for her left ankle, which she had hurt in the basketball mishap while she was on leave from her tour in Iraq. The rating qualified her for monthly payments of $115, backdated to 2005. The injury had little effect on her work performance, but other issues were creeping up. She submitted new disability claims to add more conditions and increase her ratings.

Concussions she had sustained during service were compounded by new head injuries from snowboarding and roller derby. In one incident, she was driving to the local gym one morning when a drunk driver smashed into her car. His blood alcohol level, it later turned out, was nearly three times the legal limit. Molly was still in Officer Candidate School at the time; her car was hit so hard her equipment had blown out of the trunk and scattered across the road. She remembered calling out to passersby, "Please secure my gear. Please—it's Army property," even as she was spitting up glass and getting cut out from the driver's seat. "I was lucky to be alive," she said. In response to symptoms that likely involved physical trauma to the brain, the VA issued a 50 percent disability rating for PTSD.

With a newly earned bachelor's degree and the military behind her, Molly threw all of her energy into her job. Within a year, she was promoted at Planned Parenthood, then, in March of 2009, she was hired by the North Carolina Department of Health and Human Services. Around the same time, her five-year relationship with her partner ended in a whirl of rage and pain. In November, she went in for another VA evaluation and received treatment for "major depressive disorder." The VA increased her PTSD rating to 70 percent, and her compensation payments rose to $1,228 per month.

As a disease intervention specialist in Winston-Salem, her job was to meet with patients diagnosed with communicable diseases. It felt like a different frontline, this time in the underbelly of American public health. The task often fell on her to inform patients—and frequently their partners—that they had HIV/AIDS, or syphilis, or any from a long list of diseases that represents the worst news a person might ever hear. "It was real stressful," she said.

But she kept pushing, kept pouring more of herself into her work. Even as the country's economy collapsed and home prices tanked during the Great Recession, Molly managed to earn enough to be able to buy a home. It was "an amazing house," she recalled— four thousand square feet on three acres of land, a converted turn-of-the-century barn once used for drying tobacco leaves. She had a stocked fishpond. She had a small pasture for goats.

However, as the holidays approached in 2010, she felt she was barely holding on. "What I know for sure, is that I'm getting worse," she wrote in a blog post. "I can't be around people, crowds, loud noises or close quarters. I get anxious and then my mind turns into a foggy nothingness. I can't concentrate, focus or make decisions." Even the smallest interactions, the most trivial decisions, wore her out. She constantly felt the urge to nap. "I don't know how much longer I will be able to keep this going," she wrote. "I'm exhausted. My mind is Jello and I'm just going with the flow—following others around and trying to lay low so that I don't get in trouble at work. It takes every ounce of energy to wake up and do it all over again."

Then at the end of 2011, she got word that Planned Parenthood wanted her back in Asheville to fill a director role. "It was the job I always wanted but it was never available," Molly said. She didn't hesitate to say yes.

Molly's career appeared to be thriving. She kept saying yes. As the new regional director of quality and risk at Planned Parenthood, she was in charge of managing twelve health centers across four different states. "I didn't allow myself time to reflect," she said. "I was going 110 miles per hour. I just kept going, kept going." At the same time, the disturbances kept piling up. At work, Molly's boss kept demanding more, and Molly kept saying yes. When her boss assigned her a full review of the organization's compliance operations, the stress blew through what she could handle. In addition to suffering from an autoimmune disorder, her nightmares, panic attacks, and feelings of depression had become overwhelming.

One morning in November 2012, "my brain just stopped," Molly recalled. "It stopped working. It was like having a stroke or something. I wasn't able to read anymore." She checked into the hospital and went on medical leave from work. When she couldn't return to the office, she eventually lost her job. She lost her car. She lost her home in foreclosure. One step forward, two steps back. "I couldn't hold my life together," she said. "It slipped right through my hands."

MOLLY LIFTED THE BINDERS one at a time. This one carried her military service records. That one held her medical documents.

The thickest by far, she noted, contained all the various letters and pamphlets she had received from the VA. She grunted as she dropped them on the kitchen table. "It's oppressive," she said.

It was the summer of 2018, and Molly was sorting through all the paperwork she had compiled from a turbulent decade since leaving the military. Her thirty-eighth birthday was coming up in a few weeks. She was married now—to a partner who helped stabilize her, who put up with her, who pushed her in the direction of recovery, though never at a faster clip than what she was ready for. Her wife had been the one who suggested moving to Philadelphia. They had met in North Carolina; Molly was in a slump at the time and her wife thought the change might present a reset of sorts. Besides, she joked with Molly, "you could be miserable anywhere." They moved in March 2015.

The sun lit up the living room inside their cozy two-floor unit on Philadelphia's south side. A green mountain bike leaned against the couch. On top of a nearby bookshelf were ticket stubs from the previous week; Molly had surprised her wife by taking her to a Beyoncé show at Lincoln Financial Field. Going to a concert—the crowd, the noise, the lights—would have been unimaginable to Molly just a couple years prior. In fact, the late night was still more disruptive than they had hoped: Molly had trouble sleeping and had to cancel her physical therapy appointment the following day. Even so, she could see her progress. "The problem used to be if I ever did anything like this, it meant never returning to my previous routine. At least now I know this is a one-day thing. I know tomorrow I'll be back on track," she said.

A monthly calendar, the size of a movie poster, hung from the wall. Handwritten entries were color-coded to indicate which appointments belonged to Molly, her wife, or both.

For almost three years after her crash in 2012, Molly said, she could hardly read. Before that period, she had kept a regular journal, and some days all she wrote about were her frustrations with the VA. During one period in the fall of 2011, she had felt herself sinking into thoughts of suicide. She drove to the Asheville VA seeking immediate help, but the inpatient facility turned her away. "I should have been admitted," Molly wrote at the time. "However there were only six beds available and the closest place to go was the Richmond VA. I ended up staying with my cousins until I was stable enough to read right and drive back to my apartment. No job, no caregiver, no hope, no plan. Just VA benefits." She put down the journal with a sigh. "Yeah, good times."

The VA had raised Molly's disability rating for PTSD from 70 to 100 percent, effective November 2012. Her monthly benefits rose to $2,816. "At first the money part is helpful," Molly said. "It's very much a relief." But the benefits pulled her into a sense of dependency that she found increasingly discomforting. "I've reached a point in my healing where I want to be useful and have a purpose. I feel like discarded government waste. Earlier this year, I began feeling emotions again and my issues with crowds started getting better. But, the emptiness associated with having no expectations/purpose/routine is painful," she wrote in a 2016 email.

"I'm trying not to be the guys who hang out at the VA with all the service medals stuck in their hats," she said. "But I see how easily I could be. I have nowhere else to go. I have nothing else to do."

The impermanent nature of PTSD is well-documented in the scientific literature, yet Molly was finding few outlets that accounted for this in the civilian world. According to a 2008 *Journal of Behavioral Medicine* study, 80 percent of people exposed to traumatic experiences eventually recover, while only a fifth develop long-term, chronic PTSD. "From an evolutionary perspective," writes Sebastian Junger, "[short-term, acute PTSD] is exactly the response you want to have when your life is in danger: you want to be vigilant, you want to react to strange noises, you want to sleep lightly and wake easily, you want to have flashbacks that remind you of the danger, and you want to be, by turns, anxious and depressed. Anxiety keeps you ready to fight, and depression keeps you from being too active and putting yourself at greater risk. This is a universal human adaptation to danger."[1]

From Molly's perspective, the problem was not that her condition kept beating her down. It was how to construct a life that allowed for the natural course of PTSD to occur, for the disorder's reactionary symptoms, incongruous now with civilian society, to recede and be replaced by a more suitable set of adaptations. The military, she felt, had left a hole in her life, as wide and deep as anything she ever knew. What the VA didn't seem to understand is that benefits are not only an insufficient filling, but a corrosive one. "The military was your family," she said. "Once you're not active duty anymore, you're excommunicated. You literally lose your family, your friends, and your job all at once. You lose your whole identity."

ON A TUESDAY MORNING in August 2018, Molly zipped up I-95, relieved to be leaving Philadelphia behind. The speed limit didn't mean much to her, an instinct she blamed on her time in Iraq. For the past year and more, she had been making weekly trips to Shamrock Reins, a nonprofit specializing in equine-assisted therapy for veterans. Molly had first encountered equine therapy in February 2017, when she enrolled in a seven-week PTSD residential program at Fort Thomas near Cincinnati. From day one, the program reminded her of boot camp. "Everyone had the same stuff. We all had to get up at the same time, have our meals at the same time, attend all the same classes," she said. Outside contact was limited; they weren't even allowed to watch the news. Molly found the routinized structure immensely soothing.

In one of the activities, they packed into a van and drove to an off-site arena. Inside on the field, a team of mustangs bellowed and bristled. A "Cowboy Bill-type character" taught Molly and her cohort the principles behind equine therapy and guided them through their first tentative interactions with the horses. "It's basically bio-feedback," Molly explained. "The horses are sensitive to what's going on in their surroundings—they'll mirror you. If you're all fidgety, they're all fidgety. But if you're chill, they'll become chill. I was well enough to appreciate the challenge. And if you do have a really sweet horse, it's very comforting just grooming them."[3]

A stretch of highway opened and Molly punched forward. The lush green plains of Bucks County, Pennsylvania, rushed past at seventy, seventy-five, eighty miles per hour. The commute to Shamrock's ranch, fifty miles north of the city, took more than an hour but Molly was glad to have the weekly commitment. Her time at Fort Thomas had been "very helpful, very promising," she said, but after graduating in April, she found it difficult to maintain her progress. "You're kinda like a baby bird being kicked out of the nest at the end," she said. She tried finding VA support classes in the greater Philadelphia area, but discovered that many of the notices were outdated. A weekly PTSD group, exactly what she felt she needed, hadn't met for months. One program she went to was specifically geared for drug addicts, and the staff gently suggested she wasn't the right fit. She visited another program but all the veterans there were significantly older, and the services resembled hospice care more than mental health support. She could feel herself starting to backslide. "Once you get home you assume the things you set up are going to be correct," she said, "but that was not the case with me and not the case with most people in my cohort." One step forward, one step back.

Molly pulled off the main road and crunched up a small gravel lane before parking outside a big barn house. Her psychologist at the VA was the one who had found Shamrock Reins, eventually convincing Molly to give it a try. After booking her first session in April the previous year, she had been going back more or less every week since. She grabbed a light khaki shirt from the backseat and put it on over her sleeveless black tank, covering the colorful tattoos that wrapped around both her arms. Since December, she had been working with a new horse, a formidable dark buckskin named Clancy. Unlike Molly's first horse, the ranch's exceptionally friendly boss mare, Clancy could be stubborn and occasionally irritable. Molly had only managed to ride Clancy once, but it had been one of the highlights of her year.

"It's such a confidence booster when it goes well like that," she said. "But Clancy can be funny. She's not out there just to walk around for no reason. She wants to feel like you know what the hell you're doing, like you have a plan. And there are some days when I just don't have that confidence to show. She knows it and she'll just be an ass."

After Molly signed in, a trainer named Tina wandered over to ask about the Beyoncé show. Molly talked it up, leaving out the extra day it had taken her to level back. They briefed on the day's session. "It's hot so let's just do some grooming and grazing today," Tina said.

Clancy's head bounced as Molly approached her stall. A strand of coarse brown hair shook loose and fell between the horse's eyes. "You're ridiculous," Molly said, patting Clancy's face. "I love you." A thick dribble of spit leaked from Clancy's mouth. "Ew, that's pretty gross, Clancy," Molly said. "I thought you were going to say something sweet."

Another veteran walked through the stable with his young daughter. They wore matching black T-shirts, the words "Operation Enduring Freedom / Operation Iraqi Freedom" inscribed around a graphic of an eagle. Molly ran a comb through Clancy's hair, then switched to a soft-bristle brush and rubbed circles across Clancy's body.

Inside a dirt pen nearby, Andrew, a tall Iraq War vet wearing a stretched white shirt and blue jeans, led his horse in small circles. "That's it, Emerald," he said in a loud, slow drawl that carried across the field. "Come, Emerald. Come. Good."

After a walk and a bath, Molly returned Clancy to her stall. A bucket of apples and carrots was waiting. Molly ran her hand through Clancy's hair while she fed her, then planted a kiss on Clancy's face when she finished.

"Ha! I kissed you!"

In her post-session assessment, across more than half a dozen measurements like anxiety, irritability, and vigilance, she marked that she was feeling better, calmer. It had been a good morning.

LUNCH WAS SERVED. Janet Brennan, Shamrock's founder and director, removed a stack of paper plates from their packaging and placed them on the table in the barn house kitchen. "We've got barbecue beef cups, chicken potato and bacon salad, homemade brownie bites and a big tray of fruit. Debbie made that salsa," she said, pointing.

Molly smiled. "Chicken potato bacon salad?" She had family members who were vegetarian; they likely would have objected to calling such a dish a "salad."

"It's like potato salad, but it's chicken that's the main star," said Janet, missing the irony. "The table is set up under the tree. The Adirondack chairs are out by the pool, too."

Outside, Molly, Tina, Andrew and Andrew's guest, Dre, settled around the picnic table. Molly examined the stack of meat on her plate before taking a bite. "It's like a barbecue sandwich meets a sloppy joe meets a Bisquick muffin."

Andrew soon brought up politics. "How would you feel if you had to serve under Trump? It's a question I often think about."

Molly poked a piece of melon with her fork. "It's so weird because I went to Iraq under Bush, right?"

"Mhmm, me too," said Andrew.

"And I *hated* him at the time," said Molly. "But now I'm like, he's *amazing* compared to this guy."

Everyone laughed. "My mother loved Bush," Andrew said. "I remember she used to always say to me, 'He's a faith-based man. He prays.' And I would tell her, 'Yeah, he *preys*—on the innocent!'"

A native of Kutztown, Pennsylvania, just an hour west of the ranch, Andrew had joined the Air Force Reserves after high school and trained as a flight medic. Soon the war mobilized his unit and he deployed to Iraq. After separating from the military, he applied for disability benefits. "It took me almost four years of fighting to get my compensation," he said. "I have big-time issues with the VA."

Andrew initially filed his claims through Disabled American Veterans, a national VSO with more than one million members. The

VA rejected them. He tried again, working with a different DAV officer, but for over two years, he kept getting the same unsuccessful results. His frustration grew. One day, he met another VSO officer who took pity on him. "I'm not supposed to tell you this but contact this guy," the man said, sliding a business card across the table. "If anyone asks, I don't know who this person is. I didn't give you his name."

The person on the card turned out to be a civilian therapist who had been assisting vets with their VA benefits since the Vietnam War. "I hired him, and I paid him cash, and I didn't go to see him for therapy," said Andrew. "I went to see him to fight for me." The therapist reviewed Andrew's records and wrote a long letter detailing all the afflictions Andrew had sustained in service, including sinusitis ("I was in sandstorms on the regular," Andrew said, "you breathe all that junk in and I lost my smell"), hearing loss ("not because of any traumatic event but you hear the vibration from the airplane floor and it damages those bones in your inner ear"), and PTSD from multiple deployments. This time it took just three weeks for Andrew's claims to be approved.

With the VA's spending on disability-related benefits reaching well over $100 billion per year, the massive disability apparatus has spawned a cottage industry of doctors, attorneys, consultants, and organizations who profit from the system. This itself is not new: some of the earliest pension programs for American veterans were beset by grifters and opportunists, even in the early decades of the republic.[3]

Then, as now, doctors and others who perform disability examinations have financial and emotional incentives to validate veterans' claims. For one thing, such appointments can be quite lucrative—several hundred dollars per evaluation—though they are undoubtedly unethical and, in some cases, criminal. One C&P examiner in Puerto Rico charges $200 for a ten-minute phone consultation to supply veterans with the needed evidence to get their claims approved.[4] Other actors may genuinely feel they are doing the right thing, aiding veterans who "deserve" disability compensation as a means of additional income—without seeing the larger repercussions of labeling so many men and women as disabled.[5] In either case, rather than supporting veterans in rehabilitating and achieving their full potential, these groups coach veterans to achieve a far more odious goal: a maximum disability rating.

Andrew took another bite from his beef cup then pushed his plate away. "This was good but it's too rich for the heat," he said. Following the advice from his therapist, he had continued to press for a ratings increase. "I contacted my senator and did a senatorial inquiry on [my VA examiners]," he said. Within two weeks, his disability rating was raised to 100 percent. His benefits, too, were retroactive; Andrew received three years of back pay.

From contacting their policymakers to petitioning medical licensing boards, veterans have many avenues of recourse against VA disability specialists whose decisions they don't agree with. Most immediately, a veteran whose claim has been denied, or returned with a disability rating lower than what he wanted, has three ways to submit an appeal. First, he can file a supplemental claim to add new and relevant evidence. Second, he can ask for a senior reviewer to examine the case, and third, he can appeal to a Veterans Law Judge.[7] If his appeal is denied by the board, the veteran can appeal further to the US Court of Appeals for Veterans Claims. The VA upholds no limit on the number of new or aggravated conditions that a veteran can apply for, nor is there a timespan in which vets must file their claims.[8] Altogether, these factors—a robust procedure for appealing undesirable decisions, no prohibition on additional claims, no time constraints on applying—result in a clogged and overworked VA disability system. Combat-wounded veterans are shuffled in with opportunists, serious claims are buried among trivial ones, and righteous grievances are diluted by spurious ones.[9]

Andrew viewed himself among the righteous. "They don't want us to get our benefits," he said. "They make this damn system so muddy that you can't find your way through."

Across the table, Dre was nodding. "Is that bureaucracy or red tape or—"

"It's a little bit of everything. It's all fixed, man."

A rating of 100 percent qualified Andrew for more than $3,000 in disability compensation each month. At the time, he hadn't held a job in more than two years, and soon, his veteran friends were advising him to apply for Social Security disability as well. He contacted the civilian therapist again. "I paid him more money and said, 'Will you represent me for Social Security?' He said, 'absolutely.'" The additional benefits arrived so quickly they caught Andrew off guard.[10] "I called my sister and I'm like, 'Did you make a large deposit in your account last night that was accidentally put in mine?' Because I'm loaded overnight. It was all the back pay. You don't know it's coming in. You turn around and there's $50,000 in your account."

Andrew found himself guarding his windfall like a secret, as if it would vanish if anyone found out. "Suddenly, I felt like I have to keep this to myself," he said. "I kept thinking I was going to wake up and this was all a bad dream. It didn't really happen."

His suspicions weren't entirely wrong. His increased benefits from the VA had come through a mechanism called Individual Unemployability, which bumps a claimant's disability rating all the way to 100 percent if he is deemed "unable to hold a job as a result of service-connected disabilities."[11]

The bigger monthly checks gave Andrew an immediate thrill, but the long-term repercussions of his new designation began to sink in. "I went from being able to do everything [to the VA] telling me I'm unemployable," he said, "that I should basically go home and sit around and lick my wounds."

Andrew called the civilian therapist again. "I don't want to be unemployed for the rest of my life. What am I going to do?"

The response from the other line was clear. "You can't challenge this, because you'll lose everything that you fought for."

For a while, Andrew felt caught between the payouts he had in hand and the work they prevented him from doing. "I didn't like that, but what was I to do?" he said. "It took me about a year to make peace with the decision." He lifted his shoulders, sitting a little taller. Lunch was over and he had decided to take a dip in the pool.

"I realized I should count this as a blessing," he said. "I shouldn't feel bad about this."

THE SUN BEAT DOWN on the wide and empty road. After saying goodbye to Clancy, Molly set out back to Philadelphia, replaying the conversations at the ranch in her head. Though she was never designated with Individual Unemployability, she remembered vividly feeling duress during her checkup C&P evaluations, gripped by the fear that her benefits might be reduced before she was ready.

"It makes you not want to get better—or at least not tell them that you're getting better," she said. The VA, in that regard, seemed to be taking a lesson directly from the military, which from the beginning had prompted her to hide the truth. "When I enlisted, they ask you, 'Have you ever done drugs?' And you say, 'What's drugs?' Because otherwise they won't let you in. You have to say no. And then my [sexual orientation]—that's a hell to the no. I'm not going to talk about who I'm with." In time, Molly came to view disability payments as a form of "hush money"—a monthly check to keep all the compensation recipients in line, to keep them from demanding more support or other services from the VA. "That's what it seems like. They want you to be a good patient, not a rehabbed patient. You couldn't say you were getting better. You couldn't tell the truth."

Not that everyone was inclined to. "I know there are people abusing the system," Molly went on. "Without a doubt. People talking about stuff like, 'Oh I've got mine. Did you get yours?' Like it's this thing you're supposed to do." Molly had tried to be careful not to fall into that mindset, but sometimes she wasn't sure if she was successful. After her breakdown at the end of 2012, she knew she was just barely holding on. "I couldn't work. I couldn't even read. I needed about a year just to sleep and exist. But after that, I needed to get better."

Since moving to Philadelphia in 2015, she had been meeting regularly with a psychologist and a psychiatrist, a pair of ladies whose VA offices were right across the hall from one another. "They're MVP rock stars," Molly said, and their willingness to go the extra mile, to research and find the right resources for her, had helped her steadily get back on track. "Now I feel like I'm at the point where I can do something," Molly said. "But I'm also at that point where I'm like, how does that work? It's like my entire life was depending on what I get every month. I don't even know how to go about weaning off that."

The VA had referred her to its Vocational Rehabilitation and Employment program, which promises to help vets with their job search and professional development. Molly went to her first meeting at the regional office on Wissahickon Avenue in Philadelphia in the spring of 2017. She had just returned from Fort Thomas, more motivated than she had felt in years "to tackle life." A Voc Rehab counselor introduced her main choices: she could go the education route and pursue a degree, or participate in a work experience program with partnered organizations, for which the VA would supply a modest stipend. Work sounded good to Molly, but when she asked for more information, the opportunity came to sound more like a dead end.

"It seemed like they were just using veterans to fill the need of clerks at the Social Security department," she said. "Like Social Security needed people badly and they were like, 'Okay, we'll throw you some bodies.'" She decided to enroll in a summer course at the community college. It was something to fill the time and Voc Rehab later offered to pay for some of her courses. Molly signed up for biochemistry. She found the material fascinating and aced the class. *Right on*, she thought. Maybe she was getting back to her old self. Her Voc Rehab counselor suggested that she work toward an associate's degree in applied science; it would supplement the bachelor's she had earned almost a decade earlier and raise her profile for employers. Fall was just around the corner. Molly signed up for a full course load.

She lasted three days. "The noise, the crowds, the people, the requirements of it all—it just made me run out into traffic and ultimately end up back at the VA," she recalled. The VA, though, had nothing else to offer. "Voc Rehab couldn't help me after that," Molly said. "If [school] didn't work, they didn't know anything else. They didn't know what to do with me. So they ended up dropping me."

But her performance during the summer session, when the campus had felt more manageable and her efforts were focused on a single course, had reminded Molly of what it felt like to succeed. The lesson she took away was not to retreat from the world but to continue challenging herself—without taking things too far or too fast. Life after the military, she came to realize, unfurled in cycles. Sometimes, you take a step forward. Sometimes, you get pulled a step back. What mattered is taking that next step.

In February 2018, she went on a six-day trip with a group of other veterans to the Everglades, organized by Outward Bound. By the second day, she hated every second of it. But she had nowhere to go. "I had a little talk with myself," she said. She determined to block out the voice that was complaining it was too much, that was telling her she wasn't ready, that was crying to just pick up her ball and go home. The group pressed forward. Molly had never paddled so much in her life. They traveled forty nautical miles in four days. In the end, the trip marked a major turning point.

For the majority of veterans, particularly people with mental health conditions, "It's a slow atrophy," Molly said. "When you're on active duty, or even when you're in the reserves, you're constantly doing drills. Constantly, so that you can stay sharp. But when you're home twiddling your thumbs, you forget the skills you have because you're not using them. You forget you can do all this badass stuff. But if you could just be put to a little test again, then you would remember, and you would feel good about yourself again. That's what I had when I went out with Outward Bound. We had to navigate ourselves all throughout the Mangrove Islands. You know when you made a mistake because suddenly, you're in the Gulf of Mexico. And it felt so good to be like, 'Alright, I know how to do this.' It's remembering that you really are capable still. You really are worth something."

NOT ALL MILITARY SKILLS, of course, can be easily plugged into a conventional career. But what can translate is an ethic of service, a grounding in teamwork under the most exacting standards, and a proven record of overcoming adverse conditions. On better days, Molly could feel her facilities sharpening again after years of wasting under the blanket of disability that she had grown accustomed to. Her hope was to align her steady improvements with her lifelong love of animals, and angle for a job where the two might overlap. The previous winter she had volunteered at the local church, where the congregation had tried to arrange a live nativity scene as the holidays approached. With Christmas around the corner, the manger regulars arrived—goats and donkeys and other local farm animals—but few of the organizers had ever dealt with them before. One cow, Stormy, managed to escape twice in one morning, trotting with abandon up I-95.[13] Molly, who had grown up on a farm, found herself directing the team. "I did such a good job they wanted to put me in charge," she said.

Encouraged by the experience, she went online and searched for other volunteer gigs that could bring her closer to nature. Tyler State Park in Bucks County, which Molly passed every week on her way to equine therapy, had a posting for someone to help take care of its migratory birdhouses. She usually checked on them on her drive back after Shamrock.

The three birdhouses assigned to Molly were positioned in a neat row, about twenty yards apart, just outside the park's tree line. Molly pulled to the side of the road, then hopped out with a white binder under her arm. She had been checking in on the birdhouses every week since March, tracking new eggs and nests and whatever else appeared. "I haven't done anything with such consistency for years," she said. "I'm very proud of myself for that." It was exactly the kind of engagement she wished the VA had been able to connect her with, but instead, so many of her encounters with the VA had been defined by absorption into her disabilities. "For so long you're told, 'You have this diagnosis, you have that diagnosis.' You become a really good patient." The VA fixated on all she couldn't do, rarely what she could. In her first year after moving to Philadelphia, she had collected a whole shelf full of VA business cards, pamphlets and flyers: Community Healing Ceremony for Veterans and Civilians, Veterans Indoor Fun Day, Veterans Personal Needs Research Session, Veterans Fun Cooking Class, Women Veterans Extravaganza. "An evening full of festivities!" they promised. "Still time to register!"

To Molly, they all seemed to be missing the point. "I hate not having purpose," she said. What she wanted was a routine, a structure, a path on which she could measure her progress and chart her next steps. It's why she enjoyed working with Clancy, the Shamrock stable's most mercurial horse, because it forced Molly to face her own limitations each week and fight through them, because Clancy's affection had to be earned. "The biggest thing I've learned since coming back from the military is the search for meaning," she went on. "You just have to hang on and find the right fit for what you're able to do."

Molly stopped in front of her first birdhouse. A pair of tree swallows had moved in a couple months earlier, quickly improvising a home from wild grasses. The female had laid three eggs. The parents had chirped and fussed every time Molly approached, sometimes swooping at her until she had to raise her arm and duck. But it was a good sign of protective parenting, and it made Molly happy even as she braced for their outbursts.

The previous week, she had filled out a job application—her first one in years. The Pennsylvania Department of Conservation and National Resources was seeking to hire Park Rangers, and though it had been a while since Molly was staffed out in the field, it was a line of work she could see a real future in. A future of working, contributing, growing—for more than half a decade, it had been unthinkable. And if she did get the job, it represented the first step to weaning herself off the VA's disability payments, a prospect that gleamed bright. "I'll have a living wage," she said. "It's not the most money I've ever made but I can respect myself. They can take all my benefits. I don't care anymore."

Molly stopped at another birdhouse and peered inside. An egg nestled in the corner behind some straw, small and blue like an ocean jewel. The bluebirds that had been living there had moved out; one of their eggs never hatched. The others, though, had hatched and thrived, and Molly had been a doting observer to their entire life cycle: from cracking out of their shells as hungry pink nestlings, to maturing into blue and orange chicks, to becoming adults and flying away.

Molly was preparing for her own launch. Her civil service exam was scheduled one month out, enough time for her to hit the books and study the material. "And even if I don't get it, I'm proud of myself just for filling out this damn application," she said. "That hadn't been in my brain for a long time, to think I'd ever be capable of working again." Bit by bit, she was relearning what she was capable of. One step forward, one step back. She was moving forward again.

CHAPTER 19
GOOD AND FAITHFUL SERVANT

THE NIGHTMARES didn't start immediately. They appeared long after Matt had left the Army, months after he and his wife had moved back to Marion in mid-2011. At first, the couple figured they would try to ride it out, take each episode day by day. And at first, they stuck to the plan, even as things got worse and worse.

"When you're in the infantry and you have PTSD, you're around a bunch of other people who also have PTSD. There's nothing wrong with you because everyone has the same thing wrong with them. And if they don't, they understand. Some people might have it worse than others. But the whole point is that there's nothing wrong with you—when you're in the military, it's normal. When you get out, it's not normal [anymore]," Matt said.

It wasn't normal to wake up in the middle of the night, swinging in the darkness; it wasn't normal to spring out of bed, crashing into their closet's accordion doors; it wasn't normal to blow through the bedroom, sprinting down the hall as if the house were on fire. One night, Jessica woke up to find her husband, dazed and muttering to himself, almost leaving through their front entrance. She installed baby gates in the doorways, then sat down with Matt for a talk. Their marriage was still young and the strain on their relationship was evident. The conversation was difficult; Matt had been dreading it. "When the symptoms first start getting bad, you deny it," he said. "You develop a mentality to keep your eyes forward no matter how much you're suffering. You don't want to admit that there's anything wrong even when there is." But they finally agreed: he had to seek counseling.[1]

Matt met Dr. Bellman[2] in August 2011. She was the resident psychologist at the Marion VA Medical Center, with a PhD in clinical psychology. Matt felt comfortable around her instantly. "She laid out some different therapy options and away we went," he said. They skipped the ramp-up phase; from their first appointment, they began to address what Matt had always kept tightly guarded—his primary trauma, the death of his team leader.

There are many different styles of leadership, each with its own methods and virtues. For Matt, fresh and impressionable on his first deployment, Sergeant Wyckoff represented the pinnacle: he was both the kind of leader you looked upon with awe, and the type of friend you wanted to have by your side. Everyone on the team had a role. When they were out on patrol, Matt's job was to carry the shotgun for breaching doors. Sergeant Wyckoff trained him in how to use it, but his real task was teaching all of them what it meant to be soldiers, and more importantly, team members. "No matter what," he taught them, "you take care of each other."

On one mission, Matt and another private moved on to clear the compound ahead. They immediately heard about it from Sergeant Wyckoff. "He chewed our ass out," Matt recalled. "F-bombs and 'Get the hell back here!' and 'What do you think you are doing?' and this and that. But later on, he pulled us aside and said, 'Listen, I appreciate your motivation and your wanting to get this done. But it's not your job to go first. It's my job to go first.'" Matt took the message to heart. On his second tour, when he was a sergeant leading his own team, he imparted the same lesson on his privates. Their lives were in his hands, he understood, just as his life had been in Sergeant Wyckoff's. It was a sacred duty, and it came with far greater responsibilities.

What Matt remembered most about Sergeant Wyckoff, though, was his sense of humor. He was always in good cheer, always making jokes and trying to get a laugh out of whoever was around him. He loved practical jokes. Once he put a dead scorpion in Matt's gear, knowing exactly how much his newest private hated the tiny, crawling critters. Matt almost threw up. "To me it didn't look dead because they killed it with hot water. They didn't smash it or anything, it was just boiled. It was huge," he remembered. Another time, Sergeant Wyckoff bought a pack of soda cans and rigged them above the doorway to the bathroom. A string was tied from the door to the soda can pull-tab, and a bunch of paper towels had been dumped in the bathroom. One by one, he yelled at his privates to clean up the mess. As soon as they pulled the door open, they got blasted in the face with warm, sticky soda. The whole team got a taste of that one. "He was always a happy person, always relaxed, yet serious when he had to be," Matt said. "Most of my memories are of him joking around and pulling pranks of some sort." One of the last things Matt ever heard him say, in fact, was a joke. In the middle of a firefight, Sergeant Wyckoff couldn't resist cracking one about how their enemies couldn't aim.

He put the safety of his team members above his own—all the way to his last firefight. His citation would read: "Sergeant Wyckoff left his covered position without hesitation, to force the other members of his team to take cover. Sergeant Wyckoff revealed his position and fatally engaged two insurgents to save the lives of his platoon."[3]

He was awarded a posthumous Distinguished Service Cross— the nation's second highest honor for valor. But talking about Sergeant Wyckoff, remembering him in full detail, confronting the blow dealt by his death—it pushed Matt far beyond his comfort zone. He said, "You're talking about stuff that you've spent every single ounce of energy trying to suppress. You avoid it—all the sights, sounds, smells—but you can't avoid it at night because when you sleep, you're defenseless and it all comes out in the form of nightmares. It's all uncontrollable."

Dr. Bellman tried different forms of therapy—cognitive processing therapy, prolonged exposure therapy—during their twice weekly appointments inside her office, and during each hour-long session, Matt would quickly find himself starting to sweat, soon getting so hot that he would have to grab the front of his shirt and pull it in and out, back and forth, fanning himself as the sweat poured from his body. He walked out of each session, shirt drenched, looking as if he had just run a marathon.

He received his first disability benefits from the VA in December that year, just a few months after starting his treatment. Granted an 80 percent disability rating, he began to receive roughly $1,500 in compensation each month. He was bumped up to 90 percent a couple of months later, adding another $300 to his payments. Soon he had left his dad's construction company, and not long after that, he barely left the house altogether—except for his appointments with Dr. Bellman. "I used to go in and joke that she was my only friend. She was the only person I went and actually saw beside my family," he said.

IN JANUARY 2012, Matt gained another friend when he and Jessica bought a dog—a proud and upright Great Dane. Matt immediately wanted to name him Zeus, but Jessica wasn't on board with that. They settled on Sarge. "Something about holding and petting him was comforting to me and would help calm me down," Matt said. He quickly grew reliant. On top of the usual stress that gripped him whenever he ventured outside, simply being away from Sarge was enough to fill him with anxiety. He would urgently feel the need to go home and hold his dog again. "One of the things I really liked was that no matter how terrible a day was, I can go home, and my dog loves me," he said. The first several months with Sarge passed like a honeymoon. Matt and his dog became inseparable. One day during the summer, Jessica brought home more good news: while surfing on the web she had found an organization that could help train Sarge to become an official veteran's service dog.

Matt was thrilled. They signed up to start the training immediately.

Fall arrived and Matt had to admit he was feeling worse, not better. Frustrated by the VA's healthcare system, he had given up on physical therapy altogether for his knees and back. "It's like a leaky dam and you got holes everywhere," he said. "You're plugging fingers into holes and you're trying to plug everything up, but you can't. Something's squirting out here and there. At some point you just say, 'Enough is enough.' Whatever, I'm going to hurt for a while. Let's at least work on not getting angry about it."

Having left his father's business, the monthly benefits he was receiving from the VA's disability division reduced the need, and his motivation, to look for other jobs. When it came to his mental health, Matt was noticing some improvements from working with Dr. Bellman, but his progress was inconsistent and unpredictable. It felt like "being on a rollercoaster," he said. "I could be at the top of the world, then at the bottom, one month at a time." As the days grew shorter and the cold set in, he and his wife decided to apply for a benefits increase, aiming to bring Matt's disability rating all the way up to 100 percent.

They went to the VA to file another claim and met with a veterans' service officer who was clearly resistant to help. "He told us that we shouldn't even mess with it, that we were basically barking up the wrong tree," Jessica recalled. The couple was told that the VA was "really going to dig through [Matt's] records and could potentially lower your ratings instead of increasing them."

Misinformation like this feeds the widespread perception that the VA is protective of its disability pay, never hesitating to knock down an unsuspecting veteran's rating and slash his benefits. Only rarely is this true—particularly for mental health disorders. In an internal presentation, the VA reported that less than 0.1 percent of all veterans receiving disability for mental disorders had their service-connected benefits reduced. Yet, spooked by their hostile meeting, Matt and his wife went home, delaying for months before they finally felt they had to try again.

They found a much warmer response in May 2013, when they met with a representative from the Wounded Warrior Project. With the WWP's encouragement, they filed new or increased disability claims for PTSD, traumatic brain injury, concussions, irritable bowel syndrome, heartburn, an anger condition called intermittent explosive disorder, and a nerve condition around Matt's right arm. Veteran service organizations like the WWP typically have every incentive to help vets increase their disability compensation. Those veterans become lifetime clients and a ticket to further legitimacy and political influence.

"They handled everything on our behalf, so we didn't have to go through the stress," Jessica said. "It's just like, 'Sign here and here.' They take all the headaches out of it. They make it very easy."

MATT WAS BURROWING deeper into the VA, while Jeff was making every effort to move the other way. In the spring of 2015, a few months after earning his bachelor's degree, he was hired by a prominent utilities firm headquartered in St. Louis. He settled into his role in the IT department, learning many of the skills he needed on the job. The work was challenging but his improvements kept him motivated. He saw that the field was ripe with opportunities, and in the fall, he enrolled part-time in a master's program for Information Studies. A couple of months later, his wife gave birth to a baby boy.

Within a few short years, Jeff had moved from pulling odd hours at the bike shop and browsing job listings in his ample free time to juggling full-time work, part-time graduate study, and taking care of his newborn son. Something had to give, and as the months flew by, Jeff realized he hardly ever hung out with other veterans anymore. For years he had maintained regular touch with a small group of vets, including Matt, who had all joined and left the Army at roughly the same time that he did. But ever since he and his wife had brought their son home from the hospital, much of his contact with the group fell by the wayside. "They're still in my thoughts now and then, especially around the holidays, but it hasn't been my focus," he said. In fact, his only consistent tie to the veterans' world was the VA compensation checks he kept receiving, a few hundred every month for his 40 percent disability rating. Even though he wanted to reduce his disability benefits, there was no clear channel to do so. Only a few veterans every year even attempt it.

There was no forgetting that he was a veteran, though, even as he was moving on to the next phase of his life. During his active-duty days, strangers who saw him in uniform would sometimes approach to say, "Thank you for your service." Those words felt good to hear at first, but Jeff soon lost track of the times people recited them to him, and they eventually came to feel empty and hollow. During his deployments, his parents had been proud to share his updates from Afghanistan with their friends in Buffalo, and even after he left the Army, people who recognized him in town would still stop him for a word. But something about those encounters always felt a little off. "They say, 'Thank you for your service,'" and I say, 'You're welcome.' Then there's twenty seconds of awkward silence. No one knows how to follow it up."

Sometimes, without intending to, he was the one who created the awkwardness. Once at the office, his boss made reference to a big campaign the company had launched in 2010. Jeff chuckled and replied, "In 2010, I was carrying a backpack on a mountain in Afghanistan." An uncomfortable silence filled the air. Jeff instantly realized his mistake. At the company, his military experience frequently seemed to be buried in the subtext of his interactions, but he had crossed an invisible line by explicitly calling attention to it. "There's kind of a civilian guilt," he said. "Like, 'I was here working a corporate job making lots of money, while you were risking your life.' I wasn't trying to make him feel bad or put myself out like a badass. I just slipped."

For the most part, though, Jeff got along well with his team. He felt like they accepted him, and some of them became more than colleagues; he considered them his friends. Still, "it's a tenth of the connection I have with someone I served with," he said. "Living in Afghanistan, in a fifteen-by-fifteen room with the guys—the bond of going out for happy hour every quarter pales in comparison. It would be like if you were locked in with the people at your office for a year." Over time, he became better at talking about his experiences as a soldier, more open and willing to share certain stories from his previous life. Yet there was always a "missing piece," he says.

He often wished Matt were there beside him. His new friends knew how to listen, knew how to nod and gasp and laugh at the right moments, but only Matt and the other guys from their unit would ever really know all of it. Only Matt would know what it was like to patrol in full uniform under a 100-degree sun, unable to even roll up their sleeves because some faceless general far away had decided so. Only Matt would know what it was like to burn through cigarette after cigarette, cheap Korean imports from the British goods store in Kandahar, listening to rockets whistle through the air as they sat in their tent and slugged down watery coffee to stay awake.

"Should we go out there?"

The pair looked at one another and smiled.

"Nah, let's just sit here and finish our coffee."

Nothing in the civilian world ever came close. "I can try to explain it, but nothing will ever capture the true essence of what we went through—the bonding and brotherhood and emotion," Jeff said. "There's certainly a void." He had made great efforts to fill the void, planting deep and sustaining roots out in the civilian world—by tending to his family, his work, his community—but some part of it, he realized, might never be replaced.

He felt that part often. And then he would think, *Man, I wish Matt were here.*

MATT WAS ATTEMPTING to fill the void, too. He received his disability increase in January 2014, half a year after filing his claims with the officer from the Wounded Warrior Project. The VA had approved his application to raise his PTSD rating, increasing it from 30 to 70 percent and bringing his combined disability rating to 100 percent. For both Matt and his wife, the decision felt like a formal acknowledgement of the pain, the disruptions to normal living, that they have had to endure.

"It got to the point where because of the PTSD he never wanted to leave the house," Jessica said. "If he did want to go grocery shop or something, we went at one a.m. in the morning. It was terrible. Someone had mentioned to file for an increase due to the fact that they did label him ..." she trailed off. "I don't want to use a word that might make him feel not good." The VA had determined that Matt was "housebound," a designation—"label," as Jessica put it— that qualified him for a special monthly entitlement. It kept him inside even more. Yet not even being considered housebound made pursuing treatment mandatory, further entombing Matt inside his own world.

When he did leave the house, he made sure that Sarge was by his side. After over a year of training, they had finally prepared Matt's beloved Great Dane to the level where he could be recognized as a service animal under the Americans with Disabilities Act. It was a major step and a satisfying payoff; Matt had spent hours training Sarge every day for almost fifteen months, yet it was only the second important thing to happen that spring. In May, Jessica had given birth to their son. Matt had never seen such a beautiful baby. The nurses at the hospital all seemed to feel the same way—they fawned over the baby as if he were their own. Jessica had insisted, "That's it, this is my first and last baby," but they kept joking with her, "Don't worry, you'll be back." It had been a while since Matt felt the warmth of such attention. "My wife even became Facebook friends with a bunch of them. They told us we were their favorite family."

Matt was a father now. The new role, he knew, was the most important one he would ever have, and it was one that he could not refuse, could never make excuses for. He wanted more than anything to be successful, but he wasn't sure where he would find support. He was a 100 percent disabled veteran, but the VA no longer factored much into his life: its healthcare branch had done little to improve his condition and he had already maxed out within its disability system. "Once you get to a 100 percent," he said, "there isn't a whole lot you can do."

There isn't a whole lot you can do. Rather than foster resilience, the VA is responsible for breeding passivity. Ineffectual treatment services, tangled within a bungling bureaucracy, fail to deliver the results veterans need, while an inconsistent and misunderstood compensation department pushes veterans down a dangerous track. "It's not about the quality of care that people get, it's just about [sending veterans] a check every month," said Jill Wilschke, the therapist at Camp Lejeune. As many separating soldiers were processed through the med board, she observed that their disability ratings from the VA came back far higher—"without exception"—than their disability levels from the military. Even before the soldiers had transitioned out, the VA's ratings were orienting them away from their capabilities, emphasizing instead their impairments. "Real treatment is different," Wilschke said. "It's not in any way connected with this disability system we've created."

Funneled into the VA's disability apparatus and shaped by its incentives, veterans interact differently with the labor market. Economists have known for decades that disability insurance benefits create a disincentive to work. As Jonathan Leonard wrote in 1985, "A person who perceives himself as disabled may thereby disable himself. A person who is perceived by others as disabled may thereby be disabled. And a person who finds greater economic returns to disability than to work may not struggle so hard to work."[4] The economist Jonathan Gruber, who would later become famous for his work with the Affordable Care Act, described the problem in a 1996 paper detailing how trends in Social Security Disability Insurance—which is both less generous than the VA disability system and much stricter in its criteria for inclusion—were substantially impacting the labor market.[5] Another paper, by David Autor of MIT, argues that the SSDI program is "growing…because it is supporting a rising rate of dependency and a declining rate of labor force participation among working age adults."[6]

The same distortions inflict the veterans population. In the precarious battleground of mental health treatment, where a patient's conviction to move beyond what ails them can spell the difference between success and resignation, the VA's benefits-centered disability

infrastructure produces far-reaching effects. Wilschke recounts one
patient at Camp Lejeune who informed her that he was triggered
simply by being around people in uniform. She told him she could
understand. Everyone had been in uniform when the soldier was
on deployment, where he had witnessed painful episodes, and now
that he had returned to the Marine base, the visual cues still carried lingering effects. She tried to encourage him—"How about we
work through that?"—but nothing seemed to get through. "I can't
be here, I can't be at work, uniforms are triggering, I gotta get out of
here," he kept telling her. It didn't matter what Wilschke offered, the
Marine shut her down every time.

"We've instilled this idea that any sort of mental health condition is permanent—that once the box gets checked, there's no
unchecking it," said Wilschke. "Somebody told him that it was a
trigger, that 'you'll have PTSD forever so just throw in the towel and
you have to deal with it for the rest of your life.' We've forgotten that
you can get better from this."

Such cases weigh on her the most. "I think about the story
he gets told every month, when he goes to the mailbox and gets
that check."[7] It is a story of paralysis and incapacitation, Wilschke
believes. The check tells veterans, "You're going to get triggered." It
says to them: "You're not going to get better."

ONE DAY IN 2016, Matt learned that he still had thirty credit
hours from his stint in community college before joining the Army.
That fall, he decided to return to school, part-time, to complete his
associate's degree.

When he arrived on campus again, there was nothing familiar
about the setting. Every day felt like a struggle; sometimes just sitting
through a class was "stressful as hell," he said. He was in his mid-thir-
ties, almost certainly the oldest student in every room, struggling to
balance the demands of coursework and home life. "I have concentration and memory problems anyway, plus I have a family. That's
one of the biggest hurdles—the frequent interruptions [happening]

most of my daily life." *Just get through the first year*, Matt told him-self. *Just get through the requirements.* After that, he would only have electives left to complete. He figured he could handle the electives. He kept reminding himself of something his dad used to say: "You know how to eat an elephant?" The joke came up any time they were faced with a challenge. "One bite at a time."

The spring semester was the hardest, but Matt got through it—one bite at a time. In the summer of 2017, he and Jessica celebrated with a three-week road trip, their first vacation as a couple in years. They packed an RV and drove out west, stopping first in Oklahoma to stay with friends, then driving on to Arizona. They marveled at the colorful badlands in the Petrified Forest, held their breath over-looking the Grand Canyon, and stood "on a corner in Winslow, Arizona," listening to the Eagles song about that very place. They kept on moving—through New Mexico, stopping in San Diego, then driving northward until they were hiking through California's Sequoia National Forest and staring up at General Sherman, the biggest tree in the world. "Seeing the beauty of nature like that—it was a once-in-a-lifetime experience," Matt said. The sights were over-whelming; they filled him with delight and wonder.

Yet between the immense highs of absorbing the natural world, Matt found himself getting overwhelmed at times. By the end of the second week, the travel was taking its toll. When Matt and his wife had first left the plains and cornfields of Illinois behind, he felt energized by the new terrain of the American west—the barren des-erts and landscapes, the scrub brush and mountains. But after six to eight hours on the road, day after day, he started to have nightmares again. "I'm driving along and this is exactly like Afghanistan. I'm stuck in a big uncomfortable vehicle, staring off into the middle of nowhere," he said. The heat, the rocks. Even after he and Jessica got home, a shadow seemed to loom over him. "I have no idea why, but I went into a slump of depression. It took me a solid month to dig myself out. It was rough. I just didn't have the energy or motivation to do hardly anything."

By the fall, the slump had passed. Better yet, filling its place was a new perspective so upbeat and replenishing that it even caught Matt by surprise. "I think the trip exhausted me, so I had to recover from it. But the positivity was there for sure. I would do it all over again." He had spent months in the planning phase, poring over routes and maps, developing contingency plans for anything and everything—should they run low on supplies, or get a flat tire, or have to pass through a big storm—and the results had showed. Their tour of the country, largely, had been a success. In hindsight, the achievements of the summer were sinking in. "It took a lot for me to get to that point," Matt said. "My wife and I had always talked about traveling west. I'd never been further west than Texas." The Sequoia National Forest, in particular, had been the top item on Matt's bucket list, a fascination that had started in third grade when his teacher brought to class a pinecone she had picked up from the forest. Matt couldn't believe how big it was. "Those suckers were the size of a football," he recalled. "They were huge, the size of my arm." When he finally saw them for himself, scattered everywhere as he and Jessica tramped through the grounds, he felt as if he had grasped something new and important—not only insights about himself, but about the country in which he lived.

"Down here everyone is just so fricking nice and friendly," Matt said. He would pass somebody in a restaurant and find himself having a full conversation for ten, fifteen, twenty or more minutes. Along the coast, "they were nice to you but only to the point that they needed to be." At the gas station, the attendant might say, *Thank you, have a nice day*, but as soon as the transaction was finished, "their niceties toward you are completely shut off. It's like, 'Okay, our little portion of the day together is over, now get the hell out of my face so I can do what I have to do with the next guy.'" Or driving through the roads in the Midwest: "You show up to a four-way stop and even if someone is there first and they have the right of way, they'll sit there and keep waving at you, 'No you go, no you go.' Finally you're just like, 'Whatever man, alright I'm going to go.' Out in California—hell no! We were driving from San Diego all the way through LA. You can sit there with your turn signal on for ten miles trying to get to the other lane and nobody's going to let you over."

City life, he determined, was not for him. But as wide as the gap had seemed between the fast pace of the cities and the familiar cycles he knew in Marion, Illinois, Matt couldn't help feeling captive to a more personal divide, a profound chasm between the trail he trod as a veteran and the ground occupied by everyone else. He had a hunch it had something to do with the media. "There's a million different shows on every single channel. You see it a lot, actors portraying service members. They always try to show that guy or that group that went to war and came back all fucked up. They got them digging foxholes in the middle of the night in their fricking underwear or pulling guns on everyone walking up to them. Just off-the-wall crazy shit. So people associate that with veterans. That's part of the disconnect. A lot of us just want to say, 'That's not true, that's not us at all.' I just hate it when people think we're dangerous or violent or can't be trusted."[8]

On a few occasions, his wife's relatives had even called her to express their concern. "Are you okay? Are you safe?" they asked her. "Does Matt threaten you? I know he has guns in the house—are you okay with that?" Jessica would respond, "Yes, I'm okay, of course I'm safe," or "I trust my husband more than anyone I know," but just the fact that his wife had to respond at all, had to defend him against allegations and misperceptions like that, infuriated Matt and pushed him into a bad place. He had enlisted to serve and protect his country, and there was absolutely nothing he wouldn't do to protect his family. But he felt like the country didn't understand that. He felt like it didn't seem to matter. People had no clue what it was like to have gone to war, yet they thought they knew, or else they had all already made up their minds. He could see himself reflected in their eyes as someone to be pitied, someone to be careful around, someone to be on guard against. It took so much strength to believe that he was more than that. On many days, it took more strength than he felt he had.

IN EARLY 2017, Jeff was tapped for a management role at his company. That fall, his young family welcomed a second boy into the world. His two young children kept him up at all hours of the night, but if it sometimes felt overwhelming, like he had too much in his life keeping him busy and active, Jeff wasn't one to complain about that. He had come too far.

He recalled how for the longest time after he and Matt had left the Army, their phone calls to one another were just long-winding confessions, one extended sequence of bumbled interactions and flailing attempts to fit in. One day it was Jeff freaking out in the back of his class; the next it was Matt freaking out at the entrance of Walmart. One week it was Jeff feeling so overwhelmed Bethany would have to drive him home early from the concert; the next it was Matt jumping up at dinner when the restaurant's TV suddenly kicked on. Their country was no longer the same place they had left, or else they were no longer the same people. For the first couple of years, it had seemed they were struggling through their difficult transitions in lockstep.

But then the difference in their paths began to show. Jeff found his footing in school while Matt kept stumbling. At Jeff's graduation party in 2014, Matt drove down to St. Louis with Jessica and Sarge. Jeff was struck by how far their lives had diverged. "It was a little bit of awkwardness," he said. "We got out almost the exact same day. But here I was graduating from college. And here he was [getting benefits] at the VA."

Jeff reflected often on how things had developed so differently for them. Which factors had propped him up? Which forces had dragged his best friend down? He wondered if Matt's early setbacks—his troubles getting into the police force, his subsequent injuries working in construction—had produced a narrative of defeat that, once introduced, was difficult to dislodge. The centrality of work in a person's identity is well documented by researchers and social scientists, and the shift from a job of high to low perceived significance can have particularly strong effects on a person's psychology.[9]

Matt had worked as a bricklayer before joining the military; the fact that he had to return to his father's business had been humbling. "It was difficult for him to accept that role," said Jeff, who had sympathized with his friend's grievances and wished there were more that he could do to help.

The VA had stepped in then. An ineffectual healthcare branch shuffled Matt through prescription after prescription—new pills to counter the side effects of earlier pills—all the while inducing greater dependence on its disability payments, which brought their own consequences. "He's wrapped up in the system," Jeff went on. "It's providing him a home, and health insurance, and [caretaker] money for his wife. I think it's very uncomfortable for him. He was a very able-bodied man who is now being told he can't do anything. It's tough for him. He doesn't want to be looked at by society as a fragile flower."

Society's views of veterans have morphed and softened since the Vietnam era, where harmless tropes characterized them all as either killers or victims. Yet reductive binaries persist. "Since 9/11 [...] veterans are seen as victims, heroes, or victim-heroes," writes Rebecca Burgess of the American Enterprise Institute. "But that narrative stands in its own need of rehumanization—the modern-day perception of veterans needs to be brought down from mythologized heroes on a pedestal to the real world of public servants, adventure seekers, and bill payers who volunteer for military service."[10] A more nuanced understanding, however, faces a formidable task—informing a public already conditioned to the stereotypes.

In 2012, a national poll found that more than half of Americans believe the majority of recent vets from Iraq and Afghanistan suffer from PTSD[11]—assumptions that are often performed and perpetuated by vets themselves. Burgess observes that a sense of "veteranness" has developed within the community in parallel with its treatment out in the civilian world, a strain that has "mutated" and even hooked into the commercial market. A quick internet search of "veteran clothing" turns up results of apparel with an endless list of identity-affirming messages.[12] One reads: "[vet-er-uh-n] noun - 1. Person who wrote a Blank Check payable to the United States of America for an amount up to and including One's Life." Often they portray veterans as a group separate and removed from the rest of society, as in one T-shirt that says: "Assuming I was like most women was your first mistake | US WOMAN VETERAN." Frequently they evoke images of disability and loss, underscored by such phrases like: "Honor Our Veterans: Their Sacrifice = Our Freedom"; or "PTSD: It's not the person refusing to let go of the past, but the past refusing to let go of the person."[13]

Jeff recognizes the proclivity in his best friend. His graduation party had been hosted at Dave & Buster's and the moment Matt walked in with Sarge, all the attention in the room immediately turned toward the 120-pound Great Dane beside him. Jeff was frustrated by the spectacle. "You see someone with a service dog, and you think, 'Damn, what's wrong with this guy?' It paints him in a certain light and puts him in an even more conspicuous position."

One year, not long after Matt and his wife had moved into a new home, Jeff paid a visit during the holidays. They sat for lunch and Matt gave his old Army buddy a tour. It was a beautiful house, well-furnished and comfortable. Yet Jeff noticed pieces of wartime memorabilia, or references to Matt's military service, displayed in virtually every room. Paintings from Afghanistan hung from the bedroom walls; plaques and photographs sat on shelves and cabinets; military quotes and posters lined the halls. Outside in the driveway, the license plate on Matt's car bore the letters FURY—a reference to their battalion, One Fury, First of the 508th Parachute Infantry Regiment. A sticker on the bumper read: *THE VA—giving veterans a second chance to die for their country since 1930.*

"It shows something about his mindset," said Jeff. "Within thirty seconds of meeting Matt, you'll know that he is not only a veteran but a paratrooper and that he served in Afghanistan. All this imagery gives him a reflection: *I'm a veteran, I'm a veteran, I'm a veteran.*"

The problem with fixating on the veteran identity is that it is profoundly backward-looking. Like a thirty-year-old man wearing his high school letter jacket, the veteran identity ties one to past accomplishments rather than future potential. The dozens of Facebook groups that celebrate veteran status and look down upon civilians reinforce this orientation, impeding forward progress and freezing the veteran in suspended animation, unable to return to uniform yet unable, as well, to progress onto something else.

IN OCTOBER 2018, Matt and Jessica attended the annual veterans parade in Marion. The next day was his thirty-sixth birthday. Matt had seen Jeff the previous weekend, when he drove his family down to St. Louis to attend a birthday celebration for Jeff's younger son. The two fathers watched as their children played together. Matt turned to Jeff. "I'm on the wrong side of my thirties now," he said, and the two shared a laugh like old times.

Matt had completed his associate's degree earlier in the summer. After two years of chipping through his credit requirements, he had finally finished his coursework online. He downplays the achievement. "It's nothing serious. It's not like I accomplished a lot," he says. But not everyone lets him get away with it. An older veteran Matt had gotten to know at the VA told him, "Dude, you should be proud of yourself!" He reminded Matt that a few years ago, he couldn't spend twenty minutes at a supermarket without panicking, and here he was graduating college. Matt appreciated the sentiment. It was true—he had come a long way and he shouldn't lose sight of that—but he had never been the type to overly congratulate himself. "I guess I'm just that kinda person who doesn't want extra attention on himself. Just a simple, 'Good job man,' or something like that. That's all I need," he said.

A stately clock tower stood over the Marion town square, presiding over an ensemble of statues and memorials. Matt and Jessica moved along with the parade, tracing a loop around the square before coming to a halt in front of the clock tower. Matt's teeth clenched in the cold. The winter was setting in and he needed to figure out what he would do next. He craved the sense of purpose and belonging that had defined his time in the military. Without it, many of the people he once served with had fallen into depression. Some had committed suicide. He wished he could have done something, but he wasn't sure how. Sometimes he wasn't even sure how to help himself. He had never seriously contemplated suicide, but for a while, during his darkest months, the thought of not waking up the next morning hadn't really bothered him. When asked by Dr. Bellman, he replied that he simply felt numb.

The dozen or so vets he saw every Wednesday at group therapy inside the VA had fought in every service era dating back to Vietnam. A recurring theme, flipping between foreground and background but never far from their minds, was the gulf that seemed to separate those of them sitting in that circle and everyone outside of it, all those people out there in the civilian world, going about their jobs and appointments and meetings, rushing through their busy lives. Through their discussions together, Matt had come to adopt a more historical lens.

"If you look through human civilization, when we were tribes and little villages here and there, it was a fact of life that the men would go to war. Way back in the day it was survival. If we didn't fight and win, our village would be lost. Everyone knew what was at stake. They knew that the warriors would go and fight for them and come back, and they would be different. That was okay because they understood. Now we go off and we do our thing and we come back. People try to understand but they really don't. It's hard for people to connect with their warriors."

The parade filled him with mixed feelings. It meant a lot to him that his town organized such a gathering every year, and yet he also felt that the histrionics could be performative and shallow. Appreciation and pride mixed with discomfort; it was a confusing swirl that left him confused. As the national anthem ended, a man dressed in full uniform, ribbons lining his chest, stepped proudly to the front. He addressed the procession, then called the veterans in the crowd to attention. Matt raised his hand in salute. He watched as the flag was lowered, and felt struck by a familiar aching as the bugle's first searing notes of "Taps" sliced through the air. A heaviness gripped his chest. He had never been able to hear that tune without crying. Faces of soldiers he knew swam through his head, belonging to the fallen, the living, belonging even to soldiers he never knew, like the ones carried in the hearts of the Gold Star families standing nearby. When the tears came, they felt cleansing. The swirl gave way to an instant of catharsis. The air suddenly felt crisp and clean. Then, from somewhere in front of him, a confetti cannon suddenly went off, and the moment was torched in a spike of adrenaline and alarm.

Flecks of color rained down upon them. Matt's heart pounded inside his chest. He was, somehow simultaneously, worn out and startled. He knew he was done. He put his arms around his family, and they made their way home.

EPILOGUE

BY DANIEL M. GADE

AS DEMONSTRATED in these pages, reform to the VA's disability compensation system is crucial to ensuring that veterans can lead lives of meaning, purpose, and value. The current system disempowers veterans and treats them as a victim class, rather than placing them in the driver's seat of their own transitions from active service to civilian life. For some veterans, this transition is accompanied by significant physical or mental health challenges, making successful transition simultaneously more difficult and more important. For each of the veterans profiled in this book, the transition was different: Molly is not Marco, who is not Tyson. Treating them as if they were all the same is the first of many points of failure, and systems should be scalable and adaptable to the individual needs of each veteran.

Serious government reform is difficult. Reform of the VA might be the most difficult of all, and attempts at it are typically destroyed in short order. Rethinking the approach threatens the lifeblood of entrenched interest groups and politicians who serve them in order to be re-elected. A close look at almost any change shows that what survives the legislative and rule-making process are usually additions to existing programs or the creation of new programs; in effect, the VA grows like a coral reef, adding a little bit here and a little bit there. VA programs are almost never eliminated or significantly reformed. These accretions over time have created a VA system that is huge, unwieldy, and illogical, as well as being politically protected and exceptionally expensive.

Before examining a few of the failed attempts to reform the VA, it will be useful to review the reasons behind those failures. First, the VA is beset by possibly the most powerful, organized, and motivated interest groups in Washington. Those interest groups are able to claim a kind of moral superiority because of their military service (signified by special hats, pins, and other regalia). Unlike other interest groups with social power (say, the NRA or Planned Parenthood), veteran-related interest groups are explicitly "chartered" by the VA and thus are a quasi-official part of the structure of the VA itself. The economist Randall Holcombe, quoted in *Paid Patriotism*, calls veterans "the first organized interest group that was able to use the political process to systematically transfer large sums of money to themselves through the political system…"[1]

Second, non-veteran citizens generally view the military and veterans with a deference that translates into additional political power. The military is consistently one of the most respected sectors of American life, ranking just behind doctors, scientists, and firefighters in the public eye.[2] With respect comes deference, and groups translate that deference into action on their own behalf.

Third, the military and veteran spheres have their own culture and language, which is famously incomprehensible and opaque. This makes reform difficult, because the groups who are against reform are in charge of the language. The term "service-connected disabled veteran" is used to describe not just those seriously maimed in a training accident or combat situation, but also for those with minor conditions, like tinnitus, that were diagnosed during service and thus attributed to service. In the mind of the uninformed observer, the "disabled veteran" license plate is a signifier of meaning well beyond tinnitus or sore knees. Some organizations capitalize on this further by displaying photos of multiple amputees on their posters, obfuscating the fact that combat amputees make up a vanishingly small percentage of the overall population of veterans.

Finally, the political parties themselves are complicit in the beatification of veterans and the desire to bend to their wishes, but for opposite reasons. The political right, tied as it is to 'patriotism' and its highest expression in military service, never opposes any veteran-related spending or expansion. The political left views the veterans class as misguided yet basically innocent victims of a repressive system, and is deeply invested in the VA's system of "enlistment-to-grave" care as a prototype of their desired single-payer health system.

The growth of the VA and associated programs, benefits, and services for veterans has been ongoing for more than 200 years.[3] In 1818, Congress passed a pension bill that provided monthly benefits for Continental Army veterans, amidst some controversy driven by opposition based on fear of a standing army and the now-quaint idea that every man should live "by the sweat of his own brow." The flood of pension applications overwhelmed the country, and caused the share of the federal budget that went to veterans to shoot to 16 percent. After the Civil War, Union veterans were granted benefits for injury, of course, and benefits to the families of the fallen soon followed. But what followed after that was the same as what we see today: a focused effort by lobbyists and organizations to get "their fair share," resulting in expansion of veterans programs of all types. By 1893, pensions accounted for over 40 percent of federal spending.[4] In Washington, consensus between the left and right is rare. However, on this issue, both sides agree that veterans "deserve" whatever they demand.

The most famous feature of the veterans disability system did not become law until 1864, when compensation rates became dependent on the severity of the disability. Loss of sight in both eyes, loss of both feet, and loss of both hands were all compensable; new disabilities soon followed. Policy makers quickly realized that they had created a colossus that was doomed to failure, and even recognized the perverse incentives that these systems create. In 1871, Pension Commissioner Baker observed that "Many disabilities...are disappearing by recuperative energies, and the pensioner, reluctant to lose his gratuity, oftentimes tries to fortify himself by evidence, which only consumes the time and labor of the office to no purpose."[5]

Based in part on these concerns, Congress in 1872 tried to publish a list of all pensioners as a disincentive to fraudulent claims—an early and blunt attempt at reform that died in the Senate.

With the formation and increasing power of the veterans lobby in the late-1800s came a flood of attempts to loot the treasury. Some of these attempts passed and some failed; in 1887 President Cleveland vetoed a bill that would have given $12 per month to all veterans of any war (Confederacy excluded) who had become disabled *by any cause for any reason*. This brief pause in expansion was quickly overcome when a similar bill passed and was signed by President Harrison in 1890. There was some public outcry: in those days it was expected that able-bodied men were to provide for themselves, but those who opposed unchecked expansion were shouted down as ingrates or worse.[6]

The Spanish-American War and the Indian Wars of the late1800s continued this pattern, but the floodgates did not truly open until after the Great War, with US involvement from 1917-1918.[7] After that war, the American Legion and other groups agitated for a large bonus for their lost wages during the war. Amid some back-and-forth, the bill became law in May 1924, and offered a bonus to be payable in 1944. The Great Depression, however, intervened and the starving and impoverished men (and a few women and families) descended on Washington, D.C. in several infamous "Bonus Marches" which were eventually broken up by force of arms. Nevertheless, the political gauntlet had been thrown: veterans were officially a force to be reckoned with, and were unapologetic about demanding their due.

The first of two major reform efforts over the past sixty years was the Bradley Commission, launched in 1956 and chaired by Omar Bradley, the five-star general of World War II fame. General Bradley's commission was unsparing in its critique of the disability system, its perverse incentive structure, and fundamental incoherence: "[Changing conditions of national defense force] us to reshape our traditional concepts of military service as the basis for special

332

privileges and benefits."[8] The report went on: "Our present structure of veterans programs is not a 'system.' It is an accretion of laws based largely on precedents built up over 150 years of piecemeal development. The public at large has taken little interest and the laws have been enacted in response to minority pressures."[9] Perhaps the most damning sentence in the entire report is one that flies in the face of modern sensibilities and certainly was controversial even then: "...it cannot justifiably be contended that all sacrifices, however small and transient, by those in the Nation's military service should establish entitlement to monetary claims and special privileges."[10]

The Bradley Commission's doomed report recommended several fundamental reforms. First, it rightly pointed out that disability reforms had never reached the "core of the problem" and that rating standards, presumptions, and follow-ups were insufficient to bring the program to internal consistency. The Bradley Commission argued that the goal of this and all disability programs should be to return the disabled person to functionality in society. Another major reform, to which we will return shortly, would have synchronized the compensation that veterans receive based on their non-combat service with regular Social Security payments. In other words, it would cease the practice of privileging military service above any other kind of jobs for long-term pension purposes. In any case, these reform ideas went nowhere.

The next major reform effort was sparked by a *Washington Post* exposé of conditions at Walter Reed Army Medical Center in 2007 (ironically, not a VA facility at all). The President's Commission on Care for Returning Wounded Warriors—co-chaired by former Senator Bob Dole and former Secretary of HHS Donna Shalala, and called the Dole-Shalala Commission) proposed additional major reforms. First, it proposed that disability pay be separated into two parts: loss of earnings and quality-of-life. Given the agency's legal purpose to compensate for average loss of earnings, this proposal recognized the absurdity of some parts of the disability "system." That it currently compensates for quality of life issues like the loss of a penis or mere minor facial scarring stretches the legal justification. The Dole-Shalala recommendation would have given a substantial payment for the veteran whose penis was a casualty of war and returned the program to its legal foundation.

Only the quality-of-life payment would continue after the veteran began to receive Social Security, reducing the double-dipping that some veterans do. (Some veterans even "triple dip" by getting Social Security disability, military retirement, and VA compensation—sometimes for the same disability.) Other reforms were more modest, but essentially in line with the spirit of the earlier Bradley Report. Despite the bipartisan credibility and Washington clout of the co-chairs, the Dole-Shalala report went nowhere (except for one small recommendation to assign recovery coordinators for the most seriously injured).

Reforms since the late-2000s have been spotty and anemic. After leaving the White House and returning to graduate school for my PhD, I worked as a "Special Government Employee" on the VA's Advisory Committee on Disability Compensation (ACDC) from late-2008 to 2013. The ACDC's mandate, springing out of federal law, is "To provide advice to the Secretary of Veterans Affairs on establishing and supervising a schedule to conduct periodic reviews of the VA Schedule for Rating Disabilities (VASRD)." In reality, it soon became clear, the ACDC was largely focused on supervising a revision of the VASRD that would simply clear out a few obsolete diagnoses—diseases which no longer occur or have been folded into other diseases from a diagnostic perspective—while rubber-stamping increases in a variety of other disability diagnoses and ensuring that claims were processed accurately and quickly. In the whispered back-room conversations to which I was personally privy, the disability system was acknowledged as a one-way ratchet. Only higher payments and increased ratings were to be recommended.

In this context, "accurate" simply meant that the veteran was awarded compensation in accordance with the way the schedule was written, not that his condition was, in fact, as severe as the claims he made. The word "quickly," in this context, meant precisely that: the VA soon adopted an informal policy of approving claims with limited oversight. Allison Hickey, former VA Undersecretary for Benefits, was clear about this definition, once telling the department's Advisory Committee that the "backlog" was the primary concern, not whether there were a few (or many) undeserving veterans in the queue.[11] For that reason, claims processors were pressured to put as many claims through the system as they could.

That brings us to the present day, which looks similar to each and every day of the past hundred years. The VA has made some marginal changes to the system, such as allowing veterans with denied claims to choose their route of appeal, but the basics of the system remain the same: veterans are paid to be sick, and paid more the sicker or more disabled they can show themselves to be.[12] As I hope we have shown, this is a powerfully negative force in the lives of many veterans. To say it bluntly: the VA system robs veterans of vitality and then looks everywhere else for reasons for the current suicide crisis except in the halls of Congress and the VA itself.

THE FACT that this system has remained largely unchanged for so long shows that it is quite durable. This is a testament to its political viability and strength rather than to its moral value. In political science, such durability is attributed to so-called "iron triangles"— alliances between politicians, the bureaucracy, and interest groups. Nevertheless, there are some valuable counterarguments available to the critic.

First is the critique that we favor physical wounds over damage to mental health. Mental health injuries are certainly complex and multi-faceted; among their many characteristics is that they are uniquely variable—from individual to individual, certainly, but also *within a particular patient.* Someone with PTSD, for instance, might be functional on one day and then completely incapacitated for the remainder of the week or month. Certain other conditions—especially things like back pain—are also remarkably variable in their manifestation and can range from minor and inconsequential to seriously disabling. What is to be done about such conditions? The current system, outlined in detail in these pages, simply views someone with such a variable condition as if that condition were present and powerful at all times. Further, the current system does little to encourage each veteran to live up to his or her own maximum potential, instead treating such variable conditions as if they were uniformly and permanently incapacitating. The system privileges lifetime disability and malaise over recovery in mental *and* physical health, creating ever-increasing proportions of veterans who seek disability compensation.

Second, critics typically employ the "deservingness" argument. This argument basically runs like this: because veterans have at some point accepted the possibility of grave physical and emotional harm, they are therefore deserving of whatever our country can provide. In that way, past service becomes a kind of "shield of invulnerability" that provides permanent and irreducible moral certitude to the bearer. And it is, in part, true: our country does owe a debt of gratitude to those who have both worn the uniform and borne a significant and life-altering physical or mental injury. This is particularly true for those who were involuntarily plucked out of civilian life and conscripted into military service. Although that burden is surely an "obligation of citizenship," the burden of conscription often fell in past years on those without other meaningful options. For the young man who already lacks the wherewithal to attend college, the draft became a kind of double jeopardy that disproportionately affected the poor and people of color. That there are some knaves hidden among the knights is not in question, but the proportions of each are difficult or impossible to discern.

Third, those who are Constitutional absolutists would argue that any benefit given to one citizen or a class of them by the general agreement of the representative body is legitimate on its face, and, clearly, these benefits are given under the color of law. But a representative body requires full knowledge of the situation at hand so that, at least in theory, the preferences of the people can be aggregated through their representatives and formed into coherent policy. That, in fact, is the aim of this book: not to destroy current systems but to shine a light on their inner workings in hopes of finding solutions that are effective and moral for the taxpayer, the citizen, and the veteran. Our own opinions about the range of options for reform are largely irrelevant. Our goal for this work has been to inform our fellow citizens.

Some variation or combination of each of the above criticisms will likely be hurled, but we stand by our propositions. First, our current system is well intentioned but has been distorted by political pressure into something that is absurdly expensive in implementation and immoral in effect. Second, real veterans—men and women with families to support and dreams to sustain—are held in thrall to a promise of ever-increasing benefits for their otherwise proud service. This promise of benefits distorts their vision of the future and causes them to rely on benefits in a way that is deeply unhealthy. Third, this distorted vision of the future causes veterans to make suboptimal life choices and to embrace their worst, sickest selves instead of their most positive future selves. Finally, the veterans thus afflicted are far too likely to lead lives of purposelessness, lack of balance, and ultimately to suffer far more than their injuries warrant, including being one spark in the conflagration of veterans' suicide that currently rages. In the end, any reform that's implemented will be, like the current system, subject to political pressure. For that reason, we offer not concrete policy proposals, but instead a series of principles that should guide the resulting policy.

First, the goal of any system of veterans benefits and care should be to return the veteran as closely as possible to the life situation in which he would have found himself but for the service rendered. This requires not a "one size fits all" approach, but instead an approach customized to the individual veteran. Since employment is a social good, we believe that employment should be the goal of any system of benefits—hopefully to a level that results in the veteran being weaned off of whatever temporary assistance might be required. This is true even in cases where the injuries are quite severe: even in cases of high-level spinal cord injury, multiple amputations, or devastating mental illness, there are treatments that can and will result in a more positive life course than the course that would be available in their absence. Our system must reject the idea that any veteran is unemployable or permanently and "totally" disabled. The only veterans for whom employment is not a reasonable goal are those few whose brain injuries are truly devastating and impossible to overcome. For them, virtually any amount of benefits is morally sustainable.

Second, the system should incentivize desired outcomes by linking treatment for an illness with the compensation associated with it. If you don't get treatment for your PTSD, certainly you have no right to expect the taxpayer to fund its effects. This kind of approach has a dual benefit: those who are "faking bad" to get paid would begin to drop out of the system, freeing up mental health providers to see those who are truly ill. The second benefit is that those who are being compensated and are in treatment are more likely to eventually become better and graduate from treatment to a lower level of need. Critically, *they will be better off* with their health restored than if it were not intact. There might be physical incentives too: perhaps a "BMI Bonus," i.e., if the veteran keeps his body mass index within a certain range, he gets a cash bonus that is some portion of the calculated financial cost of obesity. The possibilities are endless, but the basic idea is the same: if you want more of something, then you should incentivize it.

Third, the system needs total reform in the nature and types of disabilities compensated. Those injuries not *directly caused by* military service might be good targets for treatment rather than compensation. If, for instance, someone is diagnosed with Parkinson's Disease in military service under the current regime, then he will be compensated as if that disease were the fault of the taxpayer or the military. This is wrong. Instead, that person should be treated by the VA but not compensated. This would actually allow the VA, under a budget-neutral proposal, to spend far more on the veteran whose brain is damaged due to a gunshot wound and less on the (many) veterans who present, say, adult-onset diabetes. The entire VASRD could then be written in a few dozen pages, rather than the hundreds or thousands of pages of regulations, statutory interpretations, and other bureaucratic dross.

All in all, our nation's nineteen million veterans do deserve something: they deserve lives they can be proud of, just as they are proud of their service. What they don't need and don't deserve is to be trapped in a system that is well intentioned but demonstrably harmful. We can do better as a country.

And we should.

Acknowledgements

This book had its origin at Walter Reed Army Medical Center—ironically, not a VA facility at all—in the spring of 2005, after I was maimed in Iraq. Witnessing some of my fellow wounded warriors beginning a long slide into dependency horrified me, and I decided then and there to do what I could to forestall that slide in myself, and in as many others as I could reach.

This book would not have been possible without the generosity of the Searle Freedom Trust. Thank you, from the bottom of my heart. Thank you as well to the dozens of VA and military professionals we interviewed, some of whom took substantial professional risk in blowing the whistle on the "disability-industrial complex" as it exists today. Daniel Huang was an amazing partner in this endeavor, and his mastery of the written word makes this book sing.

Finally, I want to thank my wife, Wendy. She signed up for whatever life I led her into, and she's been beside me the entire journey. "Take my hand and come with me."

— Daniel Gade

I am deeply grateful to Jennifer Forsyth and Michael Siconolfi, Investigations Editors at the *Wall Street Journal*, for providing invaluable guidance to the early articles that led to this book-length effort, and for their continued encouragement and friendship.

Thank you as well to Chris Frueh and all the sources featured in this book—both named and anonymous—for recounting their experiences to illuminate the VA's complexities. In particular, thank

ACKNOWLEDGEMENTS

you to the veterans who generously shared their time and stories, which allowed for a more nuanced portrait of the transition from soldier to civilian life. Without their commitment and cooperation, this book would not have been possible.

— Daniel Huang

NOTES

Prologue

[1] Kisbert is a pseudonym.

[2] The US military's High Mobility Multipurpose Wheeled Vehicle (HMMWV) is colloquially known as a "Humvee."

[3] Jackson is a pseudonym.

[4] Veterans Benefits Administration. (2020). *Fiscal Year 2019 Annual Benefits Report.* Retrieved from U.S. Department of Veterans Affairs: https://www.benefits.va.gov/REPORTS/abr/docs/2019-compensation.pdf

Introduction

[1] "Statistical Trends: Veterans with a Service-Connected Disability, 1990 to 2018." National Center for Veterans Analysis and Statistics. United States Department of Veterans Affairs, May 2019. https://www.va.gov/vetdata/docs/Quickfacts/SCD_trends_FINAL_2018.pdf.

Bureau, US Census. "Veteran Population Declines." The United States Census Bureau, June 2, 2020. https://www.census.gov/library/visualizations/2020/comm/veteran-population-declines.html.

[2] "Profile of Post-9/11 Veterans: 2016." National Center for Veterans Analysis and Statistics. United States Department of Veterans Affairs, March 2018. https://www.va.gov/vetdata/docs/SpecialReports/Post_911_Veterans_Profile_2016.pdf.

[3] Veterans Benefits Administration (2020).

[4] Comparison from the 2000 Annual Benefits Report pp.147 to the 2019 Annual Benefits Report pp. 9.

"Veterans Benefits Administration 2000 Annual Benefits Report," 2001. https://www.benefits.va.gov/REPORTS/abr/docs/2000_abr.pdf

Veterans Benefits Administration (2020).

[5] "FY 2021 BUDGET SUBMISSION." Benefits and Burial Programs and Departmental Administration. United States Department of Veterans Affairs, February 2020. https://www.va.gov/budget/docs/summary/fy2021VAbudgetvolumeIIIbenefits-BurialProgramsAndDeptmentalAdministration.pdf.

Chapter 1

[1] "Scholarships - Army Enlist," accessed March 17, 2018, http://www.armyenlist.com/rotc/scholarships/.

[2] U S Army, *U.S. Army ROTC Green to Gold Scholarship Option Program*, 2017, https://www.goarmy.com/careers-and-jobs/current-and-prior-service/advance-your-career/green-to- gold/green-to-gold-scholarship.html.

[3] Phillip Carter and Brad Flora, "I Want You...Badly," November 7, 2007, http://www.slate.com/articles/news_and_politics/war_stories/2007/11/i_want_you_badly.html.

[4] U S Department of Veterans Affairs, "Post-9/11 GI Bill (Chapter 33) Payment Rates for 2016 Academic Year," accessed March 17, 2018, https://www.benefits.va.gov/GIBILL/resources/benefits_resources/rates/ch33/ch33rates080116.asp.

[5] "Army Student Loan Repayments," *Military.com*, 2018, https://www.military.com/education/money-for- school/army-student-loan-repayments.html.

[6] "Thrift Savings Plan," 2018, https://www.military.com/benefits/military-pay/thrift-savings-plan.html.

[7] The share of enlistees receiving bonuses would rise during 2000 and 2001, then hold steady at about 40 percent for the next three years. In 2005, it would spike to over 80 percent as the Army failed to meet recruiting targets for its mounting engagements in the Middle East. The following year, the Pentagon would spend more than $1 billion on enlistment bonuses, and by 2007, enlistees could earn up to $40,000 for a four-year commitment, with additional payouts for recruits fluent in Arabic. Between 2000 and 2008, the Department of Defense budget for enlistment bonuses would nearly triple from $266 million to $625 million to ensure that the military's manpower needs were satisfied. Beth J. Asch et al. *Cash Incentives and Military Enlistment, Attrition, and Reenlistment.* (2010); Phillip Carter and Brad Flora, "I Want You...Badly," November 7, 2007, http://www.slate.com/articles/news_and_politics/war_stories/2007/11/i_want_you_badly.html.

[8] "Conscription in the United States," (CQ Researcher, August 14, 1940), http://library.cqpress.com/cqresearcher/document.php?id=cqresrre1940081400.

[9] Rutenberg, Amy J., (2017, October) "Opinion | How the Draft Reshaped America," *New York Times*, https://www.nytimes.com/2017/10/06/opinion/vietnam-draft.html.

[10] Ilyana, Kuziemko, (2010, January) "Did the Vietnam Draft Increase Human Capital Dispersion?," https://www0.gsb.columbia.edu/mygsb/faculty/research/pubfiles/5798/vietnam.pdf.

[11] Weigley, R.F., (1993), "Putting the Poor in Uniform," *New York Times*, http://www.nytimes.com/1993/04/11/books/putting-the-poor-in-uniform.html.

[12] Epstein, J. (2015, January) "How I Learned to Love the Draft," *The Atlantic*,

https://www.theatlantic.com/magazine/archive/2015/01/how-i-learned-to-love-the-draft/383500/.

[13] *Congressional Record, v. 152, PT. 17, November 9, 2006 to December 6, 2006,* December 6, 2006, https://goo.gl/yyfXJ2.

[14] Friedman believed that conscription violated the values of a free society and degraded the citizen's individual freedoms. Richard Nixon pledged to end conscription during the 1968 election, and appointed Friedman as an advisor after assuming the presidency.

A fixture of his presidential campaign, Nixon had hoped that removing the threat of service would deflate the anti-war movement and appease the country's youth population. After his election, he commissioned a report to examine the issue. The report concluded that the armed forces could maintain adequate manpower levels without conscription, and Nixon ultimately approved the transition. Andrew Glass. "U.S. military draft ends, Jan. 27, 1973." *Politico.* 27 January 2012. politico.com/story/2012/01/us-military-draft-ends- jan-27-1973-072085

"Selective Service System," accessed March 18, 2018, https://web.archive.org/web/20090507211238/http://www.sss.gov/induct.htm.

[15] OHanlon, M.E, (2003, January) "Forget About Military Draft," *Brookings*, https://www.brookings.edu/opinions/forget-about-military-draft/.

[16] *The All-Volunteer Military: Issues and Performance*, (Congressional Budget Office, July 2007), viii, https://www.cbo.gov/sites/default/files/110th-congress-2007-2008/reports/07-19-militaryvol_0.pdf.

[17] Epstein, J. (2018, May 8). How I Learned to Love the Draft. Retrieved from https://www.theatlantic.com/magazine/archive/2015/01/how-i-learned-to-love-the-draft/383500/.

Fallows, James. (2015, January), "The Tragedy of the American Military," *The Atlantic*, https://www.theatlantic.com/magazine/archive/2015/01/the-tragedy-of-the-american-military/383516/.

[18] Manning, J. E. (n.d.). Membership of the 115th Congress: A Profile. Retrieved from https://fas.org/sgp/crs/misc/R44762.pdf.

[19] Bacevich, A. J. (2012, February 13). The New American Way of War. Retrieved from https://www.lrb.co.uk/blog/2012/02/13/andrew-bacevich/the-new-american-way-of-war/

[20] Jerald G Bachman and John D Blair, ""Citizen Force" or "Career Force"?," *Armed Forces & Society* 2, no. 1 (October 1, 1975): 81–96, doi:10.1177/0095327X7500200106.

[21] Amy Schafer, "Generations of War," (Center for a New American Security, May

2017), 3, https://s3.amazonaws.com/files.cnas.org/documents/CNASReport-WarriorCast-Final.pdf?mtime=20170427115046.

[22] Admin. (2010, December 8). GATES PRAISES 101ST AIRBORNE AS "TIP OF THE SPEAR". Retrieved from http://www.defencenews-online.com/land/gates-praises-101st-airborne-as-"tip-of-the-spear"/

[23] "Population Representation in the Military Services," (CNA, March 2003), 8-4, https://www.cna.org/pop-rep/2001/download/download.htm.

[24] "Population Representation in the Military Services," (CNA, March 2004), https://www.cna.org/pop-rep/2002/.

[25] William Christeson, Amy Dawson Taggart, and Soren Messner-Zidell, "Ready, Willing, and Unable to Serve," (Mission: Readiness, June 3, 2015), http://cdn.mission-readiness.org/MR-Ready-Willing-Unable.pdf.

"Population Representation in the Military Services 2015," (CNA, n.d.), https://www.cna.org/pop-rep/2015/summary/summary.pdf.

Christeson, Taggart, and Messner-Zidell, "Ready, Willing, and Unable to Serve."

[26] "ASVAB Test Sample Questions," *Todays Military*, accessed March 18, 2018, https://todaysmilitary.com/joining/asvab-test-sample-questions.

"ASVAB and Army Jobs," *Military.com*, 2018, https://www.military.com/join-armed-forces/asvab/asvab-and-army-jobs.html.

[27] "Population Representation in the Military Services 2015," 64-65.

[28] *The All-Volunteer Military: Issues and Performance*, viii.

[29] Shanea Watkins and James Sherk, "Who Serves in the U.S. Military? the Demographics of Enlisted Troops and Officers," August 21, 2008, https://www.heritage.org/defense/report/who-serves-the-us-military-the-demographics-enlisted-troops-and-officers.

[30] *National Priorities Project*, accessed March 18, 2018, https://www.nationalpriorities.org.

[31] Bernard Rostker, "I Want You!," (RAND, 2006), https://www.rand.org/pubs/mono-graphs/MG265.html.

[32] Logan Nye, "This US Army Artillery Unit Savaged 41 Iraqi Battalions in 72 Hours," *We Are the Mighty*, February 5, 2016, http://www.businessinsider.com/this-us-army-artillery-unit-savaged-41-iraqi-battalions-in-72-hours-2016-2.

[33] "The Military-Civilian Gap: Fewer Family Connections," *Pew Research Center*, November 23, 2011, 33, http://www.pewsocialtrends.org/2011/11/23/the-military-civilian-gap-fewer-family-connections/.

[34] "What Makes Someone Join the Military? What Specific Reasons Do People Have for Enlisting, and How Do They Choose Their Branch?," *Quora*, January 13, 2017, https://www.quora.com/United-States-Armed-Forces/What-makes-someone-join-the-military-What-specific-reasons-do-people-have-for-enlisting-and-how-do-they-choose-their-branch.

[35] "The Military-Civilian Gap: Fewer Family Connections," 33.

[36] Glantz, A. (2010). The War Comes Home: Washingtons battle against Americas veterans. 17. Berkeley, CA: University of California Press.

[37] Schafer, "Generations of War," 5.

[38] "What Makes Someone Join the Military? What Specific Reasons Do People Have for Enlisting, and How Do They Choose Their Branch?."

Chapter 2

[1] U.S. Army. (2019). *U.S. Army Recruiting Command*. Retrieved from Army.mil: https://recruiting.army.mil/#age

44 percent of active-duty service members, and slightly more than half of all active-duty enlisted personnel, are 25 years old or younger. Psychologists refer to this period in a person's life, between the ages of 18 to 25, as "emerging adulthood," a window of time marked by "rapid development and considerable vulnerability." According to the *Clinical Psychology Review*, the process of becoming an adult "frequently brings forth key struggles surrounding personal identity and the formulation and reconciliation of beliefs and evaluations of the self."

Department of Defense. (2016). *2016 Demographics: Profile of the Military Community*. Arlington: Department of Defense.

Mobbs, M. C., & Bonanno, G. A. (2017). Beyond war and PTSD: The crucial role of transition stress in the lives of military veterans. *Clinical Psychology Review*, 9.

[2] McGurk, D., Cotting, D. I., Britt, T. W., & Adler, A. B. (2006). Joining the Ranks: The Role of Indoctrination in Transforming Civilians to Service Members. In A. B. Adler, C. A. Castro, & T. W. Britt (Eds.), Operational Stress. Military life: The psychology of serving in peace and combat: Operational stress (p. 13–31). Praeger Security International, 2.

[3] Baron, R. S. (2000, August). Arousal, Capacity, and Intense Indoctrination. *Personality and Social Psychology Review*, pp. 238-254.

[4] Quora. (2019). *What was the hardest part of boot camp/basic training for you?* Retrieved from Quora.com: https://www.quora.com/What-was-the-hardest-part-of-boot-camp-basic-training-for-you

McGurk, D. (2006). 15.

[5] Quora. (2019). *What was the hardest part of boot camp/basic training for you?* McGurk, D. (2006). 6-7.

[7] Mobbs, M. C., & Bonanno, G. A. (2017). 7.

McGurk, D. (2006). 8.

The Most Fun I Never Want to Have Again. (2016, August 23). Retrieved June, 2018, from https://oneaardvark.com/2016/08/23/the-most-fun-i-never-want-to-have-again-part-1/

[8] U.S. Army. (2019). *Basic Combat Training; Your First Steps to Becoming a Soldier.* Retrieved from Goarmy.com: https://www.goarmy.com/soldier-life/becoming-a-soldier/basic-combat-training.html

[9] McGurk, D. (2006).10.

[10] The Most Fun I Never Want to Have Again. (2016, August 23).

[11] McGurk, D. (2006). 16.

Mobbs, M. C., & Bonanno, G. A. (2017). 7.

[12] Molly Snider is a pseudonym.

[13] Bush, G. W. (2003, May 1). *George W. Bush Declares Mission Accomplished.* Retrieved from History.com: https://www.history.com/speeches/george-w-bush-declares-mission-accomplished

[14] Berenson, A., & Burns, J. F. (2004, August 18). The Conflict in Iraq: Looking Back; 8-Day Battle for Najaf: From Attack to Stalemate. *The New York Times*, p. 1.

[15] Mobbs, M. C., & Bonanno, G. A. 8-9.

[16] A 2014 study of female U.S. Army recruits found "substantially improved" cognition and mood from completing the 9- to 10-week basic combat training. Military training was determined to improve decision-making, problem-solving, and situational-analysis skills in entry-level enlistees through exercises such as land navigation, marksmanship, battle drills, and simulated casualty evacuations. As subjects began to observe enhanced cognitive performance, they also self-reported improvement in indicators associated with mood, including vigor, fatigue, and depression. The study confirmed and built upon previous research that established the key elements associated with improved cognition and mood: (a) a structured, collaborative environment that allows for positive reinforcement by peers and supervisors; (b) positive perception of social support; (c) successful achievement of goals; (d) positive group dynamics. Lieberman, H. R., Karl, J. P., Niro, P. J., Williams, K. W., Farina, E. K., Cable, S. J., & McClung, J. P. (2014, January 17). Positive Effects of Basic Training on Cognitive Performance and Mood of Adult Females. *Human Factors*, pp. 1113–1123.

[17] Mobbs, M. C., & Bonanno, G. A. (2017). 9.

[18] McGrath, J. J. (2007). *The Other End of the Spear : The Tooth-to-Tail ratio (T3R) in Modern Military Operations.* Fort Leavenworth: Combat Studies Institute Press. 66.

McGrath, J. J. (2007). 67.

Ibid. 68-69.

[19] Nye, L. (2015, May 27). *24 Jobs You Didn't Know the U.S. Military had.* Retrieved from wearethemighty.com: https://www.wearethemighty.com/articles/weird-military-jobs

[20] Defense Business Board. (2010, July 22). *Reducing Overhead and Improving Business Operations: Initial Observations.* Retrieved from https://timemilitary.files.wordpress.com/2012/03/punaro-brf.pdf

[21] Fussell, P. (1981, August). *Thank God for the Atom Bomb.* Retrieved from Newrepublic.com: https://www.uio.no/studier/emner/hf/iakh/HIS1300MET/v12/undervisningsmateriale/Fussel%20-%20thank%20god%20for%20the%20atom%20bomb.pdf

[22] Von Clausewitz, C. (1976). On War. Princeton: University Press. 95.

Nestler, S. (2019). *The Combat Patch: Binary Indicator or Something More?* Retrieved from Smallwarsjournal.com: https://smallwarsjournal.com/index.php/jrnl/art/the-combat-patch-binary-indicator-or-something-more

[23] Noncombat personnel provide command and control support for combat troops, build the military's semi-permanent camps and bases, supply healthcare, transportation, and financial services, and establish and maintain the force's morale, welfare, and recreation facilities.

[24] Lair, M. H. (2019). *Easy Living in a Hard War: Behind the Lines in Vietnam.* Retrieved from Historynet.com: https://www.historynet.com/easy-living-in-a-hard-war-behind-the-lines-in-vietnam.htm

[25] Vergun, D. (2014, May 21). *Tail as Important as Tooth in Combat, Says Top Logistician.* Retrieved from Army.mil: https://www.army.mil/article/126469/tail_as_important_as_tooth_in_combat_says_top_logistician

Santora, M. (2009, September 08). Big U.S. bases are part of Iraq, but a world apart. Retrieved July, 2018, from https://www.nytimes.com/2009/09/09/world/middleeast/09bases.html

[26] McGrath, J. J. (2007). 81.

Santora, M. (2009, September 08). Big U.S. bases are part of Iraq, but a world apart.

Angry Staff Officer. (2015, November 3). *How Forward Operating Bases Created the Illusion of War in Iraq and Afghanistan*. Retrieved from Angrystaffofficer.com: https://angrystaffofficer.com/2015/11/03/how-forward-operating-bases-created-the-illusion-of-war-in-iraq-and-afghanistan/

Chapter 3

[1] Wenger, J. W., O'Connell, C., & Cottrell, L. (2018). *Examination of Recent Deployment Experience Across the Services and Components*. Santa Monica, CA: Rand Corporation.

[2] Defense Casualty Analysis System. (n.d.). Retrieved March, 2021, from https://dcas.dmdc.osd.mil/dcas/pages/report_sum_reason.xhtml

[3] McNally, R. J., & Frueh, B. C. (2013). Why are Iraq and Afghanistan War Veterans Seeking PTSD Disability Compensation at Unprecedented Rates? *Journal of Anxiety Disorders*, 521.

Wenger, J. W., O'Connell, C., & Cottrell, L. (2018).

[4] Gade, D. (2013). A Better Way to Help Veterans. *National Affairs*, p. 6.

[5] United States Department of Defense. (2015). *2015 Demographics Report*. Arlington, VA: Department of Defense. 55.

[6] McNally, R. J., & Frueh, B. C. (2013). 521.

[7] Holder, K. A. (2016). *The Disability of Veterans*. Washington, DC: U.S. Census Bureau.

[8] Defense Manpower Data Center. (2001). *Department of Defense 2000 Military Exit Survey*. Arlington, VA: Department of Defense. 9.

[9] Zoli, C., Maury, R., & Fay, D. (2015). *Missing Perspectives: Servicemembers' Transition from Service to Civilian Life*. Syracuse, NY: Institute for Veterans and Military Families.

[10] According to a 2017 report, 30 percent of service members planning to leave the military within two years cited "concerns about the impact of military service on my family" as their top reason for exiting. 25 percent indicated "the military lifestyle did not allow me sufficient time with my family."

Shiffer, O. C., & Maury, R. V. (2017). *Military Family Lifestyle Survey*. Syracuse, NY: Institute for Veterans and Military Families. 19.

Chapter 4

[1] The Associated Press. (2016, July 6). *A Timeline of U.S. Troop Levels in Afghanistan*

Since 2001. Retrieved from Militarytimes.com: https://www.militarytimes.com/news/your-military/2016/07/06/a-timeline-of-u-s-troop-levels-in-afghanistan-since-2001/

[2] Luo, M. (2007, March 7). *Bush Appoints Dole and Shalala to Head Inquiry on Military Health Care.* Retrieved from The New York Times: https://www.nytimes.com/2007/03/07/washington/07medical.html

[3] Government Accountability Office. (2016). *Military Health Care.* Washington, DC: Government Accountability Office. 1.

[4] As the number of soldiers entering the WTU program has declined, the Army has reduced the number of operating WTUs to 14 units as of August 2016.

Government Accountability Office. (2016). 1.

[5] Tarrant, D., Friedman, S., & Parks, E. (2014, November 22). *The War After the War.* Retrieved from dallasnews.com: http://res.dallasnews.com/interactives/injuredheroes/part1/

[6] Wounded Warrior Regiment. (2015). *Fact Sheet: IDES.* Quantico, VA: United States Marine Corps.

[7] Brennan, T. J. (2012, November 20). *From Battlefield Injury Into a Functioning Disability System.* Retrieved from The New York Times: https://atwar.blogs.nytimes.com/2012/11/20/from-battlefield-injury-into-a-functioning-disability-system/

[8] Government Accountability Office. (2012). 3.

[9] Profile is a commonly used term across all military branches to describe a duty-limiting condition. A soldier is said to be 'on profile' when they have been assessed with one of these conditions. It is also often used as a term of derision, as in "that private is a profile ranger" or "he's hiding behind his profile."

[10] U.S. Army Medical Command. (2013). *IDES Guidebook.* San Antonio, TX: U.S. Army. 4.

[11] In February of 2018, there were a little over 1.3 million active duty personnel in the US military. Chapter 61 of Title 10 of the US Code gives the Secretaries of the services the authority to retire or separate members when they cannot perform their military duties. As a general rule, physical or mental health problems that are incompatible with military duty or that may prevent deployment for more than 12 months are likely to precipitate a Medical Evaluation Board, or MEB. The MEB consists of a group of active duty physicians not involved in the care of that service member who review the clinical file and decide whether that individual should be retained on active duty, using the published standards for continued military service. If the service member is expected to recover and return to full duty, the MEB may recommend placing them on temporary limited duty (TDL) for a designated amount of time, after which they must return to their command. If they are determined to be unfit for duty, then the case

is referred to a formal fitness for duty and disability determination process called the Physical Evaluation Board, or PEB. Wounded Warrior Regiment. (2015).

[12] The PEB can recommend a number of dispositions of a particular service member. It may return the member to duty (with or without restrictions), place the member on the temporary disabled/retired list (TDRL), separate the member, or medically retire the member. In some cases, the PEB may recommend retraining or reclassification into a different military duty position in order to retain an injured or ill service member on active duty (for example, allowing an infantry soldier to retrain as an X-ray technician).

[13] Fussell, P. (1982, January). My War: How I got Irony in the Infantry. Retrieved from Harpers.org: https://harpers.org/archive/1982/01/my-war/10/

[14] Meyer, B. (2009, March 10). *At Some Bases, Wounded GIs are More Likely to be Punished by the Military Than Able-Bodied Troops*. Retrieved from Cleveland.com: https://www.cleveland.com/nation/2009/03/at_some_bases_wounded_gis_are.html

[15] Dao, J., & Frosch, D. (2010, April 24). *Feeling Warehoused in Army Trauma Care Units*. Retrieved from The New York Times: https://www.nytimes.com/2010/04/25/health/25warrior.html

[16] Additionally, 37 percent had been evacuated from combat theaters for diseases or non-battle injuries, while 20 percent were soldiers in the pre- or post-mobilization stage. U.S. Army Inspector General "Results of the Warrior Care and Transition Program Inspection". September 22, 2010. A-20. Available online at: https://int.nyt.com/data/int-shared/nytdocs/docs/566/566.pdf

[17] Ricks, T. E. (2010, June 17). Here's How Screwed up the Army's Warrior Transition Units are: Genuinely Sick Soldiers try to get out of Using Them . *Foreign Policy*.

[18] Wood, D. (2013, October 14). *Thousands of Soldiers Unfit for War Duty*. Retrieved from HuffPost Politics: https://archive.fo/x5Fyv#selection-1015.0-1015.40

[19] U.S. Army Inspector General, 2010. A-17, A-18.

[20] Ibid, A-19.

[21] Ricks, T. E. (2010, June 16). Former Pentagon Official: The Warrior Unites are Holding Tanks for Misfits. *Foreign Policy*.

[22] U.S. Army Inspector General, 2010. A-18.

[23] Ibid, A-19.

[24] Ibid, 2.

[25] Ibid, A-37.

[26] Ibid, C-5.

[27] Ibid.

[28] Malik is a pseudonym.

[29] Potomac Local. (2014, November 3). *More than 40 Groups in Manassas Veterans Day Parade*. Retrieved from Potomaclocal.com: https://potomaclocal.com/2014/11/03/40-groups-manassas-veterans-day-parade/

[30] Phillips, M. M. (2009, May 23). *Stalemate*. Retrieved from The Wall Street Journal: https://www.wsj.com/articles/SB10001424052970203771904574179672963946120

[31] U.S. Army Inspector General, 2010. A-20.

[32] Wood, D. (2013, October 14).

[33] Ricks, T. E. (2010, June 16).

[34] Wood, D. (2013, October 14).

Chapter 5

[1] Jefferson Barracks Heritage Foundation. (2008, August 13). *82nd Airborne Division Reunion and Convention*. Retrieved from Jefferson Barracks Heritage Foundation: http://jbhf.org/jeffersonbarracks/past_events.html

The St. Louis American. (2008, August 11). *82nd Airborne Division Reunion Begins Tomorrow*. Retrieved from stlamerican.com: http://www.stlamerican.com/news/local_news/nd-airborne-division-reunion-begins-tomorrow/article_31229fe1-eee6-56d2-b307-ade0b862110a.html

[2] Shanker, T., & Schmitt, E. (2009, March 18). *U.S. Plans Vastly Expanded Afghan Security Force*. Retrieved from The New York Times: https://www.nytimes.com/2009/03/19/us/politics/19military.html

[3] Mobbs, M. C., & Bonanno, G. A. (2017).13.

[4] Mobbs, M. C., & Bonanno, G. A. (2017). Beyond War and PTSD: The Crucial Role of Transition Stress in the Lives of Military Veterans. *Clinical Psychology Review*, 10.

[5] Clinton, R. (2010, September 16). *Camp Bucca, Iraq Flag Presented to Namesake's Family*. Retrieved from Dvidshub.net: https://www.dvidshub.net/news/56400/camp-bucca-iraq-flag-presented-namesakes-family#.Uizxprxw9Cd

Kramer, A. E. (2011, December 3). *A New Hotel, Where the Stay Used to Be Mandatory*. Retrieved from The New York Times: https://www.nytimes.com/2011/12/04/world/middleeast/camp-bucca-in-iraq-once-a-prison-base-now-houses-a-hotel.html

[6] McCoy, T. (2014, November 4). *How the Islamic State Evolved in an American Prison*. Retrieved from The Washington Post: https://www.washingtonpost.com/news/morning-mix/wp/2014/11/04/how-an-american-prison-helped-ignite-the-islamic-state/

[7] "U.S. Troops Fire on Prison Riot as 4 Die." CNN, February 1, 2005. http://www.cnn.com/2005/WORLD/meast/02/01/iraq.prison/.

[8] Graham, B. (2005, February 21). *Prisoner Uprising In Iraq Exposes New Risk for U.S.* Retrieved from The Washington Post: http://www.washingtonpost.com/wp-dyn/articles/A40411-2005Feb20.html

[9] In essence, the VA compares an individual's profile at their point of entry with their profile at their point of exit, and considers any variation in mental or physical health to be a "service-connected disability."

According to 38 USC 1111, the VA applies a "presumption of soundness," which means that a veteran is considered to be in perfect physical or mental health condition at the beginning of service, unless their entry exam specifically notes some pre-existing disability.

Furthermore, even strictly genetic diseases, such as polycystic kidney disease, can be and are rated under the disability evaluation criteria. Since many of these are adult-onset diseases, they typically do not exhibit symptoms prior to a younger recruit's enlistment.

"Compensation and Pension Materials." Veterans Benefits Administration. United States Department of Veterans Affairs, n.d. https://www.benefits.va.gov/WARMS/docs/admin21/m21_1/mr/part4/subptii/ch02/M21-1MRIV_ii_2_secB.doc.

Legal Information Institute. (2019). *38 CFR § 4.115b - Ratings of the Genitourinary System - Diagnoses.* Retrieved from Law.cornell.edu: https://www.law.cornell.edu/cfr/text/38/4.115b

[10] Wadsworth, M. (2019). *Service Disability Compensation for Accidents Not Related to Combat.* Retrieved from Nolo.com: https://www.nolo.com/legal-encyclopedia/service-disability-compensation-accidents-related-combat.html

[11] Army National Guard. (2019). *Officer Candidate School.* Retrieved from nationalguard.com: https://www.nationalguard.com/careers/become-an-officer/officer-candidate-school

Chapter 6

[1] The current version of TAP was established by the VOW to Hire Heroes Act of 2011, which went into effect on November 21, 2012. Curtis, C. L. (2013). *The Vow to Hire Heroes Act.* Washington, DC: U.S. Department of Veteran Affairs.

[2] TAP was established through the National Defense Authorization Act for Fiscal Year 1991, Pub. L. No. 101-510, § 502(a)(1), 104 Stat. 1485, 1551 (1990). Federal law spells out many topics that must be covered in TAP, including employment and relocation assistance, education opportunities, health and life insurance, and financial

planning. Moreover, eligibility and the time frames for provision of TAP services are spelled out in law: all service members who have been on active duty for at least 180 days are eligible for TAP services, but those separating because of a disability are eligible regardless of the length of their active duty service. Eligible service members must be provided TAP while they are on active duty, either as soon as possible within the 2 years prior to their anticipated retirement date or in the 1 year prior to their anticipated separation date. In either case, TAP services must generally commence no later than 90 days prior to their discharge or release. The exceptions to this rule occur when retirements or separations are not anticipated until 90 or fewer days of active duty remain, or a member of the reserve is being demobilized under circumstances in which the 90 day requirement is unfeasible. In such cases, TAP services must be provided as soon as possible within the remaining period of service.

Rather than TAP continuing to be an end-of-career event, DOD planned to shift to a Military Life Cycle Transition Model after October 2014. This model is intended to integrate transition preparation—counseling, assessments, and access to resources to build skills or credentials— throughout the course of a service member's military career.

Government Accountability Office. (2014). *Transitioning Veterans: Improved Oversight Needed to Enhance Implementation of Transition Assistance Program.* Washington, DC: Government Accountability Office, 5-9.

[3] Curtis, C. L. (2013). *The Vow to Hire Heroes Act.* Washington, DC: U.S. Department of Veteran Affairs.

[4] In an old presentation slide about how veterans qualify for benefits, the VA provided the following examples: (1) During a weekend drill, an Army Reservist injures her knee while participating in a physical training class. She is eligible to apply for compensation for lasting effects of the knee injury. (2) An individual enlisted in the U.S Navy in June of 2002 served for a period of 4 years. He was honorably discharged in 2006. During his active duty, he fell from a bunk and injured his back. Based on his active service, he may be entitled to service-connected benefits for the lasting effects of his back injury.

"VA Benefits and Services Participant Guide." U.S. Department of Veterans Affairs. https://www.benefits.va.gov/TRANSITION/docs/VA-Benefits-Participant-Guide.pdf#

[5] Bradley, Omar. "Veterans Benefits in the United States: A Report to the President by the President's Commission on Veterans' Pensions". Washington, DC. 1956. 9. Available online at https://www.va.gov/vetdata/docs/Bradley_Report.pdf

[6] Bradley (1956). 144.

[7] Veterans Benefits Administration. (2017). Fiscal Year 2016 Annual Benefits Report. Retrieved from U.S. Department of Veterans Affairs: https://www.benefits.va.gov/REPORTS/abr/docs/2016_abr.pdf

Shane III, L. (2020, December 22). VA gets big funding increase in final fiscal 2021 budget deal. Military Times. https://www.militarytimes.com/news/pentagon-congress/2020/12/22/va-gets-big-funding-increase-in-final-fiscal-2021-budget-deal/.

[8] Submitted News. (2018, July 17). *Veterans Affairs Announces Resource Benefits Fair and Veteran Town Hall.* Retrieved from Middletown Transcript: https://www.middletowntranscript.com/news/20180717/veterans-affairs-announces-resource-benefits-fair-and-veteran-town-hall

[9] Carolina Coast Online. (2018, July 19). *Veteran's Services Bring in Millions, Provide Benefits.* Retrieved from Carolina Coast Online: http://www.carolinacoastonline.com/entertainment/around_town/article_22f82bf8-8b5a-11e8-a066-13c31415759a.html?mode=jqm

[10] Manar, G. (2010, February 24). *Examination of the VA Benefits Delivery at Discharge and Quick Start Programs.* Retrieved from VFW.com: https://www.vfw.org/advocacy/national-legislative-service/congressional-testimony/2010/02/examination-of-the-va-benefits-delivery-at-discharge-and-quick-start-programs

[11] Document provided in an email dated 11/14/2016 to author by Dan English.

[12] According to the VA, veterans with approved BDD applications could expect to begin receiving benefits within three months, compared to the six to seven months that it typically took. Bertoni, D. (2008) *Veteran's Disability Benefits: Better Accountability and Access Would Improve the Benefits Delivery at Discharge Program.* Report prepared for US Congress. Government Accountability Office. Washington, D.C.

[13] Congressional Budget Office (2014). *Veterans' Disability Compensation: Trends and Policy Options.*

[14] Satel, S., & Frueh, B. C. (2014, August 25). *The Other VA Scandal.* Retrieved from National Review: https://www.nationalreview.com/magazine/2014/08/25/other-va-scandal/

[15] Calculations based on 2016 Annual Benefits Report. Available here: https://www.benefits.va.gov/REPORTS/abr/docs/2016_abr.pdf

[16] Author interview

[17] U.S. Marine Corps. (2014, August 1). *Leading Marines.* Retrieved from https://www.marines.mil/Portals/1/MCWP%206-11_Part1.pdf

[18] Weinstein, A. (2017, December 5). *Here's the New Navy Slogan That Took 18 Months and Millions of Dollars to Think up.* Retrieved from Task & Purpose: https://taskandpurpose.com/heres-new-navy-slogan-took-18-months-millions-dollars-invent

[19] Navy Recruiting Command Public Affairs. (2017, December 5). *Navy to Launch New Branding Campaign, Tagline at Army-Navy Game.* Retrieved from Navy.mil: https://www.navy.mil/submit/display.asp?story_id=103634

[20] Gilbert, T. (2017, December 20). *Popular US Navy Sayings, Mottos, and Slogans.* Retrieved from Navycrow.com: https://navycrow.com/popular-us-navy-sayings-mottos-and-slogans/

[21] Headquarters, Department of the Army. (2012, August). Retrieved from Army Leadership: https://fas.org/irp/doddir/army/adp6_22.pdf

[22] From a 2012 Military Times survey, cited in Schake, Kori N., and James N. Mattis. 2016. *Warriors & citizens: American views of our military.*

[23] Rosa Brooks, "Civil-military Paradoxes," pp 24. Cited in Schake, Kori N., and James N. Mattis. 2016. *Warriors & Citizens: American views of our military.*

[24] Volkman, K. (2010, December 31). *Tornadoes, Storms Slam St. Louis on New Year's Eve.* Retrieved from St. Louis Business Journal: https://www.bizjournals.com/stlouis/news/2010/12/31/tornado-hits-st-louis.html

PART II

Chapter 7

[1] CNN Money. (2010). *Best Places to Live.* Retrieved from money.cnn.com: https://money.cnn.com/magazines/moneymag/bplive/2010/top25s/qualitylife/youngest.html

[2] U.S. Attorney's Office Eastern District of North Carolina. (2013, July 18). *Veteran Sentenced To Two Years In Prison For Lying To Obtain Disability Benefits.* Retrieved from Justice.gov: https://www.justice.gov/usao-ednc/pr/veteran-sentenced-two-years-prison-lying-obtain-disability-benefits

[3] U.S. Attorney's Office District of Hawaii. (2018, March 28). *Maui Man Sentenced For Theft From U.S. Department of Veteran's Affairs.* Retrieved from justice.gov: https://www.justice.gov/usao-hi/pr/maui-man-sentenced-theft-us-department-veterans-affairs

[4] U.S. Attorney's Office Western District of New York. (2017, December 5). *Holland Couple Sentenced In Connection With Fraudulent Receipt Of Over $1,000,000 In Veterans Benefits And Postal Workers Compensation.* Retrieved from justice.gov: https://www.justice.gov/usao-wdny/pr/holland-couple-sentenced-connection-fraudulent-receipt-over-1000000-veterans-benefits

[5] Louszko, A., & Valiente, A. (2016, September 7). *Man Convicted of Disability Fraud Claims he's Actually Disabled.* Retrieved from abcnews.com: https://abcnews.go.com/Health/man-convicted-disability-fraud-claims-hes-disabled/story?id=41930250

[6] Gregory, D. (2015, June 19). "Paralyzed" Vet Walks After Getting Free Home: Military Connection. Retrieved from Militaryconnection.com: https://militaryconnection.com/blog/paralyzed-vet-walks-after-getting-free-home-military-connection/

[7] Golgowski, N. (2015, May 22). 'Paralyzed' Veteran Under Fire After Video Shows

him Walking Outside Charity-Built Home. Retrieved from NYdailynews.com: https://www.nydailynews.com/news/national/paralyzed-veteran-fire-video-shows-walking-article-1.2232594

[8] U.S. Department of Veteran Affairs. (2018, August 6). *VA History*. Retrieved from va.gov: https://www.va.gov/about_va/vahistory.asp

[9] The Veterans Health Administration is America's largest integrated health care system, providing care at 1,243 health care facilities, including 172 medical centers and 1,062 outpatient sites of care of varying complexity (VHA outpatient clinics), serving 9 million enrolled Veterans each year.

U.S. Department of Veteran Affairs. (2019, July 15). *Veterans Health Administration*. Retrieved from va.gov: https://www.va.gov/health/

[10] https://www.va.gov/budget/docs/summary/fy2021VAsBudgetFastFacts.pdf

[11] https://www.va.gov/budget/docs/summary/fy2021VAbudgetInBrief.pdf

[12] Sayer, N. A., & Thuras, P. (2002, February). *The Influence of Patients' Compensation-Seeking Status on the Perceptions of Veterans Affairs Clinicians*. Retrieved from ncbi.nlm.nih.gov: https://www.ncbi.nlm.nih.gov/pubmed/11821554

Kashdan, T. B. (2014, September 9). *11 Reasons that Combat Veterans With PTSD Are Being Harmed*. Retrieved from psychologytoday.com: https://www.psychologytoday.com/us/blog/curious/201409/11-reasons-combat-veterans-ptsd-are-being-harmed

[13] Burkett, B. G., & Whitley, G. (1998). *Stolen Valor : How the Vietnam Generation Was Robbed of Its Heroes and Its History*. Dallas, TX: Verity Press Publishing, 254-261.

[14] O'Byrne, Brendan. Testimony before the House Committee on Veterans Affairs, June 7, 2017. Available online at https://docs.house.gov/meetings/VR/VR00/20170607/106073/HHRG-115-VR00-Wstate-OByrneB-20170607.pdf

[15] McVay, M. (2016, April 27). *When PTSD Benefits are Abused*. Retrieved from denverpost.com: https://www.denverpost.com/2014/06/20/when-ptsd-benefits-are-abused/

[16] O'Byrne, Brendan. Testimony before the House Committee on Veterans Affairs, June 7, 2017.

[17] American Psychology Association. (2018, September 26). PTSD Assessment Instruments. Retrieved from apa.org: https://www.apa.org/ptsd-guideline/assessment/index

Davidson, J. R. (1995). Structured Interview for PTSD. Retrieved from psychiatry.duke.edu: https://psychiatry.duke.edu/sites/default/files/field/image/sip_scale.pdf

[18] Davidson, Kudler, & Smith. (2018, September 24). Structured Interview for PTSD (SI-PTSD). Retrieved from ptsd.va.gov: https://www.ptsd.va.gov/professional/assessment/adult-int/si-ptsd.asp

[19] Colburn Group. (2013). Waddell's Signs and Workers' Compensation Claims. Retrieved from colburngroup.com: https://colburngroup.com/wp-content/uploads/2013/09/Waddells-Signs-and-WC-Claims1.pdf

[20] "4/8/15 Further Lessons." My Education at the VA., April 16, 2015. https://myvaeducation.loudunskeptic.com/2015/03/further-lessons.html

[21] Though the VA's 8,000-plus registered C&P examiners conduct evaluations solely for the purpose of helping determine a veteran's disability pay, they are employed by the VHA—the only link in the benefits chain not to fall under the VBA.

Testimony of Chairman Jeff Miller before the House Committee on Veterans Affairs, June 25 2014; https://www.gpo.gov/fdsys/pkg/CHRG-113hhrg89376/html/CHRG-113hhrg89376.htm

One Hundred and Thirteenth Congress. (2014, June 25). VBA and VHA Interactions: Ordering and Conducting Medical Examinations. Retrieved from govinfo.gov: https://www.govinfo.gov/content/pkg/CHRG-113hhrg89376/html/CHRG-113hhrg89376.htm

[22] Breed, A. G. (2010, May 2). Tide of new PTSD Cases Raises Fears of Fraud. Retrieved from nbcnews.com: http://www.nbcnews.com/id/36852985/ns/health-mental_health/t/tide-new-ptsd-cases-raises-fears-fraud/#.XXftsyhKiUl

[23] The Veterans Health Administration is the largest integrated health care system in the United States, providing care at 1,243 health care facilities, including 170 VA Medical Centers and 1,063 outpatient sites of care of varying complexity (VHA outpatient clinics), serving more than 9 million enrolled Veterans each year. U.S. Department of Veteran Affairs. (2018, January 23). Where do I get the Care I Need? Retrieved from va.gov: https://www.va.gov/health/findcare.asp

Chapter 8

[1] Burkett, B. G., & Whitley, G. (1998). *Stolen Valor: How the Vietnam Generation Was Robbed of Its Heroes and Its History.* Dallas, TX: Verity Press Publishing, 32.

[2] Ibid. xxiii.

[3] Ibid. 16, 36.

[4] Ibid. 39.

[5] Ibid. 3-6.

[6] Ibid. 10, 12, 14, 20.

[7] Ibid. 37, 39-40.

[8] Alioth LLC. (2019). *CPI Inflation Calculator.* Retrieved from in2013dollars.com: http://www.in2013dollars.com/1985-dollars-in-2018?amount=20000

[9] Burkett, B. G., & Whitley, G. (1998). 72.

[10] Ibid. 73.

[11] Ibid. 40-43.

[12] Ibid. 50.

[13] Wikipedia. (2019, September 9). *1979 in Film.* Retrieved from Wikipedia: https://en.wikipedia.org/wiki/1979_in_film

[14] Burkett, B. G., & Whitley, G. (1998). xxiv-xxv, 79.

[15] Ibid. 46.

[16] Ibid. 84-86.

[17] Hall, R. C., & Hall, R. C. (2012). Compensation Neurosis: A Too Quickly Forgotten Concept? *The Journal of the American Academy of Psychiatry and the Law,* 390-398.

[18] Keller, T., & Chappell, T. (1996, July). *The Rise and Fall of Erichsen's Disease (railroad spine).* Retrieved from ncbi.nlm.nih.gov: https://www.ncbi.nlm.nih.gov/pubmed/8817791

[19] Harrington, R. (2007). *The Railway Accident: Trains, Trauma and Technological Crisis in Nineteenth Century Britain.* Retrieved from ideas.respec.org: https://ideas.repec.org/p/ess/wpaper/id1181.html

[20] "Compensation neurosis" has not been cited in any modern edition of *The Diagnostic and Statistical Manual of Mental Disorders.*

[21] Burkett, B. G., & Whitley, G. (1998). 267-272.

[22] Ibid. 82-84.

[23] Ibid. 81-82.

[24] Ibid. 411-416.

[25] Ibid. 553-558.

[26] Ibid. 93.

[27] Ibid. 104-105.

[28] National Park Service. (2019). *The Vietnam Veterans Memorial.* Retrieved from thewall-usa.com: http://thewall-usa.com/information.asp

[29] Ibid. 588.

[30] Ibid. 582-583.

[31] Ibid. 584.

[32] Ibid. 586.

Holzer, Henry Mark, and Erika Holzer. *Fake Warriors: Identifying, Exposing, and Punishing Those Who Falsify Their Military Service*, iii. Philadelphia: Xlibris, 2003.

[33] Statistica. (2019). *Number of Recreational Visitors to the Vietnam Veterans Memorial in the United States from 2008 to 2018 (in millions)*. Retrieved from statistica.com: https://www.statista.com/statistics/254223/number-of-visitors-to-vietnam-veterans-memorial-in-the-us/

[34] Burkett, B. G., & Whitley, G. (1998). 588-590.

[35] Ibid.

[36] Ibid. 165.

[37] Ibid. 175.

[38] Holzer, Henry Mark, and Erika Holzer (2003). 14-15.

[39] Chambers, J. (2014, July 9). *'We're all liars': Intriguing yet Sobering Findings About Lying Made Over 50 Years by UAB Psychiatrist*. Retrieved from al.com: https://www.al.com/news/birmingham/2014/07/everybody_lies_the_intriguing.html

[40] Holzer & Holzer (2003). 13.

[41] In a paper published by The Journal of the American Academy of Psychiatry, the authors wrote, "although there can be financial secondary gain as part of a compensation neurosis," most times the condition involves fabricating or exaggerating accounts of trauma due to "a combination of external and internal incentives, with internal motivators being in equal or larger factor in compensation neurosis." Frueh, B. C., Hamner, M. B., Cahill, S. P., et al (2000). Apparent symptom overreporting among combat veterans evaluated for PTSD. *Clinical Psychology Review*, 20, 853–885.

[42] Burkett, B. G., & Whitley, G. (1998). 80-81.

[43] Whitley, Glenna. "Stolen Valor." Penthouse, April 1999. Pam Lambert. "Lie Detector." People, March 8, 2004.

[44] The act was passed in 2005 and fell to a Supreme Court challenge in US v. Alvarez (2012). In that decision, the Supreme Court ruled 6-3 that the SVA was an unconstitutional abridgement of freedom of speech. The DOD announced in 2012 that it would have a new website, valor.defense.gov, in order to provide a public record of medal recipients, including MoH, DSC, and Silver Star recipients. In response to the original overturning of the SVA 2005 version, Congress passed the SVA 2013, which

made it a federal crime to profit from the false claim.

Caruba, L. (2016, January 31). *To Tell the Truth*. Retrieved from Texasmonthly.com: https://www.texasmonthly.com/articles/to-tell-the-truth/

[45] United States Attorney's Office Western District of Washington. (2007, September 21). *Phony Vets Scam More Than $1.4 Million And Damage Image Of Honorable Veterans*. Retrieved from justice.gov: https://www.justice.gov/archive/usao/waw/press/2007/sep/operationstolenvalor.html

[46] Wilson, Mark. "Author Battles Military Fraud." *Hood County News*, September 22, 2012.

[47] Ibid.

Chapter 9

[1] Bush, Shane S., and Dominic A. Carone. Essay. In *Mild Traumatic Brain Injury: Symptom Validity Assessment and Malingering*, 8. New York: Springer Publishing Company, 2013.

[2] 10 US Code, Section 883. Article 83, Malingering. Available online at https://www.law.cornell.edu/uscode/text/10/883

[3] "Malingering." Psychology Today, March 2019. https://www.psychologytoday.com/us/conditions/malingering.

[4] Phillip J. Resnick, Sara West, and Joshua W. Payne, "Malingering of Posttraumatic Disorders", in *Clinical Assessment of Malingering and Deception*, 3rd ed., ed. Richard Rogers (New York: Guilford, 2008), 111.

[5] Resnick (2008). 113.

[6] Charney, D., Davidson, J., Friedman, M., Judge, R., Keane, T., McFarlane, S., . . . Zohar, J. (1998). A Consensus Meeting on Effective Research Practice in PTSD. CNS Spectrums, 3(S2), 9.

[7] Resnick (2008). 112.

[8] Resnick (2008). 112-3.

[9] Burges C, McMillan TM. The ability of naive participants to report symptoms of post-traumatic stress disorder. Br J *Clin Psychol*. 2001 Jun;40(2):209-14.

[10] Resnick (2008). 111.

[11] Blanchard, Edward B., and Edward J. Hickling. "Determining Who Develops PTSD from MVAs." *Behaviour Research and Therapy* 34, no. 1 (January 1996). https://doi.org/10.1037/10676-006.

[12] "What Are Psychometric Tests." Institute of Psychometric Coaching, n.d. https://www.psychometricinstitute.com.au/Psychometric-Guide/Introduction_to_Psychometric_Tests.html.

[13] Jane Framingham, Ph.D. "Minnesota Multiphasic Personality Inventory (MMPI)." Psych Central, May 17, 2016. https://psychcentral.com/lib/minnesota-multiphasic-personality-inventory-mmpi.

[14] Fairbank, J. A., McCaffrey, R. J., & Keane, T. M. (1985). Psychometric detection of fabricated symptoms of posttraumatic stress disorder. *American Journal of Psychiatry*, 142, 501–503.

[15] Gold, Paul B. & Frueh, B. Christopher (1999). Compensation-Seeking and Extreme Exaggeration of Psychopathology Among Combat Veterans Evaluated for Posttraumatic Stress Disorder. *The Journal of Nervous & Mental Disease*, 680-684.

[16] Gold, P. B., Frueh, B. C., Chobot, K., & Brady, K. L. (1996, August). Detection of malingered PTSD in a sample of combat veterans. Poster presented at the annual meeting of the American Psychological Association, Toronto, Ontario, Canada.

[17] Frueh, B. C., Smith, D. W., & Barker, S. E. (1996). Compensation seeking status and psychometric assess- ment of combat veterans seeking treatment for PTSD. Journal of Traumatic Stress, 9, 427–439.

[18] Frueh, B. C., Gold, P. B., & de Arellano, M. A. (1997). Symptom overreporting in combat veterans evaluated for PTSD: Differentiation on the basis of compensation seeking status. Journal of Personality Assessment, 68, 369–384.

[19] Frueh & Hamner (2000).

[20] Simonpietri, J.C. "MMPI-2 Validity Scales: How to Interpret Your Personality Test." Cognitive Dynamics, August 9, 2015. https://cognitivedynamics.blogspot.com/2015/09/how-to-interpret-mmpi-2-scores-do-it.html#gsc.tab=0.

[21] Rouhbakhsh, P., Drescher, K., Pivar, I., & Greene, R. (1996, November). Potential for secondary gain and overresponding on the MMPI-2 in an inpatient population with PTSD. Poster presented at the 12th annual meeting for the International Society of Traumatic Stress Studies, San Francisco, CA.

[22] Richman, H., Frueh, B. C., & Libet, J. M. (1994, November). Therapists' ratings of treatment modality efficacy for combat-related PTSD. Poster presented at the tenth annual meeting of the International Society for Traumatic Stress Studies, Chicago, IL.

[23] Department of Veterans Affairs Office of Inspector General, Review of State Variances in VA Disability Compensation Payments. No. 05-00765-137, Washington, DC: VA Office of Inspector General, 2005.

[24] Hall RC, Hall RC. Compensation neurosis: a too quickly forgotten concept? *J Am Acad Psychiatry Law*. (2012). 390-8.

[25] Resnick (2008). 126.

[26] Ibid.

[27] One study found that an upcoming disability examination correlated with "small but significant" increases in symptom reporting among veterans filing a claim for PTSD. Unemployed participants and those with lower incomes showed greater increases in PTSD symptoms than those who were employed and had higher incomes. Murdoch, M., Sayer, N. A., Spoont, M. R., Rosenheck, R., Noorbaloochi, S., Griffin, J. M., et al. (2011). Long-term outcomes of disability benefits in U.S. veterans with posttraumatic stress disorder. Archives of General Psychiatry 68(10). 1072-1080.

[28] Rosen, Marc I. "Compensation examinations for PTSD--an opportunity for treatment?." Journal of rehabilitation research and development vol. 47,5 (2010). xv-xxii.

Chapter 10

[1] Veterans Benefits Administration. (2018). *Fiscal Year 2017 Compensation*. Retrieved from U.S. Department of Veterans Affairs: https://www.benefits.va.gov/REPORTS/abr/docs/2017_abr.pdf

[2] James Morales is a pseudonym.

[3] Denning, John H, and Robert D Shura. "Cost of malingering mild traumatic brain injury-related cognitive deficits during compensation and pension evaluations in the veterans benefits administration." *Applied Neuropsychology Adult* vol. 26,1 (2019): 1-16.

Schroeder, Ryan W., Phillip K. Martin, and Anthony P. Odland. "Expert Beliefs and Practices Regarding Neuropsychological Validity Testing." *The Clinical Neuropsychologist* 30, no. 4 (2016): 515–35. https://doi.org/10.1080/13854046.2016.1177118.

[4] Criminal Justice Research. (2019). *Structured Interview of Reported Symptoms (SIRS)*. Retrieved from criminal-justice.iresearchnet.com: http://criminal-justice.iresearchnet.com/forensic-psychology/structured-interview-of-reported-symptoms-sirs/

Freeman T, Powell M, Kimbrell T. Measuring symptom exaggeration in veterans with chronic posttraumatic stress disorder. *Psychiatry Res.*158,3 (2008): 374-80.

[5] Veterans Benefits Administration (2018).

Robertson, J. (2006, September 15). *Iraq War's Signature Wound: Brain Injury*. Retrieved from The Washington Post: http://www.washingtonpost.com/wp-dyn/content/article/2006/09/15/AR2006091500273.html

[6] Denning (2019).

[7] Primary Psychiatry. (2005, December 1). *Determination of Malingering in Disability Evaluations*. Retrieved from primarypsychiatry.com: http://primarypsychiatry.com/determination-of-malingering-in-disability-evaluations/

[8] Merten, Thomas, Elisabeth Thies, Katrin Schneider, and Andreas Stevens. "Symptom Validity Testing in Claimants with Alleged Posttraumatic Stress Disorder: Comparing the Morel Emotional Numbing Test, the Structured Inventory of Malingered Symptomatology, and the Word Memory Test." *Psychological Injury and Law* 2, no. 3-4 (December 5, 2009): 284–93. https://doi.org/10.1007/s12207-009-9057-0.

[9] Binder, L., & Rohling, M. (1996, January). *Money Matters: A Meta-Analytic Review of the Effects of Financial Incentives on Recovery After Closed-Head Injury*. Retrieved from ncbi.nlm.nih.gov: https://www.ncbi.nlm.nih.gov/pubmed/8540596

[10] Denning (2019).

[11] Disabilityhappens.com, comment dated June 4, 2018. Available online at https://www.disabilityhappens.com/how-where-to-report-va-abuse-and-fraud/

[12] Burns, Sarah K, Kristen M. Guerrera, David E. Hunter, and Brian Q. Rieksts. "Trends in VBA Disability Compensation." Institute for Defense Analysis, June 2016. Available online at https://apps.dtic.mil/sti/pdfs/AD1015430.pdf

[13] Veterans Benefits Administration (2018).

[14] Interestingly, WWII/Korean War combat veterans and POWs (e.g., Sutker, Winstead, Galina, & Allain, 1990; Sutker et al., 1993) do not seem to show the dramatic F scale elevations found in veterans of later conflicts. [2000 Frueh, Hamner et al, 857]

[15] Philpott, T. (2013, May 30). *Attorney Urges Congress to end Sleep Apnea Claims 'Abuse'*. Retrieved from starsandstripes.com: https://www.stripes.com/news/veterans/attorney-urges-congress-to-end-sleep-apnea-claims-abuse-1.223588

[16] Veterans Health Administration: Opportunities Missed to Contain Spending on Sleep Apnea Devices and Improve Veterans' Outcomes. No. 19-00021-41, Washington, DC: VA Office of Inspector General, 2020. Retrieved from: va.gov/oig/pubs/VAOIG-19-00021-41.pdf

[17] Veterans Benefit Administration. (2018, December 1). *Veterans Compensation Benefits Rate Tables*. Retrieved from benefits.va.gov: https://www.benefits.va.gov/compensation/resources_comp01.asp

[18] Ridgway, James D., A Benefits System for the Information Age (February 2, 2015). *Glimpses of the New Veteran: Changed Constituencies, Different Disabilities, and Evolving Resolutions* (Alice A. Booher, ed. 2015). 135.

[19] Ibid.

[20] Mikulic, M. (2019, August 9). *U.S. National Health Expenditure as Percent of GDP from 1960 to 2019*. Retrieved from statista.com: https://www.statista.com/statistics/184968/us-health-expenditure-as-percent-of-gdp-since-1960/

[21] Gade, Daniel M. "A Better Way to Help Veterans." *National Affairs* no. 16, Summer 2013.

[22] Satel, Sally, and B. Christopher Frueh. "The Other VA Scandal." National Review, August 25, 2014.

[23] Ridgway (2015). 137-9.

[24] American Academy of Dermatology. (2019). *Vitiligo: Overview*. Retrieved from aad.org: https://www.aad.org/public/diseases/color-problems/vitiligo

[25] VA Schedule for Rating Disabilities, Code 7520. Available online at https://www.law.cornell.edu/cfr/text/38/4.115b

[26] Mayo Clinic. (2019). *Sleep Apnea*. Retrieved from mayoclinic.org: https://www.mayoclinic.org/diseases-conditions/sleep-apnea/symptoms-causes/syc-20377631

[27] American Academy of Sleep Medicine. (2014, September 29). *Rising Prevalence of Sleep Apnea in U.S. Threatens Public Health*. Retrieved from aasm.org: https://aasm.org/rising-prevalence-of-sleep-apnea-in-u-s-threatens-public-health/

[28] Fox, M. (2016, December 12). *One in 6 Americans Take Antidepressants, Other Psychiatric Drugs: Study*. Retrieved from nbcnews.com: https://www.nbcnews.com/health/health-news/one-6-americans-take-antidepressants-other-psychiatric-drugs-n695141

[29] Vet Comp and Pen Consulting, LLC Facebook Page, available at https://www.facebook.com/vetcompandpen/videos/1346278995480398/?fref=gs&dti=821414564586109&hc_location=group

[30] Government Accountability Office. (2017, February). *High-Risk Series: Progress on Many High-Risk Areas, While Substantial Efforts Needed on Others*. Retrieved from gao.gov: https://www.gao.gov/assets/690/682765.pdf#page596

[31] Stichman, B. F., Abrams, R. B., Spataro, R. V., & Odom, A. F. (2016). *Veterans Benefits Manual*. Washington, DC: National Veterans Legal Services Program.

[32] Committee on Veterans' Affairs U.S. House of Representatives. (2013). Adjudicating VA's Most Complex Disability Claims: ENsuring Quality, Accuracy and Consistency on Complicated Issues. (p. 99). Washington, DC: US Government Printing Office .

[33] Names have been changed to protect anonymity. The quotes are precise. //Peter//

[34] Names have been changed to protect anonymity. The quotes are precise. //Sofia//

[35] Personal communication with a VA Compensation and Pension Examiner via Google Groups, June 13, 2018.

[36] Personal communication with a VA Compensation and Pension Examiner via Google Groups, April 11, 2018.

Chapter 11

[1] Frueh, E. (2003). Disability Compensation Seeking Among Veterans Evaluated for Post-Traumatic Stress Disorder. Psychiatric Services. Retrieved from https://www.ncbi. nlm.nih.gov/pubmed/12509672.

[2] Spiegel, A. (2006, May 31). Post-Traumatic Stress Treatment Costs Soar. Retrieved from https://www.npr.org/templates/story/story.php?storyId=5441927.

[3] Jackson, A. (2015, July 4). How veterans are coping with July Fourth fireworks. Retrieved from https://www.cnn.com/2015/07/01/health/ptsd-vets-and-fireworks-irpt.

[4] Gibbons-Neff, T. (2019, April 28). Some Military Veterans Struggle with Fireworks. Is this Sign the Answer? Retrieved from https://www.washingtonpost.com/news/ checkpoint/wp/2015/06/19/some-military-veterans-struggle-with-fireworks-but-is-this-sign-the-answer/?utm_term=.3b2608d1259b.

[5] Hernandez, C., Alexander, T., Searson, M., & Bunch, A. (2019, June 19). Signs, Of Veteran Entitlement. Retrieved from https://www.breachbangclear.com/signs-of-veter-an-entitlement/.

[6] Lilyea, John, writing on his personal blog "This Ain't Hell". June 5, 2015. Available on-line at https://valorguardians.com/blog/?p=60196

[7] Hernandez, C., Reeder, D., Alexander, T., Searson, M., & Bunch, A. (2015, August 3). "Combat Vet" Yard Signs: Follow Up From a Veteran With a Sign. Retrieved from https://www.breachbangclear.com/combat-vet-yard-signs-follow-up/.

[8] Barber, M. (2011, March 22). Man who posed as Marine hero sentenced to tend military graves. Retrieved from https://www.seattlepi.com/local/article/Man-who-posed-as-Marine-hero-sentenced-to-tend-1245127.php.

[9] AP: More POW claimants than actual POWs. (2009, April 11). Retrieved from http://www.nbcnews.com/id/30168352/ns/us_news-military/t/ap-more-pow-claim-ants-actual-pows/#.XASSnxMzbnW.

[10] LA TIMES– INTERESTING TAKE ON PTSD. (2014, August 4). Retrieved from https://asknod.org/2014/08/04/la-times-interesting-take-on-ptsd/

[11] Brassaw, Richard. "How & Where to Report VA Abuse and Fraud." disabili-tyhappens.com, 2008. https://www.disabilityhappens.com/how-where-to-report-va-abuse-and-fraud/.

[12] Brosnan, S., de Waal, F. Monkeys reject unequal pay. Nature 425, 297–299 (2003). https://doi.org/10.1038/nature01963

¹³ Konnikova, M. (2017, June 19). How We Learn Fairness. Retrieved from https://www.newyorker.com/science/maria-konnikova/how-we-learn-fairness.

¹⁴ This amount is the quote from the source. A 100% disabled veteran who is single would receive around $3200—plus more with children, a spouse, or certain extra disabilities.

¹⁵ Hernandez, C., Alexander, T., Searson, M., & Bunch, A. (2019, June 19). Thieves and Liars: PTSD Fakers and the VA. Retrieved from https://www.breachbangclear.com/ptsd-fakers/

¹⁶ "American Journal of Psychiatry (Am J Psychiatr)." ResearchGate, n.d. https://www.researchgate.net/journal/American-Journal-of-Psychiatry-1535-7228.

¹⁷ National Center for PTSD. (2018, September 26). Retrieved from https://www.ptsd.va.gov/about/divisions/behavioral-science/terence_m_keane_phd.asp.

¹⁸ This conversation is reconstructed from the recollection of Chris Frueh. Dr. Keane declined to offer a formal response to the authors. He disputes the allegation that he pressured Frueh in any way. He stands by his lengthy career in serving veterans with mental health diagnoses.

¹⁹ Frueh, B. C., Elhai, J. D., Grubaugh, A. L., Monnier, J., Kashdan, T. B., Sauvageot, J. A., ... Arana, G. W. (2005, June). Documented combat exposure of US veterans seeking treatment for combat-related post-traumatic stress disorder. Retrieved from https://www.ncbi.nlm.nih.gov/pubmed/15928355

Chapter 12

¹ Dobbs, David. "The Post-Traumatic Stress Trap." *Scientific American*, April 2009.

² McNally, Richard J. "Progress and Controversy in the Study of Posttraumatic Stress Disorder." Annual Review of Psychology 54, no. 1 (February 2003): 229–52. https://doi.org/10.1146/annurev.psych.54.101601.145112.

³ Matthew Tull, PhD. "The Criteria for Diagnosing PTSD in DSM-5." Verywell Mind, n.d. https://www.verywellmind.com/ptsd-in-the-dsm-5-2797324.

⁴ Centers for Disease Control. "Health Status of Vietnam Veterans, Volume I". US Department of Health and Human Services, Washington DC. January 1989. Available online at https://www.cdc.gov/nceh/veterans/pdfs/volumei/Synopsis2_4.pdf

⁵ "New Look at Vietnam Vets' PTSD Data." Dart Center, November 20, 2015. https://dartcenter.org/blog/new-look-at-vietnam-vets-ptsd-data.

In his 2003 book, *Remembering Trauma*, McNally notes: "The onset of symptoms is usually in the first month after the traumatic event, but in a minority (less than 15%) there may be a delay of months or years before symptoms start to appear. It is also important to note that symptom severity in the initial days after trauma (up to about 1 week) is not a good predictor of persistent PTSD."

[6] Loftus, E. F., & Pickrell, J. E. "The formation of false memories." *Psychiatric Annals*, 25(12) (1995): 720–725. https://doi.org/10.3928/0048-5713-19951201-07

[7] Southwick, Steven M. "Consistency of Memory for Combat-Related Traumatic Events in Veterans of Operation Desert Storm." *American Journal of Psychiatry* 154, no. 2 (1997): 173–77. https://doi.org/10.1176/ajp.154.2.173.

[8] Southwick (1997).

[9] Ibid.

[10] Loftus (1995).

[11] Southwick (1997).

[12] Dobbs (2009).

[13] "4/3/15 Preliminaries." My Education at the VA., April 16, 2015. https://myvaeducation.loudunskeptic.com/2015/03/preliminaries.html.

[14] Silberman, Steve. "The Forgotten History of Autism." TED, 2015. https://www.ted.com/talks/steve_silberman_the_forgotten_history_of_autism/transcript#t-199897.

[15] Sayer NA, Spoont M, Nelson D. Veterans seeking disability benefits for post-traumatic stress disorder: who applies and the self-reported meaning of disability compensation. *Soc Sci Med* Jun;58(11) (2004): 2133-43

[16] "4/6/15 PTSD 101." My Education at the VA., April 16, 2015. https://myvaeducation.loudunskeptic.com/2015/03/ptsd-1.html.

[17] Ibid.

[18] Satel & Frueh (2014).

[19] Zarembo, Alan. "As Disability Awards Grow, so Do Concerns with Veracity of PTSD Claims." Los Angeles Times, August 4, 2014. https://www.latimes.com/local/la-me-ptsd-disability-20140804-story.html.

[20] From a presentation given by Dr. Erika Zavyalov (CPT, US Army) on April 5, 2017 and provided to the author.

[21] Department of Veterans Affairs "FY2019 Annual Benefits Report". Washington, DC, 2020. Available online at https://www.benefits.va.gov/REPORTS/abr/docs/2019-compensation.pdf

[22] "4/14/15 Retirement costs." My Education at the VA., April 16, 2015. https://myvaeducation.loudunskeptic.com/2015/02/retirement-costs.html.

[23] Resnick, P. J. "Malingering of posttraumatic disorders." In R. Rogers (Ed.), *Clinical assessment of malingering and deception.* The Guilford Press (1997): p. 130–152.

[24] VA Office of Inspector General, 2005.

[25] *Post-Traumatic Stress Disorder: Management of PTSD in Adults and Children in Primary and Secondary* Care. London: Gaskell and the British Psychological Society, 2005.

[26] Frueh BC, Elhai JD, Gold PB, et al. "Disability compensation seeking among veterans evaluated for posttraumatic stress disorder." *Psychiatr Serv.* 2003;54: 84–91.

[27] US Department of Veterans Affairs. "VA Mental Health Services: Public Report." Washington DC, November 2014. Available online at https://www.mentalhealth. va.gov/docs/Mental_Health_Transparency_Report_11-24-14.pdf

[28] Frueh, B. Christopher, Anouk L. Grubaugh, Jon D. Elhai, and Todd C. Buckley. "US Department of Veterans Affairs Disability Policies for Posttraumatic Stress Disorder: Administrative Trends and Implications for Treatment, Rehabilitation, and Research." *American Journal of Public Health* 97, no. 12 (2007): 2143–45. https://doi. org/10.2105/ajph.2007.115436.

[29] "4/6/15 PTSD 101." My Education at the VA (2015).

[30] Dobbs (2009).

Chapter 13

[1] New Look at Vietnam Vets' PTSD Data. (2015, November 20). Retrieved from https://dartcenter.org/blog/new-look-at-vietnam-vets-ptsd-data.

[2] Dohrenwend, B. P., Turner, J. B., Turse, N. A., Lewis-Fernandez, R., & Yager, T. J. (2006, April). War-related posttraumatic stress disorder in Black, Hispanic, and majority White Vietnam veterans: the roles of exposure and vulnerability. Retrieved from https://www.ncbi.nlm.nih.gov/pmc/articles/PMC2538409/.

[3] McNally, R., Bryant, R., & Ehlers, A. (2003). Does Early Psychological Intervention Promote Recovery from Posttraumatic Stress? Psychological Science in the Public Interest. Retrieved from https://journals.sagepub.com/doi/10.1111/1529-1006.01421

[4] "Sally Satel." American Enterprise Institute, n.d. https://www.aei.org/profile/sally-satel/.

[5] Frueh, B. C., Grubaugh, A. L., Elhai, J. D., & Buckley, T. C. (2007, December). US Department of Veterans Affairs disability policies for posttraumatic stress disorder: administrative trends and implications for treatment, rehabilitation, and research. Retrieved from https://www.ncbi.nlm.nih.gov/pmc/articles/PMC2089098/.

Chapter 14

[1] Forensic Psychology Job Description: What You'll Do. (n.d.). Retrieved from https://www.allpsychologyschools.com/forensic-psychology/job-description/.

[2] COMBAT AND OPERATIONAL STRESS CONTROL MANUAL FOR LEADERS ... (2002). Retrieved from https://usacac.army.mil/sites/default/files/misc/doctrine/CDG/cdg_resources/manuals/fm/fm6_22x5.pdf.2002 PTSD Manual; 22.

[3] Huang, D. (2014, October 28). VA Disability Claims Soar. Retrieved from https://www.wsj.com/articles/va-disability-claims-soar-1414454034

[4] Huang, D. (2014, October 28).

[5] Ibid.

[6] Compensation: Public Disability Benefits Questionnaires (DBQs). https://www.benefits.va.gov/compensation/dbq_publicdbqs.asp.

[7] Huang, D. (2015, May 12). Automated System Often Unjustly Boosts Veterans' Disability Benefits. Retrieved from https://www.wsj.com/articles/automated-system-often-unjustly-boosts-veterans-disability-benefits-1431387826

[8] Poyner, G. Psychological Evaluations of Veterans Claiming PTSD Disability with the Department of Veterans Affairs: A Clinician's Viewpoint. *Psychol. Inj. and Law* 3, 130–132 (2010). https://doi.org/10.1007/s12207-010-9076-x

[9] VA Office of Inspector General, 2005.

[10] Levin, Aaron, and Search for more papers by this author. "VA to Keep Using DSM To Diagnose PTSD in Vets." Psychiatric News, July 21, 2006. https://psychnews.psychiatryonline.org/doi/full/10.1176/pn.41.14.0001.

[11] Institute of Medicine and National Research Council. 2007. *PTSD Compensation and Military Service*. Washington, DC: The National Academies Press. https://doi.org/10.17226/11870. 154.

[12] Merten, T., Lorenz, R., & Schlatow, S. (2010). Posttraumatic stress disorder can easily be faked, but faking can be detected in most cases. *German Journal of Psychiatry*, 13(3), 140-149.

[13] Poyner (2010).

[14] Jackson, J. C., Sinnott, P. L., Marx, B. P., Murdoch, M., Sayer, N. A., Alvarez, J. M., et al. (2011). Variation in practices and attitudes of clinicians assessing PTSD-related disability among veterans. *Journal of Traumatic Stress*, 24(5), 609-613. doi: 10.1002/jts.20688.

[15] Arbisi, P., Murdoch, M., Fortier, L., & McNulty, J. (2004). MMPI-2 Validity and Award of Service Connection for PTSD During the VA Compensation and Pension Evaluation. Retrieved from http://psycnet.apa.org/record/2004-14833-007.

Worthen, Mark, Psych C&P Exams are Unfair to Veterans (January 15, 2018). Available at SSRN: https://ssrn.com/abstract=3102447 or http://dx.doi.org/10.2139/ssrn.3102447. 30-31.

[16] Evans, F. B. (n.d.). Psychological Injury and Law (Vol. 4).

[17] The Associated Press. "Navy SEAL Sleuths Expose Those Who Have Faked Service." Penn Live, May 12, 2011. https://www.pennlive.com/midstate/2011/05/navy_seal_sleuths_expose_those.html.

[18] Russo, Arthur C. (2014). "Assessing Veteran Symptom Validity." *Psychological Injury and Law* 7, no. 2: 178–90. https://doi.org/10.1007/s12207-014-9190-2.

[19] Russo (2014).

[20] Percy, Jennifer. "The Things They Burned." *The New Republic*, December 2016.

[21] "4/6/15 PTSD 101." My Education at the VA (2015).

[22] Russo (2014).

PART III

Chapter 15

[1] Fort Bragg. (n.d.). Retrieved from http://www.militarybases.us/army/fort-bragg/

[2] George Washington to Continental Army: Farewell Orders, November 2, 1783 - American Memory Timeline- Classroom Presentation: Teacher Resources - Library of Congress. (n.d.). Retrieved from https://www.loc.gov/teachers/classroommaterials/presentationsandactivities/presentations/timeline/amrev/peace/farewell.html.

[3] Burgess, R. (2018, March 7). Beyond the 'Broken Veteran': A History of America's Relationship With Its Ex-Soldiers. Retrieved from https://warontherocks.com/2018/03/beyond-the-broken-veteran-a-history-of-americas-relationship-with-its-ex-soldiers/

[4] As the conclusion of World War II drew near, nearly 16 million American service members were poised to return from the war. The sociologist Willard Waller deliberated on their homecoming: "Our kind of democratic society is probably worse fitted than any other for handling veterans. An autocracy, caring nothing for its human materials, can use up a man and throw him away. A socialistic society that takes from each according to his abilities and gives to each according to his needs can use up a man and then care for him the rest of his life. But a democracy, a competitive democracy like ours, that cares about human values but expects every man to look out for himself, uses up a man and returns him to the competitive process."

How a veteran was to navigate such a society, structurally and culturally pitted against his re-integration, was one question. Another was the veteran's own attitude, which Waller saw as inextricable with his psychology as a soldier. "We must learn what it is," he wrote, "to be, for a time, expendable, and then to be expendable no more."

Burgess, R. (2018, March 7).

[5] The Constitution for officers and the President and "officers appointed over me" for enlisted members.

[6] Klay, Phil. "The Citizen-Soldier: Moral Risk and the Modern Military." Brookings Institution, May 24, 2016. http://csweb.brookings.edu/content/research/essays/2016/the-citizen-soldier.html.

[7] Junger, Sebastian. "HOW PTSD BECAME A PROBLEM FAR BEYOND THE BATTLEFIELD." *Vanity Fair*, June 2015.

[8] A 100 percent disability rating, in theory, therefore means that a veteran retains no functional ability to work because of it.

[9] For example, a veteran with a below knee amputation at 40 percent, a bad back at 10 percent, and hearing loss at 10 percent would not be 60 percent disabled. The first disability would leave 60 percent of his capacity intact. The next disability (10 percent) would reduce his remaining 60 percent capacity to 54 percent, and the next 10 percent disability would reduce the remaining 54 percent capacity down to 49 percent. His final disability rating is calculated to be 50%. This all can be quite befuddling, but has an important purpose in that it prevents a litany of minor conditions from directly adding up to be as "severe" as a major disabling condition.

[10] According to the VA, only about nine thousand of the 4.7 million veterans receiving disability compensation in 2018 had a combined zero-percent rating (although many more had single conditions in their list of conditions rated at that level). Department of Veterans Affairs "FY2019 Annual Benefits Report". Washington, DC, 2020.

[11] A zero percent disability rating may open the gates for a veteran to access a higher priority group for health care. It may also allow him to apply for subsidized life insurance through the service-disabled veterans' insurance program.

Chapter 16

[1] Treatment. (n.d.). Retrieved from https://www.clarematrix.org/treatment/

CLARE Foundation in Santa Monica, CA. (n.d.). Retrieved from https://www.rehabs.com/listings/clare-foundation-1902553965/

[2] Alcoholics Anonymous (AA): 12-Step Program for Alcoholism Recovery. (n.d.). Retrieved from https://www.alcohol.org/alcoholics-anonymous/

[3] FAQ Friday: Permanent and Total (P&T) Disability. (2017, July 17). Retrieved from https://cck-law.com/blog/faq-friday-permanent-and-total-pt-disability/.

[4] Watts BV, Schnurr PP, Mayo L, Young-Xu Y, Weeks WB, Friedman MJ. (2013). Meta-analysis of the efficacy of treatments for posttraumatic stress disorder. *J Clin Psychiatry,* 74(6), 541-50. doi: 10.4088/JCP.12r08225. PMID: 23842024.

[5] Heuvel, vanden. (2015, June 29). Why Is the VA Suffering From a Lack of Resources in the First Place? Retrieved from https://www.thenation.com/article/why-va-suffering-lack-resources-first-place/.

[6] Scott, C. (2012, June 13). Veterans Affairs: Historical Budget Authority . Retrieved from https://fas.org/sgp/crs/misc/RS22897.pdf

[7] Calculated by comparing the VA's 2021 budget request with its 2000 spending (48 billion) adjusted for inflation to 73 billion 2021 dollars. Retrieved from https://www.va.gov/budget/products.asp

[8] "Front Matter." Institute of Medicine. 2000. Veterans and Agent Orange: Herbicide/Dioxin Exposure and Type 2 Diabetes. Washington, DC: The National Academies Press. doi: 10.17226/9982.

[9] Liu, Ying, Sonica Sayam, Xiaonan Shao, Kesheng Wang, Shimin Zheng, Ying Li, and Liang Wang. "Prevalence of and Trends in Diabetes Among Veterans, United States, 2005–2014." Preventing Chronic Disease 14 (2017). https://doi.org/10.5888/pcd14.170230.

[10] Toone, Angie. "VETERAN'S DAY: WHAT IT'S LIKE TO LIVE WITH A VETERAN WHO HAS PTSD." Thank You For Your Service, November 11, 2016. http://www.thankyouforyourservicethefilm.com/news/2016/11/11/veterans-day-what-its-like-to-live-with-a-veteran-who-has-ptsd.

[11] Author interview with Angie Toone

[12] Recipients can qualify for more benefits when they have a spouse and dependents

[13] Nunn, T. (2015, April 15). The New Veteran, A Culture of Entitlement and Peter Pan. Retrieved from http://rhinoden.rangerup.com/the-new-veteran-a-culture-of-entitlement-and-peter-pan/

[14] Bennett, James T. *Paid Patriotism? The Debate Over Veterans' Benefits.* Routledge, 2017. 4.

Chapter 17

[1] "Most previous research has shown that veterans benefited from the funding for education provided by the Servicemen's Readjustment Act of 1944, commonly known as the GI Bill. It has been shown that economic opportunity is more strongly linked to the GI Bill than to military service itself (Sampson and Laub, 1996), and veterans had

higher earnings if they used the educational benefits provided by the GI Bill (Angrist, 1993; Sampson and Laub, 1996; Stanley, 2003)." Institute of Medicine. 2010. *Returning Home from Iraq and Afghanistan: Preliminary Assessment of Readjustment Needs of Veterans, Service Members, and Their Families.* Washington, DC: The National Academies Press. 81.

[2] "It has been noted that young military families have been targeted for predatory payday and car-title loans, which resulted in substantial debt (DOD, 2006; Oron, 2006; Tanik, 2005). Many military families are young and inexperienced in managing finances. About 48% of enlisted service members are under 25 years old (DOD, 2007) and are without financial experience or savings to cushion them in an emergency. Car-title loans enable borrowers to secure loans with their car titles. The typical loan is a small fraction of the car's worth, has a 300% annual interest rate, and has a 1-month loan term. Failure to pay can result in repossession of the vehicle. The high cost and the risk of losing one's car often result in borrowers' repeated loan renewal (DOD, 2006). Payday loans are small loans secured by borrowers' personal checks or agreement to automatically withdraw money from their accounts. Loans average $350, are due in full on the next payday (typically in 14 days), and have 390–780% annual interest rates (DOD, 2006). Payday lending can be found in storefronts, check-cashing outlets, pawnshops, and so on, and are heavily concentrated around military bases. DOD (2006) notes that the area around the southern gate of Camp Pendleton in Oceanside, California, has 22 payday lenders—17 more than would be expected for that ZIP code. Similarly, in the ZIP code in Killeen, Texas, outside Fort Hood, there are 7.3 more than would be expected for the population in that ZIP code (DOD, 2006). Graves and Peterson (2005) documented the number of payday lenders near military bases by surveying 20 states, 1,516 counties, and 13,253 ZIP codes; 15,000 payday lenders; and 109 military bases. They looked at states that are home to military communities—such as California, Texas, and Virginia—and analyzed data on the distribution and density of payday lenders and banks by ZIP code. Their findings indicated that there are large concentrations of payday-lending businesses in the counties and ZIP codes near military bases (Graves and Peterson, 2005). Active-duty service members are three times more likely as civilians to have taken out payday loans. It has been reported that one in five active-duty service members had used payday loans, which cost military families over $80 million in fees every year (Tanik, 2005)." Ibid. 83.

[3] Harris, S. (2019, March 4). Making Sense Podcast #149 - The Problem of Addiction. Retrieved from https://samharris.org/podcasts/149-problem-addiction

[4] Pollack, Stacey. "Mental Health and Veterans Benefits Administration Collaborations." Veterans Health Administration, Washington, DC. N.d Available online at https://docplayer.net/11356718-Mental-health-and-veterans-benefits-administration-collaborartions-stacey-pollack-ph-d.html

Chapter 18

[1] As noted by the combat journalist Sebastian Junger: "A 2007 analysis from the Institute of Medicine and the National Research Council found that, statistically, people who fail to overcome trauma tend to be people who are already burdened by psychological issues—either because they inherited them or because they suffered trauma or abuse as children. According to a 2003 study on high-risk twins and combat-related PTSD, if you fought in Vietnam and your twin brother did not—but suffers from psychiatric disorders—you are more likely to get PTSD after your deployment. If you experienced the death of a loved one, or even weren't held enough as a child, you are up to seven times more likely to develop the kinds of anxiety disorders that can contribute to PTSD, according to a 1989 study in the British Journal of Psychiatry. And according to statistics published in the Journal of Consulting and Clinical Psychology in 2000, if you have an educational deficit, if you are female, if you have a low I.Q., or if you were abused as a child, you are at an elevated risk of developing PTSD. These factors are nearly as predictive of PTSD as the severity of the trauma itself." Junger, Sebastian. "HOW PTSD BECAME A PROBLEM FAR BEYOND THE BATTLEFIELD." *Vanity Fair*, June 2015.

[2] Johnson, R. A., Albright, D. L., Marzolf, J. R., Bibbo, J. L., Yaglom, H. D., Crowder, S. M., … Harms, N. (2018). Effects of therapeutic horseback riding on post-traumatic stress disorder in military veterans. Military Medical Research, 5(1). doi: 10.1186/s40779-018-0149-6

[3] Bennett (2017). 16-18.

[4] In the words of one VA compensation and pension examiner: "I have come across SEVERAL of these recently here in [redacted] and have collected data from others nationally who are seeing these as well...in some cases these diagnosis for hire companies are not just charging for the initial DBQ but then taking a percentage of the Veteran's SC for X amount of months if they get SC on this erroneous disability. They also appear to be templated exams as was previously mentioned on this list and the DBQ's all pretty much look the same and state that the Veteran has impairments in most areas of their life secondary to the 10% SC back condition etc... The ones I have seen are completed by non-VA providers in Puerto Rico, California, Texas, and 2 different providers in Florida. It appears they are hired through a couple of different companies who also take a cut." Personal communication with a VA Compensation and Pension Examiner via Google Groups, June 7, 2017.

[5] Lawyers, too, can and do get in on the act. For a fee, firms such as Attig|Steele of Little Rock, Arkansas will represent veterans in their appeals or help veterans prepare their claims. Chris Attig, a former Army Captain and the founder of the firm, is also the author of a so-called "field manual" about how to get a *sleep apnea* claim approved. (1) In any such environment, the morality of such claims is secondary to their monetary value. The value of a sleep apnea claim, which can be worth a 50% rating and

more than $10,000 per year (not counting state benefits, education benefits, and so much more), is so high that it is certainly attractive to land such a lucrative fish.

One particularly oleaginous kind of firm is the so-called "disability consultant firms" that haunt Facebook and the internet, as well as market books for veterans such as "*The Complete Guide to Veterans' Benefits: Everything You Need to Know Explained Simply,*" which helpfully shows veterans how to get their benefits while reassuring them of the morality of doing so. Another group of companies, called "VA Claims Insider" and "Military Disability Made Easy" have a massive reach and an interesting business model: for 50% of the *increase* in a veteran's claim amount for a period of 5 months, these companies will help the veteran fill out his claim, gather medical evidence (see the difficulties with this approach above) and submit the claim to the VA. The CEO of these companies, Brian Reese, is himself a disabled Air Force veteran whose Afghanistan service as a contracting officer caused him severe and permanent PTSD. (2)

Numerous Facebook groups have also sprung up that encourage veterans to claim disability, and then celebrate their "accomplishment" in "achieving" high disability ratings. These groups offer a remarkable insight into the world of veterans who have embraced the disability mindset and view it as an important part of their identities. One common kind of thread is one in which a veteran who has filed a claim and been denied is offered advice on how to get a perfect "buddy letter" or other evidence including referral to one of the disability consulting firms to achieve a full disability rating. Another is one in which a veteran is coached on exactly what words to use to get a disability claim approved.

(1) Mr. Attig declined to be interviewed for this book, but has many online videos about how to win a claim against the government and encouraging veterans to claim disability.

(2) Reese, Brian, and Follow. I'm a CEO with PTSD, February 9, 2019. https://www.linkedin.com/pulse/im-ceo-ptsd-brian-reese/?published=t.

[6] Although the VA rates disabilities in 10-point increments, this "85%" is from our interview with Andrew. It is likely either 80% or 90%.

[7] This option, called a Board appeal, and others are laid out on the VA's website, at VA Decision Reviews and Appeals. (n.d.). Retrieved from https://www.va.gov/decision-reviews/.

[8] Take, for example, a veteran who feels that his knee pain has worsened, or that his knee pain is beginning to affect his opposite hip. The VA allows him to file a claim connecting the two conditions; indeed, these so-called "secondary" claims are a huge portion of the claims that veterans file. In some instances, this may make some sense: the healthy remaining limb of an amputee may wear out faster than it otherwise would have. But frequently, such 'secondary service connection' cases have a more tenuous

claim to disability. For instance, the VA is prevented by statute from making substance abuse (alcohol or drugs) a service-connected disability. But it is possible (and encouraged by some of the law firms in the 'disability industrial complex') to get service connected for alcohol abuse if the veteran first has PTSD or a pain disorder. (1) It is also possible to get secondary service connection for diabetes related to weight gain if the veteran can prove a condition that made exercise difficult—say, knee pain. (2) The financial incentives for this kind of behavior are enormous: the knee pain itself may only garner a 10% disability rating, whereas getting diabetes can result in a disability rating of up to 100%.

At the same time, the absence of any time limit for filing claims enables some absurd results. In a 2015 Board of Appeals for Veterans Claims decision, a man who served in the Marines from 1960 to 1964, and was briefly treated for a back strain in 1962. *More than 4 decades later*, in 2004, he complained to a doctor about his lower back pain, telling them that it began in 1995 (three decades after service). Further, he claimed that he had tingling in his legs and other problems related to the back pain. Instead of informing the veteran that 40 years as a gas station attendant, pilot, and night club owner might have something to do with degenerating health and increased lower back pain, the Court of Appeals directed the VA to re-examine the veteran with an eye toward increasing his disability payments. (3)The basis for this decision? The veteran had evidence of a brief period of a sore back after lifting weights in 1962, for which he was prescribed some medicine and heat therapy.

(1) "Secondary Service Connection & Aggravation." CCK Law, n.d. https://ccklaw.com/video/secondary-service-connection-aggravation/.

(2) Board of Veterans Appeals, Citation Number 1626442, Decided July 1, 2016. In this case, the veteran successfully argued that his type II diabetes was caused in part by his weight gain secondary to knee and spine problems. Available online at https://www.va.gov/vetapp16/Files4/1626442.txt

(3) In one case before the Court of Appeals for Veterans Claims, the veteran applied for disability benefits based on a period of service ending in 1964, thirty years before symptoms first appeared. While his claim was denied, many equally absurd claims are not. Court documents here: https://efiling.uscourts.cavc.gov/cmecf/servlet/TransportRoom?servlet=ShowDoc&dls_id=01203414875&caseId=85861&dktType=dktPublic

[9] The "Monday Morning Workload Report" on 12/31/2018, for instance, showed 111,152 claims for new entitlement and 196,350 for "supplemental entitlement," i.e. claims for increased evaluation. For every new disability claimant, there were almost twice as many veterans seeking additional compensation. Department of Veterans Affairs, Veterans Benefits Administration, & Office of Performance Analysis and Integrity. (n.d.). Veterans Benefits Administration Reports. Retrieved from https://www.benefits.va.gov/reports/detailed_claims_data.asp.

[10] When Mark Duggan, an economics professor at Stanford University, began research-ing federal entitlement programs two decades ago, he found that the much-maligned programs of the Social Security Administration were operating strangely. "[Even though other economic indicators in the 1990s were very positive], SSI and SSDI... had been growing really rapidly throughout the 90s [which was] very strange given what was happening with other programs like welfare, like unemployment insurance, and so forth." That finding spurred Duggan's interest in the operation of federal disability programs, leading him and a colleague to begin to explore other programs. "The thing that struck me the most was that there was this sharp break in 2001, that over time people were becoming more and more likely to have like very high benefits. So as opposed to having 10 or 20 percent, to have like 70, 80, 90 or 100 percent rating. So there was this rapid increase both in how many people were getting it, and in the generosity of the benefits, and this was happening in a period where the number of veterans actually was declining. So it struck me as like kind of odd that we have this program that serves veterans, and their populations are shrinking, and yet it's growing at this incredibly rapid rate." Author interview, August 25, 2017.

[11] Veterans Benefits Administration. Individual Unemployability Factsheet. Retrieved from U.S. Department of Veterans Affairs: https://www.benefits.va.gov/BENEFITS/factsheets/serviceconnected/IU.pdf

[12] Andrew has apparently fully embraced his new status: a review of his Facebook page shows a happy, well-adjusted, and fit man in the prime of his life enjoying his trips to Italy, Munich, and elsewhere, paid for my taxpayer dollars that foot the bill for his Social Security Disability, VA disability, and other benefits.

[13] Stamm, D. (2017, December 15). Holy Cow! Bovine Escapes Live Nativity, Again. Retrieved from https://www.nbcphiladelphia.com/news/local/Cow-Live-Nativity-464115753.html

Chapter 19

[1] So-called "wounded, ill, or injured" soldiers come in many varieties. Those with physical wounds, such as amputations, burns, or other kinds of obvious physical injuries enjoy a kind of social bonus: since they clearly were injured, their eligibility for benefits and assistance is not in question. It is not "weak" to have been burned or had a limb amputated: it is simply a matter of combat trauma, well understood by soldier and civilian alike.

The situation for those with mental health conditions is much different, however. In a famous scene in the 1970 movie *Patton*, based on a real incident, the General is tour-ing a field hospital in Sicily in 1943. Upon seeing a soldier with mental health trauma, he becomes enraged and yells "Your nerves? Why, hell, you are just a goddamned coward...I won't have sons-of-bitches who are afraid to fight stinking up this place of honor." (1)

While this type of treatment for traumatized soldiers is a thing of the past, there exists a strong stigma in society against mental health sufferers. This stigma is particularly strong in the military context, in which service members pride themselves on resilience and are loathe to self-identify as having a mental health condition. (2)

Similarly, other invisible disabilities have different levels of stigma but similar problems in that they are not seen and thus are easily ignored or discounted. For example, a soldier may have a significant brain injury that results in real cognitive or behavioral problems and yet not have any outward sign of the injury.

In any case, the service member or veteran with invisible injuries faces at least three interrelated problems: first, the disease process or injury itself may cause ongoing suffering or cognitive effects. Second, the individual may face perceived or real stigma and associated behaviors (including people doubting the facts). Finally, there is a real social and emotional cost to constantly having to explain to other people how or why you are disabled without any visible injuries.

(1) Patton. United States: Twentieth Century-Fox Film Corp., 1969.

(2) For a full review of the military context around mental health stigma, see Acosta, J., Becker, A., Cerully, J., Fisher, M., Martin, L., Vardavas, R., ... Schell, T. (2014). Mental Health Stigma in the Military. Retrieved from https://www.rand.org/content/dam/rand/pubs/research_reports/RR400/RR426/RAND_RR426.pdf.

[2] Bellman is a pseudonym.

[3] Charles E. Wyckoff. (n.d.). Retrieved from https://valor.militarytimes.com/hero/3666.

[4] Leonard, J. S. (1985, October). Labor Supply Incentives and Disincentives for the Disabled. Retrieved from http://www.nber.org/papers/w1744.pdf.

[5] Gruber, J. (1996, December). Disability Insurance Benefits and Labor Supply. Retrieved from http://www.nber.org/papers/w5866.pdf.

[6] Autor, D. H. (2011, December). The Unsustainable Rise of the Disability Rolls in the United States: Causes, Consequences, and Policy Options . Retrieved from http://www.nber.org/papers/w17697.pdf.

[7] The vast majority of the VA's payments are by electronic transfer; references to checks are largely colloquial.

[8] Matt said about the Sutherland Springs church shooting: "It kills me when one of these stupid crack-headed veterans goes out and does some dumb shit. And then media goes, Well he was an Army veteran. Okay, I get it, he was in the military but why don't you talk about him getting booted out of the military because he was a bad apple to begin with. The guy didn't want to serve with honor and distinction and then gets out and does some crazy shit.

"That dude in Texas who did the shooting at the church. That dude was at the Airforce, he was booted out for domestic violence, he should not have been allowed to purchase a firearm but the Airforce dropped the ball on that. That's stupid but people want to talk about him being in the military and associate him with us. I'm like, 'Come on CNN show the real thing.' This guy fricking beat up his wife and his kid. He wasn't a good person.

"Typically when you see a veteran do something above and beyond like save the day, you don't hear about it a whole lot. The last time was the terrorist attack in France, a couple military veterans or active duty guys that subdued the guy, they got all beat up and everything. That was good news but there was yet again a shooting in a community college in the northwest, and some former military guy held the door to keep the guy from getting in but he got shot up. Police officers probably go through the same thing, you always hear about the cop shooting someone, you don't ever get to see the stories about them diving into a frigid lake to rescue an old lady, they don't put that shit on CNN because it's not popular I guess. It's highlighting the bad."

[9] Mobbs, M. C., & Bonanno, G. A. (2017).

[10] Burgess, R. (2018, March 7). Beyond the 'Broken Veteran': A History of America's Relationship With Its Ex-Soldiers. Retrieved from https://warontherocks.com/2018/03/beyond-the-broken-veteran-a-history-of-americas-relationship-with-its-ex-soldiers/

[11] Iii, L. S. (2012). Poll: Civilians believe veterans are valuable, but lack education and suffer PTSD. Retrieved from https://www.stripes.com/news/poll-civilians-believe-veterans-are-valuable-but-lack-education-and-suffer-ptsd-1.180277.

[12] The number of such products is astounding, and speaks to the demand for them. Likely most veterans have not considered the negative social effects of this self-isolating behavior and branding. See, for instance, here: https://www.zazzle.com/awesome_veteran_shirt-235517348910820616

[13] Phillip Brown, the commander of the Fort Bragg WTU, had this to say about the phenomenon of veterans and their disability: "Your condition is not your identity. Be a man. Be a woman. Be proud of your veteran service, and be proud that you volunteered in a time of war. Absolutely be proud of that. But don't wrap yourself in the identity of who you are as a [disabled veteran]."

Epilogue

[1] Bennett (2017). 1.

[2] McCarthy, Niall. "America's Most Prestigious Professions In 2016 [Infographic]." Forbes, March 31, 2016. https://www.forbes.com/sites/niallmccarthy/2016/03/31/americas-most-prestigious-professions-in-2016-infographic/#4931b1001926.

[3] Bennett (2017). 2-3.

[4] Ibid, 3.

[5] Ibid, 35.

[6] Ibid, 69.

[7] WWI began in 1914, but US involvement did not begin in earnest until 1917.

[8] Bradley (1956). 4.

[9] Ibid, 9-10.

[10] Ibid, 10.

[11] Author served on the Advisory Committee from 2008 to 2013, and was present for this exchange.

[12] Office of Public and Intergovernmental Affairs. "VA's Appeals Modernization Act Takes Effect Today: New Law Streamlines Department's Current Claims and Appeals Process for Veterans." VA Office of Public and Intergovernmental Affairs, February 2, 2019. https://www.va.gov/opa/pressrel/pressrelease.cfm?id=5207.